A TREATISE

ON THE

CHRISTIAN DOCTRINE OF MARRIAGE.

BY

HUGH DAVEY EVANS, LL. D.

WITH A

BIOGRAPHICAL SKETCH OF THE AUTHOR,

AND AN APPENDIX CONTAINING BISHOP ANDREWES' "DISCOURSE AGAINST SECOND MARRIAGE," ETC., NOW PRINTED FOR THE FIRST TIME IN THIS COUNTRY.

NEW YORK:
PUBLISHED BY HURD AND HOUGHTON.
Cambridge: Riverside Press.
1870.

RIVERSIDE, CAMBRIDGE:
PRINTED BY H. O. HOUGHTON AND COMPANY.

PREFACE.

This work is published in accordance with the express desire of its learned author, who died lamented and beloved in the city of Baltimore, on the 16th of July, 1868, at the good old age of seventy-six.

"It is divided," to use his own words in a letter written a few months before his death, "into fifteen chapters, of which the first two are introductory and the last supplementary. The first chapter treats of the relations between law, public opinion, and conscience, asserting the supremacy of the Divine over all human law. The second treats of the relation between the sexes, which is maintained to be that of complements to each other, by which they are fitted to be companions to each other. This is proved and its ethical consequences enforced by an examination of the moral and intellectual peculiarities of the two sexes.

"The next ten chapters treat strictly of the Christian Doctrine of Marriage. They teach that marriage is not only a civil contract, but also a Divine institution, the essence of which is the indissoluble union of one man to one woman. To the formation of this union, two things are necessary — the consent of the parties, and the blessing of God. The consent must be to live together in the Holy State of Matrimony according to God's Ordinance. When this consent and the Divine blessing concur, they produce a mysterious unity between the parties and a mysterious sanctity in their union. From this unity and sanctity follow three practical consequences, involving three moral obligations, which, while they can be logically deduced from the nature of marriage, are also plainly laid down in the Holy Scriptures. They are the exclusiveness of marriage as opposed to polygamy, its indissolubleness as opposed to divorce, and the obedience of the wife to the husband.

"With respect to the rule of indissolubleness, it is admitted that there is one exception made by our blessed Saviour Himself. It is the adultery of the wife. Except in that case, all separation of married persons is forbidden and *prima facie* sinful, so that it can only be excused by an overwhelming necessity. When a legitimate divorce takes place in the excepted case, both parties are held to be absolutely at liberty, and may marry.

"The thirteenth and fourteenth chapters relate to impediments to marriage — that is, to facts which will render void an actual formal marriage. These may be all resolved into a want of consent. The want may be of three kinds. No actual consent may have been given, though an apparent one was obtained by force or fraud. The consent may have been void for want of intellectual capacity by reason of nonage or unsound mind. It may have been void for want of moral capacity to consent, in the case of a person already married, or where the persons are so connected as to render their union incestuous. The eighteenth chapter of Leviticus is adopted as the law to determine what is incest. The case of marriage with the sister of a deceased wife is discussed, and such marriages pronounced incestuous; not, however, on the authority of the eighteenth verse, which is regarded as a prohibition of polygamy. The authority relied on is the sixteenth verse, combined with the obvious principle, that what is prohibited to one sex is prohibited to the other. The supplementary chapter relates to the choice of a partner."

The necessity of a work of this description had long been present to the mind of Dr. Evans. Men called to the responsible office of legislating for the well-being of society in the different States of the Republic, seemed scarcely to dream that there was any Christian doctrine of marriage at all, or to acknowledge its binding force; while, on the other hand, Christians of all persuasions allowed themselves to accept these loose laws — framed without any reference to the Bible — as their guide in forming and dissolving marriage ties. These facts being so notorious, and the results already reached so disastrous, Dr. Evans thought that a calm and patient investigation of the subject, such as his reading and his legal experience would enable him to make, might be of use not only to his fellow-churchmen, but also to his countrymen generally. Though written from the stand-point of the Protestant Episcopal Church (and the author could write from no other point of view on such a theme), there is yet nothing in this treatise to render it unacceptable to any candid Christian who is willing to accept the Bible as a Divine rule of life and conduct.

In strongly condemning the laxity of American legislation on marriage, the author is, of course, far from maintaining that human law should attempt to cover the whole field of Christian morality. "This," in the language of Mr. Liddon, "has been from time to time the dream, the aspiration, of noble souls, longing to heighten the functions of law, and to give forcible expression to the obligations of morality; longing, for their country's sake, to make civic virtue, as nearly as might be, a convertible term for absolute virtue, and to see the good man, without further doubt or inquiry, in the good citizen. It is to the honor of Puritanism that, in its earlier days, when it was morally and intellectually stronger than it is now, it cherished this aspiration with a self-denying fervor. And if the legal annals of the New England Colonies provoke the indignation or the amusement of the modern historian, this should not prevent our doing justice to a sincere, albeit a mistaken effort, to identify absolutely the interests of religious morality with those of law. Such an effort, indeed, was only possible in a small community; and it has left, we may fear, the almost inevitable legacy of a reaction against the moral ideas which prompted it; a reaction which has not yet died out."[1]

Few will deny that our country is now suffering from this reaction, nor will any thoughtful person fail to sympathize with the desire of Dr. Evans to excite in the public mind that high appreciation of the sacredness of marriage which pervades every page of this treatise. Moreover, as Mr. Liddon also points out, "every human code must aim at enforcing more or less perfectly the Sixth, Seventh, and Eighth Commandments, if it is to

[1] *Christ and Human Law.* A sermon preached before the University of Oxford. Second edition, with a Note on Divorce. London: 1869, pp. 13, 14. The reader who desires to see a very forcible statement of one of the views which Dr. Evans opposes lucidly presented in the compass of a few pages, will find precisely what he wants in this sermon of Mr. Liddon.

do its work of protecting society against dissolution;" and civil laws concerning marriage and divorce, since they touch the very foundation of society, ought, even on the very lowest ground of expediency, to conform as far as possible to the rule laid down by our blessed Lord in the gospel.

That rule itself, the reader needs not to be reminded, has been the subject of grave dispute, and one of the most remarkable parts of this volume is the author's discussion of the well-known difficult texts in the New Testament on divorce. It cannot be disguised that one of the conclusions at which he arrives, which has been already stated in his own language, will cause surprise and regret to many (including some of his dearest friends), who will highly approve the rest of the book. Indeed, it has even been feared that positive harm might result from the publication of the author's argument, since he advocates an interpretation which differs, as he acknowledges, from that of some of the highest authorities on this question. Such fears are, of course, groundless if the author's conclusions be *true*, and it is very certain that a full, honest discussion of the matter, in all its bearings, is indispensable if Holy Matrimony is to be restored to its proper place in our theory and practice. There are many indications that the attention of the public is at last aroused, and it seems to be just the time for a thorough investigation of the whole subject of the Christian Doctrine of Marriage. An elaborate, reverent inquiry therefore, by a distinguished lawyer and theologian, who was ever more anxious "to be on the side of truth than to have truth on his side," cannot but be a valuable contribution to the literature of the question, and an aid to those who may be called upon to legislate on the matter whether in Church or State. As to the other chapters of the volume, no serious difference of opinion is likely to arise, and those to whom the memory of the venerable author is dear will greet with pleasure the appearance of this his last and favorite work, in which they will find further illustration of his fearless, yet reverent, pursuit of truth, and which will enable them to examine in detail his reasons for a position to which he had already, in other publications, given the sanction of his name.[1]

The editor has taken pains to present the *ipsissima verba* of the author's MS., with the exception of a few manifest slips of the pen. He is responsible also for the indexes, and for the biographical sketch, which he hopes will prove acceptable not only to the friends of Dr. Evans, but also to others into whose hands the work may fall.

For kind assistance in the correction of the press, his special thanks are due to his friend and Dr. Evans's friend, the Rev. Joseph H. Coit, M. A., of St. Paul's School.

Requesting the reader to remember that this book had not the benefit of those finishing touches which an author can give as his work passes through the press, it is now submitted to the candid judgment of the public as a memorial of the learning and piety of a man who has left a name that will not soon be forgotten.

HALL HARRISON.

ST. PAUL'S SCHOOL, CONCORD, N. H.,
March 22d, 1870.

[1] See further on this subject in the Appendix to this volume.

BIOGRAPHICAL SKETCH OF THE AUTHOR.[1]

I.

"I WAS born in the city, then town, of Baltimore, on the 26th day of April, 1792. My father, whom I never knew, was a merchant in a small way, and unfortunate in business. His name was Joseph Evans; he was a native of Wilmington, Delaware, of Welsh extraction through his father, and English through his mother. His paternal great-grandfather came over with William Penn, and settled, under grants from him, in what is now Cecil County, Maryland, where his descendants were long respectable. The family in the male line is, I believe, except for me extinct.

"My grandfather, George Evans, was a deacon among the Baptists. His wife, my grandmother, was a Quakeress. Her name was Rachel Gilpin. She could trace her descent from a brother of BERNARD GILPIN, the 'Apostle of the North,' and one of her lineal ancestors was an officer under Cromwell at Worcester.

"My mother was a native of Philadelphia, and was descended from all the nations which inhabit Great Britain·

[1] Abridged from a book recently published by the editor, entitled: *Hugh Davey Evans, LL. D. A Memoir, founded upon Recollections written by himself.* Hartford: Church Press Co. The opening paragraphs of the *Recollections*, which were condensed in the *Memoir*, are here given at length, and one or two other passages from them have been added. The *Recollections* were drawn up in 1862. Dr. Evans presented an autograph copy to a dear friend of himself and the editor. These extracts are made from that copy, by permission of that friend, to whom the editor tenders his grateful acknowledgments.

and Ireland, except, perhaps, the Scotch Highlanders. Her maiden name was Elizabeth Wilcox Davey. Her father, Hugh Davey, after whom I was called, was a native of Londonderry in Ireland. He was originally a Presbyterian, and educated for the ministry, but became a merchant and settled in Philadelphia. He died in the communion of the Church, but I imagine, without embracing Church principles. His wife, my grandmother, was a native of Philadelphia, but her mother was a Londoner.[1] It is only through these ladies that I have any hereditary claim to be a Churchman, and it was through them that my traditionary religious teaching was derived. It was consequently somewhat tinged with that Puritanism which has always been connected with London Churchmanship.

"In consequence of my father's connection with the Baptists, I was not baptized until I was about three years old. The sacrament was administered by the Rev. Joseph G. J. Bend, the rector of St. Paul's Parish, Baltimore, in the church building which was the immediate predecessor of that which was burned a few years ago. In the same building I was catechised, worshipped for many years, and was confirmed. I received the sacred rite at the hands of Bishop Claggett in 1809, having just completed my seventeenth year. My Confirmation was by my own entirely free choice, but I doubt whether that choice was the con-

1 "Having mentioned my great-grandmother I am tempted to say something of her husband. His name was Alexander Woodsop. He was born towards the close of the reign of Charles I., or perhaps a little later. on the frontier of either New York or Connecticut. While an infant, his father, working in his field, was surprised by the Indians. He returned to his house, hopelessly wounded, and supporting his bowels in his hands, and told his wife to save herself and leave him to die. She caught up the child, fled, and begged her way to the city of New York. How she lived there I know not, but she soon married a sea captain, who brought up her child to his own profession. The youth profited by his instructions and at one time commanded a ship out of the port of London, where he met with his wife. The family tradition is that his life was full of vicissitudes: that he was three times a beggar and three times very rich. He died in the latter condition at Philadelphia in 1743."

sequence of any very profound religious feeling. The idea of immediate Communion was not brought before me, and if it had, I suspect it would have prevented my Confirmation. I did not become a communicant until about ten years later.

"My earliest instruction, of all sorts, I received from my mother, who was a woman of a strong but uncultivated mind. I could read so early that I cannot remember when books were not my chief pleasure. Before I was eight years old, I read books written for men, and had acquired a stock of general information very unusual at that age. The first man's book which I read was an anonymous translation of Livy, to which I was attracted by having met in a school book with the story of the Horatii and Curiatii.

"This gave me a taste for history which has never left me, and has had much to do with the formation of my intellectual character. In what is called school-learning, I had studied English grammar very well for my age and had learned a very little geography, but had gone no further.

"The religious instruction which I had received was sound but defective, and was, as I have said, somewhat tinctured by Puritanism, though it did not include the self-confidence and insubordination which are among the worst portions of that system. . . . . It was very much the same with the affirmative teaching of our Low Church brethren, but included no negations, though many things were omitted. But after all the Church Catechism was its basis.

"My moral education was a great deal better, the virtues of truth, fidelity, and integrity were impressed upon me by constant precept and example. Submission to authority I was taught by a kind, but strict discipline. Frugality I learned from necessity. I have now completed my seventieth year, and have never been in other than very narrow circumstances. My mother was poor, and I was made aware of the fact at a very early age. In that and other matters I was her confidant, while I was still only a child.

"At eight years old I went, for the first time, to school. The expense of my education was defrayed by my mother's brother, Alexander W. Davey, so long as he lived, which was until March, 1803. I was first sent to what was really a girls' school, although a very few little boys were admitted. I was sent there that I might be taught to write, a thing which no one has yet been able to do for me. I remained at this school only two months, and I believe learned nothing. This was in the spring of 1800. In the fall of the same year, having spent the intervening time in the country, I was put to school to Mr. Samuel Brown, who kept one of the two best boys' schools in Baltimore. I remained with him until I had received all the school education which it was the will of Providence that I should receive, with the exception of one interval of a few weeks.

"This time was spent in a country school, to which I was sent in the summer of 1803, with the vain hope that I might be taught to write. The master proposed to teach nothing but spelling, reading, writing, and arithmetic. The two first I understood as well or better than he did. The third I seem to have been incapable of learning, partly, I believe, from physical defects, and partly from an early bad habit of seeking to do everything too fast. No doubt the master knew much more of arithmetic than I did, but he did not attempt to teach me anything of it which I did not know. On the whole, the result was that I learned nothing. In the fall I returned to Mr. Brown, and remained with him until July, 1805, when, at the age of thirteen, I was withdrawn on account of the state of my health. I never went to any school or college afterwards, except attending to take lessons from several celebrated writing masters at different times, who all failed to teach me their art. When I left Mr. Brown I was reading the Epistles of Horace and the Orations of Cicero, and had read a good deal of Latin. In consequence of what I now think very injudicious advice, I did not begin Greek with my classmates, and taking it up alone many months after them, I was not diligent for want of competition. Moreover, I think it was at a time when my mind had been much drawn off from study to play, by my having formed new intimacies with boys who were not studious, and who did not learn the languages. These circumstances may perhaps account for what would be otherwise strange, that I never took any interest in Greek. I never got through the grammar, and soon forgot the alphabet. This defect in my education has been in after life a great disadvantage, and a subject of no little regret. The instruction which I received in Latin was very superficial, but what I was taught I learned thoroughly. It was a great surprise to me to find that after a disuse of thirty years, I could still read Latin, although, of course, not easily.

"In April, 1806, my mother opened a small dry-goods store, which, like everything in which my pecuniary interests have been involved, proved unsuccessful. I was her only assistant [then 14 years of age]. In February, 1810, I commenced the study of the law, under the direction of the late Judge Heath, then a very young practitioner. But during the whole of my studentship, and even after I had begun to practice, I occasionally assisted in the shop. In the spring of 1813 my legal studies were interrupted by a failure of my health. My mother removed to Martinsburg, Virginia, where we lived about twenty-two months. This was the only part of my life during which I was not a resident of Baltimore. On the 19th of April, 1815, I was admitted to practice law, and I followed the profession with very indifferent success until June, 1856.

"This want of success was the more remarkable, because I always had among my brethren the reputation of being a learned lawyer. But in the earlier part of my career I could not speak. I was never an adroit man of business. I had not that general acquaintance in the city which is so great an assistance in both getting and doing business, nor had I that sort of knowledge of human nature, which makes a man skillful in cross-examination. I am inclined to think that the public were right and that I was, although a pretty good lawyer, inefficient both as an advocate and an agent." [1]

It is very certain, both from the modest expressions in these "Recollections" as well as from the universal testimony of those who knew him, that he was always an unusually upright, good boy, particularly remarkable for his obedience and devotion to his mother. None but those who were privileged to be his intimate friends can form an adequate conception of his integrity and spotless character as he grew up to manhood. The "Recollections" continue as follows: —

"During my boyhood, I was for the most part religiously disposed, although there were intervals in which I was not so. I have said that at my Confirmation the idea of immediate Communion was not presented to me, and I do not remember that I ever thought of it. I was soon engaged in the study of the law, and fell in with young men who had no religious impressions; their influence was very unfortunate. I never became what the world calls an immoral youth, but this period of my life is stained with many great sins, chiefly of the heart and tongue.

"In 1819, it pleased God to call me to reflection, by the death of a family connection. I then became a communicant, and, although unworthy, have been a regular one ever since. One consequence of this change was that I studied Hooker, and imbibed from him what are called High Church principles; though I was not for some years so decided upon the doctrines of the Holy Communion and

[1] *MS. Recollections*, pp. 1–6.

the Apostolic Succession as I now am. I learned these doctrines from Bishop Seabury's "Sermons,"[1] a copy of which I bought at the sale of Bishop Kemp's books, in 1829. I read them immediately, and adopted all the doctrines taught in them which I had not previously held."

II.

"Haud facile emergunt quorum virtutibus obstant
Res angustæ domi."

No one had ever more reason to feel the truth of Juvenal's words than Hugh Davey Evans. His father's death left his widowed mother to struggle against the privations which poverty entails, and almost all the ordinary opportunities which surround even a poor boy now, were denied to him. How then did he become so learned and useful as a man, who as a boy had so many obstacles to surmount? We will reply in his own words: —

"It is perhaps proper to say something, in this place, of the formation of my intellectual character. My school training, as I have already said, was confined to Latin. In Greek I failed, and in Mathematics, beyond a little arithmetic, I was never tried. But before I left school, and indeed before I went there, I had become very fond of books, and have always continued so. For science I never had any taste and I read no language but English. But English books, not scientific, I read greedily and rapidly, chiefly history and voyages and travels.

"The Baltimore Library was the source from which I drew the books, which I devoured. It was a joint-stock institution in which my uncle had left me a share. The librarian was the Abbé de Persigny, a French emigrant, with whom I believe I was rather a favorite. When I was about twelve years old I asked my mother what History of

[1] [May we be permitted to repeat the hope, which we have heard Dr. Evans express, that Dr. Seabury will give the Church a new edition of his grandfather's *Sermons*? — H.]

England I might read. She told me to ask M. de Persigny, in her name, to recommend one. When I delivered the message he was conversing with Dr. Bend, who was not only our parish clergyman, but an intimate friend of my mother. The librarian referred to him; he suggested *Hume*. The answer was a French shrug and the remark 'He is your parishioner, not mine.' 'You may trust him,' said Dr. Bend. I did not understand the precise difficulty, but I was not a little proud that I was thought trustworthy.

"My reading in works of fiction was in boyhood restrained by authority and very limited. As I approached manhood the restraints were released and I became a great reader of such things. There are none of long continued reputation in our language which I have not read. The number of those of no value which I have also read, is very great. I was in the strictest sense of the word a desultory reader, for I read without guide or plan, but unlike most other desultory readers I read very attentively, and had the habit of observing closely and gathering up things which were introduced incidentally, without strictly belonging to the main scope of the work. In this way I acquired a tolerably extensive though superficial acquaintance with old-fashioned English literature. American literature could hardly be said to exist in my youth. I also picked up a considerable amount of what may be called general information, and a pretty good knowledge of history. Polemical theology had been a prohibited subject during my years of pupilage, and I never, until it became my duty, read much of it; but of sermons, and what may be called practical theology, I always read much, and thus learned more of theology than is usually known by laymen.

"My professional studies were very differently conducted. I read very little and thought much on the subject. As I had not much practice, I had not the opportunity of learning much by the examination of particular questions, which is the way in which lawyers generally acquire most of their professional knowledge. The consequence was that my learning was far less extensive and minute than that of many others. But it was more profound, and rested more upon principles. This was another great impediment in the way of my professional success. The best possible argument from principles weighs less with a jury than an authority decided by a respectable court. This is in the main right, although I think that it is carried too far.

"My mode of studying law strengthened my reasoning faculty, and my mode of reading on other subjects my memory, while my imagination, which was naturally the weakest of the three, was left to starve. My memory was much aided by another circumstance connected with my mode of study. I never took notes. This plan was designed in part to produce that very effect; in fact, it was fallen into because I wrote badly and with difficulty, — perhaps mere laziness had a good deal to do with it; a further reason was my doing everything in as little time as possible. This habit was connected with, but did not entirely grow out of, a sense of the value of time. I took very few notes even in the trial of causes. This I found often inconvenient, as I had nothing to show in case of dispute. I find, too, that in writing I am at a disadvantage for want of reference to authorities. I know the fact or the quotation, but not where to find it. I may mention in this connection a curious fact: it is that, as I grow older, I am more apt to quote, and seem thus to have developed a familiarity with Shakespeare, for instance, which I took no pains to acquire, and did not imagine myself to possess.

"Having mentioned my sense of the value of time, I may as well speak of the habit of carelessness in dress, amounting to slovenliness, by which I was distinguished in early life, and of which strong traces still remain. The two things were undoubtedly connected, for I valued time chiefly because it might be employed in reading. The same feeling was one of the causes of the awkwardness which has prevented my learning to do the small duties of life properly, though the peculiarity of my vision — my two eyes having different focuses, — and my great nervousness have, no doubt, been coöperating causes. Perhaps both these peculiarities had something to do with the retirement from society in which I have, for the most part, lived.

"Intercourse with cultivated society is a great means of mental culture. In this I was sadly deficient. I mingled little in society. This was partly the effect of poverty; partly of the attention which I paid to my mother, who had no other resource; partly of the consciousness of my slovenliness and awkwardness. The society in which I did move was not instructive. Eminent men were not common in Baltimore, and to those who were there I had no access. Not being in society, I had few opportunities of meeting them, and if I had, they would scarcely have taken much notice of an awkward and slovenly boy. On my side they would have had to encounter a vast amount of shyness, compounded of pride, modesty, and awkwardness, and a consciousness of ignorance of the manners of society. I have seen familiarly very few men of much culture and ability, and these chiefly when I was so far advanced in life that they were my juniors.

"It was perhaps owing to this seclusion, that I took little or no interest in party politics and contemporary history. There was a time when the first Napoleon was in the height of his power and glory, that I did not know how he was employed. Of the party history of my own country I know much less than most intelligent men.

"In my youth, I considered myself to belong to the old Federal party, — the only one for which I have ever felt much respect. My mother and her immediate friends had not been Tories during the Revolutionary War, but their Whiggism was of a very mitigated type. They were nevertheless great admirers of Washington; perhaps more for his conscientious devotion to duty than as the leader of the Revolution. They were, and they taught me to be, willing to be governed in everything by a sense of duty and of right.

"My mother's admiration of Washington, combined with her strong conservative feelings, a horror of the excesses of the French Revolution, and some Anglican feeling, made her a Federalist; hence I considered myself from boyhood as belonging to that party. Moreover my Anglicanism was much strengthened by the continual reading of English books. But when I came fully into life, and thought more for myself, I found that the position of the Federal party was much changed. It had lost, by long continuance in opposition, much of its conservative character. The rivalry between France and England had become less keen, the war in Europe was over, and there was less scope for my Anglicanism. I confess that I adhered to my party less from any deep conviction than from the pride of not deserting it when it was down. But though I refused to give up the name, I frequently said that, did I live in a doubtful county, I would vote the Democratic ticket, because I thought the party which bore its name was the least democratic of the two. For democracy, in the proper sense of the word, — government by the majority of the whole people told by the head, — I have always had the greatest aversion. This feeling no doubt combined with pride in making me reject the name of Democrat, — a name, which I now more than ever rejoice I have never borne. I dislike as much the narrow oligarchy, an attachment to which is now called democracy, as I do that which the word properly signifies.

"When the Federal party was broken up, I adhered to that party which seemed to have least of the democratic spirit, though I was aware that there was little to choose between them in that respect. But in time I withdrew from all parties, and do not consider myself a member of any. I am, however, a decided Union man as a duty, because the United States is my country, and its constituted authorities the power that be, which are ordained of God, and to which I am bound to be subject not only for wrath but for conscience sake.[1] . . . .

"Although I avoided party politics, I have thought much on the science of politics. I early discovered that the advantages, which we Americans attributed to our form of government, were really the consequences of our extended territory and comparatively small population. From this it was an easy step to the conclusion, that the form of government itself was an effect of the same causes. This led to the idea, that all forms of government grew out of the forms of social organization, and they out of circumstances not to be controlled by man. A government must be developed, not extemporized. Of course I could not believe in the fancy of extemporizing an aristocracy in this country.

"These ideas render it useless to consider much the question, Which is, in the abstract, the best form of government? Yet I have spent time in thinking on the question. My early speculations tended toward absolute monarchy. But I have long settled in the opinion, that the perfection of government would be a very widely extended aristocracy. A society in which there should be several strongly marked grades, each of which should be connected with those above and below it by the bonds of mutual interest, and by the possibility — facility might be too much — of passing from the lower to the higher.

"The higher classes should be sufficiently numerous to furnish a body of men, liberally educated, from among whom might be chosen governors of the country; men

[1] *MS. Recollections*, p. 9.

who should undertake that duty, not in the spirit of trading politicians, but who should have influence enough with their inferiors to guide them in the right direction upon political questions. The class must be large enough to furnish a supply of such men, which should leave room for a choice of governors, after deducting those who may prefer other occupations, or pursuits, or amusements, or whom nature may not have qualified for office.

"The choice of governors from among this superior class, should be committed to those of the lower classes, who possess sufficient knowledge to choose intelligently, and sufficient independence of position to enable them to choose honestly. It will be seen, that this is substantially the organization of the British nation and government. But, as might have been expected, the working reality is not so perfect as the ideal model."[1] . . . .

Dr. Evans considered the troubles of the country at the time he was writing (and the same may be said now) to be due in large measure to the prevalence of a willful spirit among our people. He used to think the reading of the "Declaration of Independence" on the Fourth of July positively injurious, and calculated to increase this willfulness.[2] His remarks deserve to be quoted: —

1 *MS. Recollections*, pp. 14, 15.

2 [When he was at the College of St. James, Maryland, delivering his lectures on History and Law, we have known him to take pains to avoid being present at the celebration of that day, which included a reading of the Declaration. We would not have him misconceived on this important subject, and will therefore add a few words more. His doctrine of passive obedience — which the reader will find explained by himself in the 8th volume of *The True Catholic*, p. 493, note — made him adverse to all revolutions. In the 6th volume of *The True Catholic*, in 1848, he reprinted a sermon of Mr. Keble's *On the Danger of Sympathizing with Rebellion*, prefixing this note: "The views of this discourse seem particularly suited to the times and to the bias of our national character." He used to say that had he lived during the American Revolution he could not have taken part in it. When, however, he came to lecture on the reign of George III. he modified these views considerably. He told his class that his particular investigations into the subject had led him to believe that the Americans

"How has this willful spirit grown up? It has its root, where all evil has its root, in the corruption of human nature. Why has this corruption taken that particular form? Perhaps because willfulness is the primary form of moral evil. But it has among us received a special cultivation; we have been taught that our wills are sufficient reasons for anything. So far is this carried, that the Bible is no longer regarded as the rule of life.

"There are several reasons for this. The great majority of the people have no intention of submitting their wills to any rule, and know little and care little about the Bible in any way. An abolitionist may quote the prohibition of giving up a refugee to the heathen, which is in the Mosaic Law, against the Fugitive Slave Law. A slaveholder may quote St. Paul in defense of slavery. But neither of them have the slightest intention of compiling a slave code from the Bible. Still less do they think of regulating their whole life according to the Scriptures.

"Even religious men and women, who study the Bible and accept it as a rule of faith, do not really accept it as a

were at first only agitating, lawfully, for their rights as British subjects, which were denied them, and that, in the actual outbreak of hostilities on the night between April 18 and 19, at Lexington, Massachusetts (the accounts of which vary in details), the English were the aggressors. Self-defense on the part of the Americans became necessary; one thing led to another, and thus the War of the Revolution arose, for which the English were responsible. But he regretted the Revolution, however necessary a separation might have become, and he thought it a mistake to glory in it, and to boast of our national qualities, in the style usually adopted by the Fourth of July orators. In the lectures just mentioned, on the reign of George III., he said the mysterious illness of Lord Chatham, in the spring of 1767, was the occasion, and might almost be called the cause, of the American Revolution. Lord Chatham was so prostrated that he refused to see anybody or to attend to any business whatever. Meantime the Government went on as it could. During his absence, Charles Townshend, Chancellor of the Exchequer, brought in the celebrated Stamp-act. Had Lord Chatham been at the helm of the Government that act would never have been passed; had it not been passed, the American Revolution would not have taken place when and as it did, and perhaps a separation might have come in time without any Revolution at all. —H.]

rule of life. The whole Christian doctrine of marriage is frequently rejected by such persons, and the law of the land and a certain public opinion substituted for it.

"The reason of this is, that in the pulpit, religion is too much divorced from morals. The doctrine of justification by faith has been so perverted as to obscure the whole code of Christian morality. The clergy are now afraid to teach Christian morals rested upon the Bible as a rule of life, lest they should be accused of preaching justification by works. It is much safer to expound the symbolism of the Bible, or to extol free grace, than to touch upon moral questions, which may interfere with the practice of some of the congregation. It is not wonderful that the precepts which require obedience to every ordinance of man for the Lord's sake, and submission to the powers that be, because they are ordained of God, have been forgotten.[1]

"It is now time to return from this long digression to my proper subject of the formation of my intellectual character. From a very early period I had a fancy of writing for the public; of doing that, which, when done by others, had given me so much pleasure. I did not indulge this fancy to any great extent. When I was young, I thought it would be presumption in me to attempt to instruct the public. When I was older, I feared that my professional prospects might be hurt if I became known as a writer. I did, however, publish some articles, and wrote some which were never published, though in form they appeared intended for publication. These last were, for the most part, imitations of the 'Spectator,' though rather as to the form than the style. I do not know that anything that

1 [It is to be remembered, in applying these most true remarks, that the question between the contending parties, in the late American civil war, was precisely this: Are the powers that be, which are ordained of God, to be found ultimately in the General Government at Washington, or in the State to which each citizen belongs? — H.]

I published ever attracted much attention. But I acquired some power of composition, at least some practice and facility in putting words together.

"Thus, by the time I had reached middle life, I had collected some aids for what may be called, though perhaps with a too ambitious use of language, my public career. I had acquired habits of thinking and reasoning, and of considering the precise meaning of language, a facility in speaking, and a tolerable stock of knowledge upon which to employ my powers.

"What I have ventured to call my public career, consists of two parts, which, by a like liberty, may be called my literary and ecclesiastical careers. The ecclesiastical began first, but made but little progress until it received an impetus from the literary. Both were preceded by some professional works, which might possibly be considered as belonging in some sense to the literary career.

"In the year 1817, I was appointed reading clerk to one of the branches of the City Council. This led to my being employed in 1825, to revise the Ordinances of the City, and, in 1826, to superintend a revised edition of them. I have been employed in the same way twice since; but I mention the first time, as it was my first connection with the press.

"Having thus dipped in printer's ink, I conceived the idea of writing a pamphlet on the 'Law of Special Pleading,' and the means of improving it. It expanded under my hands into a thin octavo volume, and was published in 1827. I think that the title was, 'An Essay on Pleading, with a View to an Improved System.' It attracted no attention, and was in fact, a dead failure. But most of the improvements which were suggested, having occurred about the same time to Mr., now Lord, Brougham, he brought them before Parliament, and they are now part of the law of England.[1]

[1] [It is singular that the work attracted so little attention. Its value

"I was soon afterwards employed by a printer to give a new edition of a Maryland law-book, entitled 'Harris's Entries.' The work which I produced was in fact a new one, in which much use was made of the materials of its predecessor, while it was really composed on different principles. It had to contend with a strong prejudice in favor of the original, and was long very unpopular. It however gradually rose in public estimation, and has been long out of print. It proved profitable to my employer, but my compensation was very inadequate. Both 'Harris's Entries, and 'Evans's Harris' are now obsolete books, in consequence of modern legislation.

"In the year 1836, I was induced to deliver a course of lectures on the practice of the Maryland County Courts. They were afterwards published in a changed form, and with very considerable additions as a volume. It was entitled, 'Maryland Common Law Practice: a Treatise on the Course of Proceedings in the Common Law Courts of

was testified to by ex-President John Quincy Adams, Mr. Justice Story, Chancellor Kent, Mr. William Johnson, Mr. Bushrod Washington, and above all, by Chief Justice Marshall, who addressed to the author the following letter: —

"RICHMOND, *December* 27, 1827.

"SIR, — I have deferred making my acknowledgments for your *Essay on Pleading*, and for the very flattering letter which accompanied it, until the rising of the court should afford leisure for giving it an attentive reading. That is now accomplished, and I have derived much gratification from the perusal.

"You have certainly examined the science of special pleading with the eye of a critic, who looks through the subject, for the purpose of becoming master of the object of its rules; and you have taken a just and truly common sense view of the whole.

"The statutes of amendment have certainly accomplished much, and have left not a great deal to be done; but you have shown that they have left something. I confess I can perceive no reason why one thing should be averred which is not essential and consequently traversable, unless it were a narrative necessary to the understanding of the case.

"Be so good as to accept my thanks for this very polite mark of your attention, and be assured that I am, with great respect,

"Your obedient servant,

"J. MARSHALL." — H.]

the State of Maryland.' This work became popular, and is the only one of my writings not published in a periodical form which has afforded me an adequate compensation. It was, I think, published in 1837. [A new edition, revised by the author, appeared some thirty years afterward.]

"In January, 1835, I wrote my first theological article. It appeared in the May number of the 'Protestant Episcopalian,' a monthly magazine, at that time published in Philadelphia. My article was an honest attempt to obtain a solution of certain difficulties which I felt as to the validity of Lay Baptism. This subject was, at that time, more discussed than it has ever been since. I sincerely wanted light, by which to form my own opinion. I was answered by the late Bishop H. U. Onderdonk, who undertook to prove the validity of Lay Baptism. His article was an able one, but notwithstanding its ability, it did not satisfy me: *on the contrary it convinced me of the invalidity of Lay Baptism.* I replied, which brought out a rejoinder from the Bishop. From this I discovered, what I had not before suspected, that my antagonist was the Bishop of the diocese in which the articles were published. Of course I stopped the discussion, but my opinion against the validity of Lay Baptism was fixed. From that time I was a frequent correspondent of the church papers, but without the slightest expectation of ever being an editor.[1]

[1] [In this first theological article, on Lay Baptism, there occurs a passage which so excellently expresses the fairness of mind which was such an eminent characteristic of Dr. Evans's career as an editor that we must lay it before our readers. It was signed H. Y. S., the last letters of his name: —

"GENTLEMEN: My attention has been much attracted by several articles which have appeared on the subject of Lay Baptism in your magazine and in the *Churchman.* On this and on every other subject truth ought to be our first object; yet our nature is so constituted that we can scarcely avoid having a bias on one side or the other of every question, and wishing, as it has been well expressed, 'to have the truth on our side;' our true duty and interest being all the time that we should be on the side of truth. I do not pretend to be free from this failing, to which I am very sensible the habits of my profession, the bar, very much expose me, and I am accordingly sensible of a desire, that the validity of Lay Baptism should be

"In 1843, Mr. Joseph Robinson, a bookseller in Baltimore, conceived the idea of a monthly magazine, to be conducted on Church principles, and under the patronage of Bishop Whittingham. He applied to the Bishop to name an editor. The Bishop asked me to act in conjunction with the late Judge Alexander Contee Magruder, and Mr. Samuel Johnston Donaldson. I did not feel at liberty to refuse, and therefore said that I would do so, expecting to fill a very subordinate position. This short conversation gave a new direction to the rest of my life.

"The two other gentlemen declined, and I undertook the task of conducting 'The True Catholic' as senior editor. The junior was the Rev. John W. Hoffman, who was much younger than I was and had no experience of the press. From the first, the burden of the editorship rested upon me. Mr. Hoffman being, in truth, nothing more than a stated contributor whose articles were regarded as editorial. . . . . Mr. Hoffman soon formally retired. The work was continued under my sole direction until it reached ten volumes. . . . .

"Throughout the work I wrote the first article in each number. I wrote also most of the Notices of Books. Mr. Hoffman wrote about half of those in the first volume, and a very few — not more I think than three or four — were afterwards written by other friends. I also wrote the papers headed 'Church Affairs,' and not unfrequently one or more 'Original Papers,' besides the first in the number. The contributions of correspondents became fewer and

established. Yet I am compelled to say that the papers alluded to have induced me to doubt whether it can, and have fully convinced me that it cannot be sustained on the principles of those of its advocates who have borrowed from my profession the maxim *fieri non debet, sed factum valet,* as the text of their discourses. That it may be sustained on other grounds I hope, and partly believe, though not without doubting; but this ground is untenable, and therefore the sooner it is abandoned, the better for the cause of truth and for the advocates of Lay Baptism themselves."

He then demolishes this argument, as Bishop Onderdonk in his reply virtually admitted. — H.]

fewer, until I was left to depend upon myself and selections. There have been very few periodical works which came so near being sustained by a single mind.

"When the work had completed ten volumes, the first series closed, and a second commenced. . . . . The second series only existed for four years. No doubt this was one cause of the decline of my professional business, which rendered it necessary for me to give up the pretense of practice. Certainly the long illness of my mother, who was a paralytic for three years and a half, was another cause. She died on the tenth of October, 1846, in the 89th year of her age. The 'True Catholic' finally closed its career in December, 1856."

Such is the author's own account of this most important work, "The True Catholic," the most useful Church periodical of its day and generation. Some of the readers of this sketch will of course hear of it for the first time, for its career was closed thirteen years ago. But to very many others, and especially to those in the diocese of Maryland, it will revive the most pleasing reminiscences. We all know the pleasure which we experience in reading an author from whom we think we derive real instruction. We place his works upon our shelves to be referred to again and again, and count him our friend. Few there must be who cannot enter into Bishop Andrewes' meaning, when he blesses God "for true friends; for all who have in any way benefited me by their *writings, sermons, discourses.*" (Devotions for Thursday.) And when this author is one whose writings come to us regularly, week by week, or month by month, an acquaintance grows up scarcely less real than that of personal intercourse. We get into the habit of looking for his advice and watching eagerly for his good words.

Such was the relation which the "True Catholic" filled during a long and eventful period. It was the time of the publication of the Oxford "Tracts." The great stir produced by Tract No. 90 had been felt on this side of the Atlantic; controversy on the vital doctrines of the Church ran high, especially in Maryland, and people needed a guide. Just then the "True Catholic" began its career. Those who looked up to Bishop Whittingham as their leader, and who soon became the majority in the diocese, found in the clear style and irresistible logic of the editor a great help toward understanding the nature of the questions at issue. Many who read these lines will remember when they used to say to themselves or others, "We must wait and see what the 'True Catholic' will have to say about this"; as if it were certain that the difficulties would seem less formidable after the editor had sifted and discussed them. And so wise and learned were the arguments in its pages that the periodical soon became an authority outside of the diocese in which it was published, and established for its editor a reputation among Churchmen which no American layman has ever excelled.

For a more detailed account of the literary career of Dr. Evans, the reader is referred to the "Memoir" already mentioned. Some notion of the extent of his labors may be had from perusing the list of his works appended to this sketch.

III.

Our limited space forbids our entering into a detailed history of the ecclesiastical career of Dr. Evans, an account of which will also be found in the volume just referred to. We must, however, remark that although he was for many years one of the leaders of the High Church party, and although his periodical, "The True Catholic," was regarded as a sort of standard of Churchmanship in other dioceses besides Maryland, yet Dr. Evans was in no sense a party man. He, if any one could, was able to see that a question had more than one side. He recognized very distinctly the existence of two or more schools of thought within the

Church. Nor was he afraid to call them (for convenience among other reasons) by their well known names. While he would by no means have admitted that the doctrines of his school were not in the truest sense "Evangelical," he did not object that the principles he had "imbibed from Hooker" (whom Keble also called his "Master") should be marked by an appellation which brought out boldly the *high* place assigned by the greatest names in English theology, and equally, as he conceived, by the Holy Scriptures, to the *Church* or Body of Christ in the Christian system. Yet he could do justice to the teaching of earnest men among the "Evangelicals," so far as it was positive, and his language about his early religious instruction is singularly like that of Mr. Liddon with reference to Bishop Hamilton, who also was not brought up in childhood under the influence of those decided Church principles of which he afterward became such a fearless champion.[1]

All manœuvres and tricks, adopted in imitation of political parties, Dr. Evans detested, but "it is all nonsense," he would say, "to talk of ignoring parties in the Church. As long as the different schools of thought exist it is better there should be parties, whose conduct is, or may be, comparatively open and above-board. The moment you get rid of parties you will find that you will have to deal with the spirit of *clique*, which, being secret and underhand, is far worse than the party spirit you were afraid of." It may be said that he was a *High* Churchman because he was a *Churchman*, and he found himself associated with that party because he loved the Prayer Book; and only High Churchmen it seemed were able to accept the Prayer Book without reserve, qualifications, or explanations.

The following remarks on the questions between High and Low Church are particularly valuable, and well illustrate the writer's ability to see both sides of an argument: —

"The questions between the two parties practically re-

1 See Mr. Liddon's *Sketch of Bishop Hamilton*, p. 16. London, 1869.

solve themselves into three classes: those which relate to the doctrine of Baptism; those which relate to the doctrine of the Holy Eucharist; those which relate to the doctrine of the Episcopate. All other questions seem to be obsolete, except just so far as they are absorbed into one of these classes.

"The questions in the first class grow chiefly out of a misapprehension of the meaning of the word *regeneration.* Low Churchmen taking that word in its modern sense, and being very much afraid of attributing any efficacy to an external rite, lest they should diminish the value of internal spiritual operations, seem, in controversy, to attribute less importance to Baptism than they really do. Although the controversy about Baptism has never been lost sight of in Maryland, it has never been brought prominently forward.

"The questions connected with the Holy Eucharist do not grow out of a misapprehension as to the meaning of a word, but like that touching Baptism, they are connected with a fear of over-valuing the outward and visible sign. The Oxford Tracts had been mentioned in one of our Convocations, in which not a single member had seen them, as a sort of test of orthodoxy, or perhaps, to speak more accurately, of heterodoxy. This gave keenness to the sacramental controversy; for the Tracts were commonly believed, by those who had not read them, to teach transubstantiation. The Zuinglian doctrine was apparently adopted by Low Churchmen. *But they really all held a much higher doctrine than they were willing to acknowledge.* The heats growing out of these questions were really connected with the sermon of Mr. Johns.[1] That sermon really taught Zuinglianism. But they readily combined with the third class of questions, which were those by which the Diocese of Maryland was chiefly disturbed."

The fairness and breadth of view in these extracts must commend themselves to every reader, especially when it is

[1] See *Memoir of Hugh Davey Evans*, etc., p. 28.

remembered that the author had been for twenty years in the fore-front of the controversy.

Dr. Evans served with distinction as a delegate from St. Paul's Parish, Baltimore, in the Convention of the Diocese of Maryland in 1828, and from 1836 to 1862, with the exception of two or three years, when he refused to sit as a member of the Convention, because he could not conscientiously vote for his friend the Rev. Dr. Wyatt for Bishop. He did not believe that Dr. Wyatt, whom, however, he admired and loved, would be the best choice for the office. Yet he could not represent Dr. Wyatt's parish (St. Paul's), and vote against him when he was probably the only man in it who did not desire to see Dr. Wyatt elected. Dr. Evans therefore announced his determination not to sit in any Convention until a Bishop should be chosen. In 1840, after an exciting contest of three years' duration, the Rev. William Rollinson Whittingham, D. D., Professor in the General Theological Seminary in New York, was elected Bishop, to the great joy of the High Churchmen of Maryland, and to the satisfaction of many of the Low Church party also. Many serious controversies, however, arose in which Dr. Evans took a very prominent part. Of these no account can be given here.

In 1847, Dr. Evans was chosen lay deputy to the Triennial General Convention. The Editor of "The True Catholic" was warmly welcomed as a valuable addition to the House of Deputies, and was at once placed on the important *Committee on Canons*, where he rendered very great assistance in drawing up the Digest of the Laws of the Church. He continued to represent Maryland in the General Convention, as one of her most honored laymen, until the unfortunate breaking out of the civil war. After grave consideration, Dr. Evans determined to support the Union cause, which he did with great ardor. He believed it to be his duty to do so for the reason which he himself gives in the passage already quoted from his "Recollections."[1] On

[1] See *supra*, p. xx.

the other hand, the majority of the clergy and laity of the Diocese of Maryland sympathized with the South, agreeing with the Southern view of the rights of the States. Dr. Evans thought it his duty, in November, 1861, to address a letter to the London "Guardian" on the subject of the arrest of the Maryland political prisoners. His design was to correct certain statements in a letter of a clergyman of Baltimore, which had been published in that journal, and which he (Dr. Evans) believed conveyed an erroneous impression. The main facts stated in the clergyman's letter could not be denied, whatever defense might be set up for those who did the acts complained of. This letter, which was republished in Baltimore, and various reports that were circulated about the opinions and speeches of Dr. Evans, some of them much exaggerated, gave rise to an impression that, in case any political resolutions should be introduced into the conventions, diocesan or general, he would lend his support to them. Accordingly, the vestry of St. Paul's parish refused to elect him, as usual, as their delegate. It was as painful an act to some of those who voted against him as the refusal to vote for his friend Dr. Wyatt for Bishop, must have been to Dr. Evans himself in 1837. The Convention of Maryland also refused to send her old and learned deputy to the General Convention. This was an unspeakable blow to Dr. Evans. He delighted in the honorable position which he held; he loved the Church ardently, and rejoiced to feel that he really was of use in her councils, but he bore the disappointment with great patience and without any ill-will toward his opponents. The writer believes that, while Dr. Evans was unquestionably a very decided Union man, he was entirely misinterpreted with respect to introducing politics into the conventions; he believes that he would have been sound and conservative in the General Convention of 1862, and would have acted with the large and respectable minority in that body, who opposed, at the risk of misconstruction, the various political resolutions which were introduced at that exciting and important crisis. The reasons for this opinion will be found, by those who are interested in the subject, in the Memoir previously mentioned.

IV.

OUR plan in this sketch has been to follow Dr. Evans in his "Recollections," transcribing some of the most interesting passages, and supplying such a narrative as might serve to connect the extracts together. In doing this, we necessarily brought into view his opinions on many important subjects which are still matters of controversy. We have now finished with the "Recollections," and it remains to give some further notion of his character, and the estimation in which his memory is held by his friends.

Before passing to this, however, we will mention some of his opinions on topics not touched upon in the "Recollections," which were finished in the year 1862.

His intense interest in public affairs, especially his favorite subjects, the English Church and English Politics, continued to the very last. He was a constant reader and subscriber to the London "Guardian," for a great many years, and his initials H. D. E., were well known to many readers of that journal.[1] He greatly admired the "Guardian" (in which many of our readers will sympathize with him), and he wished that the condition of things in our country and Church admitted the publication of a news-

1 "From across the Atlantic is announced by telegraph, the death of Thaddeus Stevens. . . . . A far different character has passed away, whose death is recorded in the New York church papers. Hugh Davey Evans, of Baltimore, was a lawyer of great reading and historical experience, whose counsel and example stood high in the American Church. His initials will be familiar to those of our readers acquainted with the inner life of the sister church, whether in her literature or in the more active life of the Convention. The body of H. D. E. was carried to its resting-place in a good old age, on the 17th ult." — From *The Guardian* of August 19, 1868.

paper of similar character. In general, he agreed with the political and ecclesiastical views of which that journal was the exponent up to the time of his death in 1868. He read many other English newspapers also, especially "The English Churchman," "The Saturday Review," "The Literary Churchman," and others.

Of English public men of the present day, he admired Mr. Gladstone most of all, and his appreciation of that statesman's genius in finance and politics dated very far back. Of course he was delighted to see such a sound and stanch churchman (as he believed Mr. Gladstone to be) taking a leading rank among the statesmen of the day. The writer remembers Dr. Evans saying to him some fifteen years ago or more, in answer to a question, "Gladstone! — he's the greatest man in England."

The "Register's" short-lived career[1] was in the days of the Aberdeen Ministry, — one of the best administrations England had had of late years, according to Dr. Evans, who could never forgive Lord John Russell for breaking it up. During this period Dr. Evans had of course much to say of Mr. Gladstone in his "Thoughts on Current Events," contributed to that journal, one of the best church newspapers ever published in this country. The question came up then in a very forcible shape which has so often since that time been presented to the University of Oxford, Whether Mr. Gladstone deserved the confidence of English churchmen. The Tory party had been much startled by his great speech in answer to Mr. Disraeli on the 17th of December, 1852. Mr. Disraeli, "after four nights' criticism" of his Budget, delivered what was said to be one of his greatest efforts. Mr. Gladstone, contrary to custom, was allowed to deliver a long speech after the "reply" of the leader of the House. He rose at two o'clock in the morning, and for about two hours kept the excited and weary House of Commons enchained. The division was

[1] *The Register* was a newspaper published in Philadelphia, in the interest of the Protestant Episcopal Church, in 1852 and 1853.

taken at four o'clock. Mr. Disraeli was defeated (and with him Lord Derby's Ministry) by a majority of nineteen in a full House. The Aberdeen Administration was then formed, including Lord John Russell, Lord Palmerston, and Mr. Gladstone as Chancellor of the Exchequer. Thereupon, Archdeacon Denison wrote a letter to Mr. Gladstone, in which he told him, as one of his constituents, that since he had taken his seat in a government in which Lord John Russell sat, from that time he could place no confidence in him as representative of Oxford, or as a public man. The loss of the venerable archdeacon's confidence Mr. Gladstone seems to have survived, but this was the beginning of that tremendous opposition to the present Prime Minister which has been so frequently repeated. Dr. Evans says in his "Recollections," that he by no means suspected himself of a want of power of saying sharp things, though he could keep it in check. That he had the power, he showed by his ridicule of the Archdeacon's letter. He made up his mind then, that he would continue to believe in Mr. Gladstone, and that the course of that statesman was right.

Mr. Gladstone has indeed changed greatly since Lord Macaulay, in his brilliant essay in the "Edinburgh Review," spoke of him as "the rising hope of those stern unbending Tories who follow, reluctantly and mutinously, a leader whose experience and eloquence are indispensable to them, but whose cautious temper and moderate opinions they abhor." But if Mr. Gladstone has changed considerably, the times have changed still more. A man's opinions may be modified, while the great principles of his life remain the same. Dr. Evans agreed with Mr. Gladstone's own statement, that while change of opinion in public men is an evil to the country, it is "a much smaller evil than their persistence in a course they know to be wrong." ("A Chapter in Autobiography," 8th edition, p. 10.) So much has been written on this subject, and Mr. Gladstone's opinions and conduct are of such deep interest to all American churchmen — especially to those who would agree with Dr. Evans and the present writer, in both of whom the feeling of admiration almost blended with affection, — that it is worth while to say that in all those important changes, from the Jews' Disabilities Bill to the Disestablishment of the Irish Church, Dr. HUGH DAVEY EVANS — by universal consent second to none in this country as an intelligent observer of English affairs — was able to keep step with Mr. Gladstone. On this last momentous subject we will quote Dr. Evans's own words: —

"As to English and Irish affairs, I think Gladstone is right, though for reasons he does not assign, although they are, no doubt, in his mind. The Church of Ireland ought to be a missionary church, and it cannot be useful as such while it is the object of the hatred of the people, which it always will be while it is established. To get rid of that difficulty, and have the power of regulating its own affairs, it may well give [up] the endowment. Gladstone very properly proposes to leave untouched *modern* endowments. I think the English are mad not to accept these terms, but raise an outcry that the Church of England is in danger. The Church of England *is* in danger, and will be disestablished in a few years, and everything confiscated. Her true policy is to get a safe precedent set in Ireland. Disraeli's plan is to plunder the Irish Church and leave her enslaved, and disabled as a mission church; but it saves the Queen's supremacy, and the patronage. Nothing, I think, gives stronger evidence that Gladstone is right than the meeting at St. James's Hall. Even the Bishop of Oxford could only declaim commonplaces, and all the arguments of the other speakers were mere Erastianism." [1]

The character of Dr. Evans can be judged, in great measure, from his own writings and his long life of self-denying labor — and labor unrequited in this world — for the Church and his fellow-men. Whatever else may be

[1] MS. letter to the Rev. Hall Harrison, June 5, 1868.

desired in the way of drawing a portraiture of him as a man, has been so well done by two of his friends that our readers will thank us for presenting what they have written.

We print first an interesting and valuable communication from an old friend of Dr. Evans and ourselves, who lived for many years in the Diocese of Maryland: —

"WOOSTER, Ohio, *January* 15, 1870.

"REV. AND DEAR BROTHER,—I will most cheerfully comply with your request to furnish the substance of the remarks I had the honor to make in my brief address before the 'Church Brotherhood' of Baltimore, about the late HUGH DAVEY EVANS, LL. D.

"Having been, for some years, the intimate personal friend of the learned lay theologian and canonist, and the transcriber of the MSS. of all the articles he wrote as editor of the 'True Catholic,' contributor to various periodicals, editor — and, in part, author — of 'Theophilus Americanus,' author of 'Anglican Ordinations' (a work of two series), and a number of smaller publications — I enjoyed almost daily intercourse with him for a period of years, and perhaps saw as much of his daily life as any one now living. For this reason, I confined my remarks before the Brotherhood to his personal character, and mentioned such facts only in his private life as I knew would illustrate the lofty principles which constituted his invariable rule of action under all circumstances, for it must be remembered that Dr. Evans was in no sense a mere *expediency-man.* Few men in our times have succeeded so well in defining clearly the principles by which they chose to be governed through life, and none, I will venture to say, have left behind them a more beautiful and instructive record of consistent and rigid adherence to them than our departed friend.

"The first question that seemed to occur to his mind, in view of anything proposed to him to do, was, '*Is it right?*'

and his remarkably quick discernment of all the elements involved, or consequences to be apprehended, enabled him to decide immediately on the course to be pursued. But if, from the nature of the case, it was necessary to adopt a course of action at once, that his after-judgment, enlightened by the teaching of subsequent events, would be constrained to regard as a mistake, he would not rest until he had made every possible effort to rectify the error; and if the interests of others were involved, to repair any damage that it might have caused to them.

"As an illustration of his conscientious adherence to this principle, I will state that on one occasion, when I entered his private office, I found him engaged over some business papers. In a few moments he tied them up in a bundle and deposited them in his desk; when turning to me with his countenance lighted up with unmingled gratification, he remarked that he felt very thankful and comfortable, and that he must tell me the cause. He then stated that, in the course of his professional business, he had become executor upon an estate, which, on being settled, was found to yield, for the benefit of a widow, some three thousand dollars, and which constituted her entire resources for her support.

"He consulted her respecting the investment of the money, and was requested to use his own judgment in the matter. At that time he kept an account with, and deposited his own funds in the Bank of ——, and believing it to be in a prosperous and safe condition, he concluded to deposit there the funds of his widowed client. Subsequently the bank failed. Many persons lost their money, among them Dr. Evans and the widow whose legal adviser he was.

"Years passed away until the day above referred to, when in his private office he stated the facts to me, adding that, soon after his own loss and that of his client, he felt that although he had acted according to the best judgment he could form at the time, — his perfect confidence in which was evident from his having his own funds in the same bank, and although he was aware that he was under no obligation, either legal or moral, to repair the loss to the widow, he could not feel at liberty to disregard the pleadings of *Christian charity,* and at once determined to do what he could. He mentioned the subject to several of his brethren in the legal profession, and as he was not then in full practice, asked a share of their excess of business, which, in admiration of his motives, they readily granted. 'And,' said Dr. Evans in conclusion, 'I have this morning paid the widow the last cent of principal and interest, so that she loses nothing.' I will only add that in accordance with another of the Doctor's established principles (as I have reason to believe and remember), *he made a special contribution to the work of the Church as a thank-offering to God for enabling him to effect the object for which he had so long labored and prayed.*

"The above case was by no means the only one known to me, in which that able and good man manifested the power of Christian principle, and the constraining influence of Christian charity. I know of another instance in which several hundred dollars, the amount of professional fees from a deceased husband, were returned to the widow and orphan children on learning that they were left without support. And I was myself the medium through which he restored to another family in need a considerable sum of money, received as fees from the deceased father and husband.

"Dr. Evans, moreover, was one of the few who kept a regular tithe-account, obligating himself to pay into the Lord's treasury *at least* one tenth of his income. He not only faithfully complied with that Scriptural rule, but greatly exceeded it. And yet he was not lavish of his means, and was a stranger to every species of extravagance. He was never known to purchase anything for which he had no particular use. Had he had the wealth, he would have shown the munificence of a Peabody;[1] but the *Church* would have been the depository of his benefactions, as her literature has been enriched by the contributions of his powerful pen.

"As a Christian Dr. Evans was childlike in his faith, and the fruit of this was an implicit, unquestioning obedience to all the requirements of religion. The mysteries of the faith were as welcome to his belief as were the plainest and most easily understood truths; but only after he had perceived them in the light of Holy Scripture, and traced them in the Church to primitive authority. Dr. Evans was also a *devout* man. He had his set times for closet exercises, and delighted in devotional reading. [Dr. Pusey was a very great favorite with him.[2] His copy of the 'Parochial Sermons' was so worn from constant use that he was obliged to have the volumes rebound. He always carried the 'Book of Common Prayer' in his pocket.] His place

[1] [Some people will think it a startling thing to say, but if we are to be guided in our judgment by the principle implied in St. Luke xxi. 1–4, it can hardly be a question which of the two men here brought in contrast was the more generous. Our valued correspondent would agree with us in this we know. It is just as well to realize it and say it right out. All honor to the good and generous man whose elaborate and costly funeral the people of two countries — while we are writing these lines — are uniting in celebrating. May he find as many to imitate him as he has had to come to bury him and to praise him!

Dr. Evans gave of *his penury;* not indeed all his living like "a certain poor widow," but it must have been very near it. He must have reduced his expenses to the minimum. Out of his small income to give three thousand dollars with the interest! And perhaps at this very time he was paying tithes over and above this. What daily self-denial it must have involved! No wonder his library was but a small one and restricted to books of great value absolutely necessary for the prosecution of his studies. Here is a "beautiful deed" — a καλὸν ἔργον — which speaks volumes, and further words seem quite out of place. — H.]

[2] [From among many passages in the writings of Dr. Evans showing his opinion of this saintly man, we select these few words which occur in a review of *The Entire Absolution of the Penitent.* The sermon, he says, "is pervaded throughout by that spirit of meekness and charity, by which his writings are distinguished beyond those of any living man with whose works we are acquainted." — *True Catholic,* vol. iv. p. 186. — H.]

in the sanctuary was but rarely vacant. In the Liturgy of the Church he found an ample provision of helps in spiritual communion with God, but it was in the Holy Supper that he found the greatest enjoyment and renewal of his spiritual strength. He was regular and systematic in self-examination, and longed to experience more and more the 'love of God shed abroad in his heart by the Holy Ghost.'[1]

"With a powerfully argumentative mind, and a singular capacity of understanding and analyzing evidence, Dr. Evans was eminently qualified as a polemic. His style of composition was remarkably clear, with no waste of words for the sake of embellishment. His propositions were

[1] [A clerical deputy from Maryland to the General Convention of 1850 (now one of our Bishops), lately told us that he journeyed in Dr. Evans's company to Cincinnati on that occasion. He was much with the Doctor, occupying the same room with him, and he distinctly remembers how much he was impressed by the glimpse, thus unavoidably afforded, of his devotional habits. On this same journey a little incident occurred that showed how great a reputation Dr. Evans had out of his own diocese. The Maryland party passed a Sunday at Niagara, where they were joined by others. A gentleman came up to our informant and said, "Who is this Mr. Evans that seems to be such an important member of your company?" "Well, sir, that is Mr. Hugh Davey Evans, a man of some note among us in Maryland." — "*Hugh Davey Evans!* Not the editor of *The True Catholic?*" — "Yes, indeed, the same." — "O! why he's a *very* famous man; I must go and get introduced to him." He then devoted himself to Dr. Evans during his stay at Niagara, or on the journey, for we forget whether the gentleman was himself a deputy to the Convention.

We add here another anecdote, because we have no better place for it. One day, during one of his courses of lectures at the College of St. James (we think it was in 1859, or 1860), Dr. Evans came into our study and asked for a Horace. "One of my young friends in the College," said he, "has requested me to write my name and a line in his Album, and I thought I might get something out of Horace that would answer my purpose." After finding the line, —

"Nil desperandum Teucro duce et auspice Teucro," —

he said; "I want you to tell me whether there would be any *metrical* objection to substituting *Christo* for *Teucro* in that line." We replied there was none, and remarked what a beautiful verse it made. "Then," said he, "that will do," and went and wrote the verse, with his signature appended, thus, —

"Nil desperandum *Christo* duce et auspice *Christo*." — H.]

always well stated, his positions distinctly taken, his analysis clear, and his illustrations striking. Among all the authors in the Church's literature, the judicious Hooker was his favorite. But his reading of that great writer was not after the manner of some who are fond of citing him in support of laxity of discipline or a latitudinarian interpretation of church doctrine. Dr. Evans read Hooker in the light of Hooker; and when he cited his opinions, it was not to extract a few lines, here and there, to present a view contrary to the general tenor of his teachings. On the contrary, he always exhibited the Master of the Temple as consistent with himself.

" Our departed friend will also long be remembered for his genial spirit. He was a great favorite with the young of both sexes, and he loved them in return. Often have I known him, after hours of study, to throw aside the manuscript over which he had been closely engaged in profound thought, and take a part in the sports of a juvenile circle, or amuse his friends with anecdotes drawn from the abundant store with which his mind was supplied. But even then he was ready to instruct, and would spare no pains to gratify any reasonable demand for information.

" In a word, it may be said that no layman of the American Church has exhibited a more laborious devotion to the interests of the Church of Christ, or has given more convincing evidence of his deep devotion to her interests, than has Dr. Evans.

" The 'Treatise on the Christian Doctrine of Marriage' was often the subject of conversation between the Doctor and myself, and in my very last interview with him he expressed the hope that it would be published after his death, if not before. With Christian regard,

" Your friend and brother,

" JAMES MOORE,

" Rector of St. James's Church, Wooster, Ohio."

The very great Christian self-denial, of which the foregoing letter gives such touching examples, becomes the more remarkable when we remember what Dr. Evans has said incidentally of his narrow means in his "Recollections."

The following extracts from a letter from one of the ladies with whom he lived for many years, will enable the reader still better to appreciate the great generosity of his character, and his deep religious feeling: —

"The first year of taxation upon incomes we were on our way together to the tax-office. He remarked, 'My income is larger this year than it ever has been, or ever will be again. I want to lay up enough for my funeral expenses, and if possible, save a little to buy a small annuity.' In December, 1867, he resigned his position as Justice of the Peace. He told me his great object in accepting that position was to make enough to purchase a tombstone for his mother's grave. In this he succeeded. On the day of his resignation he came home and said, 'So closes my office-life. I have now nothing to do but to work for the Church and prepare to die.'

"For a man of his taste and attainments, it was wonderful to see the quiet contentment with which he bore the pinch of narrow means. Upon several occasions he grew a little desponding, fearing he might not be able to meet his necessary expenses. He often had to give up articles of dress really necessary for him to have. He once said to me, 'My whole life has been filled with self-denial. I have never been able to purchase books, and one great cause of my shabby dress is that I am never able to lay aside my clothes until they are thoroughly worn out.' Economy had become so habitual that even when his wants were found out and supplied he would lay the things aside, fearing a time of greater need. And yet so easily contented and satisfied was he that he often said, 'I live in too much luxury for a Christian man; my home is too comfortable, but I cannot give it up.' When I was one day in his library he picked up a volume of Shakespeare, saying, 'When I bought these books I was like Charles Lamb; I had to stand and reflect whether I was *able* to purchase them. I was a young man, had my mother to support, and my means were small.'

"Some months before his death there was a manifest change when in the home circle. There was no abatement of pleasantry, or readiness to engage in lively conversation, but when all was quiet he was deeply engaged in pious meditation, repeating aloud, unconsciously, portions of the Prayer Book. On the Easter before his death, he went to the early celebration of the Holy Communion at St. Paul's Church (a distance of nearly a mile). That evening I told him I wished to illuminate a sentence for his room, and should like to know what he would prefer. He replied: 'I never come home from Holy Communion, but I enter my room repeating, LORD, I BELIEVE, HELP THOU MINE UNBELIEF. If this is too long give me FAITH, HOPE, CHARITY.'"

With respect to the rule of paying tithes, which Mr. Moore says Dr. Evans laid down for his own practice, it may be remarked that he obeyed the precept of the Sermon on the Mount (Matt. vi. 3), and observed such reticence about all these things that even one intimate with him would scarcely know, except by accident, that such was his rule. The following is an instance in point: he had spoken with one of his friends of making an investment; we think it was about the purchase of an annuity, that he might have something to depend upon in his old age, but he had not quite the amount of money requisite. Not long after, some money was paid him. His friend, who knew of this, said to him: —

"Now, Doctor, you can accomplish your purpose, and buy that annuity."

"No. I haven't got quite enough money to do it."

"Why yes. I think you must have; you know it only requires so much."

"Yes, but I haven't got that much."

"That money lately paid you would buy it."

"O but *my tithes* you know! I've got to take my tithes out of that."

He was evidently a little annoyed at having to make the explanation. It was in such ways as this that the strictness of his rule of life would be disclosed.

The meeting of the Church Brotherhood to which Mr. Moore refers, was mainly devoted to a pleasant conversational review of Dr. Evans's life and character. It was suggested to his friend Mr. J. G. Proud, of Baltimore, to contribute some notes illustrative of his social qualities. These MS. notes he has very kindly placed at our disposal, and we shall proceed to make large extracts from them.

"After briefly adverting," says Mr. Proud, "to the request and its object, I said I could relate perhaps the earliest known anecdote of him, which I had heard from my mother. It was but a trivial one, but going back to the years of his early childhood, it furnished an indication of character.

"A lady one day, rather thoughtlessly, taunted him playfully with his homeliness. 'Hugh,' she said, 'you're certainly not a *pretty* boy.'—'I don't tare if I ain't' (was his answer in the imperfect accents of childhood),—'I don't tare if I ain't, I'se dood; *dood* is better than *pootty*.'[1] All who knew him will recognize in this reply the germ of what became a leading trait in his character. He always preferred the '*good*' to the '*pretty*,' the practical to the merely ornamental. His taste in this respect was perhaps too severely simple. He rejected the graces of manner with too

[1] [Some persons have discovered a touch of vanity in this little speech of the child; it is certain that there was the most marked absence of that foible in the character of the man.—H.]

sweeping a judgment. This sometimes gave an abruptness to his style which may have occasionally detracted from its effectiveuess. But it secured its simplicity and directness. He always went straight to his purpose.

" Dr. Evans was eminently social in his habits and feelings; he *enjoyed* compauy, but not indiscriminately. He preferred intimacy with a few to mingling in general society. How it may have been in earlier life, I know not, but certainly in his later years he seemed to limit his intercourse chiefly to a few friends, with whom he could lay aside ceremony and feel perfectly at home. With such he was a most welcome companion, his spirits gushing out with a genial flow, and delighting in playful humor. Sometimes he would indulge in a strain of raillery, in which, in an ironical way, he would say some sharp things; but his friends understood his humor, and knew that no real bitter ness lurked beneath his words. Especially did he delight to affect the misogynist, and to make satirical remarks to the ladies, pretending to depreciate the qualities of their sex, his eyes, meanwhile, sparkling with fun and mischief. It is needless to say that their sex had no warmer or more chivalrous admirer, and, bachelor as he was, he had not among his own sex more earnest or devoted friends than he had with them. His well-known devotion to his mother would vindicate him from the charge of having for her sex any other sentiment than one of reverence and esteem.[1]

[1] [The never-failing devotion of Dr. Evans to his mother is one of the most noble traits of his character. It was this that prevented an engagement to be married from being carried into effect.

Some may perhaps think that this should not have been mentioned lest it should prejudice the reader against some of the author's views in the following work, or make him think that we have here a case in which the proverb applies, *Ne sutor ultra crepidam.* On the contrary, the fact that Dr. Evans was unmarried is one of the remarkable points of his history necessary to be known in forming an estimate of this volume. An elaborate treatise by a bachelor on the Christian Doctrine of Marriage, is in some respects a curiosity, and while all the friends of Dr. Evans knew the fact already, it is proper that the general reader should also be made acquainted with it. — H.]

"Dr. Evans could not be called a great talker, he rarely attempted to lead in conversation. He preferred to listen to what was said by others, which he always did attentively, however humble the speaker, throwing in occasionally some pointed remark of his own. His friends had generally to draw him out by questions for information, or by starting some favorite topic, and then, when you had struck a genial vein, it was a real pleasure to listen to him.

"He was remarkable for condensation of thought and expression, and his words were always ready, going right to the gist of the subject. . . . . Sometimes when opposed in argument on a subject in which he had a deep interest, he would show a degree of warmth — almost of excitement, — but the feeling, if any existed, always passed away with the occasion, and left no bitterness behind.

"He had some strong prejudices, and would sometimes amuse his friends by the earnestness with which he expressed them. He had no taste for music, and I have heard him say that he would go a square out of his way to avoid a band of players. [He used to say, "'Music hath charms to soothe the *savage* breast,' but my breast is not savage."] He was as deficient in knowledge of tune as the learned Dean Hook, who told an American clergyman of my acquaintance that he had a short time before mistaken 'Old Hundred,' played as a compliment to him before his own door, for 'God save the Queen!'

"Dr. Evans loved to talk of our mother Church of England, and her leading men. Indeed, everything conneoted with England was familiar to him, — its history, its politics, its localities, its public men, and its ancient manners and customs. He seemed to have a minute acquaintance with the genealogies of the leading families, and could trace the connections between them by intermarriage. Suggest the name of some prominent man, and you would be likely to obtain from him all you would desire to know. Ask from him an explanation of some phase in English politics, and he would give you a clear and intelligent exposition of the principle involved, and its bearing upon the interests of Church and State. In fact, his knowledge of history, both ancient and modern, was minute and accurate, and his memory exceedingly retentive. I remember once mentioning some obscure facts in Carthaginian history which I had read a few days before in a rare old book, when he immediately took up the subject, and showed not only that he was familiar with them, but had forgotten no material incident. I have known him also to show a minute recollection of facts in legal causes with which he had been professionally connected many years before.

"Although he possessed such vast stores of knowledge, there was never any ostentatious display of learning; his conversation was marked by that unpretending simplicity in manner and language, which was so conspicuous a trait of his personal character.

"Notwithstanding the very great mental disparity between us, it was my high privilege to enjoy an intimacy with him of many years' standing. For years it was his custom to spend an evening of almost every week in our family; and how we miss his pleasant converse we cannot express.

"The last time I saw him alive was when taking leave of him at his own door after a meeting of this Society, or of the Missionary Committee, from which he had walked home leaning upon my arm. How little I thought that it was for the last time.

"At that meeting he had taken great interest in the discussion of the affairs of the Church Home in our city, and had headed a subscription, suggested by himself, toward the maintenance of free beds at that excellent institution. With the exception, perhaps, of a meeting of the Missionary Committee a few days after, this was the last Church work in which he publicly took part, and it seems now to have a peculiar and beautiful fitness. His kindly heart was then moved to aid in providing a bed for the sick and destitute, little knowing that he was so soon to be stretched in mortal sickness upon his own. But doubtless in that trying hour he fully realized the promised blessing. In the loving hearts and gentle ministrations which were about him, and in the tranquil submission of that closing scene, we seem to read the fulfillment of the words, 'Blessed be the man that provideth for the sick and needy; The Lord shall deliver him in the time of trouble. The Lord will strengthen him upon the bed of languishing: Thou wilt make all his bed in his sickness.'"

But little remains to be told. Dr. Evans kept up his habits of untiring industry to the very last. He was constantly reading and writing.

"During the winter before his death he was very much engaged in reading, collecting materials for the enlargement of some future edition of his work on the 'Christian Doctrine of Marriage,' which was then in the hands of publishers in Chicago. Two valuable note-books, greatly increased by the winter's reading, were left by him. These books cost him much labor and covered an immense ground of reading. He said to me one day when reading extracts, 'How tiresome it is to copy, but I must have notes to refer to.' During the latter part of the winter he was greatly interested in the early English writers, — Piers Ploughman, and the publications of the early English Text Society, Chaucer, and others. It seemed to him truly a season of rest from all out-door work, and he gave himself to literary pursuits, — the first time in his life, perhaps, that he was ever able to gratify his taste." [1]

Our own last interview with him was on Monday, July 13, 1868, three days before his death. We had called, not knowing that he was ill. He was in bed, but he talked as readily and as instructively as usual. Among other subjects

1 MS. letter from Miss M. B. to the Rev. Hall Harrison.

we spoke of Ritualism; of the approaching General Convention; of his work on Marriage, and, in particular, of certain objections which had been taken to his views about divorce. The propriety of the marriage of first cousins was also discussed. He asked if we had ever read the answer of Pope Gregory the Great, to the questions of St. Augustine, of Canterbury, on the subject. On our replying we had not, he at once referred to a particular shelf in his library, and told us to take down the first volume of Johnson's "Laws and Canons of the Church of England" (Oxford, 1850), and carry it home with us.

An attack of pain which came on brought our visit rather abruptly to a close, but we left him fully expecting to see him well in a few days. But this was not to be. His disease was an acute attack of dysentery, from which his physician and intimate friend (Dr. Samuel Chew) thought he would, humanly speaking, have recovered beyond doubt, had not one or two days of, perhaps, the hottest weather ever known in Baltimore, set in just as he was getting better. He was entirely prostrated, and sank rapidly. We shall continue the account of his last hours in the simple and unaffected language of one of the ladies, with whom he found for so many years a comfortable and much-loved home.

"The Doctor anticipated a long spell of illness, thinking he would have the same disease of which his mother died. He had made every preparation for this illness; often spoke of it, saying what he wished done, whom he wished sent for. It was evident that he dreaded falling into the hands of a hired nurse. My sister and myself assured him that such should never be the case; that we would take care of him, and never permit him to be moved from our house. I must think that he thought of that promise when he was taken so much worse. He grasped my hand so tightly, that I could not release myself. I leaned down to listen, and heard him say, 'Don't leave me.' When I told him I must send for the doctor, he let me go.

"On the Monday after you left him, he told me what a pleasant conversation he had had, adding, 'Difference of political opinion has never made any coolness between H—— and myself. I am very fond of him, and believe he is a strong friend of mine. I have always been sorry that I had to express myself as I did in my letter to 'The Guardian' about W—— H——. I did not agree with him, but he is a good man. It was my opinion, and I think the same now.' He then went on to tell me what a sore trial it was to him, and how deeply his feelings had been wounded by the coldness of some of his friends. That a few days before, when at the library, he met an old friend, who turned his back upon him. 'The war has taken ten years from my life.' We then had a long conversation in which he expressed his sentiments at length. He had been making preparations, even at that early day, for the approaching General Convention. [He had also drawn up and published a *canon*,[1] which he intended to propose, on the degrees of relationship within which marriage might not lawfully be contracted, and on divorce.] Among other things, he said, 'Six years ago and three years ago, they would not elect me, because they thought I was a violent party man; they thought I would bring politics into the Church. They never were more mistaken in their lives. I was for keeping politics out of the Church; I was then very anxious to go; I could have done much good, for they knew my political sentiments. That time has passed; I suppose, after next October, I shall never be at another General Convention; I shall in three years more be too old.' His face brightened up as he added, 'And W—— H—— told me he would take me under his care next October.' Then he said, 'I am quite sure I shall live to go to the General Convention; this will not be my last illness; I shall be up to-morrow.'

"Though he was such a strong Union man, there was

[1] See Appendix.

no bitterness in his feelings toward the people of the South, though when excited he would say things that he afterwards told me he was very sorry for, 'but I could not help it,' he would say. He told me, too, that he had always given as much as he could spare whenever a collection was taken up for Southern orphans, or for any other charity connected with the South.

"On Wednesday I was at his bedside all day. He was very talkative, in full possession of his intellect, constantly making quotations from different authors. I remarked, on giving him some food, that there was but a trifle left. He replied, with a smile, 'Your trifle 's no trifle I ween, to a customer prudent as I am.' Several times during the day, after waking from a short sleep, he would say, 'I thought you were my mother; I was dreaming of her.' A volume of 'Notes and Queries' lay upon the table, which he wanted to read, but we objected to it. We did not then consider him very ill; he was decidedly better; but there was danger lest the tropical heat of those few days, might cause a relapse.

"At seven o'clock in the evening, the great change came. We sent for his friends, Messrs. R. and J. Proud, fearing he might become restless, but such was not the case. All was calm, quiet peace. He continued perfectly conscious up to twelve o'clock at night, when it became evident that he was sinking. At five o'clock in the morning, we sent for an old colored woman who had been much with his mother. When she came she fell upon her knees at his bedside, and prayed that the Lord would receive his spirit, and that she might be permitted to see his face in heaven. At six o'clock on Thursday morning, July 16, 1868, he fell asleep, as calmly and quietly as an infant going to rest.

"The deep solemnity of that peaceful death-bed scene is still before me. Living in such a constant state of preparation, when the hour came there was no need for more than to lie down and fall asleep.

"For seventeen years the Doctor had been the pleasant companion of our home circle. You can readily imagine, as the long winter evenings come on, how much I miss the literary conversation, the pleasant and instructive reading, that filled up the spare moments of home life.

"I have now given you a faithful account of the last illness of our dear old friend. You must glean from it such portions as may be suitable for publication. I have entered into these lengthy details that you may understand how fully his private life accorded with his outward profession, — an humble, self-denying member of Christ."[1]

On Friday afternoon, July 17, he was followed by his friends, including many of the clergy, to his resting-place, beside his mother, in St. Paul's Church-yard, Baltimore. The funeral service was held in St. Paul's Church, of which he had so long been a vestryman. It was immediately after the regular Evening Prayer, and one of those beautiful and remarkable coincidences occurred which are constantly happening in our services as prescribed in the Prayer Book. The next to the last verse of the first lesson appointed (Job v.) is as follows: —

"THOU SHALT COME TO THY GRAVE IN A FULL AGE, LIKE AS A SHOCK OF CORN COMETH IN IN HIS SEASON."

Scarcely had these words been read when they seemed to receive an illustration, for the doors of the church were thrown open, and the funeral train entered bearing the mortal remains of HUGH DAVEY EVANS, in the 77th year of his age.

It is proper to subjoin the opening paragraphs of his Will: —

"IN THE NAME OF GOD, AMEN. I, Hugh Davey Evans, of the city of Baltimore, Counsellor and Attorney at Law, do make, publish, and declare, this my last Will and Testament, written with my own hand, I being in sound

[1] MS. letter from Miss M. B. to the Rev. Hall Harrison.

health, both of body and mind, hereby revoking all former Wills, Testaments, and Codicils heretofore by me made.

"*Imprimis:* I commit my soul to the infinite mercy of God, the Father, Son, and Holy Ghost, its Creator, Redeemer, and Sanctifier, praying that through the merits of Jesus Christ our Lord, the only begotten Son, my many sins may be forgiven, and that I may have the benefit of His Atonement in departing this life in the Communion of His Holy Catholic Church, and in a joyful Resurrection. I make this declaration, not as a matter of form, but because I think it becomes a Christian, in an act which is always a solemn one, because it is done in contemplation of death, to confess those truths which are to be his support in that awful hour.

"*Item.* — I desire that my body may be buried in my mother's grave, in St. Paul's Church-yard, in the city of Baltimore, or in any other place to which her remains may have been removed. But if I should die at such a distance from her grave that my body cannot be transported thither without expense, or inconvenience greater than usual, I desire that I should be buried at the most convenient place. In every case I direct that my funeral shall be as plain and inexpensive as possible, conformable to my circumstances, which are very narrow.

"*Item.* — I direct my executor, hereinafter named, to erect over my mother's grave a plain, white, marble slab, with the inscription of which the form will be found in the trunk with this Will, filling up the blank left for the time of my death. Should I have erected such a slab, let as much of the inscription as may not be already on it be added, with the blank filled. This paragraph of my Will is to be executed literally, wherever I may be buried." [1]

Such a man was Hugh Davey Evans. The facts that have been related speak for themselves. From them —

[1] The inscription will be found at the foot of the next page.

from his life and his works — his character is to be judged, and not from any words or opinions of others.

It frequently happens that people who perhaps think they are following the maxim, *de mortuis nil nisi bonum*, write in an extravagant and unreal way of those who have gone from us. They pervert that true maxim. It is great injustice and wrong, when a good man dies — one who did his work quietly, according to the light which he had, but without displaying any remarkable ability, or really attaining any very high standard — to heap upon him flattery and panegyric so overstrained that what there was of real goodness and usefulness is hidden from our eyes.

We would fall into no such error in writing of one who had "that chastity of honor which felt a stain like a wound," and who never went beyond the bounds of what he believed to be the truth in all his numerous writings — thereby laying himself open at times to the appearance of

IN MEMORY OF
Elizabeth Wilcocks Evans,
BORN
April 9, 1758,
DIED
October 10, 1846;
AND OF HER ONLY DAUGHTER,
Elizabeth Woodsop Evans,
BORN
April 7, 1791,
DIED
July 19, 1791;
AND OF HER ONLY SON,
Hugh Davey Evans,
BORN
April 26, 1792,
DIED
July 16, 1868.

"*As it is appointed unto men once to die, but after this the judgment; so Christ was once offered to bear the sins of many; and unto them that look for Him, shall He appear the second time without sin unto salvation.*" *Hebrews ix.* 27, 28.

"*For yet a little while and He that shall come will come and will not tarry. Now the just shall live by faith; but if any man hold back, my soul shall have no pleasure in him. But we are not of them that draw back unto perdition; but of them that believe to the saving of the soul.*" *Hebrews x.* 37-39.

having less deep feeling than he really possessed. But facts are facts, and HUGH DAVEY EVANS, if any man ever did, practiced the great rule of Christian life as laid down by our blessed Lord Himself. That daily self-denial, that hidden taking up of the cross, that bountiful almsgiving out of his penury, that love for even the least of Christ's brethren, — all these were, beyond any question, leading traits in the noble character which we have so imperfectly sketched.

Who can fail to be affected by his own simple story of his early years? Born of parents of very limited means, with the poorest schooling, and compelled to give up even that at the early age of thirteen to aid his widowed mother in making her living, he yet proved his commanding intellectual ability and indomitable strength of character, by surmounting the most crushing obstacles, and attaining real eminence in various branches of learning, — in Law, in History, in Theology, three of the largest departments of human knowledge.

Add to these mental accomplishments, his noble private character, and all will admit that we have here a man whose friends may, without any sense of unreality or extravagance, look up to his bright example as one of the very salt of the earth, — a man to be admired, to be loved, to be imitated. To be admired for his great mind devoted to the service of the Catholic Church, and that branch of it in which his lot was cast, — both of which he loved with all his heart and soul, — as well as for his spotless character; to be loved for his affectionate, kindly, genial nature; to be imitated in his child-like spirit, his Christian courage, his perfect truthfulness, his unaffected piety. Forget for a moment the vulgar standard of the world, and it must be acknowledged that HUGH DAVEY EVANS had in him the elements of real greatness. For in what does true greatness consist? We answer the question in the words of a clear and philosophic writer: —

"A man's greatness lies not in his wealth or station, as the vulgar believe; nor yet in his intellectual capacity, which is often associated with the meanest moral character, the most abject servility to those in high places, and arrogance to the poor and lowly; but a man's true greatness lies in the consciousness of an honest purpose through life, founded on a just estimate of himself and everything else, on frequent self-examination, and a steady obedience to the rule which he knows to be right, without troubling himself as the emperor (M. Aurelius) says he should not, about what others may think or say, or whether they do or do not do that which he thinks and says and does."[1]

The same thought essentially, only made beautiful by the coloring of deep Christian feeling thrown over it, is thus expressed by one of the most remarkable writers of the day: —

"What we are outwardly in this world, what men think or say of us, of our titles, of our incomes, or of the absence of them; all this matters but little; all these are leveled by death. But what we are in ourselves, in our consciences, our hopes, our affections, and wills, before God our Father in Heaven, and His blessed Son our Divine Redeemer; this is a matter of an importance that is simply unspeakable, fraught to each one of us with consequences more lasting and more momentous than the mind of man can conceive."[2]

In this light then, and not with eyes blinded by worldly station or the dazzling show which in this age mere money brings with it, let us form our estimate of this good man; a man who, after doing valuable, and, in great measure, unrequited service to the Church, lost his honorable seat in her Councils from a misconception, on the part of others,

[1] *The Thoughts of the Emperor M. Aurelius Antoninus.* Translated by George Long. Introduction, p. 27: London, 1869.

[2] *Life in Death.* A Sermon in Memory of Bishop Hamilton, by H. P. Liddon, M. A., p. 28.

of his principles and purposes, as we verily believe and have tried to show;[1] and who, having borne this grievous disappointment for many years, not only without repining, but in a spirit of beautiful patience, has left to those who knew him best a touching and never-to-be-forgotten example of that —

> "Calm old age which conscience pure
> And self-commanding hearts insure;
> Waiting his summons to the sky,
> Content to live, but not afraid to die."

[1] See the *Memoir* from which this account is abridged, pp. 63 *et seq.*

CATALOGUE OF THE PRINCIPAL PUBLISHED WRITINGS OF HUGH DAVEY EVANS, LL. D.

1. An Essay on Pleading, with a View to an Improved System. 1 vol. 8vo. Baltimore, 1827.
2. Harris's Entries. Revised by Hugh Davey Evans. (Year of publication unknown.)
3. A Treatise on the Course of Proceedings in the Common Law Courts of the State of Maryland. 1 vol. 8vo. Baltimore, 1837. A new and revised edition was published some thirty years afterwards.
4. A Letter to the Rev. Henry V. D. Johns, occasioned by the Publication of his Sermon entitled, "The Protestant Episcopal Pastor." Baltimore, 1842. (Pamphlet.)
5. Essays to Prove the Validity of Anglican Ordinations. 1 vol. 12mo. Baltimore: Robinson, 1844.
6. Essays to Prove the Validity of Anglican Ordinations. Second series. 2 vols. 12mo. Baltimore: Robinson, 1851.
7. Remarks on the Correspondence between Bp. Whittingham and the Rev. Mr. Trapnell, in a Letter to the Laity. Baltimore, 1846. (Pamphlet.)
8. A Second Letter to the Laity of the Diocese of Maryland, by one of their Number. Baltimore, 1846, or 1847. (Pamphlet.)
9. The Unholy Alliance of Church and State: By a Lay Communicant. Printed in New Hampshire, and published in Richmond, Virginia, 1846. (Pamphlet.)

This pamphlet did not, as its title might lead one to suppose, discuss the condition of the Church in England. The writer of it "considers that the Church *in this country* has not yet fully thrown off the domination of the State." He regards the admission of worldly men to a share in the government of the Church, for worldly considerations, as a great evil which had its origin in the Alliance of Church and State. . . . He concludes with *recommending that Churchmen shall "determine not to aid in sending to legislate for the Church, any man who is not a dutiful son of the Church, as well in practice as in theory, — who has not ratified his baptismal vows, and does not habitually seek for spiritual strength and grace at the table of his Lord."* Notice in the "True Catholic," vol. iii. p. 562.

10. Some Observations on some Remarkable Passages in Mr. Goode's Work on Baptism. Baltimore: Robinson. (Pamphlet.)

11. Theophilus Americanus; or, Instruction for the Young Student concerning the Church and the American Branch of it. Chiefly from the fifth edition of "Theophilus Anglicanus." By Chr. Woodsworth, D. D., Canon of Westminster; Late Head Master of Harrow School. Edited by Hugh Davey Evans, LL. D. 1 vol. 12mo. Philadelphia: Hooker, 1851. 2d edition, *Ibid.*, 1852. 3d edition, *Ibid.*, R. Macauley, 1870.
12. An Essay on the Episcopate of the Protestant Episcopal Church in the United States. 1 vol. 12mo. Philadelphia: Hooker, 1855.
13. The True Catholic: A Monthly Magazine. 14 vols. 8vo. 1843–1856.
14. A Treatise on the Christian Doctrine of Marriage. New York: Hurd and Houghton, 1870.

CONTRIBUTIONS TO "THE TRUE CATHOLIC," VOLS. II.–VIII.[1]

VOL. II. (*May*, 1844 — *April*, 1845.)

1. The Connection of Church Principles.
2. The Authority of the Church.
3. Private Judgment.
4. The Rights of the Laity.
5. Episcopal Authority.
6. Dissent and Semi-dissent.
7. Defective Views.
8. Rationalism.
9. Importance of Words.
10. Rationalism (continued).
11. Discipline.
12. The General Convention of 1844.
13. The Truth.
14. German Theology — a review of Mr. Dewer's Work.
15. Non-essentials.
16. Romanizing.
17. The Unity of the Church.
18. The Proceedings against the Bishop of New York.
19. The Unity of the Church (continued).

[1] No list of articles in Vol. I. is given, because it was impossible to distinguish with certainty those of Dr. Evans from those of his coadjutor the Rev. Mr. Hoffman. Nearly all however were written by Dr. Evans. The catalogue which is given of the leading articles in Vols. II.–VIII. (we regret that we had not the remaining six volumes at hand), presents a most inadequate idea of the vast amount of work which Dr. Evans did in those days. No mention is made of the notices of books, which formed an important feature of the periodical. They were written in a vigorous and spirited style — often displaying considerable caustic humor, — and conveyed valuable theological teaching. The articles (begun in the 4th vol.) called "Church Affairs," are also not included in this list. These were often very elaborate, and must have cost immense labor. They discussed, in a style far more graphic and interesting than he generally employed in his leading articles, all the important doings in the Church both in this country and in England. For example, apropos of the *Gorham* controversy, these articles on Church Affairs contained valuable discussions of the Baptismal question now, unhappily, revived among us.

VOL. III. (*May*, 1845 — *April*, 1846.)

20. On the Respect due to Ecclesiastical Authority.
21. Our Common Christianity.
22–24. Church Law.
25. Necessity (on the Apostolic Succession).
26, 27. The Principle of Protestantism. (Review of Dr. Schaff's Work).
28. The Diseases of Protestantism.
29. Christian Politics.
30. On Mr. Newman's Secession.
31–33. Lay-Baptism.
34. Development. (Review of Dr. Newman's Work.)

VOL. IV. (*May*, 1846 — *April*, 1847.)

35. Schism.
36. Religious Symbols.
37. Faith and Opinion.
38–40. The Mystical Presence. (Review of Dr. Nevins' Treatise, which is most highly commended as a most valuable theological work, entitled to the confidence and gratitude of a true Catholic.)
41. Conscience.
44. Episcopal Authority.
45. The Dangers of the Church.
46. Individuation.

VOL. V. (*May*, 1847 — *April*, 1848.)

47. Aggregation.
48. Ought the Minister to Preside in the Vestry?
49. Assimilation.
50. Church Law.
51–53. The Episcopate.
54. Extremes.
55. Private Interpretation.
56, 57. Suffragan Bishops.
58. Romanism.

VOL. VI. (*May*, 1848 — *April*, 1849.

59, 60. The Progress and Prospects of the Church.
61. Church Finance.
62. The word "Catholic."
63. Duty and Authority.
64, 65. The Generative Principle of Political Constitutions. A review of De Maistre's Essay on the subject.
66. Development and the Papacy.
67. Church Unity.
68. Sectarianism.

VOL. VII. (*May*, 1849 — *April*, 1850.)

69. The World in the Church.
70. Sacrifice.
71–72. The American Epoch.
73. The Missionary Society.
74. The Philosophy of Religion. A review of Morrell's Work.
75. Revelation.
76. Inspiration.
77. Confession.
78. Development.
79. Regeneration. Apropos of the Gorham Controversy.

Vol. VIII. (*May*, 1850—*April*, 1851.)

80. The Articles.
81, 82. Bishops in the United States.
83. The late Maryland Convention—Bishop Whittingham and Dr. H. V. D. Johns.
84, 85. Interpretation.
86, 87. The Visibility of the Church.
88. Amusements.
89. The Pursuit of Wealth.
90. Education.

The following articles were contributed to the first and second volumes of the "American Church Monthly" (in 1857), edited by the Rev. Henry N. Hudson, M. A., who says of H. D. E.: "Our most sound and solid contributor of Baltimore, at whose feet the best of us may sit, and that to learn theology as well as law." Vol. I. p. 396.

91. Ecclesiastical Polity.
92. Moral Theology and Moral Philosophy.
93. Providence.
94. Reverence.
95. Divorce.
96. Inter-dependence.
97. The Reformation.
98. City Amusements.
99. Christian Morals.
100. Marriage.—The Choice of an Associate.
101. Cities.
102. The Relations of Church and State.

CORRIGENDA.

P. 48. *The first line of the second paragraph from the bottom should read:* Each of the others rests upon a merely false notion. One rests, etc.

P. 296, note. *For* others, *read* other States.

P. 321, § 7. A reference should have been made here to Bp. COXE's *Moral Reforms*, Philadelphia, Lippincott, 1869.

CONTENTS.

A TREATISE

ON THE

CHRISTIAN DOCTRINE OF MARRIAGE.

CHAPTER I.

INTRODUCTORY — OF SOCIETY, LAW, PUBLIC OPINION, AND PRIVATE CONSCIENCE.

§ 1. Necessity of Society. — § 2. The Family. — § 3. Law of God. — § 4. Customary or Traditional Law. — § 5. Necessity and Nature of Authority and Law. — § 6. The Three divinely appointed Societies. — § 7. The Church. — § 8. Comparison of the Family, the Church, and the State. — § 9. Private Conscience. — § 10. Morality. — § 11. General Society and Public Opinion. — § 12. The three authoritative Societies designed for different Purposes. — § 13. Constitution of the Family. — § 14. Departments of Government. — § 15. Government of the Family. — § 16. Paternal Government in the State. — § 17. General Principles of Civil Government. — § 18. General Principles of Church Government. — § 19. Relations of Church and State. — § 20. Conflicting Laws. — § 21. Matrimonial Causes. — § 22. Civil Jurisdiction in Matrimonial Causes. — § 23. Ecclesiastical Jurisdiction in Matrimonial Causes. — § 24. Four Classes of Matrimonial Causes. — § 25. Proceedings for Divorce *a Mensa et Thoro* and for Restitution of Conjugal Rights. — § 26. Proceedings to obtain a Declaration of Nullity of Marriage. — § 27. Jactitation of Marriage. — § 28. The State of Things in America. — § 29. The Object of the Work.

§ 1. Society is necessary to the well-being of man. God has declared that "it is not good for man to be alone." It is true in a much wider sense than that which is usually given to it. The connection with the creation of woman, of this declaration, shows that its application is in the first place to the relation between the sexes, and especially to marriage; but it also means that society is necessary to the well-being of man. The broader sense includes the narrower, for woman was created for marriage and marriage is the foundation of society. Out of it arises the family, which is at once the germ of all other societies and the material of which they are made. The well-being of every society depends upon the well-being of the families of which it is composed, and that upon the laws and opinions by which marriage and the relations between the sexes are governed. A right understanding upon these subjects is of the highest importance, and is, unfortunately, very rare in this country. Hence the need of some such work as the present.

§ 2. The word family has several meanings, of which it is only necessary to mention two. The primary sense is that of a household composed of a man, his wife, children, and dependents living together under his authority. It is to such a family that what has been said is to be applied. In the only other sense, which will be mentioned, a family includes all persons who have a descent from a common ancestor, which can be traced through males. This idea may also be expressed by the word race.

The household, as appears by the Holy Scriptures, once existed in a state of independence, and was not included in any other society. It would in that state have whatever is essential to a family. It would be a society for the worship of God and the preservation of religion, and so would be a church. It would have the right of protecting its members from injuries, whether offered by other members of the same family or by members of other families. These rights are the germs of judicial authority and of the rights of war and peace. Such a family is, therefore, the germ of a state.

§ 3. As the members of such a family grew up and established themselves, they would frequently settle in the neighborhood of the parent stock. There would thus arise a community formed of households. The necessity of rules to regulate the conduct of men to each other would then be felt. In a single household, the head might govern without much regard to rule; but the chief of several households would be liable to suspicions of partiality from which he would gladly take refuge in rules and laws.

Law is well defined by Blackstone: "A rule of action which is prescribed by some superior, and which the inferior is bound to obey."[1] The superior must possess that right to control the actions of the inferior, which is called authority, or the inferior would not be bound to obey the rule. God is the only being of whom man can conceive as possessing underived power or authority. His law is paramount to all other laws, which must derive their authority from it. No man and no number of men, unless they have an authority given to them by God, can have any right to control any other man, or to make any law which shall bind him.

§ 4. In primitive societies, the rule of action is generally a revelation, real or pretended. In either case, it is preserved by traditions, which grow into usages and customs. These are supposed to be conformable to the Divine will, because they have been handed down to the existing generation from their forefathers. They constitute customary law. This seems to exist everywhere, and to be assumed and implied in all written law. It is enforced by those to whom Divine providence has given authority, and thus acquires, although not in a very strict sense, the character of a rule prescribed by a superior, which an inferior is bound to obey.

§ 5. Marriage produces a family. Families expand into races, which are sometimes called clans or tribes. These break up and unite in various ways, and thus a community is formed, which is not all of one race. New members are added to it by birth and by aggregation. The common

[1] 1 *Comm.* p. 38.

descent of the original members is forgotten, and thus it appears to be a mere aggregation of human beings. Such a community needs authority and law more than a family, or even a clan or tribe. Without them it could never have been formed, and if they ceased to exist it must be dissolved. They are necessary for the protection of the weaker and simpler members of the society.

Laws must be made by persons who have authority, and authority must be derived from God. There are but two modes in which it can be shown to have been so derived. It must rest on a direct revelation, or on the fact that God, in his providential government of the world, has permitted certain persons to have the power of enforcing their decrees. It is not an exception to this rule, that authority sometimes rests on a combination of the two things. In the case of the Church, authority was at first committed by direct revelation to a body of men, with power to perpetuate themselves by a continual admission of new members. Still the new members are providentially designated.

Authority and human law are necessary to society, for God does not, in this world, enforce his law by a direct manifestation of his power. He leaves it to be enforced by men, and that it may be so enforced it must be interpreted by men. Human laws are nothing more than rules laid down to govern those to whom the enforcement of the Divine law is committed. The law of God is his will as to the conduct of men. It is to be gathered from three sources; his Word, his works, and his providence. From the last, taken alone, his will in particular cases may be learned, but it scarcely gives any general rules. These must be found in the Revealed Word or gathered from observation of the works of God in connection with his providence. Those contained in the Word are called, collectively, Moral Theology, Christian Law, or Christian Ethics. The rules inferred from the observation of God's works are called, collectively, Moral Philosophy or Natural Law, as actions are viewed in connection with duties or rights. It may be remarked that no system of moral philosophy or natural law, which shall approach to completeness, can be framed without the aid of revelation.

§ 6. All laws require to be enforced and, therefore, to be interpreted. For these purposes God has instituted three classes of societies, to which it is his will that every human being shall belong. As these societies have duties to perform, they must be organized. The organs of an animal are the parts by means of which it performs its natural functions. The officers of a society, by means of whom it performs its functions, may therefore be called its organs. A society which has duties must have such functionaries, and must have rules by which their powers and duties are defined, distributed, and limited. Those rules are its organization and constitute it an organized society.

There are, as has been said, three classes or kinds of organized societies, which have divinely given authority. To some particular organization in each class, it seems to be the will of God that every human being should belong. Each has authority over its own members within its proper sphere.

A particular society may take many forms without losing its title to a place in its proper class. Each of the three classes was instituted for a particular purpose: churches to take charge of the spiritual welfare of men; states to take charge of their temporal welfare; families to provide for the education and training of young persons, so as to promote their welfare in both spiritual and temporal affairs.

§ 7. The Church is perhaps not so much a class of societies as a single society, extending in design, although not yet in fact, throughout the world. But its very extent involves the necessity of its including many lesser organizations. The general society is really a federation in which practical power is committed to lesser federations included within the larger. It is, therefore, not improper to speak of churches in the sense of such lesser federations, and of the Church as a class of societies.

Organized societies differ very much in the number of their members, in the extent of territory over which they spread, and in the principles upon which membership rests. The authority of the family extends, in each case, over a few persons, mostly bound together by a common descent, and living in a single house. Wherever it is attempted to extend the authority of the family much beyond these limits, the experiment fails. To give it even the appearance of success, the society must be organized upon principles which are not consistent with the character of the family.

The authority of the state extends over all persons living within a certain territory. It may be large or small, populous or otherwise, but it is assumed that the persons occupying it are a community, that is, have a body of interests and opinions in common. The constituted authorities of the state represent this community. They exercise authority over its members, over the territory which it occupies, and over all persons and things within that territory.

The Church has, by Divine appointment, authority over all mankind, all of whom ought to enter into the one Church by connecting themselves with some one of her federated societies. But as she has no means of enforcing her authority, except exclusion from her privileges, which is of no avail against those who do not desire them, she has practically no members who have not joined her of their own will.

The federated societies which constitute the one Church are really branches, which have grown out of one root and therefore historically are not federated; yet they are so practically. In fact, they are very loosely bound together as to externals, though spiritually they are one, at least in theory. The units of which the great society is composed are collected into smaller societies. These are bound together in federations, which are much more closely united than the great society. The lesser federations generally have territorial boundaries, within which they have authority over all the members of the Church, and are missionary societies for the conversion of all who are not members. These boundaries not unfrequently coincide with those of particular states.

There are several differences between the particular churches, as the smaller federations are called, and the particular states within whose territorial boundaries they exist. They differ as to their organization, their objects, and the nature of the matters about which they are occupied.

The identity of territory, and consequently of the persons who ought to be subject to the authority of particular churches with those who are subjects of particular states, has led to the notion that the Church and State are two manifestations of one society. This notion is the basis of the doctrine of the union or rather the unity of Church and State. It has been said that the two organizations are merely two manifestations of one society, because the members of both are the same persons. If it were assumed that both organizations were created by the society itself, this might be true; but if one of them be of Divine institution, it is not a manifestation of the society. It is an instrument appointed by God, through which to instruct and rule the members of the society.

§ 8. In some sense both Church and State are of Divine appointment. This is true also of the Family. But it is true in each case in a different way. The organization of the Family is settled by a Divine law, which has been plainly revealed. In the Church, the general principles of the organization have been revealed; but many things are left to be regulated by the authority of the Church herself, "according to the diversity of countries, times, and men's manners, so that nothing be ordained against God's Word."

As to the State, very little more has been revealed than that it is agreeable to the Divine will that there should be such an organization and that it should be obeyed. Everything else has been left to human law and the disposal of Divine providence. The only rule seems to be: "Let every soul be subject to the higher powers. For there is no power but of God: the powers that be are ordained of God."[1]

The Church and the State have their proper spheres, and have authority each within its own sphere; but the authority of both is limited, because it is a derived and therefore a subordinate authority. They may, each within its own sphere, interpret, apply, and enforce the law of God. Neither ought to erect any rule inconsistent with that law, for from it all human authority is derived.

§ 9. This is the foundation of the right and duty of private conscience, which is commonly confounded with private judgment. The two things are as different as judgment and conscience. Judgment may be occupied about anything, may decide all questions as well those of mere expediency as those of right and wrong. The difference may be illustrated by a case of very common occurrence. A man in authority decides what is the true interpretation of a law. Another man who is under his authority appeals to his own private judgment, and says, "You are mistaken in your interpretation; I will disregard it and follow my own." This is private judgment, and unwarranted. But if a man appeals to his private conscience, and finds that he cannot comply with the law as interpreted by his superior, he is bound to disobey. It is disputed whether conscience is an independent faculty or a mere function of the reason, while it is agreed that judgment is a mere function of the reason. Whether they be functions of the same faculty or not, it is clear that they operate in different spheres. Judgment may decide any question; conscience can only act upon questions of right and wrong.

[1] Romans xiii. 1.

A man may give up his judgment to authority, but not his conscience. That which he is convinced is wrong in the sight of God, he may not do upon man's authority. But if that which he is required by human authority to do, be not contrary to the law of God, his conscience has nothing to do with the question of obedience, except that it ought to tell him that it is his duty to obey the powers that God has set over him. To such authority he should submit his private judgment, except when it clearly contravenes the law of God. Moreover men should remember, what they too often forget, that their private consciences are strictly private, and that the conscience of one man is no guide to another, nor is it any authority for him who has never been subjected to it by Divine authority.

The office of private conscience with respect to human laws, is to decide whether they are inconsistent with the Divine law. Its office ascertains its limits; in this, as in other cases, a right cannot extend beyond the principles upon which it rests. The function of private conscience is to inquire whether an inferior law is so inconsistent with a superior one that one cannot be obeyed without disobeying the other. It is to do this only for the person whose conscience it is. When both laws cannot be obeyed, because one commands what the other forbids, men are obliged to obey the higher authority. When the conscience of a private person instructs him that such is the case, he has no choice but to obey the higher law; yet every other person has the same right of inquiring and deciding for himself. No private man has the right of dictating to another. Nor has any private man a right to inquire further than into the lawfulness, so to speak, of the inferior law. The charter of private conscience is [in] the book of the Acts of the Apostles: "We ought to obey God rather than man."[1] Where it is possible to obey both, private conscience has no rights. He is not the

[1] Acts v. 29.

handmaid of private will. Men are apt to forget this and to confound her with private fancy and private caprice as well as with private judgment.

Private judgment is usually applied to decide whether a private man, or perhaps a public officer, is bound to obey the law as interpreted by human authority, or, as it is more usually put, to obey a human law or follow a human decision. It is generally called into action when a person is unwilling to obey a law or accept an interpretation of a law. Her voice is willingly heard when, as under such circumstances she generally does, she decides in favor of private will. The liberality of her decisions has raised her many friends under her false name of private judgment. Almost every man is an advocate for private judgment. The decisions of the private conscience ought to be made with freedom from the bias of private inclination, after fair inquiry and within its proper sphere. Above all they should be made under a deep sense of responsibility to God and his law. Under these conditions the conscience of each man is for him the ultimate human judge. Questions about its authority may generally be disposed of by remembering that its office, with respect to public law, is only to prevent inferior authorities from overruling the decisions of their superiors. All questions of authority must be settled by it. This function of the conscience men are apt enough to maintain and enlarge, even till it is confounded with private judgment, and decides questions of expediency and even of taste. This is because they can thus contrive, under its protection, to evade obedience to any authority.

Unfortunately it has another office, which is, at this time, very important. It is perhaps only a form of the other. It is to decide between rival claimants to be the Church. The Church, having no right or power to apply external force, cannot prevent the formation of other organizations which assume her name and claim her authority. Private conscience, from the necessity of the case, must decide between the contending claimants. The law of God has made it the duty of every man to join the true Church. Two organizations each claim to be that Church. The man who proposes to join either, must then decide for himself which is the true one; that is, which of them is obeying, and which is disobeying the Divine law.

§ 10. The private conscience has another office which men are less fond of calling into exercise. It is that of interpreting the Divine law, and applying it to one's own conduct, in cases which have not been provided for by any human law. Conscience is far less readily attended to here, when it appears in its proper character of a restraint, than when, under the name of private judgment, it acted as a liberator from restraint. This function of conscience is very important. For no human laws interpret or enforce the whole of the Divine law, or even pretend so to do.

The law of the land only enforces those portions of the Divine law which the State judges important to the temporal welfare of her subjects or citizens. These she reënacts and enforces by human sanctions. The Church professes to enforce the Divine law in its entirety. But she has not interpreted it in a legislative form, except to a very small extent. She generally leaves the interpretation to her judicial authorities, who interpret the law as cases arise. She even allows them a wide discretion as to enforcing the law by human sanctions.

This has led some persons into an error; they suppose that the Church has adopted the interpretation of the State. But no church or pretended church has ever done this. The interpretations of the State are made for her own purposes, which are very different from those, which the Church is bound to keep in view. They are, therefore, entirely inadequate to the wants of the Church. Moreover, there are many State laws, which are founded upon mere notions of expediency, without any reference to the Divine law. Again, the State laws are only designed for the security of men in temporal affairs. They take no notice of anything simply as it is a sin. For all these reasons it is impossible that any sound church should ever adopt the principle, that it is bound by the State's exposition of the Divine law.

A very large domain is left for private conscience, in the interpretation and application to men's private conduct of that portion of the Divine law which has received no public interpretation. This portion of the Divine law is generally known as morals or morality. It is so called from the Latin word *mores*, which means customs, usages, because men's opinions about it are very much governed by the usages of society.

In English we have two words, which together are equivalent to the Latin word *mores*, morals and manners. We apply the first to those usages which have a direct effect upon society at large, and which it is generally understood ought to be regulated by some Divine law, either revealed or natural. The other is applied to usages which only affect the comfort of particular circles which it is rightly thought may well be regulated by the opinions of those circles. Morals and indeed manners ought to be governed by the Divine law, which it is the duty of private conscience to apply and enforce. To relieve it from that duty men have set up public opinion. This formally governs in the region of manners and practically in that of public opinion.

§ 11. Besides the three organizations which have been mentioned, and which have each an object, functions, and organs, every community may be considered under a fourth phase. This is called simply Society. In this sense Society has no functions and therefore no organs. It is not unfrequently spoken of as organized; in fact social organization is a very familiar phrase, but nothing more is meant by it than social arrangement. Society is arranged into classes, orders, grades, cliques, circles, coteries, professions, trades, and into what are called worlds, which last are composed of persons of similar tastes, habits, and modes of thinking. These various divisions each include many members who are also included in other divisions, so that men may be, and most men are, members of several of them. This arrangement has practically great effect on the political and ecclesiastical organizations of the same community, which, in their turn, react upon the social arrangement, which is sometimes called the social organization. It is even said that society, in the sense in which the word has just been used, has organs, and that some at least of its divisions have organs; but what are so called are not really organs. They are only persons, or perhaps periodical publications, who undertake without authority to pronounce and so to make the opinion of society, perhaps to promote the interests or spread the opinions of some portion of society.

Public opinion is that which prevails in society and is a matter of great importance. It undertakes to mould and to overrule the law of the land and of the Church, and even to supersede the Divine law. It is thus formed: each of the many divisions of society, all of which it may be convenient to include under the general term of classes, has its own manners, customs, and morals, which are adapted to the promotion of its own interests and form its public opinion. Each of these classes has taken morals under its charge so far as they affect its interests, and in an informal way has enacted a code of morals. From these codes general society has compiled one for itself, which is called Public Opinion. It adopts and enforces the observance of the special codes modifying them by the friction of one against another. It indirectly professes to be an exposition of the Divine law; but directly scarcely recognizes its existence, and practically pays little or no attention to its precepts.

The codes of the different classes are all marked by a

strong leaning to class interests. They therefore fall short of, if they do not contravene the Christian law; yet they are all admitted into the general code of public opinion, when they are not grossly inconsistent with the public interest, and sometimes when they are. Every class is willing to overlook the vices in the codes of other classes, that those of its own may also be overlooked. To the particular codes are added some maxims and rules which are found convenient in the general intercourse among men without regard to other relations.

Thus is formed that code of morals which is called Public Opinion. It is made by society in its unorganized form, in which it is regarded without reference to any of the three divinely appointed organizations. It is enforced by that society by the penalty of social degradation or social excommunication.

The society by which it is made, being composed of men who are corrupt in their nature, it cannot be otherwise than imperfect and corrupt. Society has the power to enforce its code, and is not slow to exercise its power. Having been permitted in the course of Divine providence to possess power, it has some right to exist, although it has no no direct gift of authority in the Divine law. It does not claim any such right; it does not claim any legitimate authority whatever; it only claims power. Nevertheless Society has a right to be heard, subject to the claims of private conscience to compare its laws with the Divine law, or with the legitimate human laws of the Church and the State. Yet in this matter, private conscience is as sluggish and slow to act as private judgment is forward and determined in ecclesiastical matters. Men are also slow to appeal from the law of the land to private judgment, or even to private conscience. The reason for both these things is the same; civil and social penalties are more feared by common minds than the censures of the Church. The *ultimum supplicium* of the Church is exclusion. That is no penalty to those who are without her pale, or who do not care to remain within it. But fines and imprisonment and the scorn of those with whom they associate are feared by all men.

Public Opinion has become very powerful. It sometimes dictates the laws of the State, and sometimes forbids the execution of them. In the Church it has an undue and pernicious influence, which shows itself rather in preventing proper enactments than in procuring improper ones. It affects very injuriously the enforcement of discipline. Being itself unsound, and neither knowing nor regarding the principles of the Church, it is scarcely possible that public opinion can have a beneficial influence upon the Church.

§ 12. There are three distinct organizations or classes of organizations to which authority has been divinely committed. They are the Church, the State, and the Family. Every human being ought to join himself to the Universal Church, and to commune with it through the particular church which exists in the place in which he lives. Every human being owes obedience to the State, within the territory of which he or she lives; from the nature of the State there is no choice, whether that obedience shall be paid or not. Every human being is born into some family, and generally ought to be connected with one either as head or members through life; though God in His Providence sometimes releases a person from that obligation by rendering a compliance with it impossible. These three organizations have power to enact laws, and [appoint] governors, who make and administer their laws.

They have been instituted for three different purposes. The Church is to provide for the eternal well-being of all mankind. The State is to provide for the temporal well-being of its members and of all who reside within the territory committed by Providence to the charge of each particular state. The Family is to train up members for both, with reference to the wants of both. It is divinely appointed, as fully and clearly as either of the others; yet it is a constituent part of both, and subject to the authority of both, within the proper sphere of each. The Church and the State are also divinely instituted organizations, to which the families and persons of which they are respectively composed are united by other ties than those of a voluntary aggregation.

§ 13. The internal organization of the family has been made the subject of direct revelation; all authority is vested in the head, that is, in the father if there be one, and if not, then in the mother. "Honor thy father and thy mother."[1] "Children obey your parents in the Lord, for this is right."[2] "Children obey your parents in all things, for this is well pleasing unto the Lord."[3] "Wives submit yourselves to your husbands as it is fit in the Lord."[4] "Let the wife see that she reverence her husband."[5] "Likewise ye wives be in subjection to your own husbands."[6]

Such texts leave no room for question as to the internal constitution of the family. It is a monarchy, without any checks upon the authority of the monarch, except those that are within the bosom of the monarch. Yet the constitution itself sets limits to his authority, although it provides no external means of confining him within those limits. In close connection with the texts which have been cited as giving authority to the head of the family, are others, which regulate the exercise of that authority. "Husbands love your wives even as Christ also loved the Church and gave himself for it."[7] "So ought men to love their wives as their own bodies. He that loveth his wife loveth himself."[8] "Let every one of you in particular so love his wife even as himself."[9] "Husbands love your

[1] Exodus xx. 12.
[2] Ephesians vi. 1.
[3] Colossians iii. 20.
[4] Colossians iii. 18.
[5] Ephesians v. 33.
[6] 1 Peter iii. 1.
[7] Ephesians v. 25.
[8] Ephesians v. 28.
[9] Ephesians vi. 4.

wives and be not bitter against them."[1] "Fathers provoke not your children to wrath."[2] "Fathers provoke not your children to anger lest they be discouraged."[3] "Ye husbands, dwell with them according to knowledge, giving honor unto the wife, as unto the weaker vessel, and as being heirs together of the grace of life; that your prayers may not be hindered."[4]

This class of texts sufficiently indicates the check that God has placed upon the authority conferred by the others. It is that kindly affection which He, in his infinite wisdom and goodness, has decreed shall be the natural product of the family relations. The smallness of the community, the identity of interest among its members, their intimate connection and their constant interchange of benefits. combine to produce strong feelings of affection. The head participates in these feelings, and thus is provided a check upon the abuse of power, which must always be wanting in such organizations. If in any case this check should be wanting, or insufficient, another is to be found in the authority of the Church and of the State. The family is now always a subordinate society, so that its head, as well as each of its members, is subject to the authority of both the others. The external checks in the authority of the monarch of the family are to be found in the higher authority of the Church and the State.

§ 14. The heads of families do not exercise their authority in the same way with the rulers of the other two organizations. The powers of government are usually divided into three classes: the judicial, which decides controversies and punishes crimes; the administrative, sometimes called the executive, which disposes of the common resources for the common benefit; the legislative, which superintends, directs, and restrains both the others. In the State, and in some degree in the Church, attention is paid

[1] Colossians iii. 19.
[2] Ephesians vi. 4.
[3] Colossians iii. 21.
[4] 1 Peter iii. 7.

to the distinctions between these classes of powers, but in the family they are neglected. Hence a government which neglects them, and professes to do what is most for the happiness of its subjects without regard to them, is called a paternal government.

It is commonly said that it is the office of the legislature to make laws, of the judiciary to expound them, and of the executive, as the administrative power is generally called, to execute them. These notions are superficial and in fact erroneous. The administrative power has very little to do with the execution of the laws. The judiciary is the department which is really charged with that duty. It applies the laws to particular cases, and superintends the execution of its own decrees. That is the real execution of the laws. The decrees of the judges, when disobeyed or resisted, are enforced by a class of officers called ministerial, who act under the authority of the judges. These ministerial officers do not belong to the administrative department. They are the hands of the judiciary department, and are as much a part of that department as the hands of a man are a part of his body. The so-called executive department has really nothing to do with the execution of the laws, except in very extreme cases. If the resistance to the ministerial officers should be so strong that they are unable to overcome it, with the local aid for which they have authority to call, the administrative, or so-called executive power must suppress the rebellion, as it must any other rebellion. This, however, is not so much executing the laws as preserving the existence of the State.

The proper duty of the judiciary department is to apply and enforce the laws, and the right and duty of expounding them is merely incidental. The power of expounding would be of little use without the power of enforcing the exposition. In the infancy of government the leading ideas are to decide disputes and punish crimes, that is, to apply and enforce the Divine law. In all primitive societies these are the only offices of internal governments which are known. When government comes to be divided into departments these offices are allotted to the judicial department. But laws to be applied must be interpreted. Thus the interpretation or exposition of the laws comes to be a secondary and incidental duty of the judges, growing out of their primary duty of enforcing the law. This truth is universally admitted in practice. No judge would promulgate any exposition of a law, unless in the act of applying it to a particular case in which he had been called upon to enforce the law. If a judge were to do so, his exposition would be treated with so much respect as his private opinion might deserve and with no more. No one would regard his exposition as a judicial act, because it was not put forth in the legitimate execution of his office.

The legislative department has the power of making laws. Such laws are strictly only interpretations of the Divine law, fitted to classes of cases, and intended for the guidance of the judicial and administrative departments. It also promulgates decrees, which, although called laws, are not properly laws; they are rather rules of expediency, which the administrative department is bound to obey. It has a third power, that of taxation. This is really a very important function of the administrative department, which experience has shown may be more safely intrusted to a legislative body than to the ordinary heads of the administrative department.

§ 15. In the family monarchy, the monarch, whether male or female, has administrative and judicial authority, without the restraint of legislative supervision. He may by his own authority lay down rules which his subjects are bound to obey. These are or ought to be interpretations of God's law; but he can lay down no rules for the administrative or judicial departments, for all administrative and judicial authority is exercised by himself. He will very rarely lay down any rules, because as he is the only judge, his interpretations of the Divine law will be extemporized as they are wanted. The principles upon which he proceeds can only be gathered from the decisions which he makes, and which will come in time to be regarded as a sort of usages or customs of the family. Besides his decisions, he will issue commands, directions, or instructions to particular persons, for he is a teacher as well as a judge and an administrator. These may also enter into the customary or traditional law of the family. This kind of government, it has been already remarked, is called paternal government.

In interpreting the Divine Law, the head of a family is subject to the authorities of the Church and State and must take into view their human laws. He must follow their interpretations within their respective spheres; but in the outlying field, which is called morality, he must interpret for himself. Here, however, he will be apt to avail himself, perhaps too much, of the aid of public opinion.

In his task of interpretation, the head of a family will be little embarrassed by the opposition of private judgment, because a large proportion of his subjects, having no power of forming opinions, are incapable of private judgment, and therefore of any private conscience, which would be entitled to consideration. The combination of this fact, with the narrowness of his jurisdiction, and the absence of any legislative check, gives a peculiar character to his government. His modes of proceeding are all informal. Having, if he choose so to do, consulted with such members of the family as he may select, he makes up his mind and proceeds to declare or to execute his decision. Should the case partake of a judicial character, he in his discretion either wholly neglects or very slightly uses the forensic forms. This is all rendered tolerable by the affection which he generally feels for each person under his authority.

§ 16. In the family this paternal government answers

very well; because it is there usually directed so as to promote the welfare of the governed. In the State it always fails; because the paternal solicitude is not real. The exercise of power is not checked by the tenderness of parental affection, and there is not the sameness of interest which binds together the head and members of a single household.

§ 17. The State, like the Church and the family, is a divinely appointed organization. Unlike them, it has no divinely appointed form. Government is needful to the well-being of man. In this truth all are agreed, notwithstanding the assertion, still sometimes made, that it is a necessary evil. The true meaning disguised under that phrase is that it is a disagreeable good. The inference which used to be drawn from it, that the best government was that which governed the least, was once very popular. Like many other popular doctrines, it was a gross exaggeration of a truth. That truth was, that government ought not to subject private persons to any restraints without good reasons. Man cannot exist without government, therefore government is an ordinance of God. Thus much may be gathered from the light of nature, that is, the exercise of the human intellect upon the works and the providence of God.

The sure word of Revelation teaches the same doctrine. The written charter of the State is to be found in the first part of the thirteenth chapter of St. Paul's Epistle to the Romans: "Let every soul be subject to the higher powers. For there is no power but of God: the powers that be, are ordained of God. Whosoever therefore resisteth the power, resisteth the ordinance of God: and they that resist shall receive to themselves damnation. For rulers are not a terror to good works, but to the evil. Wilt thou then not be afraid of the power? Do that which is good, and thou shalt have praise of the same. For he is the minister of God to thee for good. But if thou do that which is evil be afraid; for he beareth not the sword in vain; for he is the minister of God, a revenger to execute wrath upon him that doeth evil. Wherefore ye must needs be subject, not only for wrath, but also for conscience' sake."

This passage, neglected as it is, is full of instruction, and it is scarcely too much to say that it is the basis of the whole science of politics. It contains no political theory, and nothing about the form of organization. The Divine right of kings of Sir Robert Filmer, and the natural right of the majority of Thomas Paine and Thomas Jefferson, are both passed by. Neither of them have any foundation in Scripture. The right of governing is declared to belong to the powers that be. It is in the men to whom God in his providence has given the power of enforcing order. They are to be obeyed, because to resist them is to resist the ordinance of God.

St. Peter teaches the same doctrine: "Submit yourselves to every ordinance of man for the Lord's sake: whether to the king, as supreme; or unto governors, as unto them that are sent by Him for the punishment of evil doers, and for the praise of them that do well. For so is the will of God, that with well doing ye may put to silence the ignorance of foolish men: as free, and yet not using your liberty for a cloak of maliciousness, but as the servants of God." [1]

This is in some sense a digression. In this work there is no need to discuss the question of resistance and non-resistance. It is, however, necessary to say something of obedience and its limits, which are very different things. The Apostles lay down a general principle, that every ordinance of government is to be respected. St. Peter proceeds to illustrate the principle, by applying it to the government under which he and those to whom he was directly writing lived. St. Paul follows out the principle into some of its important consequences. He first tells his readers that the authority of the State extends to all per-

[1] 1 Peter ii. 13, etc.

sons, " Let every soul be subject unto the higher powers." Next that it extends to the infliction of capital punishment, and by a parity of reason to making war, " If thou do that which is evil, be afraid; for he beareth not the sword in vain; for he is the minister of wrath upon him that doeth evil." Again, he tells us that the authority of government extends to all actions, " Rulers are not a terror to good works, but to the evil." This implies that they are to judge which are good works and which are evil.

But from this power itself arises a limitation. Rulers have a right to decide what works are evil; but they must have some rule by which to decide the question. The rule is the law of God; for the ruler is the minister of God and must not counteract the will of Him who is the only giver and source of his authority. All human laws are therefore only expositions of the Divine law. They may be erroneous, and even contravene the Divine law. When they do contravene it men are bound to disregard them, which is a very different thing from resisting the authority which enacts them. " We should obey God rather than man." [1] To decide when such cases arise is the office of private conscience, but that office should be exercised according to the rules which have been already laid down.

Again: the office of the State is to promote the temporal welfare of those who are under its authority. With the spiritual welfare of men it has nothing to do. Its powers are all external, and the spiritual well-being of man depends on his internal condition, which cannot be reached by any external power. Religious actions done from the fear of human laws are not pleasing to God. Outward compliances with religious observances are not faith. Faith and obedience constitute religion; but they must be faith in Christ and obedience to God. Those the State cannot command, and it has therefore no right to meddle with religion, and its acts about religion are not binding upon the

[1] Acts v. 29.

conscience. The great limitation upon the authority of the State is, that the State cannot justify any man in committing a sin. What is a sin is a question for the private conscience, and the rule by which it is to be decided is the law of God.

§ 18. God has committed religious questions to the care of another organization. The Church differs from the State in this, that the form of its organization is partially prescribed in the Divine Word, and from the family, in that the form is not fully prescribed. It was called into existence for a purpose different from that which the State was designed to serve. Its object is to promote the spiritual welfare of mankind. The spiritual well-being of men depends upon faith and obedience, an obedience not merely formal and external, but arising from a lively internal faith. The Church has to deal altogether with that which is internal, and has, therefore, no right to use external force. She cannot compel any person to unite with her. She may divide the world into territories for particular churches, which will be missionary bodies for the conversion of all the inhabitants of their respective territories, and will have ecclesiastical jurisdiction over those who have voluntarily become their members, or who while they were incapable of acting for themselves were placed under their authority by their parents. She has no right and no means to compel submission, and the State, which has means, has no right to act in the matter.

Every member of the Church must become such by his own free choice. This appears from the nature of the Church, which was instituted only for spiritual purposes, and from the means by which only she can enforce her authority. A man, so long as he is a member of the Church, is bound to respect her authority. But the only means which she has to enforce obedience, is exclusion from her pale. It is not here meant to deny the awful meaning of the words upon which the power of excommunication rests.

But to those who lack faith, whether they are formally in connection with the Church or not, excommunication is nothing more than an exclusion from church membership, and a denial of church privileges. This to such men is only expulsion from a voluntary society. Yet excommunication is the *ultimum supplicium* of the Church, as death is of the State. The power of excommunication was given to the Church in these words of our blessed Saviour: "Whose soever sins ye remit, they are remitted unto them; and whose soever sins ye retain, they are retained." [1]

The duty of the Church is to watch for souls, and this is in another text expressly made the foundation of her authority, "Obey them that have the rule over you, and submit yourselves: for they watch for your souls, as they that must give account, that they may do it with joy and not with grief: for that is unprofitable for you." [2]

§ 19. The Church and the State are two organizations founded upon different principles, but both having divinely given authority. The Church has authority over her own members; the State over all persons found within her territories, including the members of the Church. Each has jurisdiction over all actions, when circumstances bring them within its sphere. For the two societies exist for different purposes, — one for the eternal, the other for the temporal benefit of mankind. Each may have jurisdiction over any conceivable action. For there is no voluntary action which may not affect the spiritual welfare of the agent or the temporal welfare of some person. Many actions do both, and are thus at once within the jurisdiction of the Church and that of the State. There must then be danger of collisions between the two societies. On two points there is, however, no danger of collision. The Church has no jurisdiction over things or over persons who are not her members.

Yet the Church has an independent authority which may

[1] John xx. 23. [2] Hebrews xiii. 17.

be exercised without any regard to the decisions of the State. She may enact the same laws with the State, and so her authority will come in aid of that of the State; or she may enact laws which contradict those of the State, and so the two authorities will be antagonistic to each other. The Primitive Church was antagonistic to the Roman Empire. This antagonism is possible, because the two societies are both independent; they are so, because such is the will of the God who has appointed them both, and from whom both derive their authority. But He has also confined each of them to its proper sphere. Neither has any right to interfere with the decisions of the other, or to restrain it from enforcing them. It is possible that the two authorities may come to decisions which clash with each other, for both are administered by fallible men; one or the other, or both may mistake the Divine law. Both are administered by peccable men, and one or the other, or both may neglect the Divine law.

The State never recognizes the law of the Church as a reason for disobeying her laws, and she is not bound to do so. Neither is the Church bound to recognize the law of the State as a reason for disobeying her laws. Nor should either, in making laws, attempt to conform them to those of the other. Their laws are made for different purposes and enforced by different penalties. Every one who is subject to both, is bound to obey both. When they clash, each person must decide for himself which he will obey, according to the dictates of his private conscience. The question for his conscience to decide is this, Which of the two is conformable to the Divine law? If private conscience cannot answer this question, then every one must choose between church privileges and temporal advantages, between church censures and temporal penalties.

The authority of the Church is given to her to promote the spiritual welfare of mankind, and it is given to her as an organized society. She is, in the Divine intention,

Catholic and Universal. Her mission is to bring all men within her pale. To do this she must be a city set on a hill, which cannot be hid, and she must be so pure that men may see her purity and be attracted by it. It is therefore necessary that unworthy members should be excluded and unworthy officers degraded. The puritan notion of a perfectly pure church is a chimera. For every member of every church, "although baptized and born again in Christ, yet offends in many things, and if we say that we have no sin, we deceive ourselves, and the truth is not in us."[1]

Yet the purity of the Church must be vindicated by removing from among her members, and especially from among her officers, gross and notorious offenders. It is right that censures should be passed upon offenders even for the sake of the offenders. It was the theory of the Church for several centuries, that all proceedings in ecclesiastical courts were for the benefit of the accused. The memory of this theory has been preserved in the English ecclesiastical courts, whose articles of accusation against a man were, and perhaps still are, said to be for the good of his soul,—*pro salute animæ suæ.*

The Church is an organized society having authority. She has officers who are pastors, whose duty it is both to govern and to feed the flock, functions which imply the teaching them by good example. The faith and morals of these men are objects of peculiar solicitude to the Church, which everywhere enacts special laws concerning them. These provide for an inquiry into their fitness both in faith and morals, before their admission to office, and for their removal from office, when found deficient in either. They can properly be removed only after a judicial inquiry.

There are thus two kinds of church discipline, which are respectively known as clerical discipline and lay discipline. In lay discipline the *ultimum supplicium* is excommunication; in clerical degradation ecclesiastical law is composed

[1] Article xx.

of the rules which the Church lays down for the administration of these two kinds of discipline.

So long as church discipline is enforced only by the suspension and degradation of offending clergymen, and the suspension or excommunication of offending laymen, there can be no reasonable cause of complaint on the part of the State and so no hazard of collision. The State can only regard the Church as a voluntary society, excommunication as an exclusion from that society, and degradation as the removal of one of its officers. She can do nothing but acquiesce in the exclusions and removals. If the offenses which led to them are also violations of her laws, she is still free to punish them. If the exclusion or removal directly affects civil or material rights, she may inquire in her civil courts whether the ecclesiastical proceedings have been conducted according to the law of the Church. Thus much can scarcely be denied to her, and in this country she claims no more. While these principles are acted upon on both sides, there can be no collision.

The old collisions arose out of the old unions between the Church and the State, in which each delegated some portion of its authority to the other. Each moreover claimed an exclusive jurisdiction over some persons who it insisted should be exempted from the jurisdiction of the other. The State even allowed the Church in some cases a jurisdiction over things. The Church on her part allowed the State a large share in the appointment of her chief officers. The plain boundaries between the two jurisdictions, which are marked out by the different objects of the two institutions and their different modes of enforcing their authority, were forgotten. The ideas of men on the subject became confused, and their interests and passions excited them against each other. The ecclesiastical history of Europe for several centuries is little more than a record of collisions with the State.

This state of things was made worse by the theory that the two societies were identical. Of two organizations governing one society, it was thought that one must be superior to the other. The question which was the superior must arise. Both had assumed a federative form, and each was composed of lesser federations having each its own head. These were all subject to the head of some larger federation, all being at last subject to the head of one great federation, of which all were members. The Church federation was the largest and in moral and intellectual force the strongest. The State was stronger in physical force. Hence the long struggle between intellectual and physical power.

The whole Church of Western Europe was combined under the Pope. The clergy all acknowledged his authority, and they had influence everywhere. The largest of the State federations was by no means so extensive. Hence every temporal prince in Europe felt that it was his interest to be on good terms with the Pope, who was thus enabled to command that military force, which the Church had not, and ought not to have, by playing off one temporal prince against another. This emboldened him to claim a superiority over the heads of the States. The claim was everywhere resisted, and was the cause of many collisions between the Church and the State. Happily this and all the other causes of collision which have been mentioned are now at an end in this country.

The struggle for superiority had a great effect in bringing about the Reformation, which decided it in favor of the State. Where the Reformation prevailed, the authority of the Pope was at an end. The local clergy having no longer a protector beyond the limits of the State, were brought entirely under the power of the State. In those countries which did not throw off their allegiance to the Pope his power was nevertheless much abridged, and that of the temporal sovereigns advanced. The State has now become the great advocate for the union of Church and State and the great enemy of the independence of the Church.

In this country there has grown up a great aversion to the union. A sound feeling, though scarcely resting upon the true grounds. The union has produced many great evils, but more to the Church than to the State or to private persons. Popery itself is nothing but a recoil from it. The Church had once a financial system, which was voluntary, although based upon the idea of duty. When the alliance between Church and State was formed the Church gave it up, and undertook to live upon her endowments eked out by State aid. The State soon ceased to give any aid, and falsely took credit for having given the endowments. The wants of the Church outgrew the endowments, and it became necessary to return to the voluntary system. But the old mode of conducting the business was forgotten, and men had but the sense of duty and the habit of giving. Hence the poverty of the Church.

People in this country profess to dread the union of Church and State. What they really dread is the domination of the Church over the State and over themselves, things of which there is no danger. In Europe the union has terminated in the domination of the State over the Church, which is undoubtedly a great and unmixed evil. In former times the English people looked to the State as their protector from the Pope. The State was the champion of Protestantism. Englishmen now affect to do the same thing; but there is reason to fear that too many of them value the State as the champion of religious libertinism. Many Englishmen profess a strong attachment to the Church, who really dislike the idea of an independent ecclesiastical jurisdiction; but they are sincerely attached to the existing establishment, because they look upon it as a mere creature of the State.

The American people have inherited from their English

ancestors a great jealousy of the Church, meaning any religious organization which claims authority. They profess a great dislike to any connection between the Church and the State. But there is a covert willingness to subject the Church to general society and public opinion. This feeling may be detected by its effects. The secular newspapers, the would-be organs of public opinion, are fond of meddling with church affairs and judging of them by their own standard. Some Church papers and some members of ecclesiastical bodies are fond of appealing to public opinion, because they are themselves under its influence. Such appeals and those who make them are always popular with people outside of the Church.

Society is always ready to take the part of the State against the Church. She is still more ready to press her own notions upon the Church, and to dictate her laws, as she does, to a great extent, those of the State. She really prefers the State; temporal interests are better understood and more valued by the public at large than spiritual. The State too can enforce her laws by temporal penalties, and so has a more tangible authority than the Church. The authority of the Church is spiritual, her censures [are] only felt by those who have faith. It is disregarded by the great mass of mankind, who regard it as a mere usurpation. The Church is moreover suspected of seeking to impose a code of morals more strict than that of society or that of the law of the land. Public opinion is, therefore, adverse to the Church.

The Church is perhaps over careful to avoid collisions with the State or with society; but it would be really unwise for her to bring about a collision with either if it could properly be avoided. Either the State or society can rally a large portion of the Church's own sons against her. Yet a case may arise in which it may be her duty not to decline a conflict.

§ 20. If the State were to pass a law requiring anything

to be done which is against the law of God, it would be the duty of the Church to censure any of her members who should obey the law. Men must then choose, according to their private consciences, which of the two authorities they will obey. If they choose to obey the State, the Church can do nothing but exclude them from her pale.

Such collisions are not very likely to occur. The laws of the State which contravene the Divine law chiefly relate to marriage and are not very numerous. They are practically only permissive. The State leaves every person at liberty to marry or not at his or her choice, and, with a few exceptions, to marry whomsoever he or she will. But it compels no person to marry, still less to marry any particular person. When a person contracts a marriage which is against the law of God and not against the law of the land, he has offended and is liable to Church censures; but if he do not contract such a marriage he offends neither the Church nor the State, for the law of the State is only permissive. It is more correct to say that there is no State law on the subject. When, therefore, the Church censures a person for a marriage which the State does not forbid, there is no collision between the Church and the State. What one permits the other forbids, and a person who is subject to both ought to obey the stricter law. There is really no difficulty until a case shall arise in which one forbids what the other commands.

Thus the laws which allow the dissolution of a valid marriage, and the marriage of the parties to it to other persons without waiting for the death of either, are really only permissive. No person is obliged to apply for a divorce, or having obtained one, or having been forced to submit to one, is obliged to marry again. The State does not command either of these things, and the Church does not provoke a collision by forbidding them.

The legislation of the American Church is peculiar. Its discipline is applied to offenses which are not defined in the canons otherwise than by the most general reference to the Divine law. The effect is that the interpretation of the Divine law is committed to the judges who administer Church discipline. Public opinion requires that they shall take the law of the land for their guide, or, as the framers of public opinion prefer saying, that they should obey the law of the land. They should obey the law of the land when it is not in conflict with the law of God; but they should not subject the law of God to the law of the land.

When a question arises whether the law of the land conflicts with the law of God, it cannot be decided by the law of the land, which is of inferior authority to the law of God. The law of God, which is the higher law, must be the rule, and conscience the judge to apply that rule. Every one who is called upon to act upon the question must decide it for himself, as every one who is called to act upon any question must decide it for himself. The private man must decide it according to his conscience. The officer of the Church, who is called to advise, direct, or judge the conduct of the private Christian, must decide according to his private conscience, unless the Church has furnished him with a rule. The Church herself, in her legislative capacity, must be governed by what may be called her aggregate, or public conscience.

If the two laws do not conflict, every one, including the authorities of the Church, must obey both. If one permit what the other forbids, men should respect the prohibition. If one command what the other forbids, we must obey God rather than man. Suppose a man should apply to be received into the communion of the Church who had married after a civil divorce which was contrary to God's law. How ought the rector of the parish to act? Public opinion would perhaps say that the twice-married man should be received, because he had done nothing not allowed by the law of the land. But the true question is,

Has he done an act contrary to the law of God? The law of the land, which is, at best, an interpretation of the law of God, made by temporal rulers for temporal purposes, has nothing to do with spiritual questions.

The State may interpret the law of God for her own purposes; but she has no right to interpret it for those of the Church. She may decide what actions are injurious to the temporal interests of men, not what are injurious to the spiritual welfare of the agent. Moreover, it is notorious that the rulers of States do not now even pretend to interpret the law of God. They avow that they act only upon their own notions of expediency. This is an abuse of power, but the legitimate authority of the State is not impaired by it. To suppose that her authority could be forfeited by abuse, would render all government impossible. The laws of the State, however they may conflict with the law of God, are binding in the courts of the State. A judge whose conscience will not permit him to execute a law of the State should resign his position.

In the supposed case the second marriage is not legally bigamy. The husband has the same legal control over his *de facto* wife and her property as any other husband. The so-called wife has a legal right to be supported by the *de facto* husband according to his means and condition. At his death she will be entitled to a wife's share of his estate. The true wife has lost her right to a support and to a share in the distribution of her husband's estate. The children of the second marriage are legitimate. All these effects the act of the State can produce; but it cannot make a sin to be no sin.

The Church has neither the right nor the power to interfere with these civil matters; but she has a right to declare that such an union is sinful and prejudicial to the spiritual interests of those between whom it has been formed. It is not necessary that the declaration should be a legislative act, which would give no additional force to a Divine law, though such an act might be of great service to individual clergymen as a defense against public opinion.

The true idea of a legislative act is that it is an exposition of the Divine law, of the meaning of which, or of its application, there may be some doubt. St. Germain, an old writer on the Common Law, states this truth thus: "The law of man (the which sometimes is called the law positive) is derived by reason as a thing which is necessary and probably following of the law of reason and of the law of God. And that is called probable, in that it appeareth to many, and especially to wise men, to be true. And therefore in every law positive well made, there is somewhat of the law of reason, and somewhat of the law of God." [1]

A legislative act is binding upon all persons who are providentially under the authority of those by whom it is made, so far as their jurisdiction extends, but no further. The jurisdiction of the State does not extend to spiritual matters, except just so far as it may be necessary to protect herself, or her citizens or subjects, from injuries attempted to be cloaked under spiritual forms. Even then it does not extend to the decision of what is, and is not sin. Her exposition of the law of God for such a purpose is without authority. The exposition of the Divine law for spiritual purposes, belongs to the Church. But a legislative interpretation of a plain Divine law is unnecessary. The church may therefore leave such a Divine law to be interpreted by her judicial and administrative officers. It does not follow, that they are to follow the interpretation of the State, when it contradicts the true sense of the Divine law.

§ 21. Both the Church and the State have jurisdiction over matrimonial causes, each in its own sphere and for its own purposes. One acts with regard to the temporal welfare of the community under its care; the other with regard to the spiritual welfare of mankind. They enforce their decisions in different ways: one punishes that which it con-

1 *Doctor and Student*, Chapter iv., at the beginning.

siders as bigamy, by forced labor; the other censures that, which in its judgment is the same offense, by suspension from the Holy Communion. The Church has no right to complain of the State for punishing a man who has married again during the life of a former wife, although the Church may regard the first marriage as against the Divine law, and void because contracted with a brother's widow, or for any other reason. So the State has no right to complain if the Church censure a man who has married a second time during the life of his wife, although the State has released him from his civil obligations to her.

There seems, however, to be a notion, that questions concerning matrimony are peculiarly within the jurisdiction of the State. Like all other questions they are within her jurisdiction, so far as the temporal welfare of the people and the administration of the temporal laws are concerned; but like all other questions, they are within the jurisdiction of the Church, so far as they bear upon the spiritual welfare of mankind. To suppose the contrary is to fall into the old error, which grew out of the old union between Church and State, that some questions are, in themselves, of spiritual, and others of temporal jurisdiction; whereas, in truth, all questions of right and wrong belong to both; though each is to treat all questions for its own purposes and in its own manner.

In former times many attempts were made to settle the questions between the Church and the State, by allotting certain causes and questions to one, and others to the other. In the course of these attempts, matrimonial causes were assigned to the ecclesiastical courts, to be decided according to church law. In England they remained in that position until very lately. They are now held to be of civil jurisdiction, as well in England as in France, Scotland, the Protestant portion of Germany, and some other parts of Europe. They really belong to both, to each within its own sphere, and for its own proper purposes, according to its nature, and the object for which it was instituted.

§ 22. Marriage, which lies at the root of all society, must concern the temporal welfare of the community. It is therefore impossible that the State should not have a right to make laws about it. They, like all others, ought to be true expositions of the Divine law. Yet if the State err in her interpretation, or even make a law without reference to the Divine law, there is no earthly power which can set her right. Happily, she leaves every one at liberty to abstain from marrying, or to marry whomsoever he or she will, except in a very few cases. In these she recognizes a few of the Christian impediments to marriage between particular persons. At least in this country, she requires no clergyman to solemnize any particular marriage. Her erroneous laws are then practically only permissive, and cannot interfere with the conscience of any one. In the Middle Ages the State made no laws on the subject, and her courts entertained no matrimonial causes. The whole matter was remitted to the Church, which made and administered the law. The State only accepted her decisions as final.

§ 23. The Church had a right, for her own purposes, to expound the law of marriage. This was not derived from the State, and did not involve any right to impose her decisions upon the State, or to affect, in any way, temporal rights. The State, however, chose to accept for civil purposes the decisions which the Church made for spiritual purposes. The State had always a right to withdraw the power which she had thus delegated to the Church; but not to withdraw the original right, which the Church had, to legislate about marriage in a spiritual view. The contracting an unlawful marriage, the living in one after it is contracted, or living separate from a lawful husband or wife, are sins, and, like other sins, damage the spiritual state of those by whom they are committed. All sins are within the jurisdiction of the Church.

Matrimonial causes were, in the Middle Ages, regarded as belonging to the canon law and the ecclesiastical courts. According to English usage, they were of three classes: proceedings for divorce, for restitution of conjugal rights, and for jactitation of marriage. Under the first class were included two kinds of proceedings, which were of very different characters, and neither of them properly proceedings for divorce. A divorce is a dissolution of a valid marriage. But it is a principle of the canon law, that the dissolution of a valid marriage is impossible.

§ 24. That law, however, recognizes two things, which it calls divorce: one is a declaration that a supposed marriage is void. The form of a marriage may have been gone through, but the persons were not *married*, because a marriage between them is unlawful. It was competent for the ecclesiastical courts to declare such marriages void. Such a declaration was called a divorce *a vinculo matrimonii*. The other thing, which was called a divorce, was a permission or command to married persons to live separate from each other, while the bond of marriage remained unbroken. This was called a divorce *a mensa et thoro*. Matrimonial causes were then of four kinds: proceedings for divorces *a vinculo matrimonii*; for divorces *a mensa et thoro*; for restitution of conjugal rights, and for jactitation of marriage.

§ 25. Passing by, for the present, the first of these proceedings, the second and third may be considered together. They are correlatives to each other. The question in both is the same, but it is raised in different modes, under differing circumstances. In one, the person who is desirous of living separate from his or her companion, applies for permission so to do, which implies protection in so doing. In the other, the person who is desirous to separate has departed from his or her companion without permission, and the person deserted seeks to compel a return. Both these proceedings were, no doubt, in their origin, applications to the bishop of the diocese for his counsel and assistance. The general principle is plainly laid down by St. Paul, that it is the duty of married persons to live together as man and wife Yet particular circumstances may arise which may render it difficult to perform that duty. The difficulties may be so great as to render it impossible for one of the parties to the marriage to live with the other. When such cases arose, the bishop, who knew the Divine law, stood impartial between the parties, and had authority over both, was the fittest person to decide them. The question which he was to decide was, Whether the peculiar circumstances of the case were such as to make it an exception to the general rule?

In a conscientious age, persons who were in doubt as to the course which it was their duty to pursue, naturally applied to their bishop for instruction. His decision would often settle the matter; if it did not, the primitive discipline gave him the power of enforcing it by excommunication. But excommunication was, after all, only an appeal to the conscience. The conscience of the offender, called into action by the decision of the bishop, and if necessary by the excommunication, might so work as to produce a thorough reconciliation.

When ecclesiastical proceedings took a forensic form, the seeking for the bishop's advice became a direct application to his authority. It took one of two forms. When the persons were still living together, the application was for a separation which came to be called a *divorce a mensa et thoro.* When one of them had left the other, it was open for the person who had departed to make a similar application, in order to legalize the existing separation. This came to be the usual mode of action, the dissatified person departed and applied for a legal separation, or as it came to be called, a divorce *a mensa et thoro.* But the person who did not wish for a separation, might apply for an order on the person who had departed to return, which came to be called a decree for the restitution of conjugal rights.

In process of time ecclesiastical causes ceased to be tried by the bishop in person. They were tried under episcopal authority by judges, who, whether in holy orders or not, were practically lawyers, and decided questions according to rules and precedents and in a lawyer-like spirit. Now, another change has taken place; matrimonial causes are tried by a mere lay judge acting under the authority of the State. Under such circumstances the proceedings for the restitution of conjugal rights can be nothing but a delusion.

Under the original system, the return of the person who had departed, being either directly or indirectly the effect of conscience, might have led to a reunion of feeling. Under that which followed, the ecclesiastical court could make its decree, but it was not likely to be attended with any very beneficial effects. If it were against a recusant wife, it would place her person in the custody of her husband. Formerly the law of the land and the usages of society armed the husband with means to enforce outward obedience. But it is impossible that the affections, the most valuable conjugal rights, would be restored at the mandate of a judge. Now, the law has been much changed, and the usages of society more. The same court which restored a recusant wife to the custody of her husband, would grant her a judicial separation for cruelty, if she were treated with harshness. It is not easy to see that a decree ordering a husband to return to his deserted wife could produce any good effect.

So in the case of a divorce *a mensa et thoro*, which the late act of Parliament calls by its right name,—judicial separation, a formal decree is seldom sought, until after a separation by agreement or otherwise has taken place. It is then sought for merely civil purposes. It will give the separation a legal existence, be an answer to any proceeding for the restitution of conjugal rights, relieve the wife from the shadow of legal authority, which the husband still retains, and be a foundation for an application for alimony, or a provision for her support at the expense of her husband. But husbands and wives do not now live together, because a judicial separation has been refused. The State has a right to make provision for judicial separations for the purposes to which they are actually applied. But whatever human laws may be made upon the subject, there will still remain a grave question for the conscience of a Christian. A person who thinks of asking for a judicial separation, or, as it is still called in this country, a divorce *a mensa et thoro*, has still to ask, Can I, under the circumstances in which I am placed, avail myself of the human law, without breaking the Divine law?

§ 26. The proceeding to obtain a declaration of the nullity of a marriage in fact, which is commonly called a divorce *a vinculo matrimonii*, had a different origin. It was at first a proceeding instituted by the authority of the Church, *pro salute animarum*, — for the health of the souls of the persons concerned. It was intended to put a stop to the sin in which they were living. As the discipline of the Church declined, it was left to the consciences of the sinners themselves to apply the remedy.

In the mean time, the Latin Church had multiplied the prohibitions to intermarry, until it was difficult for any person of any rank to find a person within reach and of equal rank whom he or she might lawfully marry. This multiplication of prohibitions was probably intended to increase the revenue of the Popes, who had the power of granting dispensations and sold them at high prices. They answered that purpose, but became a great moral evil. The fact, that they could be purchased with money, prevented the prohibitions from taking hold of the conscience. They were costly; marriages, for which they were necessary, were solemnized without them, sometimes in ignorance that the parties were related within the forbidden degrees. It was possible too that a dispensation might be defective in form, and forms were rigidly enforced when it was profitable so to do. Such dispensations were set aside. If a dispensation contained no formal defect, it was easy to say, often with truth, that it had been obtained by fraud or misrepresentation. Upon the whole, the effect of the system was that the great men had such a facility in getting rid of their wives, as almost amounted to a power of arbitrary divorce. The women had in theory the same facility, but not in practice.

§ 27. The proceeding for jactitation of marriage rested on a still different set of principles. Its object was to restrain persons from falsely jactitating, or boasting that they were married to particular persons. It is not probable that such a practice was ever so common or so mischievous as to require a remedy. Yet one was provided. In order to obtain a decree forbidding the person complained of from repeating the boast, it seems to have been only necessary to show that he or she had made it, unless he set up as a defense that the boast was well founded. It would then be necessary to inquire, first, whether any marriage in fact had been solemnized between the parties, and next, whether the marriage solemnized was valid. Both these inquiries were within the province of the Church. For the State had adopted the ecclesiastical law of marriage, and had committed to the Church the entire jurisdiction in matrimonial causes. It is still the law of England, — at least there has been no direct legislative change, — that when an issue is joined in the civil courts directly upon the question of marriage, without involving any other question, the court refers it to the bishop of the diocese. Such cases now scarcely ever occur. Where the issue of married or not is, as it generally is, complicated with any other question, it must be tried by a jury in the ordinary way. When, therefore, it was intended to provide a remedy for such a wrong as jactitation of marriage, it was natural to give the jurisdiction to the ecclesiastical courts.

The proceeding is of very rare occurrence; but there was a very remarkable case in the last century. An ingenious attempt was made to use it as a means of liberating married people from engagements of which they were weary. A proceeding for jactitation of marriage was commenced against a real husband. The marriage had been private, and never publicly acknowledged. The evidence was suppressed by collusion, and the husband prohibited from asserting the marriage. The lady considered herself to be legally unmarried, and of Mrs. Hervey, or Miss Chudleigh, her maiden name by which she had passed, became Duchess of Kingston. She was afterwards tried for bigamy, and it was decided, that the sentence of the Ecclesiastical Court had produced no effect on her condition. The proceeding has since been once resorted to, for the purpose of showing that the use of the marriage ceremony in sport had not made two young persons man and wife.

In time a change in the policy of the State took place. Instead of handing over to the Church any part of her jurisdiction, she encroached on that of the Church, and at length undertook to dictate the ecclesiastical law. Thus marriage came to be considered in England as exclusively of State jurisdiction. Yet matrimonial causes continued to be tried in courts which were nominally ecclesiastical, but which had become so secularized, as to have lost every trace of their religious character. A very few years ago the jurisdiction in matrimonial causes was transferred from these courts to one which was avowedly civil.

§ 28. In this country there were never any ecclesiastical courts, in the European sense of the words. Before the Revolution, the law of marriage was the same in the colonies as in the mother country; but there were no courts to administer it. Among a scattered population of comparatively pure morals, there was little occasion for them. At the Revolution there was no provision made for the administration of justice in matrimonial causes. But in time questions about divorce appeared. The State legislatures, with the honorable exception of South Carolina, assumed, one after the other, the power of authorizing married couples to live separately from each other, and even of dissolving the bond of marriage. These assumed powers they exercised according to their notions of expediency, without reference to the Divine law. They even came to exercise them corruptly. Members sold their votes for popularity, for assistance in carrying favorite measures, or for the mere hope that the favor might be in some way returned. Divorces could be obtained for any cause, and without any inquiry into the truth of the matters alleged. The whole law of marriage became daily more and more relaxed. No provision has ever been made for the restitution of conjugal rights or the jactitation of marriage. Such cases are entirely unknown in America.

Soon after the Revolution, laws were made imposing restraints upon the marriage of minors, and upon marriages within the degrees forbidden in Leviticus. In most of the States these laws have been modified, so as to legalize many incestuous marriages, although there is perhaps none, in which the grosser kinds of incestuous mixture are not forbidden and punishable in the civil courts.

The consequences of these repeals and of the legislative divorces have been a general looseness of opinion on subjects connected with marriage. From this a few persons are partially preserved by religious principle, and a few more by a certain worldly refinement. This state of things has even alarmed the legislatures, who have generally relinquished the power of divorce, which they had usurped and abused. As a substitute for it, they have authorized the civil courts to grant divorces, both *a mensa et thoro* and *a vinculo matrimonii*, in cases provided for by law. The laws are framed upon the loosest principles, often contravening the Divine law. Every step which has been taken, tends to strengthen the false notion that the State has sole jurisdiction in matrimonial causes. From this the conclusion seems to have been hastily drawn, that she is an infallible guide to the true interpretation of the Divine laws about marriage. This is not true, and besides, she does not even pretend to interpret it. She legislates upon her own notions of expediency, which are often very crude.

It is therefore necessary that Christians should make use of private conscience in the matter, and that private conscience should have some rule whereby to judge the questions which may come before it. The rule is that of the Revealed Law, and is for the most part plain enough; although men have contrived to raise many questions about the meaning. These questions Church authorities and private persons are left to settle for themselves.

Church authorities have done very little. The Romish Church has her own laws, which are seemingly very strict, and much more burdensome than the Divine law. But between her avowed system of dispensations, and her unavowed system of connivance, her laws are not very strict, although, perhaps, more so than those of any other denomination. The Protestant Episcopal Church has done almost nothing. The Presbyterian Communion has gone further than any body of Protestants; but even her steps have been wavering and uncertain. The other denominations have done literally nothing. People, who have not the moral courage to adhere to the Divine law and interpret it for themselves, have adopted the law of the land and the conventional law of public opinion as their rules of action.

§ 29. Men are apt to consider themselves without blame when they conform their actions to those rules. They do not always think themselves bound to obey the law of the land. They will often disobey it if they think that they can escape disgraceful punishment, and that the conventional morality of society will excuse their conduct. But both these codes are very insufficient guides. Neither of them has, practically, any reference to the relation of man to God, or to the Revealed Law, which man is bound to obey. Men have consequently fallen into a very low tone of morals, especially upon subjects connected with marriage.

The Divine Word contains rules upon these subjects, the obligation of which all Christians acknowledge. Those rules constitute the Christian doctrine of marriage. Very few of them are enforced either by the law of the land or by public opinion; some of them are contradicted by both. Hence there has arisen a great looseness of practice, which can only be corrected by infusing a better tone into the public opinion of general society. The only agent which can be employed in that work, is the private conscience. There is no great hope that the thing can be done, but it ought to be attempted. Perhaps all that is left to Christians is to preserve, by the Divine aid in each case, a conscience void of offense. The object of this work is to assist them in so doing, by enlightening the private conscience, which requires to be reminded of the rules that are laid down in the Holy Scriptures.

CHAPTER II.

OF THE RELATION BETWEEN THE SEXES IN GENERAL.

§ 1. The Connection of the Subject of the Chapter with that of the Work. — § 2. Five false Theories. — § 3. The Scriptural Doctrine. — § 4. Headship of the Family. — § 5. Subordination of Woman. — § 6. Qualified Equality. — § 7. The Combination of those Relations. — § 8. Safeguards provided for Women. — § 9. Five Relations of Woman to Man. — § 10. The three Duties of Wives, and Correlative Duties of Husbands. — § 11. The Effect of Subordination and Authority, with Relation to the Affections. — § 12. Coöperation of the Sexes. — § 13. Diversity in Unity. — § 14. Amiability of Women. — § 15. The Image of God reflected in the Union of the Sexes. — § 16. Woman the Complement of Man. — § 17. Instincts. — § 18. Directing Instincts. — § 19. Inciting Instincts. — § 20. Emotions. — § 21. General Description of the Diagram. — § 22. Lowest Division of the Diagram. — § 23. Second Division of the Diagram. — § 24. Third Division of the Diagram. — § 25. Highest Division of the Diagram. — § 26. Intellectual and Moral Constitution of the Sexes. — § 27. — Female Imagination and Impulsiveness. — § 28. Female Benevolence. — § 29. The Higher Reason. — § 30. Passions and Affections. — § 31. Moral Nature. — § 32. Woman's Faith, Hope, and Charity. — § 33. Woman as Man's Adviser. — § 34. Disadvantages of the Female Constitution. — § 35. Woman as Man's Companion. — § 36. Woman as Man's Help. — § 37. How Woman is fitted for Subordination. — § 38. The Diagram.

§ 1. THE relation between the sexes is something different from the law of marriage, yet the two subjects are so intimately connected, that one cannot be treated of without some reference to the other. It is, therefore, proper in an inquiry into the Christian doctrine of marriage, to introduce some notice of the other subject. This is the design of the present chapter, which will not treat directly of the doctrine of marriage while it must speak of it incidentally, and anticipate some ideas, which will be repeated in subsequent parts of the work.

On the relation between the sexes as on most other moral subjects, there is a Scriptural doctrine and several false theories. These will be first stated, then the true doctrine, and the greater portion of the chapter will be devoted to some observations on the moral and mental constitutions of the sexes, with reference to the relation between them, and to the important fact that each of them is the complement or completion of the other.

§ 2. The relations between the sexes constitute the most important element in the social arrangements. Where sound ideas upon the subject prevail, society is generally in a sound state. Where false notions about the sexes are dominant, the social arrangements are generally bad. There is a revealed doctrine upon the subject, which is of course the only true one. There are also at least five false theories, of which three are very ancient and two are very modern.

The oldest of the five false theories has the advantage of resting upon a conception as to the reason for the creation of woman, which so far as it goes is true, and is only false, as it is imperfect. It is, that the final cause of woman is the continuation of the species.

Each of the other rests upon a merely false notion, and rests on the notion that woman was designed for a drudge. It has been well said, that half truths are whole falsehoods, but this is not even half of a truth. The truth, of which it is a perversion, is that woman was created a sa help to man, not as a mere servile worker, and she was created to. be something more than a mere help. If she were created to be a mere drudge, the logical inference is that a wife is a slave. These notions prevail wherever the intellect and the affections are in a low state of development. They are enforced by the superior strength and courage of man.

A third false notion is that woman was created to be an instrument of sensual pleasure to man. According to this theory a wife is a toy. It prevails among half civilized nations, who have made some progress in sensual refinement. Among them, it by no means excludes the second theory. The third also exists in more highly advanced communities. It is there seldom avowed, but it lurks in every grade of society, and not least in the highest. This notion lies at the root of all sexual immorality.

The fourth notion is modern. It is that woman is superior to man, and was created to be flattered, pampered, and adorned. Man is to do all this, and is also to venerate her as of a higher nature than himself. On this theory a wife is an idol. It cannot be really held by a man, and can scarcely be seriously stated by a woman, yet it influences more or less the opinions of most women, and of many young men. It has thus power to produce much evil in society. It is only a reproduction and development of the third theory in a more cultivated state of society. Woman is still regarded as a means of sensual pleasure, although not merely in the coarsest sense. She is to be flattered, pampered, and adorned, that she may be more able and more willing to give pleasure.

The last theory rests on the notion, that woman was created for herself without any reference to man, except so far as both sexes are necessary to the propagation of the species. According to this theory a wife is a business partner. It supposes that the sexes differ only as they do in the lower animals, and that their occupations, rights, and duties should be the same. These notions seem to be a reaction from the second and third theories. This fifth theory, which is the most modern of all, is so unnatural, that it can never be generally received. There are women, in whom the characteristic qualities of their sex are not well developed. They have adopted this theory, and try to propagate it, not without much noise. They find abettors in a few men, to whom it is a sufficient recommendation of any theory that it is new, startling, unchristian, and unfavorable to the idea of authority. It has also a great influence on the thoughts and conversation of a very numerous class of people, who do not take the trouble of arranging their thoughts into systems, and are content to talk of the Bible without adopting it as the rule of life. The members of this class govern their opinions more by each other's idle talk than by any settled convictions of their own. Few of these people accept the fifth theory as a whole, but they all take many notions from it. Much false doctrine and wicked practice thus finds its way into society.

These false notions about women have led to evil practices with relation to marriage. Out of the three ancient errors have grown the compulsory marriage of women, polygamy, and divorce at the arbitrary will of the husband. Out of the modern have grown domestic insubordination, and separations by consent, which are really divorces.

§ 3. The Scriptural doctrine is first introduced in the earlier chapters of Genesis, and is more fully developed in other parts of the Bible; which it pervades throughout. It is this: woman was created to be a wife and a mother, and a wife is to be the companion, the adviser and the assistant of her husband, who has authority over her. The proper position of a wife has not been left to be inferred from any theory. It is expressly revealed that a wife is to be the companion of her husband, and his help in the performance of his duties. It follows that she is his adviser, especially as she is also the mother of his children. She is not a dictator to rule, but she is an adviser to give counsel, of the soundness of which he is to judge. She is the better fitted for these functions, because her animal, intellectual, emotional, and moral natures all differ from his. They so differ, that each sex supplies that in which the other is wanting. Each is the complement, or completion of the other. The companionship of the woman is more delightful, and her advice and assistance the more valuable for that reason.

A family, like all other societies, requires a head, which

implies subordination in all the other members. The man is by Divine appointment the head. The moral constitution of the woman fits her, in a very remarkable manner, for the subordinate position thus assigned to her.

The earliest indications of the Scripture doctrine are to be found in the following texts: "So God created man in his own image, male and female, created He them. And God blessed them, and said unto them, Be fruitful and multiply, and replenish the earth and subdue it." It is remarkable, that in this first mention of woman, there is an intimation, that she is the complement, or completion of man, without which the image of God is not complete. It is first said, "in the image of God created He him," and then immediately, "male and female created He them."[1]

In the next chapter, it is recorded, "And the Lord God said, It is not meet for man to be alone: I will make an helpmeet for him."[2] With reference to this text it is worthy of notice, that the word "meet," that is, fit, proper, has passed out of the ordinary vocabulary. This has led to a misunderstanding of the text, which has given rise to the common use of the word "helpmate" for a wife. It is not impossible that, in this popular expression, and the misunderstanding connected with it, there may lurk some false doctrine. The true meaning of the text is, that God would furnish Adam with a help, who should be meet, that is fit, for him; but no idea of equality is implied.

In these texts the reasons for the creation of woman seem to be disclosed; from them the relation between the sexes may be inferred. Woman was created for three purposes: for the continuation of the species, to be a companion to man, and to be a help to him. As his companion and help she would naturally be his adviser. For the performance of these functions, it is necessary that her nature should be the complement of his, supplying that wherein his is deficient. Such is found to be the case.

[1] Genesis i. 27, 28.

[2] *Ibid.* ii. 18.

§ 4. The man and woman were to form a society with children, when born, which would require a head. The headship belongs to the man. But as the woman was created for his companion, there cannot be a very wide interval between them; yet her position as a help implies subordination. The third relation, which is inferred from these two, is, that woman is the counselor, or adviser of man. She is not designed to govern him; one who helps does not direct the work. It is not her office to overrule his judgment by authority, by violence, or by persuasion; but to present for his consideration that side of every question which the intellectual and moral constitution of her sex enables her to see more clearly than he can. She was designed to be his counselor, but in that, as in every other relation, to be subordinate to him.

§ 5. Even in Paradise, woman was subordinate to man. Subordination is inequality for the sake of order. A subordinate position is one which is under another in the established order of things. The inferior position of woman is not the consequence of any want or defect in her physical, intellectual, or moral constitution; but it implies a physical, intellectual, and moral constitution, differing from that of man, and adapted to a subordinate sphere of action.

If this subordination did not exist in Paradise, it was established immediately after the Fall. "Unto the woman, He said: I will greatly multiply thy sorrow and thy conception; in sorrow shalt thou bring forth children, and thy desire shall be to thy husband, and he shall rule over thee."[1]

This law is fully recognized in the New Testament, in which there are many texts bearing on the subject; some of them have been quoted in the first chapter, and more will be quoted hereafter. These texts, for the most part, relate primarily to the duty of a wife to her husband; but the relation between the sexes is very closely connected

[1] Genesis iii. 16.

with that of husband and wife, which may be said to be its final cause. Still there are not wanting texts which teach the doctrine of the subordination of the female sex, not merely that of the wife to the husband. This doctrine is the foundation of the general exclusion of women from political power.

St. Paul writes thus, " I would have you know, that the head of every man is Christ; and the head of the woman is the man, and the head of Christ is God. Every man praying or prophesying, having his head covered, dishonoreth his head. But every woman that prayeth or prophesieth with her head uncovered dishonoreth her head; for that is even all one as if she were shaven. For if the woman be not covered let her also be shorn; but if it be a shame for a woman to be shorn, or shaven, let her be covered. For a man indeed ought not to cover his head, forasmuch as he is the image and glory of God; but the woman is the glory of the man. For the man is not of the woman, but the woman of the man. Neither was the man created for the woman, but the woman for the man." [1]

In this passage there is no mention of the relation of husband and wife; yet the doctrine of the inequality of the sexes is plainly taught: "Man is not of the woman, but the woman of the man. Neither was the man created for the woman, but the woman for the man."

In another Epistle, the same Apostle again insists on the inequality of the sexes, " Let the woman learn in silence with all subjection. For I suffer not a woman to teach, nor to usurp authority over the man." [2]

§ 6. The Scripture doctrine of the relation of the sexes is, that woman is the equal companion and subordinate help of man, and consequently his adviser. To fit her for all these functions, her nature is made the complement, or completion of his. These relations, according to the sacred writers, exist in an inchoate state, independently of

[1] 1 Corinthians xi. 3–8. [2] 1 Timothy ii. 11, 12.

marriage, and are provided for in the very nature of the sexes. When St. Paul, in a passage just quoted, teaches the subordination of woman, he takes care lest too much should be inferred from his words; he adds: "Neither is the man without the woman, neither the woman without the man in the Lord. For as the woman is of the man, even so is the man also by the woman; but all things of God."[1]

Here again there seems to be a recognition of the fact, that woman is the complement, or completion, of man's nature. Her subordination implies inequality; but a qualified inequality, which exists in some respects and not in others, and which is nowhere very great. God, in his infinite wisdom, has ordered these things with reference to the holy state of matrimony. The practical holiness of that state depends very much upon the acknowledgment of these truths.

§ 7. In these complicated relations each modifies and is modified by the others. The subordination in one capacity modifies the equality in another; while the equality, in its turn, modifies and softens the subordination. The two ideas are so mingled that neither is absolute or unchecked by the other. Such is the equality of the sexes and such is the subordination of woman. An apt illustration may be found in the usages of the military profession. It is well understood that a subordinate officer, as a gentleman, is the equal companion of his superior. He is, moreover, his adviser upon proper occasions; yet, as an officer, he is bound to obey his orders. The result is that the equality of companionship is never felt to be perfect, while the duty of subordination cannot, unless under very peculiar circumstances, be harshly enforced. This relation seems, in these respects, to be an imperfect image of that of husband and wife.

The relation of companion implies a near approach to equality, while that of help involves the idea of subordina-

[1] 1 Corinthians xi. 11, 12.

tion. It is not easy to preserve a just equilibrium between these things. The most obvious danger, and the evil which history shows to have occurred most frequently, is that man has abused his position. He is physically stronger than woman, and his intellectual and moral nature is of a harder texture than hers. Not but that the modern theories have actually produced evils of an opposite character.

§ 8. It has too often happened, that the equality of woman has been forgotten, and her subordination exaggerated. It was, therefore, necessary to provide safeguards for her. They have been provided by divine authority, in the revealed laws of the exclusiveness and indissolubleness of marriage. A third of great importance is not directly revealed, although it seems to be implied in the general tone of revelation. It is the freedom of a woman in choosing her husband. This ought to extend so far that no woman should be compelled to accept of a man for her husband against her will. Compulsory marriage, polygamy, divorce, and the seclusion which the two first make necessary, have been great instruments in the degradation of woman. As much may be said of the practice of taking women captives and reducing them to slavery.

It was, therefore, provided by God himself, that a man should have one female companion, and but one. She is to be his help and his deputy in the government of his family, as well as his companion and the possessor of his undivided affections. He is not to be separated from her but by death. He is to rule her, but with an authority tempered by love.

Both the exclusiveness and the indissolubleness of marriage are plainly taught in the Book of Genesis. Indeed, the exclusiveness was intimated in the creation of only one woman. The Prophet Malachi takes this view.[1] But both are taught in the account of the creation of woman: "And the Lord God caused a deep sleep to fall upon Adam, and he slept; and He took one of his ribs, and

[[1] Chap. ii. 14, 15.]

closed up the flesh instead thereof, and the rib, which the Lord God had taken from man made he a woman, and brought her to the man. And Adam said, This is now bone of my bone and flesh of my flesh she shall be called woman, because she was taken out of man. Therefore shall a man leave his father and his mother and shall cleave unto his wife, and they shall be one flesh."[1]

St. Paul makes use of this passage in pressing the necessity of those kindly affections, without which there is danger that the authority of the husband may become a burdensome yoke. He writes thus: "Husbands, love your wives, even as Christ loved the Church, and gave Himself for it; that He might sanctify and cleanse it with the washing of water by the Word, that He might present it to Himself a glorious Church, not having spot, or wrinkle, or any such thing; but that it should be holy and without blemish. So ought men to love their wives as their own bodies. He that loveth his wife loveth himself. For no man ever yet hated his own body, but nourisheth it, and cherisheth it, even as the Lord the Church; for we are members of His body, of His flesh and of His bones. For this cause shall a man leave his father and his mother, and shall be joined unto his wife, and they two shall be one flesh."[2]

There is more doctrine in Ephesians than in Genesis, but the allusion to the passage in Genesis, its adoption and extension, are very evident. There is, in St. Paul, a plain allusion to the "flesh of my flesh and bone of my bone" of Adam. Moreover the words, which deliberately declare the unity of man and wife, are quoted in such a manner as to furnish a commentary pointing [out] their meaning. Adam says, "A man shall leave his father and his mother, and shall cleave unto his wife, and they shall be one flesh." St. Paul says, "They two shall be one flesh." He thus gives his readers to understand, that the unity cannot be so extended as to admit more than two persons. It may

[1] Genesis ii. 20–24. [2] Ephesians v. 25–31.

include one man and one woman, but not one man and several women. In making this addition St. Paul has done no more than our Blessed Lord himself. He quoted the text in the same way, and the fact is recorded by two Evangelists.[1]

It seems clear, both *a priori* and from history, that the entire oneness does not admit of a plurality of wives. It is hard to see how it can admit of the dissolution of the marriage. The great causes of the degradation of women, which history shows to have been so general, have been compulsory marriage; polygamy, including concubinage; seclusion, which was a consequence of the first two; the slavery of captive women, which was intimately connected with concubinage, and divorce. Polygamy in any form deprives woman of her proper position, and lessens her authority in the household. It is very likely to put an end to the affection of the husband, or rather to prevent its formation.

Arbitrary divorce, which is the most ancient form of divorce, reduces women to slavery, by placing them entirely in the power of their husbands. A man may drive his wife from her home with little or no provision for her support, and thus separate her from her children. The power of life and death could scarcely make him more absolute. This is not the place to discuss the question of divorce in its modern form, which calls in the authority of the state to decide judicially the questions connected with the separation.

§ 9. The relations of woman to man, passing by what belongs to the continuation of the species, about which it is not necessary to say much, are five in number. She is his companion, his adviser, his help, and his subordinate. She is all these, because her nature is the complement of his. That circumstance fits her for and puts her in her other relations. It also shows that she was never intended to be his slave, a position which is inconsistent with at least two of the other relations.

[1] Matthew xix. 5; Mark x. 8.

Subordination is not slavery. The subordinate person is placed under the authority of the superior for the benefit of the whole community, and, therefore, of both parties. The authority of the master over the slave is to be exercised principally for the benefit of the master, although not without some reference to that of the slave. In practice the interests of the slave are generally forgotten, and men act upon the idea which is expressed in some definitions of slavery, that is, the absolute subjection of one person to another for the exclusive benefit of that other. But no human authority can be absolute; it must be always limited by the Divine law. This is as true of authority over a slave as of any other authority. Still authority for the common good is very different from authority held for the benefit of him who holds it. To confound the two has always been the vice of those who had power, if it be not nearer the truth to say that the last-mentioned kind of authority is nothing more than the abuse of power.

§ 10. The Scripture doctrine of the relation of husband and wife, as developed in the Book of Genesis, involves three duties on the part of the wife: companionship, assistance, and obedience. Man has three rights correlative to those duties or obligations. These rights, like all others, involve correlative duties or obligations. If woman be the companion of her husband, he is bound to be hers, and must fulfill the obligation as well as claim the right. If she be his help, she is entitled to a provision out of the proceeds of their common labor, as well as to the consideration which belongs to her in her capacity of his companion. If he has authority over her, it should be exercised with moderation and mildness and tempered with affection. All these duties and rights resolve themselves into the unity of the two persons, which enforces the duties and limits the rights. The relation, consisting of three elements, which have a certain connection with each other, is liable to be perverted by the exaggeration or neglect of any one of them, or by the introduction of new principles. It has been perverted in all three ways.

§ 11. The Holy Scriptures everywhere teach the authority of the man and the subordination of the woman. Subordination seems to be, in a relation so intimate as that of marriage, necessary to the development of the kindly affections. Authority kindly exercised, and subordination quietly acknowledged, promote the development of the affections, to which there is nothing more dangerous than rivalry. A superior may have a strong affection for an inferior, as a mother for her child. An inferior may have a strong affection for a superior, as a child for its parent. In neither case is affection lessened by the exercise of authority; on the contrary, the kindly exercise of authority seems to strengthen the attachment. Affection may exist among equals, when there is no rivalry and no claim to authority or occasion for its exercise; but rivalry and disputes about authority are fatal to affection. In the family a supreme authority is necessary; it cannot be divided or jointly held between the husband and the wife. Under such circumstances, equals must be rivals. Thus those who act upon the fifth of the false theories which have been mentioned, take away from marriage the principle by which it is cemented, and expose the weakened fabric to unnecessary storms.

§ 12. Men and women were created to coöperate with each other, by the performance of different functions. God has assigned to the sexes different spheres, and different physical, mental, and moral constitutions adapted to these spheres. Both were designed to take part in the business of life; each that part for which the other was less fitted. This involves a diversity which affords greater play to the affections. The two sexes form one species and live together in communities each of which is a unit, while particular men and women are united to each other in marriage, that is, made one. The result is diversity in unity.

But diversity sometimes leads to disagreement; to settle such disagreements the principle of the subordination of the woman was introduced, by God himself.

§ 13. It is a general law in the physical and moral world that diversity in unity is necessary to perfection. True unity cannot be obtained by simple repetition without subordination. This law is applicable to the relations between the sexes, as well to those between men and women in general, as between particular men and women in the state of matrimony. Woman repeats man subordinately, and so is another and the same. Yet she is not, according to the error of Pope, merely "a softer man." She has her own peculiar constitution, the elements of which are the same as those which enter into the male constitution, but they are introduced in different proportions. This fits her for her peculiar functions, while she is still a variety of man, who is not fit for them. She has much in common with him and much that is diverse from him. She is thus fitted to be his companion, his help, and his adviser. But the same circumstances which fit her to perform her proper functions unfit her for those of the man.

§ 14. It is often said, that as woman is a more loving being than man, she reflects the Divine image more perfectly than man, since God is love. The Scriptures teach that God is love; but they do not teach that He is nothing but Love. The phrase, like many others in the Holy Scriptures, is not a full expression of the whole truth; but requires, to be compared with other texts, which will limit and modify its meaning. God is Love; but He is also a consuming fire. Wisdom, and Justice, and Power as well as Love enter into His nature, and none of them extinguish or override any of the others. Man excels woman in some of these things. The image of God is not so fully reflected in woman as in man. St. Paul says, "He is the image and glory of God; but the woman is the glory of the man."[1]

[1] 1 Corinthians xi. 7.

§ 15. But the image of God is not so perfectly reflected in either as in the combination of their two natures. This truth has been happily expressed by Mr. Gladstone in a single sentence: "When Christianity wrought out for woman, not a social identity, but a social equality, not a rivalry with the functions of man, but an elevation of her own functions as high as his, it made the world and human life, in this respect also, a true image of God." [1]

§ 16. The more perfect reflection of the image of God in the combined natures of man and woman than in either separately, implies that these two natures are complements to each other. This is equally true, whether it be viewed in connection with the combination of the two natures in the persons of one married pair, or in the whole human race, of which both sexes are portions. If neither of the sexes can reflect the Divine image so perfectly as the union of the two, each must have some qualities answering to something in the Divine nature, which the other wants, or has but imperfectly. Each must, therefore, be the complement of the other; so that, when joined, they constitute one whole. This is the explanation of the unity and sanctity of marriage.

The Scripture doctrine of the relation between the sexes may be summed up in a few words. Woman is the companion, the help, and the adviser of man, as he is her companion, maintainer, protector, and governor. The nature of each has been made the complement, or completion of the other. In order to show this it may be proper to take a summary view of some of the elements of human nature, and even of some of the elements of animal nature.

§ 17. Much has been written about the nature of the inferior animals, which has not been very well considered. Their nature contains what may be considered the germs of all the principles of human nature, except perhaps conscience. The outward manifestations which dogs some-

[1] *Studies on Homer*, vol. ii. p. 480.

times exhibit, and which have been supposed to indicate the presence of conscience, may more probably be referred to fear. But dogs and elephants, and in a lesser degree other animals, do manifest, at least the germ of the reasoning faculty. Some notice, although but little, has been taken of this fact, as well as of others connected with what may be regarded as the super-animal part of the merely animal nature. These expressions seem strange, but they will probably be understood.

Perhaps the most mysterious part of the animal nature, as it is usually treated of, is that which is called instinct. It seems to be taken for granted, that the distinction between men and animals consists in this, that men are governed by reason, brutes by instinct. This seems to be a mistake. The true distinction lies in the possession by man of a moral nature, which is wanting in the brute. They have not even its germ; but they have an undeveloped and imperfect reason. Still, it is true that they are, in the main, governed by instinct. But what is instinct?

Few subjects have been more carelessly handled. In fact, three classes of things which are essentially distinct, are generally grouped together under the general name of instincts. One of these is sometimes distinguished from other instincts by the name of appetites. The other two have been inextricably confounded under the name of instincts. It would be hopeless to attempt to introduce any other name for either. Yet they are two distinct classes of things, and may be distinguished into inciting instincts, or those which incite to action, and directing instincts, or those which regulate action. The first class is the germ of that which has been most happily termed the emotional nature of man. The other supplies to animals the place of reason; but it is not the germ of reason, as the other class is the germ of the passions and affections. The appetites are to be distinguished from the inciting instincts in that they are really physical wants, which act upon the physical nature.

These appetites exist in man as in beasts, although modified by their coexistence with the higher parts of human nature. They are three in men and three in beasts, and are not to be confounded either with instincts or emotions. In man or in beast they are merely animal, and directly connected with merely animal sensations.

§ 18. Both in men and in other animals the appetites are directly under the control of directing instincts, and it is remarkable that the very few directing instincts which man possesses are connected with the appetites. All the actions of brutes are under the direction of such instincts. The little reason which they possess is only occasionally called in as an aid to the instinct, supplying its place a little way beyond its limits. On the other hand, men are placed under the dominion of reason as the ordinary guide of their lives. It is more fallible than instinct, but is capable of being applied in a much greater variety of cases, and is, moreover, capable of being improved by exercise. It is therefore the fitter guide for a moral being. The directing instincts operate each within a narrow compass, but direct the animal to results at which reason could only arrive by long and tedious processes. They are very useful to animals incapable of reasoning, or only capable of reasoning imperfectly; they are unnecessary to a being who possesses a faculty capable of being made to supply their place by labor and industry. Perhaps, also, they are less suited to the condition of a being in a state of probation; where an infallible guide constantly at hand would relieve one from a wholesome responsibility, which is enforced by the necessity of using the services of a fallible guide, like reason, and of making exertions to improve the quality of the guide. This seems to be the difference between instinct and reason.

The bee, under the guidance of an infallible instinct, forms its combs into hexagons, without knowing any reason for so doing. The man, who desires to unite strength of construction with economy of materials, adopts the same form under the guidance of a fallible but instructed reason. The one comes to the conclusion at once; the other after long study, in which both his intellectual and moral natures have been, or at least may have been improved. The directing instinct might have been very convenient so far as material interests were concerned, but would not have been so advantageous to the moral nature. Hence, man has no directing instincts except such as are connected with the merely animal appetites; which it is not convenient should be made the subjects of much thought or attention. Even with respect to these, the directing instincts are inferior to those of the beasts. For man has no instinct which points him unerringly to food, medicine, or poison; most beasts have.

§ 19. The inciting instincts are something very different from the directing, and may undoubtedly be considered as the germs of our emotions. They differ from directing instincts in that they do not govern action, but only incite to it. They differ from appetites, in that they are not merely animal sensations, the results of certain physical processes which have been going on in the animal system. In fact, they testify very distinctly to the existence of that, which the wise man calls "the spirit of the beast, which goeth downward to the earth."[1] By those words Solomon probably intended to intimate that the inferior creatures were not merely material, but that there existed in their nature a principle which, although mortal, was spiritual.

The proofs of the existence of such a principle, which observation furnishes, are chiefly derived from the inciting instincts. It is not easy to account for these things, so different from mere appetites, upon any theory which does not allow, to the beings by whom they are possessed, something more than a mere organization of matter. They are not, like appetites, the results of known physical causes;

[1] Eccles. iii. 21.

yet they are seen to affect the conduct of animals. They differ from directing instincts in that they are not unerring, and seem only to incite, not to govern.

The inciting instincts may be reduced to three classes, each of which is composed of the developments of a single instinct. These three instincts may, in a certain sense, be called primary; although, in a certain other sense, only one of them is primary. They are self-love, malevolence, and benevolence. Of these, self-love is a primary instinct in a different sense from the others, although also in the same. For the malevolent and benevolent instincts alike give pleasure by their gratification, which pleasure is a gratification to self-love. Hence a school of moralists have denied the existence of any other principle of action than self-love, or, as they prefer to call it, selfishness.

But it is plain that there are principles in our nature, and even in that of beasts, which derive gratification from the well-being or the suffering of other sentient beings. These are something different from the principle which seeks and rejoices in our own well-being, without reference to any being without us. This last principle is properly self-love, and, when over indulged, selfishness. Selfishness is the exaggeration and abuse of self-love. Self-love, then, seeks simply the advantage and well-being of the self-lover. Malevolence seeks the gratification of the malevolent being through the sufferings of another being, which has become the object of his ill-will. Benevolence seeks the gratification of the benevolent being through the well-being of another being, which has become the object of his kindness. The existence of the first of these principles in human nature is universally conceded. It is to be feared that there are not many human beings who will not, upon a strict self-examination, find the evidence of the second in their own hearts. It is to be hoped, also, that there are not many who need go further for the evidence of the third.

§ 20. Suffice it to say, that the three primary instincts of self-love, malevolence, or ill-will, and benevolence or good-will, are all found in the nature of the inferior animals, and are transferred, so to speak, into our human nature, where they are developed into a vast variety of emotions. These emotions are capable of being classed, and in fact have been classed, under the three instincts out of which they are developed. They differ from the secondary inciting instincts of animals, in that they are connected with the intellectual faculties of memory and imagination. The first of these faculties is certainly, and the other probably, possessed by animals. But both, especially the imagination, in a degree very inferior to that which is exhibited in man. When, therefore, the primary instincts are combined with the stronger memory and enlarged imagination of man, they produce emotions of greater intensity and longer duration, as well as of greater variety, than the secondary instincts of animals.

In men as in animals, the benevolent part of our nature seems to be the weakest of the three. This is most probably an effect of our fallen condition. But, whatever be the cause, the existence of the phenomenon is certain. Language bears a striking testimony to this. The selfish and malevolent emotions are called passions, sufferings; they are supposed to carry away the man with an irresistible force. In fact, their power is irresistible, except by the aid of Divine grace. The benevolent emotions are called affections; things which affect us, but not with an irresistible, or overwhelming power. These feeble affections, feeble by comparison with the passions, constitute one portion of our emotional nature. The passions constitute others.

Those which are directly connected with self-love, have been called the concupiscible passions, because, for the most part, they relate to things which are desired. The word is used for passions connected with desires of any sort, not merely for passions or appetites of a particular class. In Johnson's "Dictionary" there is a quotation from

Dr. South, which is very apposite: "The schools reduce all the passions to these two heads, the concupiscible and the irascible appetites." Richardson gives a quotation from Bishop Beveridge, which is still more to the purpose: "Now there being a double object for the will of man to work upon, there is likewise a double faculty considerable in it: the one we call a concupiscible, the other an irascible faculty; by the one we follow that which is good, by the other we run from that which is evil."

These quotations speak of but two classes of passions, and Bishop Beveridge seems to include fear among the irascible passions. It is certainly something different in its nature from anger, and equally so from desire, though it is as certainly connected with self-love. It has, too, a large class of passions which are connected with it. It then seems better to acknowledge three classes of passions: the desires, which grow out of self-love; the fears, which have the same root; and the irascible passions, which are connected with malevolence. The two last-mentioned classes combine to produce a third, which leads men to contend with danger, not to shun it. This class of passions is connected with the instinct of self-defense, which may be considered as a compound of fear and malevolence. The affections, which grow out of benevolence, are a fifth class. In order to illustrate these views a diagram has been prepared and placed at pages 72 and 73, an explanation of which will now be inserted.

§ 21. The diagram is an attempt to exhibit to the eye. the connection of the principal Virtues with the principal Emotions, Faculties, and Instincts. It takes the form of what architects call a section of a building; which may be regarded as of four stories.

The lowest division, or story, represents the Animal Nature, common to man and other animals. Here are Instincts without any government. This division corresponds to that part of human nature, which the Apostle to the Thessalonians calls Body.

The next represents the Intellectual Nature, in which Emotions and Faculties are found under the dominion of Intellectual Choice, that is, an exercise of the Intellect without reference to moral considerations. This answers to what the Apostle calls Soul.

The third represents the Moral Nature, which the Apostle calls Spirit. Here are the Emotions and Faculties, under the government of the Conscience, assuming a moral character and ripening into Virtues.

The highest division represents the Sanctified Nature of the regenerate and renewed man under the Influences of the Holy Spirit. From these Influences descend the Sanctified Conscience, the Sanctified Reason, and the Sanctified Will. The Virtues, by passing under these Influences, assume a different and higher character, and may be called Saintly.

The lines drawn up and down show the connection of particular Instincts with particular Emotions and Virtues, and of the Faculties with each other. Sometimes particular Emotions, Faculties, or Virtues, are united by lines across the page, which show a connection between them, a marriage as it were, from whence arises a new line of Emotions, Faculties, or Virtues, traceable to the combination of those so united.

§ 22. In the lowest division are placed three Primary Instincts: Self-Love, Benevolence, and Malevolence. All of these, men have in common with other animals; although Benevolence is not usually regarded as belonging to them. The word is not, however, used in a very high sense, but only to express the power of kindly feeling; neither is Malevolence used in the sense of malignity. Both words are used in the primary sense indicated by their etymology, for the willing, by one being, of good or evil to another. They are thus distinguished from Self-Love, which has no reference to any other being than the self-lover. It is, therefore, a Primary Instinct in a stricter sense than the others; because they are instruments by which it receives gratification, but a gratification connected with the well or ill-being of others, and therefore, where moral responsibility exists, with virtue and vice.

These Instincts are all Primary, in that they are the germs out of which are developed all other Inciting Instincts. Directing Instincts are of a separate and very different class. All the Inciting Instincts, except the three named — and they are very numerous — may be called Secondary; because they are only manifestations or developments of one or more of the three Primary Instincts. Thus Benevolence, even in the inferior animals, is developed into several kindly Instincts; in many species into an attachment to a mate, in many more into fondness for offspring, in a few into an attachment for human beings, in some cases into kindly feeling for individual animals, sometimes of a different species. Malevolence also manifests itself in the form of many like Secondary Instincts. The developments of Self-Love are even more numerous, and may be regarded as divided into two classes: those which are connected with Pleasure or Comfort, and may be collectively named Desires, and those which are connected with Self-Preservation, which may be collectively named Fears. Out of a combination of Self-Love and Malevolence arises the Secondary Instinct of Self-Defense.

§ 23. For the present purpose, the two classes of Secondary Instincts, which grow out of Self-Love, Desires and Fears, have been treated as single Secondary Instincts, to which there have been given the names of Pleasure and Preservation. From these and from the Secondary Instinct of Self-Defense and the Primary Instincts of Benevolence and Malevolence, have been drawn five lines into the second division of the diagram, which represents the Intellectual Nature, or what St. Paul calls the Soul.

This is that part of human nature which includes Faculties, by which it acts, and Emotions by which it is incited to action. The latter are developments of the Inciting Instincts, in connection with the Faculties. The dawn of the Faculties may be perceived among some of the lower animals; but they are there only subsidiary to certain Instincts, which may be called Directing Instincts. These do not pass, like the other class of Instincts, which may be called Inciting Instincts, into the Intellectual Nature. In fact, man has very few of them, and the infant more than the adult. They relate chiefly to animal wants. Beyond that sphere their place is supplied by the Faculties, which differ from them in kind not in degree. In the Animal Nature, the Instincts are the ruling power; in the Intellectual, the Faculties and Emotions are under that rule which is called Intellectual Choice, because it decides without reference to Moral Considerations. It is either a function of the Higher Reason or closely connected with it. The two names are placed in a line, at the top of this division.

The three Primary Faculties, Memory, Imagination, and the Understanding, or Lower Reason, are introduced into this division on the left hand side near the bottom. The Lower Reason is the Faculty by which we understand or judge of objects of sense. From the union of this Faculty with that of Imagination springs the Higher Reason, by means of which we consider things not patent to sense. Intellectual Choice is very probably a function of this Faculty; where it is weak or neglected, the Emotions domineer over the Faculties.

The Inciting Instincts on passing into the Intellectual part of our Nature become Passions or Affections, which are designated by the general name of Emotions. The five lines drawn from the lower division show their particular connections. Thus Benevolence becomes the Benevolent Affections; Pleasure, or the Desires, the Concupiscible Passions; Preservation, or the Fears, the Apprehensive Passions; Self-Defense, Courage; and Malevolence, the Irascible Passions. The Concupiscible Passions, or Desires connected with Self-Love and the Instinct of Pleasure, cannot rise beyond this stage. They are incapable of becoming the grounds of moral action, until they are connected with some other part of our Nature. But one very important passion of this class, combining with a Benevolent Affection develops that mixed Emotion, which brings the sexes together, and which may be called Amorous Emotion.

§ 24. The third division shows the Emotions or Affections and Passions, transplanted into the region of Morals, under the Dominion of Conscience, with which is associated, at the top of the Division, the Higher Reason, now become Moral Reason, because judging of everything with reference to Moral responsibility. It is not desirable to enter upon the question whether Conscience be an independent Faculty or only a function of the Higher Reason. The Emotions passing into this sphere become Moral Emotions, and pass on into Moral Virtues. Thus the Benevolent Affections become Love and pass into the Virtue of Kindness. Amorous Emotion becomes Conjugal Affection and the Virtue of Conjugal Fidelity; the Apprehensive Passions are represented by Moral Fear, or Fear connected with Conscience. From this proceed the virtues of Prudence, Temperance, and Chastity. Courage becomes Confidence and Moral Courage, and the Irascible Passions are reduced to Indignation, or a keen hatred of wrong as such. Moral Fear combines on one side with Love, and produces Reverence, which rises into the Virtue of Docility; and on the other with Indignation and produces Remorse, which, until it passes into the highest division, is nothing but a painful Emotion.

§ 25. In the upper Division, the Virtues and Emotions are connected with the Influences of the Holy Spirit. From these Influences come the Sanctified Conscience, the Sanctified Reason, and the Sanctified Will, which are all his Instruments. From Him descend the three Evangel-

THE CONNECTION OF THE VIRTUES.

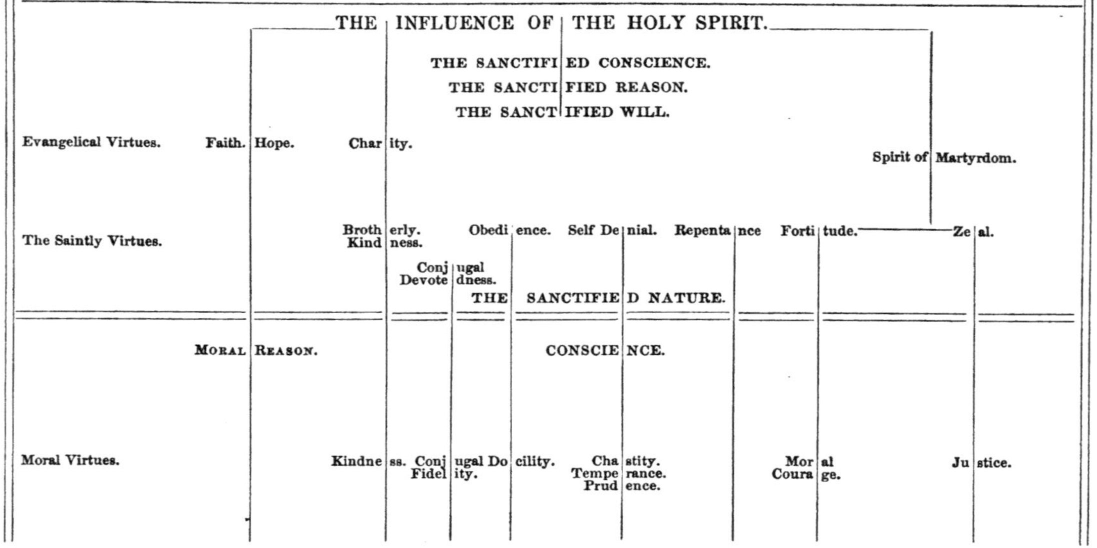

THE INFLUENCE OF THE HOLY SPIRIT.

THE SANCTIFIED CONSCIENCE.
THE SANCTIFIED REASON.
THE SANCTIFIED WILL.

Evangelical Virtues.	Faith.	Hope.	Charity.						Spirit of Martyrdom.
The Saintly Virtues.			Brotherly Kindness.	Conjugal Devotedness.	Obedience.	Self Denial.	Repentance.	Fortitude.	Zeal.
					THE SANCTIFIED NATURE.				
	Moral Reason.				Conscience.				
Moral Virtues.			Kindness.	Conjugal Fidelity.	Docility.	Chastity. Temperance. Prudence.		Moral Courage.	Justice.

Moral Emotions.	Love.	Reverence.	Moral Fear. Remorse.	Confidence.	Indignation.
		Conjugal Affection.			
SPIRIT.—1 Thess. v. 23.		THE MORAL NATURE.			
HIGHER REASON.		INTELLECTUAL CHOICE.			
		Amorous Emotion.			
Emotions.	Benevolent Affections.	Concupiscible Passions.	Apprehensive Passions.	Courage.	Irascible Passions.
Faculties. Memory. Imagination. Lower Reason.					
SOUL.—1 Thess. v. 23.		THE INTELLECTUAL NATURE.			
Secondary Instincts.		Desires. Pleasure.	Fears. Preservation.	Animal Courage. Self-Defense.	
Primary Instincts.	Benevolence.	Self-Love.		Malevolence.	
BODY.—1 Thess. v. 23.		THE ANIMAL NATURE.			

ical Virtues of Faith, Hope, and Charity. Of these the two first connect themselves with Human Reason, and the third with Human Affections. Below the Evangelical Virtues there are placed other inferior, but still Saintly Virtues, which are Sanctified modifications of the Moral Virtues. Thus Brotherly Kindness is a Sanctified modification of Kindness, Conjugal Devotion of Conjugal Fidelity, Obedience of Docility, Self-Denial of Prudence, Zeal of Justice, Fortitude of Moral Courage. The two last named combining, under the Influence of the Holy Spirit, produce the still Higher Virtue of the Spirit of Martyrdom. Remorse, which, in the merely Moral Nature, is only a painful Emotion, becomes the Saintly Virtue of Repentance, when brought under the Influence of the Holy Spirit.

§ 26. The diagram, having been explained, may be used to illustrate the intellectual and moral constitutions of the sexes. Of the three primary instincts, one, self-love, seems to be equally the property of both. Benevolence is stronger in woman, and malevolence in man. Of the secondary instincts, desire predominates among men, fear among women; courage is a male quality. All the emotions of the human heart spring from these six instincts. All human beings have them all. Neither sex is destitute of any one of them, or of any of the emotions, of which they are the germs; although each has its peculiar instincts and emotions, which are stronger in it than in the other. These generally prevail in the sexes to which they belong, though not in every man or woman. Most women are more affectionate than most men. Yet all women are not equally affectionate, and some may be found whose kindly feelings are cold and slow. Most men are more given to hatred than most women, while some men hate more heartily than others, and some are not easily roused to hatred. Some women, Fulvia and Herodias are instances, have hated as bitterly as any man.

A similar difference exists in the distribution of the intellectual faculties. The three leading faculties are memory, imagination, and reason, or the logical faculty. The first is possessed equally by both sexes; in woman the imagination predominates, in man, the reason. This does not mean that man has no imagination. Or what should we do with Shakespeare. Neither does it mean that woman has no reasoning powers. Or what of the thousands of women who have reasoned well upon many subjects. But, as a general rule, imagination is stronger in women, and the logical faculty in men. These differences in the instincts, emotions, and faculties color the whole character of the sexes. It is owing to them that the nature of each sex is the complement of the other.

§ 27. The impulsiveness of women arises from the strength of their imagination, and the delicacy of their bodily organizations. It renders them unfit to have the absolute decision of important questions, and thus makes their subordinate position beneficial to themselves. When a question is brought before a woman, the strength of her imagination brings the materials for a decision rapidly and vividly before her mind. The decision is soon made, and is generally right. It is always as near right as the woman could make it, after long examination. But imagination sometimes introduces materials which do not belong to the case, especially if it is disturbed by any emotion. It has sometimes not produced all the materials. It has neglected the dark side of a lover's character, or the advantages of withdrawing from the gayeties of a city. The decision will be erroneous, and the woman can never correct it.

The bringing forward the facts which imagination has dropped, and setting aside those which it has improperly introduced, are works of patient labor, for which woman's impulsive nature unfits her. Women have more patience than men, but it is of a different kind. A woman can endure anything but delay in deciding. Men decide more slowly, because they decide by some logical process. A man may thus often correct the hasty conclusions of a woman; though he will seldom be able to convince her, for she cannot follow the logical process, by which, consciously or unconsciously, he works. This is another reason for the authority of man, and the subordination of woman. Yet her quickness of apprehension makes her invaluable as an adviser to slower man, especially as the facts and the feelings, which she brings to the consultation, are precisely those which a man is most likely to overlook or to want.

§ 28. There are other modes in which the peculiar constitution of woman fits her to be the adviser of man. Her greater benevolence, and her more vivid imagination, make her feel for distress more readily and more keenly. She is thus in a better condition to obey the great law: "All things, whatsoever, ye would that men should do to you, do ye even so to them." But in some cases, something more than benevolence and imagination is necessary to the proper application of this text. When the question is a simple one, between a person who is to decide and one who is to suffer, the female character will generally make the best decision. But there may be cases even of that sort in which it may be proper to appeal from the hasty decisions of a benevolent imagination. Where a question is complicated by the number of the parties, and their various interests, man with his feebler benevolence and slower imagination, is better able to wait, until his cooler and stronger reason has unraveled the intricacies. Woman is the fairer decider between herself and others. Man is the best judge. He is not less so, because he is able to form judgments, from which the benevolence of woman would shrink, and sternly to carry them into effect. The male character is not amiable, but it is strong. Woman is amiable in her very weaknesses, because they are connected with benevolence.

§ 29. Instincts pass into the intellectual nature, and there become emotions. In this state they are governed by intellectual choice, which decides without reference to the rules of right and wrong; but which, nevertheless, deals with matters, which are veiled from sense. It therefore acts by the highest reason with which the whole emotional nature is intimately connected. The higher reason is the union of the imagination with the logical faculty. It is a very different thing in the different sexes, because the elements which compose it are present in different proportions. The peculiar character of the higher reason in woman is reflected upon all her affections and passions, in all which the imagination plays a great part. Her benevolent affections are the instinct of benevolence, which has passed into the intellectual nature, come into contact with the imagination, and passed under the jurisdiction of the higher reason. But the higher reason imposes very little restraint upon it, for in it, as well as in the affection, imagination is the larger ingredient.

In man the higher reason is sterner, because in him the imagination is the feebler of the two elements of which it is composed. In both sexes the emotions are nothing but instincts coupled with imagination. Men govern them more easily than women, because the sympathy between the higher reason and the emotion growing out of the imagination which enters into both, is not so strong.

§ 30. The emotions are compounded of instincts and imagination, and may derive strength from the strength of either element; where the instinct is strong as benevolence is in woman, the emotion will be strong. But even where the instinct, as that of hatred, is weak in woman, the emotion may be strong, stronger even than in man, because her imagination is stronger than his. A man's emotions are strong because his instincts are strong; a woman's, because her imagination is strong. The emotions are under the government of the higher reason. In governing, the logical faculty, which is one of its elements, is that which is chiefly to be relied on. For the imaginative element in the higher reason may combine with that in the emotion to be governed. Thus the higher reason of man is fitter for its office than that of woman. It is, perhaps, on this account, that the Holy Scriptures designate woman as the weaker vessel. She is so, but it cannot be denied that, morally as well as physically, she is the more beautiful.

Desire and malevolence, when they come in contact with the imagination, are developed into the concupiscible and irascible passions. These emotions are stronger in men than in women, because the instincts, out of which they grow, are so. They require the restraining influence of the higher reason, which is also likely to receive valuable aid from the influence of woman. Her benevolence will be especially useful in softening the irascible passions, and her prudence in checking the concupiscible. She is thus again, by her peculiar constitution, fitted to be the adviser of man.

§ 31. The effects of the specific character of the feminine higher reason do not stop here. The emotions pass on into the moral nature, in which they are under the dominion of conscience. The higher reason passes with them, and becomes the moral reason. It now takes into view the distinction between right and wrong, and is closely connected with conscience. Conscience, according to some philosophers, is only a function of the moral reason; according to others, it is a distinct faculty. This is not the proper place to decide the dispute, which is perhaps only verbal. No one doubts that the two things are closely connected. Both are employed about ideas connected with responsibility, and with right and wrong.

The higher reason becomes the moral reason, but it is still only a compound of imagination and the logical faculty. Without its aid, the problem of right and wrong could never be worked; for without the imagination the mind cannot receive any idea which does not come through the senses, or the internal consciousness. The judgments of the moral reason may be the work of the element of pure reason which it contains; but the evidence upon which they are founded is collected and arranged by the imagination. The more vivid the imagination the greater is its influence upon the judgment. It is thus owing to the larger infusion of imagination in the moral reason of women that they have more tender consciences than men.

§ 32. Woman derives another advantage from the same fact. The higher reason is the faculty by which the gift of faith is received, and chiefly through the imaginative element. The imagination performs precisely the same office in the moral world as in the intellectual, and it is precisely the same with that which faith performs in the spiritual nature. It is, in a lower sense, "the evidence of things not seen." By means of it, the higher reason grasps the subjects with which it deals, and with which the lower reason cannot deal, because they are veiled from sense. Thus is produced that human belief of Divine things, upon which the Holy Spirit grafts the Divine Gift of Faith. Hence it is that women have more Faith and Hope than man. Their constitution is better fitted to receive the Divine Graces. Their stronger instinct of benevolence is the reason that they have more charity than men. They are thus better fitted to receive all the three evangelical virtues than men; they are, therefore, more religious than men.

§ 33. The value of woman as an adviser to man rests upon the faculty of imagination, both pure and as an element of the higher reason, and upon the instinct of benevolence. These render her more humane, more conscientious, and more religious than he is, as well as of quicker comprehension. In consultation he will bring enough of the wisdom of the serpent; it is for her to supply the harmlessness of the dove. She brings precisely those elements in which he is probably deficient, — kindness, conscientiousness, and comprehension of the feelings of others.

This is not the only reason of the fitness of woman to advise man. His instincts of desire and malevolence are strong, and the passions developed from them are also strong, and require a powerful check. The best is only to be found in the sanctified nature. Those provided in the intellectual nature are the instinct of fear, and the emotions developed from it. In the moral nature, the same office is performed by the virtue of prudence, which is also a development of the instinct of fear. In man that instinct is comparatively weak, while in woman it is strong. In the moral nature her timidity grows into prudence. Hence her counsels tend to check the passions of man.

§ 34. Yet the constitution of woman's nature is not perfect, but requires the aid of the masculine complement, as much as the nature of man requires that of the feminine complement. The female imagination works readily, and produces a lively impression, but that impression is apt to be one-sided. The ideas, which imagination presents, must be examined by the slower operation of the reason, before the mind can come to a safe conclusion. Passions in man derive their power from the strength of his instincts; in woman, from the vividness of her imagination, which draws a lively picture of the good which she desires, of the wrong which she has endured, or of the crime which has been committed. In the two last-named cases, her resentment or her indignation is thus easily carried beyond due bounds. Even her conscientiousness may then be enlisted on the side of malevolence.

So the vividness of the female imagination shows the object of desire in the most brilliant and attractive colors, and thus makes up for the weakness of the instinct of desire. This is the cause of the female tendency to extravagance, which requires an external check, such as has been provided in the authority of the husband. Female spite and female extravagance grow out of the exuberance of the female imagination, as well as female conscientiousness and female piety.

§ 35. The peculiar constitution of woman makes her a suitable companion for man, because her lively imagination presents things under an aspect which he would never have observed. He looks at everything through his reason, and thus attains to views which are new to her. This diversity of views makes the intellectual intercourse of persons of different sexes agreeable and instructive. The natures of the two sexes again appear as the complements to each other. Each brings to the conversation as to the consultation, that which the other wants. Another effect of the livelier imagination of woman is a quicker and keener sense of the disagreeable qualities of everything. She is easily shocked by whatever is coarse or impure, whether physically, intellectually, or morally. This is what is called refinement; in which men are naturally far inferior to women. Man's ruder contact with the world tends to diminish the scanty stock of refinement with which he is endowed. It is only by intercourse with women that the refinement of men can be increased, or even preserved. Thus again the peculiar constitution of woman fits her to be the companion of man.

§ 36. Nor does it less fit her to be his help. It is a part of the aid which she is to give him that she is to be his assistant and deputy in the government of his household. In this position, her kindness qualifies his sternness, and her conscientiousness supplies his neglects. The same qualities, together with her patience, prudence, and affection for her husband and children, render her eminently fit to have charge of the internal arrangements of the house. Her refinement is also no small advantage in that office.

§ 37. The constitution of woman is such as to prepare her for subordination. Many reasons why the subordinate place was assigned to her have already been mentioned. It remains to point out why it is less irksome to her than to man. The emotion which becomes conjugal affection is compounded of a passion and an affection. These are introduced in different proportions in the two sexes. In man the passion, which is a development of the instinct of desire combined with the imagination, is the stronger element. In woman the affection is the stronger element; it is an offshoot from the instinct of benevolence. Affection lasts longer than passion. When passion is gone the attachment is much stronger on the side of the woman, and renders the obedience, which her subordinate position requires, comparatively easy. Her timidity, the weakness of her malevolence, and the strength of her conscientiousness, all work in the same direction.

CHAPTER III.

OF THE NATURE OF MARRIAGE.

§ 1. Marriage in the largest Sense. — § 2. Concubinage. — § 3. Morganatic Marriages. — § 4. Polygamy. — § 5. Popular Notions of Marriage. — § 6. Civil Laws of Marriage and Divorce. — § 7. How far Marriage is a Civil Contract. — § 8. How Marriage differs from other Civil Contracts. — § 9. American Views. — § 10. American State Law of Divorce. — § 11. Marriage a Divine Institution. — § 12. Reasons for the Institution of Marriage. § 13. Continuation of the Species. — § 14. Help. — § 15. Distribution of Labor. — § 16. Various Developments of the Principle. — § 17. General Admission of the Principle. — § 18. Government of the Family. — § 19. Training Children. — § 20. Mutual Duties. — § 21. Society. — § 22. Importance of a True Idea of Marriage. — § 23. Definition of Marriage. — § 24. Its Laws. — § 25. Its Elements. — § 26. False Notions about Marriage. — § 27. False Notions about its Elements. — § 28. The Five Sides of Marriage. — § 29. Christian Marriage.

§ 1. Promiscuous sexual intercourse has always and everywhere been held unlawful. No people has been found so savage as not to consider the appropriation of particular women to particular men an important point of morals. This appropriation is called marriage. In a narrower sense, the equality of the parties in social position entered into the notion of marriage. When the woman was of inferior rank to the man, the appropriation was early called by a name which was equivalent to concubinage. Sometimes the woman was a slave to the man and the appropriation was slave concubinage. There were, thus, three kinds of relation which fell within the meaning of the word marriage, taken in its largest sense. All three were permanent. The largest sense which can be given to the word "marriage," is the permanent appropriation of a woman to a man.

§ 2. The association was, nevertheless, considered by most nations to be capable of dissolution; but at the time of entering into it a dissolution was not expected. It did not come to an end without some action, by which it was broken off, and but for which it would have continued during the lives of the persons concerned. A connection with a slave was more easily dissolved than one with a free woman; and one with a free concubine than one with an equal wife. Hence the meaning of the words "concubine" and "concubinage" have changed. The idea of permanence has disappeared from them. Concubinage now means cohabitation without the contract and the ceremonies which the law or the religion of the country require as a security for permanence.

§ 3. A woman who is, by such a contract and such ceremonies, appropriated to a man, who is her superior in rank, is generally considered an equal wife. But in some countries such marriages were sometimes contracted with stipulations that neither the woman nor her children should share the rank of the husband and father. A woman so married was called a morganatic, left-handed, or unequal wife, but never a concubine. A concubine is now understood to be a woman who cohabits with a man without any security for the permanence of the union and without any religious or legal ceremony.

§ 4. Among many nations a man is allowed to cohabit at the same time with several women, either as equal wives or as free or slave concubines. This is polygamy, and is not allowed in any Christian country, either by religion, law, or public opinion.

§ 5. The popular definition of marriage is different in different countries and among the followers of different religions. In the East there are but two classes of people: free persons and slaves. Concubinage with free women, in the ancient sense, is therefore impossible. In the modern, it is condemned by religion, law, and public opinion. But polygamy and arbitrary divorce are allowed, so that their notion of marriage does not, practically, differ much from our notion of free concubinage. Slave concubinage is moreover legal, consistent with the morals of the Koran, and extensively practiced; but it is not regarded as marriage. The popular Eastern definition of marriage is, the cohabitation of a man with a free woman, who is appropriated to him permanently, unless he shall choose to dissolve the connection. Such a marriage may subsist between a man and any number of women not exceeding four.

The popular Western definition is, the cohabitation of one man with one woman, who is permanently appropriated to him by a tie, which can only be dissolved by a legislative act or a judicial decision.

In these definitions, the word permanent is used to signify that the tie to which it is applied is designed to continue during the lives of the persons bound, though capable of being dissolved. An indissoluble tie would be one which was incapable of being dissolved. The phrase, however, may be applied, a tie which cannot be dissolved except under peculiar and exceptional circumstances.

§ 6. This Western notion of marriage seems to prevail in legislative bodies throughout Europe and America. Laws are provided which prescribe certain modes of entering into the married state, and also other laws regulating the mode of dissolving such an union, which is regarded as permanent but not indissoluble. The State, however, acting upon motives of expediency, will not allow it to be dissolved, except for causes approved by her, and shown to exist to the satisfaction of her tribunals.

She has a clear right to regulate the mode of entering into marriage. For it is important to the welfare of her citizens that it should be known who are married persons and to whom they are married. The law of the land regulating the modes of marrying is, therefore, to be obeyed, because it is founded on that part of the popular definition which is sound, and the observance of it is necessary to the welfare of the community. Such laws are in no way inconsistent with the Divine law.

The laws touching divorce stand upon a different ground. They rest on the notion that marriage though permanent is not indissoluble, which is involved in the popular definition, or perhaps on the idea, that marriage is indissoluble only in the modified sense which has been mentioned in the last section. If the last notion be adopted, it must be coupled with another that is absolutely false, that the State has a right to decide what are the exceptional circumstances which will justify the dissolution of a marriage. The first notion is itself false. A Christian can only avail himself of these laws in an exceptional case, in which the dissolving the marriage is consistent with the Divine law. But in such a case the State law must be obeyed as to the manner of proceeding, for in that matter the State has a right to prescribe.

It concerns the public to know whether a marriage has been dissolved or not. It concerns moreover the temporal welfare of the parties to the marriage, that it should not be dissolved unless for proper reasons. It concerns also the public morals, that marriages should not be surreptitiously dissolved. The State has, therefore, a right to see that the allegations upon which the case depends are sufficiently proved, and are in themselves sufficient to justify a dissolution of the marriage; although she has no right to dissolve a marriage for reasons which are not recognized by the Divine law, yet if she undertake to dissolve a marriage, when according to the law of God it ought not to be dissolved, it must be considered as dissolved for all civil purposes; though it still continues to bind the consciences of the parties and of all who are aware of its existence. It does not take away the sin of one of the parties who may marry, or of any one who may intermarry with either of them.

States undertake to dissolve marriages which ought not

to be dissolved under various circumstances. Divorces are sometimes granted upon grounds, which, by the Divine law, are insufficient. In such cases no Christian can avail himself of a decision which is in conflict with the law of God. In other cases, a civil tribunal may have been mistaken about the facts, and so have dissolved a marriage erroneously, which if the allegations of the party had been true, might have been properly dissolved. The decision of a competent tribunal ought to be presumed right, and to satisfy all persons who are not so well acquainted with the facts, as to know that the tribunal was deceived. No person, however, has a right to act upon a decision, which rests upon facts that he believes did not occur.

§ 7. The root of all the many errors respecting the doctrine of marriage, which exist in this country, is Paley's notion, that marriage is a civil contract and nothing more. This proposition would be assented to by every lawyer in the United States, except the very few who have examined the subject upon Christian principles. It is the predominant notion among all classes of people, except the Roman Catholics and a few religious Protestants.

It is true, that the State can only regard it as a civil contract. Blackstone is right when he says, "Our law considers marriage in no other light than as a civil contract." The State and the Law, which the State makes, can consider nothing but as it is civil, that is, as it affects the *cives* and the *civitas*. They have nothing to do with the consciences of men; though their laws, when not inconsistent with the Divine law, bind the conscience. The law of the land considers marriage only as it is a civil contract, that is, as it falls within the jurisdiction of the State; but it has qualities not within that jurisdiction which make it more than a civil contract. It is a civil contract, but it is also a religious vow. The State cannot release the conscience from this vow, and cannot and does not declare that marriage is a civil contract and nothing more. Paley, who professed to be a moralist not a lawyer, was very wrong when he wrote, that "marriage is a civil contract and nothing else." This is a totally different proposition from that of Blackstone, and is not true.

§ 8. Marriage contracted according to the civil law of the land, is a civil contract, but it is also much more. If it were merely a civil contract it would follow that it might be dissolved by the consent of the parties agreeably to the law maxim, "*omne ligamen dissolvitur eo ligamine quo ligatur.*" "Every obligation may be dissolved by the same power by which it was created."

When any other civil contract has been broken, the law allows the injured person to recover compensation; that done, the contract is at an end. It is scarcely an exception to this rule, that in some cases the injured person has the right to compel performance of the contract. For marriage the law recognizes no compensation which shall be a satisfaction for the injury and put an end to the contract. It always continues until it has been dissolved by a legislative act or a judicial decision. In other cases the performance or the damages may be released. It is not so in the case of marriage. The law distinguishes between a contract to marry and a marriage. The first is a mere civil contract, for the breach of which the law will give damages, and the damages or the contract itself may be released. It is quite different where there has been an actual marriage, of which the law knows no release. It punishes certain gross violations of the contract, but gives no compensation for any. It regards marriage as incapable of being dissolved by mutual consent, directly or indirectly.

This is the rule among all Christian nations. A marriage once contracted can only be dissolved by a direct act of the legislature, or for certain reasons which are prescribed by law, and must be judicially established. The sentence must be pronounced by a public tribunal, which has examined the case, and is satisfied, both of the sufficiency and the truth of the reasons alleged for the dissolution of the marriage. The only exception to this rule is when a legislature chooses to interpose, by the use or abuse of its supreme power. Both legislators and judges assume that marriage is a civil contract. But the necessity for their action shows that it is not a mere civil contract.

Most men hold that marriage is a civil contract, but one which cannot be dissolved on account of its peculiar nature. They also hold, very correctly, that it is an entire contract, which cannot be modified by the will of the persons concerned, as all other civil contracts can. They perhaps attribute these peculiarities to the law of the land. If that were their true origin, an act of the legislature might change the law of marriage, and make it as easy to dissolve a marriage as a contract of hiring. Perhaps a majority of the American people would assent to that proposition, although most of them would regard such a change in the law as inexpedient.

§ 9. The doctrine that marriage is a mere civil contract, so far prevails in this country, that in a large majority of the States the union may be formed in the presence of a mere civil officer, without any religious rite. This is consistent with sound principles, provided that religious rites are not prohibited, which no American State has yet done. Marriage being a civil contract, although not merely a civil contract, the State has right to insist that it shall be celebrated by her officer, and even to require it, before she will recognize the union. None of the United States have gone so far. They all recognize the validity of marriages solemnized with such religious ceremonies as are conformable to the opinions of the persons married, by any one whom they may acknowledge as a minister of religion. If there are any exceptions, they go no further than to provide some means of assuring the civil authority, that the minister is recognized as such by some religious body. The States generally allow both religious marriages and those celebrated before civil officers, looking upon them with indifferent eyes. In Maryland, however, every marriage must be celebrated either by some minister of the Christian religion, or in the manner used among Quakers or Jews, unless the persons to be married, or one of them, make oath that they are conscientiously scrupulous of being so married.

The public opinion of the more educated classes looks with disapprobation upon marriages before a civil officer; which does not seem, however, to be connected with direct religious feeling. A marriage without religious rites is considered as ungenteel, not as irreligious. It is thought bad taste not to connect so important a contract with an outward ceremony of religion. It were well if all those who hold that opinion acted consistently upon it, and did not desecrate the solemnities upon which they insist. The irreverent conduct of the company which is assembled, perhaps in the house of God, for the solemnization of a marriage, is a consequence of the irreligious views generally held on the subject, and tends to perpetuate them.

§ 10. Marriage is in the United States generally considered to be merely a civil contract; but the logical conclusion, that it may be dissolved at pleasure, is not drawn. It seems to be held that evil consequences would follow were that allowed. The law makes the interposition of a court of justice necessary to the legal dissolving of a marriage. Rules have been laid down according to which it must be done, and certain things declared to be sufficient causes for the dissolution. The causes in many of the States are so numerous, the rules so little stringent, and so little provision has been made against collusion, that if a married couple agree to dissolve their marriage, they will find no practical difficulty in their way. The law of the land, and the civil tribunals, will interpose none. South Carolina is the only one of the United States which has the honor of not allowing any divorce.

§ 11. Marriage is a civil contract, and as such subject to the jurisdiction of the State and the law of the land; but it is also a Divine institution, and, as such, not under their authority. God himself instituted the appropriation of one woman to one man, and subjected it to certain laws, which the State ought to enforce, but which she may, at her peril, refuse to enforce. If she refuse, there are no means of compelling her, for she has no human superior; but the Divine laws are not less binding. The State ought to enforce the Divine laws, because they would promote the temporal welfare of her citizens; but if she be of a different opinion, it only remains that Christians should obey them, and endure whatever inconveniences may arise, from their not being enforced upon others. In this country, the State declines to enforce them, and it is the more necessary that Christian men and women should be familiar with them.

§ 12. Christian marriage is, as has already been said, of Divine appointment. For that appointment there were reasons into which it may be well, reverently, to inquire. They will be found to be substantially the same with those for the creation of woman, which have been mentioned at the beginning of the second chapter. Some moralists have supposed that St. Paul indicates another when he writes, "It is good for a man not to touch a woman. Nevertheless, to avoid fornication, let every man have his own wife, and every woman her own husband."

From this text it has been inferred that one of the reasons for the institution of marriage was the avoiding of fornication. The Apostle does not say so. He only directs that particular persons should marry, as a means whereby they may avoid fornication. But for the institution of marriage fornication would be as impossible to the human race as to the lower animals. Yet there is a sense in which marriage may be said to have been instituted to prevent fornication, since it was instituted to prevent promiscuous intercourse,

[1] 1 Corinthians vii. 1, 2.

which is now fornication. But that idea is included in the idea that it was instituted for the continuation of the species. The other reasons were the same with those for the creation of woman, as set forth in the beginning of the Book of Genesis; that is to say, the continuation of the species, and the furnishing man with a help and a companion: "It is not good that the man should be alone; I will make him a help meet for him." [1]

The creation of the first woman supplied those three wants of the first man. The existence of the female sex supplies to the male sex the means of providing for the same wants. But in order that particular women might be appropriated to particular men, and become to them what Eve was to Adam, marriage was instituted. Men became husbands, and women wives, that the ends of the creation of woman might be answered in their particular cases. Hence the intimate connection between the relation between the sexes, and the relation of husband and wife. Hence, too, it is that the reasons for the creation of woman and for the institution of marriage are the same, and in the Bible are assigned together, "And the Lord God said: It is not good that the man should be alone; I will make him a help meet for him." [2] "And the Lord God caused a deep sleep to fall upon Adam, and he slept, and He took one of his ribs, and closed up the flesh thereof; and the rib which the Lord God had taken from man made He a woman, and brought her unto the man." [3]

The creation of woman, and the institution of marriage, took place at the same time. The reasons for both were the continuation of the species, and the providing for man help and companionship.

§ 13. It may, perhaps, be said, that the continuing of the species was provided for by the creation of the sexes, as it was in the case of the lower animals. But man is not a

[1] Genesis ii. 18. [2] *Ibid.* [3] *Ibid.* 22.

mere animal, governed by instinct. He is an immortal being, and must be trained for eternity. He has faculties which must be cultivated, and emotions which must be subjected to the conscience. Those things make a long course of care and education necessary. This can only be provided by parents who are permanently united. Under other circumstances, experience shows that the child either perishes in infancy, or is brought up without the proper training. Without marriage the continuation of the human race would be very imperfectly provided for. There would be none of that moral and intellectual culture, which is indispensable to the well-being of the race. For the protection and education of children, a family is necessary, and marriage is an essential condition of a family.

§ 14. This leads to the second reason for the institution of marriage, — the providing help for men. The continuation of the species makes it necessary that there should be a household, in which the young may be provided for and protected. It is the duty of the man to take care for all this, as well as for the maintenance and protection of the mother of his children. These duties he cannot perform without help. The maintenance of the household involves several operations, some of which would interfere with the proper performance of others. It is then necessary that he should have help, and that of a kind which he could scarcely have without marriage. The necessaries for the family must be provided, prepared for use, kept from waste, and finally distributed.

§ 15. Necessaries must be either directly produced by labor, or money to purchase them must be procured by labor. In either case the labor must generally be performed out of the house, and must always absorb nearly all the time and attention of the man. The other offices must be performed within the house. When the provisions for the family are purchased with money, the making the purchases, and bringing home the provisions, is a third class of duties. This third class of duties is sometimes allotted to the husband, and sometimes to the wife, and, perhaps, more usually divided between them. But the first of the two other classes is generally allotted to the husband, and the second to the wife. This distribution of labor pervades every form of society, from that in which the savage kills in the forest the game, which his wife cooks in the wigwam, to that in which the wealthy merchant, or skillful lawyer gathers up in the counting-room, or office, the money, which he hands to his wife that she may provide for the wants of his household. It is not possible for the man to perform both these classes of duties. One who has no household, or who has left his home for a time, may, if he be content or compelled so to do, both collect and administer the means of his own subsistence. But such a system in a household would be incompatible with comfort. It could only exist in the absence of any demand on the man to provide for the wants of others.

It would be very inconvenient, if not impossible, for the man and the woman to undertake both departments jointly. One or the other would be neglected, while the other would perhaps receive too much attention. Nor could the departments of foreign affairs and the interior be well filled by the man and woman alternately. Each would be compelled to hand over to the other unfinished operations, which could only be advantageously finished by the head and hands by which they were commenced.

It must not be overlooked that the mental and physical constitutions of the two sexes qualify each of them more especially for one of these two departments. The greater physical strength, and rougher moral constitution of man, fit him for the struggle with nature, or with other men, by which only subsistence can be gathered. The more delicate organization of woman, and her capacity for patient attention to little things, fit her for the superintendence, or for the work of the internal department. Hence, ever since "Adam delved and Eve span," the external affairs of the household have been committed to the man, and the internal to the woman.

§ 16. The principle is universal, though it is developed differently in different circumstances. An Esquimau takes the seal, which he has speared, home to his wife, who extracts the oil and cooks the flesh. Abraham, who was a herdsman, ran to the herd and fetched a calf, which a young man dressed, or, as we Americans would say, butchered. Sarah made ready two or three measures of meal, and baked cakes upon the hearth.[1]

Andromache and Lucretia superintend the spinning and weaving of their slaves, and, no doubt, household affairs generally. Hector and Collatinus appear only as warriors, but in time of peace they probably cultivated the soil, or tended flocks or herds, or in some way provided for their families. What they provided was administered by their wives.

In the present complex state of society, all women are not, any more than all men, called upon to do the coarser kinds of work. The principle is always the same, but it is worked with more or less coarseness, according to the various positions of different persons. One man lives by his daily earnings, and it takes them all to provide for his family. Were he to cook their food and make their clothes, his earnings would be diminished, so that he would be unable to provide for them. Those offices are therefore performed by his wife with her own hands.

In another station the man has capital, and has it in his power to purchase the assistance of others, whose labors he superintends. He enjoys a large income, which he acquires with very little manual labor. Another man has stored and disciplined his mind. He has studied the laws of the land, and the arts of influencing men's minds, or he has studied the constitution of the human frame and the

[1] Genesis xviii. 1—8.

modes of treating its diseases. In either case his knowledge and skill enable him to receive large rewards from those who require his services. In all these cases the man would suffer great loss were his attention diverted from his proper business to domestic affairs. He cannot, more than the laborer, afford to leave his occupation to take charge of the home department. He is not fit for it, and cannot become so without unfitting him for his proper work, and it would occupy time which might be more profitably employed.

It does not follow that the wives of these men are to do what the wives of laborers do, still less that they are to do nothing. They are to manage and superintend the household. The wife of a rich merchant, manufacturer, or planter commits to the hands of others whatever is coarse, laborious, or disagreeable in the affairs of her household, just as her husband commits to the hands of others whatever is coarse, laborious, or disagreeable in his business. He gives time aud mental labor to the superintendence and direction of his business, for it could not otherwise be successfully carried on. So his wife must give time and thought to the direction of the household affairs. Both husband and wife are thus occupied in their respective departments, although in a different manner from other persons in a different position. It may happen that either or both may require and obtain assistance even in superintendence and direction. But the supreme direction and superintendence must still remain with the natural head, — in the outward business with the husband, in the house with the wife. The position of a woman as the help to her husband may be modified by circumstances, but it exists under all circumstances.

§ 17. The idea that the wife is the help of her husband, and the particular distribution of labor between them, are recognized in the two extremes of American society. They have been recognized everywhere and always. The work which is to be done out of the house is allotted to the man, that which is to be done in the house to the woman. The only exception to the rule is that the duty of purchasing some of the supplies for the family is often allotted to the woman. As the family rises in wealth and social position there is a change. Both husband and wife call in assistance, and labor rather with the head than the hands.

In Europe there is a class of persons who have inherited large property, upon the income of which they can live, without any effort to acquire more. Their duties, with respect to providing for their families, are confined to taking care of their possessions and collecting and administering their incomes, and they are able to command assistance even in the performance of these duties. Yet the proper attention to their estates will consume time and require thought; still, they are men of large leisure: some of them waste their leisure as other men abuse other blessings. Others find employments by diligence in which, they may advance the state of the world. They may take part in public affairs without becoming the slaves of party for the wages of office, or they may serve the public in religious, ecclesiastical, philanthropic, scientific, or literary occupations.

Must not similar obligations rest upon their wives, as those which bind the wives of other men? Such men require to be relieved from the cares of the household just as much as the savage, the nomad, the laborer, the merchant, or the planter. It is the office of their wives, as of those of other men, "to guide the house," to rule in the domestic department. The burden is lightened to them by the possession of wealth, just as the burden of their husbands' business is lightened to them, but the duties still remain, though they may be neglected. Both men and women are under such circumstances exposed to great temptations. Many of them abandon their duties and give themselves up to pleasure and frivolity; yet many of both sexes perform their duties nobly. It is thus that the wife is a help to her husband, and thus is fulfilled in part the intention of the

Lord God in creating woman and instituting marriage. St. Paul speaks of this portion of a woman's duty, when he says: "I will, therefore, that the younger women marry, bear children, guide the house, give none occasion to the adversary to speak reproachfully."[1]

§ 18. Other duties of the man are the protection and government of his children. These also are naturally divided into two branches, as they are to be done within the house or abroad. Children are exposed at home to many small dangers, from which they can only be protected by one who is at home. They can only be effectually governed by one who is generally with them. The other duties of the wife are to be performed at home; these, then, fall more readily into her department. Her patience in small matters, her more tender and affectionate disposition, and her strong affection for the children, are peculiar qualifications for the duties of protecting and governing the children. These duties, so far as they are to be performed at home, thus fall within the province of the wife. As in the other case, her labors may be lightened, where the circumstances will admit of it, by assistants. The duties of direction and superintendence will still, however, be incumbent upon her.

§ 19. Another yet more important duty, in which man requires female help, is the training of the children. This includes the government of them in a higher sense of the word than that in which it has been just used. So far as girls are concerned a man can hardly perform this duty properly, certainly not without female advice and assistance. The same thing is true of boys during their tender years. When they are older, the deep religious convictions of woman render her aid most valuable in forming their religious and moral characters. These are also modes in which she is to show herself a help meet for her husband.

§ 20. Duties are not all on the side of the wife. It is her duty to be a help to her husband; but he is not to ex-

[1] 1 Timothy v. 14.

pect her to be a drudge, unless his own position is that of a drudge. He should lighten her labors by procuring for her assistance, and if necessary by such personal exertions as will not interfere with his own occupations. He is to protect her as well as the children, and that from the petulance and insubordination of the children themselves, as well as from external dangers. On her part she is to remember that she is a help, and, therefore, in a subordinate position. She is to administer the affairs of the household and govern and train the children in conformity with the instructions of her husband.

§ 21. A wife is not only a help but a companion; in that capacity she is her husband's equal, and he should remember that he is her companion as much as she is his. Companionship is necessary to them both. It is one of the offices of woman to refine and polish man by her society. It is the business of man, by his society, to strengthen the character of woman. The state of marriage was instituted for both these ends. It is a departure from the designs of the Almighty, when men allow business, or women permit amusements, to interfere with the duties of mutual society.

Closely connected with these duties are the position of the man as the instructor and mentor of the woman, and that of the woman as the adviser of the man. In this form of companionship, it is more especially his part to take care that their plans be such as will succeed, hers to see that they are innocent. Yet he is never to lose sight of innocence, nor she of prudence, strength, and firmness. Each has a proper place and function which the other is to respect, and the decision is to be made by harmonizing the ruling faculties and emotions of both. It may then be hoped that it will be both wise and innocent.

§ 22. All these ideas enter into the more complex one of marriage, an idea which lies at the root of all society. For all societies were developed from families, and are still only aggregations of families. The family has its root in marriage, from which sprung the first family, and from which new households are continually springing to replace those which death is continually breaking up.

It is not then wonderful that all communities have recognized marriage, or sometimes something so like it as to be called by its name, which will answer some of its purposes, though it does not come up to the true idea. Hence the words marriage, husband and wife, are used in speaking of connections which have been formed according to the notions, laws, and customs of any community, notwithstanding very defective notions about marriage may have prevailed in that community. It is very possible that many such arrangements may have been true marriages where the parties to them have entertained sound notions, and intended to act upon them. St. Paul, in the seventh chapter of the First Epistle to the Corinthians, treats them as true marriages, when one of the parties to one of them has been converted to Christianity. Still it must not be forgotten that Christians have a definite idea of marriage, to which it is their duty to conform, because it is revealed and so known to be true.

As the family is the root of society, and marriage is the root of the family; so the root of the morals of every society is to be found in the morals of the family, and those morals grow out of the ideas entertained about marriage. The notions about marriage, which prevail in any community, have an important bearing upon the morals of the people. It may be safely said that any community, which shall have really and practically adopted the Christian idea of marriage, will have made the first and greatest step toward the adoption of the body of Christian morals. Unfortunately no such community exists or has ever existed. In all parts of the world and of the Church, there is a tendency in public opinion to throw off the Christian idea and adopt much lower notions. This is at least as true in the United States as in any other country.

§ 23. Marriage is a Divine institution, resting on Divine appointment, governed by Divine laws. It is the voluntary and indissoluble union of one woman with one man for the purposes of procreation, help, and society. The union is so complete as to produce unity between two persons, and is sanctified by God Himself. Those who enter into this union in the right spirit, are entitled to the Divine aid in fulfilling its duties, provided it has been implored with due faith and devotion.

§ 24. Marriage has its Divine laws, which seem to be seven in number. First, that it shall be contracted with the free consent of both parties to live together agreeably to the Divine law. Second, that the Divine blessing be invoked upon the union. Third, it is declared that the union so blessed makes the parties to the marriage "no more twain but one flesh." Fourth, that the Divine blessing also sanctifies the union and makes it holy. Fifth, it is provided that marriage shall be between two persons only, neither of them being capable of being united to a third during the life of the other. Sixth, that marriage shall be indissoluble, except in a certain case specially provided for. Seventh, that the wife shall be subordinate to the husband and subject to his authority.

§ 25. The things required by these laws are the elements of marriage, and like the laws are seven in number. The consent of the parties, the Divine blessing, the mysterious unity which grows out of the first two, and which is the central idea of marriage, the sanctity or holiness which is produced by the Divine blessing. From the unity and the sanctity may be deduced, by strict logical deduction, the exclusiveness of marriage, its indissolubleness, and the authority of the husband. The three last-named elements are not only logical consequences of the others, but rest upon distinct Divine precepts. The elements of Christian marriage are then consent, the Divine blessing, sanctity, unity, exclusiveness, indissolubleness, and the authority of the husband. An union in which any one of these seven elements is wanting is not a Christian marriage.

They may be divided into three classes. The two first may be called the formative elements, because they form the union. Sanctity and unity are the mysterious parts of marriage, and may be called the mysterious elements. The other three are practical rules to govern the conduct of the married pair, and may be called the practical elements.

§ 26. The words marriage, husband and wife, are, as has already been remarked, applied to unions which have been formed according to the laws and customs of un-Christian communities, although they do not contain the true elements of Christian marriage. Even in Christian countries, the people, or large portions of them, entertain loose notions of marriage, which are very different from those taught in the Holy Scriptures. The word marriage is, therefore, very often used in a large sense. Hence it becomes proper, when it is used in a strict sense, to prefix the adjective Christian.

In the mouths of those who reject the Christian idea, the word is used in various senses, so that it is impossible to give a definition which will include them all. It is so used by persons of various opinions and with reference to various laws and customs, as to exclude, on some occasions, every element of Christian marriage. The definition, which would perhaps include the greater number of these notions, would be: The appropriation of a woman to a man for the purpose of procreation and help.

§ 27. Yet the fourth of the five false theories mentioned in the second chapter, which may be called the romantic theory, rejects the idea of help as well as that of authority. The fifth, which may be called the Amazonian, rejects authority, and can scarcely be regarded as accepting help. In other false theories the authority of the husband is accepted and exaggerated, while every other element of marriage is in one or other of them rejected.

The consent, which is an element of Christian marriage, being a consent to live in marriage according to God's law, cannot exist if any of the other elements is wanting. The Divine blessing, unity and sanctity are so purely Christian ideas, that it may be said that they never are accepted but as a portion of the Christian system. Exclusiveness is not recognized by the Mohammedans, the Mormons, or the pagans of Asia, Africa, or America. Indissolubleness is generally rejected wherever exclusiveness is. In many Christian countries it is by no means generally accepted. Protestant Germany and the United States of America are examples. The authority of the husband is generally recognized in false theories of marriage ; yet it is rejected in the romantic and Amazonian theories, and is not very heartily received by many women who do not exactly subscribe to either of them.

§ 28. Before quitting the subject of false notions about marriage, it may be well to say a few words about the sides of marriage. It is designed to answer certain purposes, some of which are connected with the animal nature, some with the intellectual, some with the moral, and some with the spiritual. It has, therefore, its animal, intellectual, moral, and spiritual sides, upon any one of which it may be contemplated. It is also connected with men's social position in such a way as to give it a fifth side, — the prudential. It is a false notion of marriage, which is collected from looking at it on any one or more of these sides neglecting the others.

§ 29. Amidst all these various notions, there is no sure foundation for domestic happiness, or for virtue, private or public, save in the Christian idea of marriage, an union founded on consent to live in the holy state of matrimony according to God's law, sanctified by the Divine blessing, recognizing the divinely decreed unity, and all the other divinely appointed elements. Such an union is a true marriage. The Divine blessing, and the sanctity which it gives, confer upon it a peculiarly religious character. It is not a sacrament, but it is as the Church has always called it, — the holy state of matrimony. The rite by which persons enter into that state is a holy rite, though not a sacrament, for it has no "outward and visible sign ordained by God himself," and is not, "generally, necessary to salvation." The rite is a holy rite and the state a holy state; but if used in an unholy manner they may be sources of great misery here and hereafter. The solemnization of marriage is, therefore, a very serious occasion, and should be marked by discretion, reverence, sobriety, and the fear of God.

CHAPTER IV.

OF THE FORMATIVE ELEMENTS OF MARRIAGE.

§ 1. Consent. — § 2. The Divine Blessing. — § 3. The Connection between Consent and the Divine Blessing. — § 4. Marriage Rites. — § 5. The Church of England and her American Daughter. — § 6. The Protestant Denominations. — § 7. The Church of Rome. — § 8. Evasion of Forms. — § 9. Irreverence. — § 10. The True Marriage.

§ 1. THE formative elements of marriage are consent and the Divine blessing. The consent, which is one of the elements of marriage, includes much more than the acceptance of a particular person as a husband or wife, agreeably to the usages of society. It includes an acceptance of the Christian ideas of marriage, and of the relation of husband and wife. According to the Divine law, that relation involves certain duties and rights, to which both the man and the woman are to consent. They do not merely consent to live together and to enjoy the privileges and advantages which they desire, and to perform those duties which they may find agreeable, and in all other matters to do as they please.

Marriage is a Divine ordinance, which the Divine law does not permit to be modified; it must be accepted or rejected as a whole. The consent is to live together according to God's ordinance as He hath made it, and to obey entirely and without reserve God's laws of marriage. These it is not easy to obey. On the announcement of one of them the Apostles of our blessed Lord said, "If the case of the man be so with his wife, it is not good to marry." [1]

Our Saviour admitted the difficulty, and only said that all men could not receive the saying. He did not soften the law. It is therefore unaltered, and is what many men con-

[1] Matthew xix. 10.

sider rigorous in some of its provisions, and many women in others. This may be a reason for not marrying; it is very often a reason for not marrying a particular person. It is always a reason why marriage "is not to be entered upon unadvisedly or lightly, but reverently, discreetly, advisedly, soberly, and in the fear of God."

This involves a real and sincere consent to enter into the holy state of matrimony, and to live therein according to God's ordinance. This is the more necessary, because whether the internal consent exist or not, the external marriage has created an external union. The parties are thus bound to all the duties of the state without the grace which, under happier circumstances, would have assisted in the performance of them. Such a state of things, it is highly probable, involves sin, and is certainly exposed to great temptations.

§ 2. The blessing of God is a necessary element of marriage. It is the means by which He joins the parties together and makes them one, so that man cannot separate them. In every Christian marriage it is God, not man, who really marries the pair, just as it is God who really administers every Christian sacrament, though He uses man as his instrument. It is to this that Christian sacraments owe their efficacy, and Christian marriage its holiness.

This is too often forgotten, and marriages are lightly considered and unadvisedly entered upon, to the ruin of the temporal and eternal happiness of one or both of the persons concerned. Such marriages have bound upon the consciences of those who have entered into them, a burden which they have not intended to assume. It may be feared that they have not entitled themselves to the Divine aid, without which the burden cannot be borne. Marriage is not a sacrament according to the received definition of that word. Like the sacraments, however, it fails to convey the Divine blessing to those by whom it is treated with levity as well as to those by whom it is rejected. All the

Divine ordinances are hurtful to those who receive them in an improper state of mind or heart. Their value depends upon two things, — the Divine institution, and the faith of those by whom they are received.

The institution is Divine, but it was not intended to operate by the mere exercise of the Divine power without human coöperation. It is a mere form unless it receives life from the Divine blessing in each particular case. That blessing is never withheld from those who seek it in a proper frame of mind and heart. It is never granted to those who are in a state of mind in which they are unworthy to receive it. There is no such thing among the Divine ordinances as an *opus operatum*, — a work wrought by the Divine power, without the acceptance of man.

The granting of the blessing depends upon the state of mind and heart in which the ordinance is received. A man may be baptized or confirmed or receive the Holy Sacrament of the Body and Blood of Christ externally, when no internal effect is produced, or worse, when none but injurious effects are produced. The salutary effect was lost because it was not really sought or was sought without performing the conditions upon which only it will be granted. In such cases there is an external Baptism, Confirmation, or Communion without the internal benefits with which it ought to be connected. There is, then, an external and an internal Baptism, Confirmation and Communion. The internal cannot exist without the external; but the external may exist without the internal, and is then of no spiritual value or real validity. Nevertheless, man may not dispute the validity of the external rite, because he knows not the heart and it is there that the defect lies.

So in the case of marriage, there may be an external, formal marriage, without the real, internal marriage. The validity of such a marriage man may not dispute. It is, in all respects of which man can take cognizance, a marriage lawful according to Divine and human laws. The State and society will respect it, and the Church is bound to respect it. For the Church, like the State and society, is composed of men, and men can only look upon the outward appearance. Yet God, who looketh upon the heart, may see that there has been no consent to a real Christian marriage, no Divine blessing, no unity of the persons, no sanctity of the union.

The parties may have been joined together otherwise than as God's law doth allow, and the marriage may therefore not be lawful. All this may be true, with whatever rites it may have been attempted to consecrate the union. None of the circumstances which render marriage a blessing may exist; but the indissoluble bond and the authority of the husband will exist, and will be felt as intolerable grievances.

§ 3. The Divine blessing is not tied to the blessing of a priest or to any external symbol, or any particular form or rule of celebration. Marriage, and the sanctity which is a part of its essence, may exist independently of any forms; but not without an internal consent manifested by external action in conformity with existing laws. It is only upon such a consent that the Divine blessing will descend. That it will descend upon such a consent, if earnestly implored, is certain. Such a consent and such a blessing constitute marriage.

§ 4. This brings up the consideration of marriage rites, or the external form of manifesting consent, and invoking the blessing of God. There must be an external form of marriage, which should involve an external expression of the internal consent. It is right that the parties to the marriage should be formally assured of the consent of each other, which can only be by some such outward expression. It is also right that each of them should be well assured of his or her own consent, which can scarcely be, unless it is brought out in an external shape, and reduced to a form which will compel attention, and bring the matter distinctly before the mind. The external and formal consent has other uses. The Church is the guardian of the spiritual welfare of her members, and the superintendent of their morals. The State has her own interest in the purity of morals. Society, irrespective of both, assumes a right of protecting itself from immoral intruders. Each claims to be satisfied of the fact of the marriage by means of some prescribed ceremony.

The State prescribes no form, but throws around the contract of marriage such guards as she thinks sufficient to prevent the violation of her laws. For this purpose, she takes care that the consent which unites the persons shall be pronounced in whatever form, before witnesses whom she can trust. The witnesses whom she selects are, in very many cases, the ministers of the Church. Society having no right or power to dictate a form is satisfied whenever either the Church or the State is satisfied.

Most churches have set forth a form for the solemnization of Matrimony, and have therein introduced the minister of God, and instructed him how to lead the devotions of the persons to be married, and to bless their union in God's name. These forms are so much alike, that they may be spoken of as one. It sets forth the Christian doctrine of marriage, and the duties of husbands and wives. It is highly unbecoming the character of Christians, for persons not to avail themselves of the advantages thus provided for them, although some of them may not be of the essence of marriage. Marriage, and the sanctity which is of its essence, may exist independently of these forms, but not independently of the Divine blessing, or of the sincere and fervent prayer, by which that blessing should be sought.

The Church for many ages insisted upon what she called a marriage in the face of the Church, as being the most perfect form of marriage. The phrase suggests the idea, that at one period the marriage took place in the face of the ordinary congregation, assembled for their ordinary worship. This is the principle of the form of marriage among the Quakers. But the ascetic notions of the Middle Ages, which much obscured the idea of the sanctity of marriage, drove the celebration of the rite out of the church into the porch. The phrase, *ad ostium ecclesiæ*, was substituted for, in the face of the Church. For a long time the last phrase has only meant, in the presence of a minister of the Church. In the Church of Rome it is understood that the persons who are to be married are the ministers of the sacrament, and the blessing of the priest is not of its essence. His function, which is, however, essential, is that of a witness, which he performs not so much in the character of priest as in that of *parochus*, in which he symbolizes the Church.

The duties of marriage have been prescribed by God himself, and though He has never reduced them into the form of a precise promise, it has been done by His servants. The forms of marriage used by all churches and denominations in this country are substantially the same. They are really the same with those of other churches throughout the world, and contain the judgment of an immense majority of Christians, as to the nature and elements of Christian marriage. There can be no doubt that they are an exposition, by the authority of the Church, of the Divine law as to marriage.

§ 5. The marriage service of the Church of England retains traces of those ideas. The solemnization is to be in the church, not in the porch. It was not intended that it should be in the chancel, although such is the present practice. In the offices in the earlier Prayer-books, it is implied that there may be a sermon and a communion. It may be then inferred that the marriage took place in the presence of the congregation. It is historically known that it was sometimes so celebrated. It was, probably, always celebrated in the presence of a congregation; if not the ordinary one, a special one assembled for the occasion.

In fact marriages are still solemnized in the presence of a congregation, which is sometimes not a small one, although often very indevout.

The Church of England insists that, unless by special license from the Archbishop of the Province, the ceremony shall take place in a consecrated building. It must always be solemnized by one of her own ministers, who witnesses the consent, and pronounces her blessing. Her American daughter found it impossible, in the former state of the country, to insist on these things. She is, therefore, satisfied with the presence and agency of her minister. The feeling of her members is, however, growing in the direction of celebration in a Church edifice. This probably arises from a combination of the ideas of the solemnity of the occasion, and the sacredness of the building. It is to be wished that these ideas were more widely diffused and more deeply felt. They would then check conduct, by which they are now set at defiance, and which cannot but lead to a suspicion that the Church is sometimes used in compliance with fashion, from motives of family convenience, or, perhaps, merely for display. Neither Church regards any of the things just mentioned as essential to the validity of a marriage. They both recognize as a valid marriage one celebrated in any form which the State regards as sufficient.

§ 6. The same is true of all the Protestant denominations in this country. They are all agreed that no particular form or ceremony is necessary to the validity of marriage. This is true, because every form involves a consent to the Divine law, unless it contain an express repudiation of that law, or one is implied because polygamy, or arbitrary divorce, are prevalent practices in the community. But a contract, which repudiates any part of the Divine law of marriage, is not a marriage. It must also be remembered that a marriage by any form may be only formal, because the internal consent may be absent.

The Protestant denominations, except the Quakers, require the solemnization of marriage to be by a minister. The Quakers, who reject a ministry, and yet hold, in a very decided manner, the Christian doctrine of marriage, have thus been driven back upon the old notion of a marriage in the face of the Church, and have substituted the congregation for the minister as the witness of the transaction.

§ 7. The Church of Rome recognizes no clergy but her own, but regards marriages, not solemnized by them, as so far valid, that she does not require the re-marriage of persons who join her communion, already married. When her own people marry, she requires that a priest shall pronounce the nuptial benediction. She does this, even after a civil marriage, or a marriage by a minister not ordained in her communion, which she probably regards merely as a civil marriage.

§ 8. A legal marriage cannot be entered into without some form of consent. Every consent implies a consent to the whole Divine law, and that idea is embodied in most or all of the ecclesiastical forms. Yet people always find some way of evading the most stringent forms. Sometimes they use the prescribed form, and delude themselves by saying, "it is only a form." It is assumed that the words of a form have no meaning, and bind to nothing. But every form is intended to bind to something, and means whatever that something is. The form used at a marriage ceremony is meant to bind those who pronounce it to a consent to live together according to the law of God. Too many persons suppose that it binds them only to that to which they in their secret minds intended to be bound. If the plain words of the form import anything else, it is only a form, and they have repeated it without any intention of being bound by its words. The form only means what they please, and they are at liberty to give it any interpretation they please, no matter how nonnatural.

Sometimes they neglect the form altogether, or substitute

one of their own, which expresses the terms by which they are willing to be bound. When this is done, with the consent of the authority by which the form is imposed, and that authority is competent to alter the substance which the form is intended to express, there can be no objection. But people alter forms, which express the substance, dictated even by Divine authority, so as to alter the substance, and then maintain that they are only bound by the words of the form which they have pronounced or subscribed. They forget that they are bound by the law, of which the form is an expression, not merely by the words of the form. The form expresses the mind of the legislator or framer, which he has reduced to a precise and stringent form, in order that it may be understood, and produce a deep impression. Whether it be used or not, it settles that which the legislator requires of the person upon whom it is imposed. It may be omitted, mutilated, or explained away, but it is still binding, in its full and natural sense, upon those who have accepted the rights and privileges which the law confers on condition of entering into its obligations. It is astonishing how much these plain principles are neglected, and that not merely with reference to the marriage rites; though they are much neglected with reference to these rites, and the neglect is the occasion of much misery.

§ 9. It is the common judgment of all Christians, who are worthy of the name, and of many who are not, that so important a step as marriage should not be taken without seeking the Divine blessing. The public opinion of the educated classes in this country enforces this as a form. Yet, with singular inconsistency, the very same persons, who would be shocked at a marriage not solemnized with religious rites, throw around these rites such accessories as render it almost impossible that they should be anything more than mere forms.

It has been remarked by a distinguished clergyman, that

the bride at a fashionable wedding has no time for reflection, except the five minutes occupied by the rite. Of late years an attempt has been made to introduce the English practice of celebrating marriages in houses of worship, and assembling a select congregation to join in the devotions. The natural effect would be, to add greatly to the solemnity of the occasion. It is to be regretted that means have been found to neutralize those measures and defeat that effect. The special congregation sometimes come to the church arrayed in the dresses in which they are to appear at the evening entertainment, and with the thoughts and feelings connected with that style of dress. On other occasions, perhaps on the same, the doors are thrown open to a crowd, who rush in as to a spectacle. They treat the house of God as a place of exhibition, just as the invited and dressed guests treat it as an extension of their friends' drawing-room. In both cases all reverence and all decorum disappears. At the conclusion of the ceremony, a scene of disorderly congratulations and struggles to get a sight of the bride, or to get into the street, ensues, which is utterly inconsistent with the proprieties of the place and the occasion.

Our ancestors brought the animal side of marriage too much into the light. We affect to veil it; but we bring forward in its place the lust of the eye and the pride of life, and a mirth which may well be likened to the crackling of thorns under a pot. The modern mode of celebrating marriages may include nothing so indelicate as the sack posset, or throwing the stocking; but it includes many things which are quite as inconsistent as those practices with the idea of a religious office. The marriage office is the invocation of God's blessing upon one of the most momentous transactions in the lives of two Christians. The object of the practices, which have been mentioned or alluded to, seems to be to divert attention from the solemnity of the occasion. It is one of rejoicing; but it should be a solemn, Christian-like rejoicing.

The five minutes of the ceremony are scarcely excepted from the prevailing frivolity. The rite is treated as a mere form, which has no other effect than to license the new married pair to live together according to the usages of the world so long as they shall both choose so to do. The promises, the vows, the pronouncing of God's blessing by his minister, are all regarded as only forms signifying nothing, or, at least, not signifying what they express. The service is hurried over, if not mutilated, and receives no attention from the parties to the marriage, who have no distinct intention of being bound by it. By these means it is practically degraded to a level with those marriages in which an irreligious lay magistrate pronounces a couple man and wife without any religious rite, and with about as much ceremony as he bestows upon a deed for an acre of land. In both cases there may be a Christian marriage, for in both there may be a sincere consent to God's ordinance, and in both the blessing of God may have been invoked and granted. Yet in both the external marriage is a legal, not a religious ceremony.

Nevertheless, the Divine blessing may be present, or it may be granted after the external marriage is over. Thus the real marriage with its unity and sanctity may be superinduced. For the Divine blessing may always be given when it is duly implored, and the proper consent has been given. There is reason for believing that this has sometimes occurred. Yet in any particular case, it is only a possible event, the occurrence of which it is not safe to anticipate. For probability is against it, and until it occurs the married couple are living in a state of sin. Hence the great importance of making sure of the Divine blessing, by coming to the marriage ceremony with the thoughts and feelings appropriate to the occasion.

§ 10. The actual consent and the actual Divine blessing form the unity and confer the sanctity, and thus constitute the true marriage. There is no reason to believe that either is tied down to the moment of the formal marriage. That is only the means of publicly expressing the consent which may and ought to have been internally given at an earlier time. [As] the Divine blessing may also have been already invoked and granted, so both the consent and the Divine blessing may follow the formal marriage, if the consent has not been given, or the conditions on which the blessing depends have not been performed until after the ceremony.

The objects of the rite are several. One is to notify the public of the fact of the marriage. Another is to comply with the legal forms exacted by the law, whether civil or ecclesiastical. A third is to call the attention of the parties to the nature of the transaction. A fourth to add to its solemnity by bringing forward its religious element. The fifth is to impress, by all these means, the minds and memories of the married pair. All these objects, except two, demand a solemn and religious state of mind. This it is designed that the rite should produce, and, therefore, such accessories should be thrown around it as will promote that design.

The blessing of God is one of the formative elements of marriage, without which there can be neither unity nor sanctity. It is best symbolized by the blessing of the Church pronounced by her minister, who is also God's ambassador; but the two things are not connected by any Divine decree. The priest, or the minister, does not pronounce the blessing in virtue of any special authorization, as in the case of the sacraments. He pronounces it in virtue of his general authority as an ambassador of God. It may, therefore, be allowable to apply to marriage, with a slight alteration, that which King James, at the Hampton Court Conference, said of Baptism, "Though the minister be not of the essence of the 'rite,' yet he is of the essence of the right and lawful administration." Marriages upon which no minister pronounces a blessing come fairly within the meaning of the old phrase, "*Fieri non debet, factum valet.*"

This phrase properly applies to cases in which people have acted irregularly, though without assuming an authority which does not properly belong to them.

Although the blessing of a priest, or minister, is not essential to the validity of a marriage, the blessing of God is necessary to its internal and spiritual validity. That blessing is always given when it is sought in a proper frame of mind and heart, and with proper intentions, and upon an union which is not forbidden by the Divine law.

CHAPTER V.

OF THE MYSTERIOUS ELEMENTS OF MARRIAGE.

§ 1. The Mysterious Unity. — § 2. Sanctity. — § 3. In what the Holiness of Marriage consists. — § 4. New Testament Doctrine. — § 5. Unholy Marriages made Holy. — § 6. Marriages with Unbelievers. — § 7. Marriage a Mystery. — § 8. Connection between Sanctity and Unity. — § 9. Marriage as a Duty. — § 10. Remarks on 1 Corinthians vi. 14, 16. — § 11. Amorous Emotion does not produce the Unity. — § 12. Incompatibility of Temper. — § 13. Conjugal Affection does not produce the Unity. — § 14. Marriage the Cause of Conjugal Affection. — § 15. Complex Nature of Man and of Marriage. — § 16. The Indwelling of the Holy Spirit. — § 17. Motives to Marriage.

§ 1. The mysterious elements of marriage are unity and sanctity, which are so closely allied that it is possible they may be only two aspects of the same thing. They both, at any rate, grow out of consent, when God has given it his blessing, and are inseparably joined together, and constitute the mystery of marriage. St. Paul in the Epistle to the Ephesians, says, " For this cause shall a man leave his father and mother and shall be joined unto his wife, and they two shall be one flesh. This is a great mystery, but I speak concerning Christ and the Church." [1]

The remark of the Apostle is sometimes understood to refer to Christ, and the Church, but it seems rather to refer to the whole passage, and perhaps more directly to the unity of the married pair, which is a great mystery. They are seen to be two persons, having two wills, each capable of performing all the functions of life. It is known that they have separate responsibilities, and that their final destinies may be different. After the death of either it is agreed that

[1] Ephesians v. 31, 32.

they are no longer one. Yet it is many times said in the Holy Scriptures that they are one flesh, and the assertion is more than once made by the Incarnate Son. It would not be easy to find anything better entitled to the name of mystery. There is plainly a discrepancy between what men know, partly from observation and partly from revelation, on one side, and that which is explicitly revealed, on the other. This clearly is a mystery.

The unity of married persons is often taught in the Holy Bible. In the second chapter of Genesis, Adam says, "A man shall leave his father and mother and shall cleave unto his wife, and they shall be one flesh." At the very close of the Old Testament the same doctrine is taught: "Because the Lord hath been witness between thee and the wife of thy youth, against whom thou hast dealt treacherously; yet is she thy companion and the wife of thy covenant. And did not He make one? Yet had he the residue of the Spirit. And wherefore one? That He might seek a godly seed. Therefore take heed to your spirit, and let none deal treacherously against the wife of his youth." [1]

In the New Testament the doctrine of Adam's speech is fully adopted. Our Lord adopted it on several occasions, and the fact is recorded by two Evangelists. In one it is thus expressed: "And He answered and said unto them: Have ye not read that He, which made them at the beginning, made them male and female, and said, For this cause shall a man leave father and mother and shall cleave to his wife, and they twain shall become one flesh? Wherefore, they are no more twain but one flesh. What, therefore, God hath joined let not man put asunder." [2]

In another Evangelist it is thus written: "And He answered and said unto them: What did Moses command you? And they said: Moses suffered to write a bill of divorcement and to put her away. And Jesus answered and said unto them: For the hardness of your hearts, he wrote you

[1] Malachi ii. 14, 15. [2] Matthew xix. 4–6.

this precept. But from the beginning of the creation God made them male and female. For this cause shall a man leave his father and mother and cleave to his wife, and they twain shall be one flesh: so then they are no more twain but one flesh. What, then, God hath joined let not man put asunder."[1]

§ 2. The sanctity of the married state is a real thing and is revealed in the Holy Scriptures, yet the idea is well-nigh lost out of the minds of men. The Church has always regarded marriage as a holy state, and most, if not all forms for the solemnization of the union speak of it as Holy Matrimony. But this is popularly understood as meaning only that it has a sort of negative holiness, a mere innocence. Holiness is merely taken as a negation of unholiness. Unholiness is the equivalent of sin; it has thus a sort of positive signification of which holiness is made the negation. It is thus brought about that holy matrimony means no more than that marriage is not fornication. This is not the full meaning of the Church or of the Holy Scriptures.

The writer to the Hebrews says, "Marriage is honorable in all, and the bed undefiled: but whoremongers and adulterers God will judge."[2] This text contains three clauses. In the first, marriage is declared honorable; in the second, the marriage bed is pronounced undefiled; in the third, judgment is threatened against sensuality. The third has no direct connection with the present subject. The two first, if they have any meaning, bear strongly upon the argument. Popular opinion seems to reduce the first clause to a mere assertion of a consequence of the second; it is more natural and more true to consider the second as an inference from the first. If it had been written, the marriage-bed is sinless, and therefore marriage is honorable, the words would have conveyed the ordinarily received meaning that marriage is sinless, but the then second clause, now the first, would have been superfluous. But it is written,

[1] Mark x. 3-9.

[2] Hebrews xiii. 4.

"Marriage is honorable in all, and the bed undefiled." The proposition in the first clause is the cause, not the effect, of the truth stated in the second. The word honorable has a positive and affirmative meaning, importing some substantial quality which produces effects and changes the character of actions, making sinless that which otherwise would be sinful. This can be nothing short of sanctity. There is a passage in Isaiah, which countenances this view: "If," says the prophet, "thou turn away thy foot from the sabbath, from doing thy pleasure on My holy day; and call the sabbath a delight, the holy of the Lord, honorable," etc.[1]

The sanctity of marriage, if it rested solely upon the passage in the Epistle to the Hebrews, must be considered as something more than the mere absence of sin. But it is implied in the Divine institution that it should be something more. It is the divinely appointed means for man to fulfill a direct injunction. Milton is right when he speaks of marriage as that "which God commands to some, leaves free to all."

§ 3. The sanctity of marriage is not a mere innocence arising out of a permission, like that granted after the flood to eat the flesh of beasts. It is a sanctity which sanctifies, conveying holiness to persons and actions. It is closely connected with the other elements of marriage. It proceeds from the blessing of God, which is only bestowed upon a marriage founded upon a consent to all the elements of a Christian marriage, and which at the same time imparts unity and sanctity. From these mysterious elements arise the practical elements. This appears in the first passage in Holy Writ, in which marriage is mentioned; it has been already referred to, when the objects for which marriage was instituted were discussed. It is this: "For Adam there was not found a help meet for him. And the Lord God caused a deep sleep to fall upon Adam and he slept.

[1] Isaiah lviii. 13.

And He took one of his ribs and closed up the flesh instead thereof; and the rib which the Lord God had taken from man made He a woman, and brought her to the man. And Adam said: "This is now bone of my bones and flesh of my flesh; she shall be called Woman, because she was taken out of Man. Therefore shall a man leave his father and his mother and shall cleave unto his wife, and they shall be one flesh."[1]

The same ideas are reiterated by the prophet Malachi, who thus connects the sanctity of marriage with its indissoluble unity: "Because the Lord hath been witness between thee and the wife of thy youth, against whom thou hast dealt treacherously; yet is she thy companion and the wife of thy covenant. And did not He make one? Yet had he the residue of the Spirit. And wherefore one? That he might seek a godly seed."[2]

This text refers to the relation between God and the Church. But the analogy between that relation and marriage is very strongly brought out, so as to show that both were in the mind of the prophet. This is also true of a passage in the Epistle to the Ephesians, which has been already referred to. The prophet in one case and the Apostle in the other looked upon marriage as an apt type of the relation between God and the Church, and spoke of both at once. Both prophet and apostle wrote under the influence of Divine inspiration. The doctrine about marriage is therefore stronger, not weaker, for its connection with yet more sacred ideas. Moreover, the different sides upon which they approach the subject, add force to their teaching.

The prophet is speaking of the relation between God and his Church, and introduces the relation of husband and wife as an illustration. He passes from one to the other in such a way as to leave it almost doubtful which he regarded as his leading subject. St. Paul is treating of the

[1] Genesis ii. 21–24. [2] Malachi ii. 14, 15.

married state, and introduces the relation of Christ and the Church as an illustration. He, too, writes of both together, as if what was true of one was true of the other.

§ 4. It is in the New Testament that the doctrine of the sanctity of marriage is most distinctly announced. The passage just mentioned is an instance. It is as follows: "Wives, submit yourselves unto your own husbands, as unto the Lord. For the husband is the head of the wife, even as Christ is the Head of the Church; and He is the Saviour of the body. Therefore as the Church is subject unto Christ, so let the wives be to their own husbands in everything. Husbands, love your wives, even as Christ also loved the Church, and gave himself for it, that He might sanctify and cleanse it with the washing of water by the Word; that He might present it to Himself a glorious Church, not having spot or wrinkle or any such thing; but that it should be holy and without blemish. So ought men to love their wives as their own bodies. He that loveth his wife loveth himself. For no man ever yet hated his own flesh; but nourisheth and cherisheth it, even as the Lord the Church: For we are members of his body, of his flesh, and of his bones. For this cause shall a man leave his father and mother, and shall cleave unto his wife, and they two shall be one flesh. This is a great mystery: but I speak concerning Christ and the Church. Nevertheless, let every one of you in particular love his wife even as himself, and let the wife see that she reverence her husband." [1]

In another Epistle the same Apostle teaches directly the sanctifying power of marriage, without any special reference to the unity of the married pair. The passage is this: "If any brother hath a wife that believeth not, and she be pleased to dwell with him, let him not put her away. And the woman which hath a husband that believeth not, and if he be pleased to dwell with her, let her not leave him. For the unbelieving husband is sanctified by the wife, and

[1] Ephesians v. 22–33.

the unbelieving wife by the husband: else were your children unclean, but now are they holy."[1]

This passage seems to teach two doctrines: The first is that for which it has been cited, the sanctifying power of marriage, which produces the effect of sanctifying the unbelieving partner and the children. This is not, as some persons think, the prospect of winning the unbelieving husband or wife to the truth, as is elsewhere said: "Likewise ye wives be in subjection to your own husbands, that if any obey not the Word they also may, without the Word, be won by the conversation of their wives, while they behold your chaste conversation coupled with fear."[2] So St. Paul, a verse or two after the passage just cited from him, says: "For what knowest thou, O wife, whether thou shalt save thy husband? or, how knowest thou, O man, whether thou shalt save thy wife?" The conversion of the unbeliever is spoken of as future and contingent. The sanctification is spoken of as present, and producing present effects. "The unbelieving husband is sanctified by the (believing) wife; and the unbelieving wife by the (believing) husband, else were your children unclean, but now are they holy."

§ 5. Another doctrine involved in this text is that a marriage, which was originally unholy, may become holy through the faith of a believing husband or wife, even though the other party to the marriage may continue in unbelief. The persons of whom the Apostle is speaking were converts, who had been married while still heathens. There had been no Christian marriage, no consent to one, no Divine blessing sought or received. The original marriage was not holy, it only became so when one of the parties to it became a believer. The faith, which worked this change, must have been a lively faith, which worked by love, produced a desire for the Divine blessing, and a consent to the Christian doctrine of marriage. The marriage then became holy, both parties were, for the purposes

[1] 1 Corinthians vii. 12, etc. [2] 1 Peter iii. 1, 2.

of marriage, sanctified, and the children became holy. Such cases cannot occur in Christian lands, but many analogous cases do occur when people have entered into marriage unadvisedly or lightly. Persons in such circumstances may derive comfort from this Apostolic doctrine.

§ 6. It may be well, in this age and country, to say that neither of these doctrines will justify the intermarriage of believers and unbelievers. Such a marriage may, like other unlawful marriages, become lawful by the subsequent faith and repentance of one of the parties to it, but in its inception it was sinful. What St. Paul, in the same Epistle, writes of widows, is true of all Christians. "The wife," says he, "is bound by the law as long as her husband liveth, but if her husband be dead, she is at liberty to be married to whom she will; only in the Lord."[1] The liberty of a virgin or of a man cannot be larger than that of a widow.

Marriage with an unbeliever is directly condemned by another text; it is: "Be ye not unequally yoked together with unbelievers; for what fellowship hath righteousness with unrighteousness? And what communion hath light with darkness? And what concord hath Christ with Belial? or what part hath he that believeth with an infidel?"[2]

A marriage with an unbeliever is, therefore, sinful, and even if not directly sinful, it exposes the unequally yoked Christian to great temptations. Those who rush into temptation can scarcely hope to share the blessing which is promised to those who only continued a contract into which they had entered in ignorance of the Christian law. Such persons the Apostle commands to respect the rights which the other party had acquired, while the newly converted Christian was still in a state of ignorance. The usual pretext of marrying in order to convert the unbeliever, receives no countenance from St. Paul or St. Peter. They are speaking of continuing in marriages, not of entering into them.

[1] 1 Corinthians vii. 39. [2] 2 Corinthians vi. 14, 15.

§ 7. The texts which have been cited prove that there is in marriage a mysterious sanctity. It will not be contended that it is a sacrament "ordained of Christ" as "a sure witness and effectual sign of God's good will towards us, by the which He doth work invisibly in us, and doth not only quicken, but also strengthen [and confirm] our faith in Him."[1] Still less will it be contended that marriage is "an outward and visible sign of an inward and spiritual grace given unto us, ordained by Christ Himself as a means whereby we receive the same and a pledge to assure us thereof." Least of all will it be asserted that it is "generally necessary to salvation." It is not then a sacrament.

But it is impossible to deny that it is a mystery, since it produces holiness or sanctity. Everything which relates to sanctity is mysterious. St. Paul, in the passage cited from his Epistle to the Ephesians, says: "For this cause shall a man leave his father and mother, and shall be joined unto his wife, and they two shall be one flesh. This is a great mystery, but I speak concerning Christ and the Church."[2]

It has been sometimes contended, that the last member of the last sentence refers the former part of the sentence to Christ and the Church. The relation between the Lord and the Church, not that between husband and wife is, upon this view, that which the Apostle pronounces a mystery. But the clause seems rather to refer to the whole passage, of the subject of which marriage is at least a great part. It is treated as a type of the union between Christ and his Church. At the same time, the conduct of the Lord towards his spouse the Church is held up as the example of husbands, and the conduct of the Church is held up as an example to wives. Such is the relation between type and antitype, that it is hard to suppose anything said of the one that is not true of the other, in its measure. Moreover, it could scarcely be necessary to

1 [Art. xxv. Of the Sacraments.]

2 Ephesians v. 31, 32.

state so distinctly the obvious truth, that the relation between Christ and the Church is a mystery.

§ 8. The sanctity of marriage seems to consist in the sanctification imparted by the Divine blessing to the unity. This may constitute its element of indissolubleness: "Whom God hath joined together let not man put asunder." There is no prohibition to put asunder those whom God hath not joined. Perhaps it may be proper to repeat here the caution, that man who can only look upon the outward appearance, cannot separate those who in outward appearance have been joined by God.

The two mysterious elements of unity and sanctity may be regarded as the essence of marriage, or rather, perhaps, as the centre with which all the other elements are connected either as causes or effects. The consent may be considered as the root, out of which, when watered by the Divine blessing, grow the unity and the sanctity. The practical elements — exclusiveness, indissolubleness, and the authority of the husband — are the effects of the unity and sanctity. It has been already shown that the indissolubleness of marriage is traced to the unity by the highest authority. It is plain to the merely human intellect, that polygamy is inconsistent with unity, which is, therefore, the source of exclusiveness. It will hereafter be shown that the authority of the husband is also closely connected with unity.

§ 9. Marriage is not a thing merely tolerated or licensed. It is a duty under the ordinary circumstances of mankind. This is implied in the Divine declaration, that "it is not good for man to be alone," which was the assignment of the Divine motive for creating woman and instituting marriage.

St. Paul has been supposed to contradict this Divine declaration, in the seventh chapter of his first Epistle to the Corinthians. This whole chapter may be taken as an instruction to be prudent in contracting marriage. In the twenty-sixth verse, the Apostle expressly says that he was speaking for the present distress. His doctrine may be reconciled with the passage in Genesis, by supposing that the two taken together mean something like this: It is not good for man to be alone; it is better that he should have a help which is meet for him; but it is better that he should be alone than that he should have a companion who is not a help, or who is not meet for him, whether from defects in her character or from other causes, which render it unmeet for him to marry.

That this is substantially the meaning of St. Paul, appears from two other passages, in which he treats marriage as the duty of women under ordinary circumstances. If it be the duty of women, it can hardly be other than a duty for men. In the first of these passages, he is giving directions about the widows who were to be "taken into the number," whether of those who were to be relieved by the alms of the Church or of official persons, is not clear. He requires that they shall not be under threescore years of age. After giving some directions about them, he goes on to speak of others who were not to be "taken into the number," and adds: "I will, therefore, that the younger women marry, bear children, guide the house, give none occasion to the adversary to speak reproachfully." [1]

In the other passage he implies that marriage is the ordinary and proper condition of woman. He says: "The aged women likewise, that they be in behaviour as becometh holiness, not false accusers, not given to much wine, teachers of good things; that they may teach the young women to be sober, to love their husbands, to love their children, to be discreet, chaste, keepers at home, good, obedient to their own husbands; that the Word of God be not blasphemed." [2]

Upon the whole it may be considered that marriage is a Divine institution, into which it is the will of God that

[1] 1 Timothy v. 14.

[2] Titus ii. 3–5.

men and women should generally enter. The rule is open to many exceptions, and in some conditions of society and stations of life to more than in others. But marriage is the appointed state of man, and is not only not sinful, but possesses one great element of holiness, perhaps the chief element, conformity to the Divine will. This renders the state so agreeable to God, that He has bestowed upon it the power of sanctifying whatever is connected with it. Yet this and all other effects of the Divine blessing are withheld from unions which are not in accordance with the Divine law.

§ 10. Various theories have been found to account for the unity of married persons. One is, that there is some mysterious connection between sexual intercourse and the unity of man and wife, or the making of twain one flesh. The idea that it is necessary to the completion of a marriage has been formerly recognized by human laws, and has still some hold upon the public mind. This might lead to other considerations for which this is not the proper place. These ideas are perhaps connected with a remarkable passage in the writings of St. Paul, which might have been cited as an additional proof that Adam, on the introduction of his wife, spoke by inspiration, but which has been reserved to this place on account of its other teaching. It is this: "Know ye not that your bodies are members of Christ? Shall I then take the members of Christ and make them the members of a harlot? God forbid. What! know ye not that he which is joined to a harlot is one body? for two, saith he, shall be one flesh. But he that is joined unto the Lord is one spirit."[1]

In this passage St. Paul seems to attribute the power of making two one flesh to sexual intercourse even when unlawful. The Reverend Hector Davies Morgan, a learned clergyman of the Church of England, published, in 1826, a work on "Marriage, Adultery, and Divorce." In it he

[1] 1 Corinthians vi. 15–17.

attempts to give another turn to this text. According to him, the word which is translated harlot means a person who is an alien from the Church of God. The meaning of the text would then be that marriages between believers and unbelievers are unlawful. This doctrine is taught elsewhere by the same Apostle, but not in this place. Mr. Morgan perhaps adopted this interpretation because it favors a notion of his, that the exception in our Lord's prohibition of divorce relates only to such marriages.[1]

He supposes that marriages with persons not members of the Church are only fornications, and that such a marriage is the fornication mentioned by our Blessed Lord in St. Matthew, as a sufficient cause of divorce. It is unfortunate for this notion, that if the passage refer to such mixed marriages, they are valid, for it attributes to them the power of making two persons one flesh. If the Apostle is speaking of mixed marriages, he treats them as sinful but valid. He regards them as among the things of which it may be said: *Fieri non debet, sed factum valet.* They ought not to be done, but being done are valid.

This is a true doctrine, but almost all commentators, ancient and modern, are agreed that it is not taught in this passage, which they think relates to simple fornication. Dr. Pusey adopts the authorized translation, and quotes St. Chrysostom, who cites the text in that sense.[2]

The text is a difficult one; it clearly teaches that fornication in some sense unites the fornicators into one flesh; but it is, perhaps, not necessary to believe that the union is indissoluble. If it be, then the world is full of polygamy and polyandry. Many men have each a great number of wives, each of whom has a great number of husbands, and all these unions are indissoluble marriages. They cannot be so; God has not joined the fornicators, and therefore they may be put asunder. Yet it has been gravely as-

[1] See Morgan *On Marriage*, etc., vol. ii. p. 134, *et seq.*
[2] *Parochial Sermons*, vol. i. Preface, p. xxv.

serted that he who has been joined to a harlot, is married to her, and cannot during her life marry another woman. This is a fearful doctrine, for it would annul a very large proportion of existing marriages. It would involve thousands if not millions of persons in sins which they have committed in ignorance of the facts which made them sins. It is more to the purpose to remark that it would be difficult to reconcile either this doctrine or Mr. Morgan's with the respect which the Apostle, in the next chapter, pays to heathen marriages, most of which would be void according to this doctrine, and all according to Mr. Morgan's.

There can scarcely be a marriage where there was no intention to marry, no consent to live together according to God's law, and no Divine blessing asked, expected, desired, or received. No Divine blessing can have been given to an act of sin, and without the Divine blessing, there can be no unity or sanctity in marriage. The sin may, nevertheless, have its own mysterious power of uniting the sinners in a mysterious unity of guilt, although not in an indissoluble Christian marriage. The guilt is disgraceful to a Christian and insulting to his Divine Head. The Divine blessing may, by the sin of those who neglected to seek it, be transformed into a curse.

§ 11. Another theory is that it is love which produces the unity in marriage. By love is meant the amorous emotion which incites to marriage, and which often but not always develops into conjugal affection. This emotion is compounded of a benevolent affection and a passion derived from the instinct of self-love, as is shown in the diagram in the second chapter. In the married state the passion fades, and the affection develops into conjugal love. But this emotion, however desirable it may be as a preparation for marriage, has no power of giving unity to a marriage. It is impossible to concede to it such a power. It is the germ of conjugal affection; but the germ may not develop into the fruit or the fruit may perish.

In either case the marriage would, on that theory, be at an end.

§ 12. The notion involves that of divorce for incompatibility of temper, that is, of marriage so long as both parties please. Frequent disagreements would arise because the parties could be relieved from their relation to each other. There would be much cruelty on the part of the man, and much petulance on that of the woman, which would be resorted to in order that the incompatibility of temper might be manifest. The end would be, that marriage would be regarded as only a temporary arrangement, and woman as merely an instrument of sensuality.

§ 13. Another theory is that conjugal affection is the uniting power in marriage. In a merely human mode of looking at things in the order of nature, it is very likely to be so considered; but in the order of grace it is not. There is an intimate connection between conjugal affection and the unity of man and wife. Conjugal affection is not an element of marriage, although it is closely connected with both the formative and the mysterious elements. In some popular theories of marriage, which are connected with the romantic theory of the relation between the sexes, conjugal affection is made the essence of marriage. In these theories, it precedes the marriage in the state of a germ, prompts the consent, joins the parties, and sanctifies in some sense the union. After marriage it develops into its full dimensions, and is itself the unity. This unity has nothing mysterious about it; it consists in a conscious affection, which combines the wills of the married persons. This is conjugal affection, but it is not the mysterious unity which makes of twain one flesh.

Conjugal affection is very important to the temporal and indeed to the eternal happiness of the married couple; but it is not the essence of marriage. Such a notion would be inconsistent with the indissoluble character of marriage, for conjugal affection does not always endure to the end. Its absence, whether it has ceased to exist or has never existed, is fatal to the temporal and hazardous to the eternal happiness of the married pair. Without it the duties of the holy state are very likely to be neglected, or carelessly and insufficiently performed. In such a state of things, hatred may take the place of love. This is highly sinful; but it does not dissolve the marriage, as it would were conjugal love the essence of marriage.

But conjugal love is necessary to the happiness and safety of the married state. Thus much must be conceded to the advocates of the romantic theory. But it is impossible to concede to them that proper conjugal affection or its germ, for conjugal affection cannot exist before marriage, can constitute Christian marriage.

§ 14. The unity and sanctity of marriage are the causes, not the effects of conjugal love. It may be urged that there are many cases of married persons who have no conjugal affection, and that, therefore, marriage cannot be the cause of that affection. The truth of the assertion cannot be denied; but the inference does not follow. There are many marriages which are external only; the forms of marriage have been gone through, but not in the right spirit. There has been no Divine blessing, no mysterious unity, no sanctity. In such cases it is not surprising that there is no conjugal affection. If marriage be, or be regarded as a mere civil contract, it cannot produce any such affection. Neither can the mere living together produce it. It may aid in its development by giving opportunities of observing the amiable qualities of the object of affection. But where it can only expose unamiable qualities, it cannot aid the development. The truth is that conjugal affection, at least in its highest perfection, belongs to the order of grace, and is connected with the Divine institution of marriage.

It has been already said that marriage is not a sacrament in which a special Divine grace, tending to the salvation of the recipient, is given. But it is a Divine institution, the blessing of which is to be sought by prayer, and will be given to those who seek it in the right frame of mind and heart. This blessing unites the persons and sanctifies the state. All this is very mysterious; but so are all the operations of Divine grace. The unity and sanctity of the marriage state are then the true causes of conjugal love, it is not the cause of them.

The unity and sanctity of marriage are so closely connected, that it is not possible for one to exist without the other. Where they are, conjugal love will scarcely be wanting; where they are not, it will scarcely be found.

§ 15. Men, according to St. Paul, are composed of three parts, body, soul, and spirit. "The very God of peace sanctify you wholly; and I pray God your whole spirit, soul, and body, be preserved blameless unto the coming of our Lord Jesus Christ."[1] There is in the regenerate and sanctified man a still higher element, which is derived from his union with Christ and the indwelling of the Holy Ghost. In every man and woman there are thus, as it were, three natures: the animal, answering to the body in the text just quoted; the intellectual, there called the soul, which includes the faculties by which the intellect works, and the emotions by which it is stirred; the moral, which is the spirit of the Apostle, in which the emotions and faculties are subjected to the dominion of conscience, and compelled to acknowledge the distinction between right and wrong. Over all these, there is, in the regenerate and sanctified man, the new nature superinduced by the indwelling of the Holy Spirit, which sanctifies the other three.

Marriage is designed for men and women thus constituted, and may, as has been intimated in a preceding chapter, be considered as having several sides adapted to the various portions of this complex nature. Each of

[1] 1 Thessalonians v. 23.

these presents a true, though inadequate and imperfect view of the subject. Marriage has its animal side, adapted to the wants of the animal nature. It has also its intellectual side, or rather two sides connected with the intellect. One of these may be called the emotional side, and is adapted to the demands of the kind affections. The other is connected with the faculties, for which it provides occupation and assistance. It has also its moral side, as it provides for the improvement of the moral nature. Marriage has therefore four sides, which are connected with as many different sides of human nature. Christian marriage has a fifth, the spiritual side, which is to the spiritual nature what the moral side is to the moral nature. It has also something, which without great impropriety may be called a sixth side. This is connected with the relations of man to society, and so far is intellectual, and also with the necessary provision for the animal wants, and so far is animal. It may not very improperly be called the prudential side of marriage.

The unity of marriage, which is its essence, has relations to the first five of these, and in a qualified sense to the sixth. The sanctity of marriage has, in a sense, relations to the first four sides; but its especial relation is to the fifth. In its highest sense, it belongs to the higher nature which has been superinduced upon the others by Divine power operating upon the coöperating human will.

§ 16. The sanctity of marriage consists in the sanctification by the Divine blessing of the consent, the unity, and all their effects, and of all the faculties, emotions, instincts, and functions with which marriage is connected. Thus it is that the unity and sanctity of every Christian marriage are inseparably joined and constitute its essence. Yet there is a higher sanctity which is wrought by the indwelling of the Holy Ghost in the hearts of the married persons, and is the same with their sanctification. This raises conjugal love into a sanctified virtue. Both this and the ordinary sanctity are the work of the Holy Ghost, and it should be borne in mind that He does not act without the coöperation of the human will.

§ 17. Those who desire to understand the doctrine of marriage, must not be content to look at it upon only one of its sides, but must examine it upon all. It ought not to be entered into with only the feelings connected with any one of them. This is generally acknowledged to be true, especially with respect to the animal and prudential sides; but the acknowledgment is more theoretical than practical. Men and women often marry for prudential reasons only; and men, at least, for animal motives. Such marriages are wrong. Those which are commonly called love-matches and grow out of emotional impulses, are no better; although young ladies are apt to fancy that they are the only right marriages. None of these things should be despised or neglected. No one should enter into a marriage which he or she has not considered on all sides. Every reason for marrying, or for marrying any particular person, is to be kept in subordination to moral and religious considerations, if the marriage is to be sanctified.

CHAPTER VI.

OF THE PRACTICAL ELEMENTS OF MARRIAGE. — I. EXCLUSIVENESS.

§ 1. The Practical Elements of Marriage. — § 2. Monogamy of Civilized Nations. — § 3. Bigamy and Adultery. — § 4. Unanimity among Christians on the Subject of Polygamy. — § 5. The Creation of Woman, and Institution of Marriage. — § 6. Polygamy before the Flood. — § 7. Polygamy not permitted to Noah. — § 8. Polygamy in the time of Abraham. — § 9. Polygamy among the Descendants of Abraham. — § 10. Polygamy in the 1st Book of Chronicles. — § 11. Polygamy under the Mosaic Law. — § 12. Exodus xxi. 7-11. — § 13. Exodus xxii. 16, 17. — § 14. Deuteronomy xvii. 17. — § 15. Deuteronomy xxi. 10-14. — § 16. Deuteronomy xxi. 15-17. — § 17. Deuteronomy xxii. 28. — § 18. Leviticus xviii. 18. — § 19. The Marginal Translation. — § 20. The Case of Jacob. — § 21. Modern Interpretations. — § 22. The Book of Judges.— §23. The Case of Elkanah. — § 24. The Kings. — § 25. Saul. — § 26. Other Kings. — § 27. Polygamy unusual among the Israelites. — § 28. Doctrine of St. Paul. — § 29. Doctrine of our Blessed Saviour.

§ 1. Some idea has been given in the last chapter of the mysterious elements of marriage, — unity and sanctity. It is now proper to pass to the practical elements which flow from them. These are three: exclusiveness, indissolubleness, and the authority of the husband, or, which is the same thing, the subordination of the wife.

§ 2. The exclusiveness of marriage is violated by polygamy, in any of its forms. The Christian rule is announced by St. Paul, "Let every man have his own wife, and every woman her own husband." [1] This rule is disregarded by the Mohammedans, the Mormons, and most pagan nations. But the more civilized of the ancient heathen generally allowed but one wife to each man. The same rule prevailed among the barbarians who overthrew the Roman Empire,

[1] 1 Corinthians vii. 2.

and of those who invaded, and partially subdued the conquerors. Modern Europe, in addition to the Christian law, received the tradition of monogamy, through all the channels through which it derived its civilization. Moreover, in civilized communities, the expense of polygamy will prevent it from becoming general. The expense would be greatly increased by the complicated arrangements of modern civilization. Even among the semi-civilized Mohammedans, the expense has confined the practice to the very rich, who can meet any expense, and men of a low class, who regard wives as profitable slaves. Moreover, polygamy is sustained upon the last-mentioned principle. For all these reasons, polygamy is not likely to become a recognized institution among any civilized people.

§ 3. It is not likely, therefore, that the Mohammedan or Mormon forms of polygamy will spread among us. Many causes will work together to prevent the growth of a system which is so contrary to the genius of the age, and bears so hardly on the whole of one sex, and the larger part of the other, that its existence anywhere is a problem very difficult of solution. No doubt an *à priori* observer would have pronounced Mormon polygamy impossible; yet its existence is a melancholy fact.

The loose ideas entertained of the marriage tie have, unhappily, made two other forms of polygamy not uncommon among us. One of these is that to which the law gives the name of bigamy. It consists in marrying several wives, who, although all living at the same time, do not know of each other's existence. This form of polygamy is rather inconsistent with the Christian idea of the indissolubility of the marriage tie, than with that of exclusiveness. The migratory character of our population, with many advantages, involves, among other moral evils, a great facility for committing this crime; for so the laws designate it. A man who finds himself linked to an ill-assorted partner, or to one with whom for any cause he is unwilling to live, divorces himself from her, and makes the divorce effectual by removing to a distance. In his new abode he passes for a single man, and has neither scruple nor difficulty in marrying a new wife. This is made the more easy by the lamentable levity with which marriage is regarded by the larger portion of the female sex in this country. This levity is again connected with the forgetfulness of the indissoluble nature of marriage, which is so very common among us.

The third kind of polygamy is also, it is to be feared, not uncommon. It is when a married man lives with his wife, and yet keeps up an adulterous intercourse with one or more other women. This is everywhere in the United States contrary to law, although not everywhere to the penal law, and also to public opinion. It is, nevertheless, extensively practiced, and involves many of the evils of polygamy.

§ 4. Upon the subject of polygamy there has been great unanimity among Christians of all ages and countries. There are few doctrines which could better stand the famous test of Vincent of Lerins, than the unlawfulness of polygamy. There were some practical violations of the rule of monogamy, chiefly by powerful men in the Middle Ages, which were perhaps connived at by the clergy, not approved by the Church. There have been some doubtful stories, perhaps only one, of dispensations granted by popes, in particular cases. There is the unfortunate case of Philip Landgrave of Hesse. He was married to a second wife, in the lifetime of the first, with the consent of Luther, Melancthon, Bucer, and other leaders of the German Reformation. They decided the case on the authority of the text in the twenty-first chapter of Deuteronomy, which forbids the preference of the son of a beloved wife, which they held to show that polygamy was lawful among the Jews. They inferred that it might be allowed among Christians by dispensation, although it was still generally unlawful. There could not have been much worse logic; but they carried their strange doctrine into effect by giving the Landgrave a dispensation to marry a second wife during the life of the first, upon certain conditions. He was accordingly married in the presence of some of the principal Reformers. The transaction has often been referred to, by the enemies of the German Reformation, as a great scandal. Yet though the fact cannot be denied, no one has ever attempted to defend it. There is no other instance of the practical allowance of polygamy by any number of Christian ministers, and it must be observed that the dispensation did not even pretend to be a synodical act. Moreover, it is apparent on the face of the papers that Luther, and those who acted with him, did not really believe that polygamy was lawful; they acted on motives of worldly expediency. There is a full account of the transaction, with translations of the documents, in Dr. Hook's "Ecclesiastical Biography," article *Bucer*.

There has never been, in truth, any instance of polygamy having been approved by any respectable Christian body. The German Anabaptists upheld, and the American Mormons now uphold, polygamy; but neither of these bodies have much claim either to the epithet respectable, or to the name of Christian. A few eccentric writers have advocated the institution, but their works have never had any influence, and are now only known to the curious. These are the only exceptions to the unanimity of Christians.

§ 5. It is easily shown that there is a sufficient basis for this unanimity in the Holy Scriptures. A strong presumption against polygamy arises from the fact that only one woman was created. The facts connected with her creation make the case stronger: "The Lord God said: It is not good for the man to be alone; I will make him a help meet for him." [1] Not two helps, one was all that was

[1] Genesis ii. 18.

requisite. It is further said: "And the Lord God caused a deep sleep to fall upon Adam, and he slept; and He took one of his ribs, and closed up the flesh instead thereof; and the rib which the Lord God had taken from man, made He a woman, and brought her unto the man. And Adam said: This is now bone of my bones, and flesh of my flesh; she shall be called Woman, because she was taken out of Man. Therefore shall a man leave his father and his mother, and shall cleave unto his wife, and they shall be one flesh." [1]

This speech of Adam may be called the marriage ceremony of Paradise. It is certain that he spake by inspiration, for our Blessed Lord attributes his words to God. "Have ye not heard," says He, "that He, which made them in the beginning, made them male and female, and said: For this cause shall a man leave father and mother and cleave to his wife, and they twain shall be one flesh?" [2]

There is no doubt of the inconsistency of polygamy with the primitive institution of marriage, and consequently none that it was from the first unlawful. The place in Genesis just cited, establishes a unity between man and wife, which precludes the introduction of a third person. That the Jews so understood it appears from the Septuagint, a translation made by Jews, and adopted by all the Greek-speaking Jews. In that translation the word two is introduced, "And they two shall be one flesh."

The Prophet Malachi, referring to the creation, says: "And did not He make one? Yet had He the residue of the Spirit. And wherefore one? That He might seek a godly seed." [3] It thus sufficiently appears by the Old Testament, that polygamy is inconsistent with the original law of marriage. The doctrine of the New Testament is, as shall be shown hereafter, even more explicit. There are, then, abundant reasons for the unanimity of the Church upon the question of polygamy.

[1] Genesis ii. 21–24. [2] Matthew xix. 4, 5. [3] Malachi ii. 15.

§ 6. It would rather seem from the antediluvian history that the meaning of the original institution was then understood. Only one instance of polygamy is mentioned, and that among the descendants of Cain. Among the descendants of Seth there is no evidence that it existed, unless, as has been asserted, it is to be found in the statement that "the sons of God saw the daughters of men that they were fair; and they took them wives of all which they chose."[1] It is by no means to be inferred that any of them took more than one wife. Noah and his sons had each but one wife, for it is said: "In the same day entered Noah, and Shem, and Ham, and Japheth, the three sons of Noah, and Noah's wife, and the three wives of his sons with them, into the ark."[2]

§ 7. Polygamy was then contrary to the original law of marriage, and there is no record of any license on account of hardness of heart, as in the case of divorce. It has been suggested that the law was relaxed at the flood. It is a sufficient answer to this, that there is no trace of such relaxation in the Sacred Record. History does not show that polygamy reappeared until long after the flood. The new law given to Noah, contains nothing on the subject, although two things are mentioned with either of which it might naturally have been connected. The command given to Adam to increase and multiply is repeated. Yet there is no allusion to polygamy as a means of obeying it. Permission to eat the flesh of animals, which was not allowed at the creation, was then given. Here the extension of privilege in one direction would have made it natural to speak of an extension in another.

The whole passage is this: "And God blessed Noah and his sons, and said unto them, Be fruitful, and multiply, and replenish the earth; and the fear of you and the dread of you shall be upon every beast of the field, and upon every fowl of the air, and all that moveth upon the earth,

[1] Genesis vi. 2. [2] Genesis vii. 13.

and all the fishes of the sea; into your hands they are delivered. Every moving thing that liveth shall be meat for you; even as the green herb have I given you all things. But flesh with the life thereof, which is the blood thereof, shall ye not eat. And surely your blood of your lives will I require; at the hand of every beast will I require it, and at the hand of every man; at the hand of every man's brother will I require the life of man. Whoso sheddeth man's blood, by man shall his blood be shed: for in the image of God made he man. And be ye fruitful and multiply; bring forth abundantly in the earth and multiply therein."[1]

§ 8. The postdiluvian history in the Book of Genesis, and the earlier part of that of Exodus, mention instances of polygamy, but they seem to have been exceptional. In a large majority of the cases in which a wife is mentioned, it appears that she was the only wife of her husband. Apart from the exceptional cases which are mentioned, the impression produced upon the mind is that of a people among whom monogamy was the rule. No instance of polygamy occurs before the time of Abraham. The first recorded is in the twelfth chapter of Genesis, and that is not a very clear one. It is there related that Sarai was taken into Pharaoh's house to be his wife or concubine; but it does not distinctly appear that he was already married.

The same remark cannot be made of Abimelech, mentioned in the twentieth chapter to have treated Sarah in the same manner. It appears from the seventeenth and eighteenth verses, that he had slave concubines; and it is mentioned in the seventeenth that he had a wife, but only one in the sense in which the word was then understood. All that can be gathered from the twentieth chapter about polygamy is that a king had slave concubines, and was not scrupulous about the mode of increasing the number. In

[1] Genesis ix. 1–7.

modern times, kings have indulged in concubinage. For aught that appears, the concubinage of the married king Abimelech may have been as irregular as that of the married King Charles. The arrangement may not have been more legitimate than that by which Charles II. had, notwithstanding his marriage, the Duchesses of Cleveland and Portsmouth, Mistress Nelly Gwyn, and other women as concubines at the same time. It is true that Abimelech says he fears God, and God himself says that Abimelech had done it in the integrity of his heart. This only means that he did not know that the woman was married, and did not mean to commit adultery against her husband. Of that sort of adultery which is committed with another man's wife, both he and his son or descendants mentioned in the twenty-sixth chapter, as well as the Pharaoh of the twelfth, had a great horror.

Between the occurrences mentioned in the twelfth and twentieth chapters, Abraham had taken Hagar as his slave concubine, which shows the existence of that institution. The circumstances out of which the arrangement grew were very peculiar.[1] It was made for a particular purpose, and there is no evidence that it continued longer than that purpose required. Moreover, that part of Abraham's conduct is never mentioned in the Scriptures with approbation. Its consequences were very undesirable, and the allegory in the fourth chapter of the Epistle to the Galatians places it in an unfavorable light.

Bethuel, the father of Rebekah, had four sons by a concubine, who was not taken only for the purpose of having issue, for he had eight sons by his wife.[2] There is, perhaps, no other instance of polygamy than these, mentioned in the Scriptures as occurring during the life of Abraham.

In the sixth verse of the twenty-fifth chapter of Genesis, mention is made of "the sons of the concubines which Abraham had." These were probably the sons of Hagar

[1] Genesis xvi.

[2] *Ibid.* xxii. 23, 24.

and of Keturah, another wife whom he took after the death of Sarah. She was probably of inferior birth, and therefore here called a concubine; while she rather resembled the left-handed wives of modern German princes. In the first verse she is expressly called a wife. There is no evidence that he had any other wife or concubine at the same time with her. The history imports that he had no concubine but Hagar, and no sons but Ishmael and Isaac during the life of Sarah.

§ 9. During the life of Isaac, and after his father's death, polygamy made great progress, though Isaac himself had but one wife and no concubine. Ishmael also seems to have had but one wife, whom Hagar his mother took for him out of the land of Egypt. But both of the sons of Isaac were polygamists. Esau had three equal wives, and Jacob two, besides two slave concubines. Yet polygamy does not seem to have continued its advance in the next generation.

Among the descendants of Esau, Amalek is the only one who is said to have been the son of a concubine. He was a grandson of Esau. Timnah, his mother, was of the race of the Horites, whom the children of Esau subdued. In the fall of her race, she probably became a slave and a concubine. There is no conclusive evidence that any of the sons of Jacob were polygamists. Shaul, the son of Simeon, was the son of a Canaanitish woman, and therefore not by the same mother with his brethren. He may have been the son of a second wife, married after the death of the first. But from the manner in which he is spoken of, it is not unlikely that he was the offspring of a passing amour, as were the twin sons of Judah.[1]

Throughout the earlier chapters of Exodus the whole history is that of a people whose custom it was to have only one wife at a time. No case of polygamy is mentioned, and women are spoken of as the wife of such a man,

[1] See Genesis xxxviii. and xlvi. 10.

10

just as they now would be. It would seem that then, as well as during the time of which the history is recounted in Genesis, polygamy existed, but that the cases were very few. Two of them, those of Abraham and Jacob, are so prominent that they fill the imagination, and lead to the notion that polygamy was common. A close examination will show that it was by no means common, at least among the chosen people. Nor does it seem to have been common among any of the nations which are mentioned in the Book of Genesis, except in the form of slave-concubinage. Such was the case in Egypt, according to Sir Gardner Wilkinson.[1]

A continuation of the history of polygamy through the Books of Chronicles, Judges, Samuel, and Kings, shows a similar state of things to that which appears in Genesis. Cases of polygamy are recorded; but monogamy seems to have been the rule.

§ 10. In the genealogies which occupy the first nine chapters of the First Book of Chronicles, care seems to have been taken to mention every case of polygamy. There are only seven, besides those mentioned in Genesis. One of them, however, includes many individual cases, being stated as the custom of a family, or tribe. It is not perfectly clear that polygamy is meant; though that is probably the meaning. The passage is the fourth verse of the seventh chapter: "And with them after their generations, after the house of their fathers, were bands of soldiers for war, six-and-thirty thousand men, for they had many wives and sons." The other six cases are each of a single man. There is besides mention made in the fourth chapter, of Shimei, who had sixteen sons and six daughters. This number is not large enough to prove that he was a polygamist, although it is quite probable that he may have been one. In the narrative there are very few cases of polygamy, except those of kings and great

[1] *Popular Account of the Ancient Egyptians*, vol. ii. p. 224.

men; while the wives of men of all ranks are so spoken of as to imply that they were the only wives of their husbands.

§ 11. It has been sometimes asserted that under the Mosaic law polygamy was lawful. The Mosaic law does not contain any direct permission of it, and it was unlawful according to the original institution of marriage. Yet it has been said by high authority, that it is "supposed as allowable in distinct enactments." Seven of these are enumerated, and it is added, "perhaps in some other places." The author has searched in vain for the other places, and believes that the seven enumerated passages are all that exist. An examination will show that some of them only suppose that polygamy will exist, not that it is allowable, while others do not imply it at all. They are, Exodus xxi. 7–11; xxii. 16; Deuteronomy xvii. 17; xxi. 11; xxi. 15; xxii. 28; Leviticus xviii. 18.

§ 12. The first of these texts is this: "If a man shall sell his daughter for a maid-servant, she shall not go out as the men-servants do. If she please not her master who hath betrothed her to himself, then shall he let her be redeemed; to sell her to a strange nation he shall have no power, seeing he hath dealt deceitfully with her. And if he have betrothed her unto his son, he shall deal with her after the manner of daughters. If he take him another wife, her food, her raiment, and her duty of marriage he shall not diminish; if he do not these three unto her, then shall she go free without money." [1]

The betrothment mentioned in the eighth verse does not imply polygamy, for the master might be a bachelor, or a widower. The tenth verse certainly implies that a man who had betrothed his slave to himself would sometimes take another wife. But it does not say that he might lawfully do so. It gives no countenance to such a step, but clogs it with an impossible condition. If the master does not comply with the condition the slave is to go out free, which

[1] Exodus xxi. 7–11.

is the same thing to her as a divorce to a free woman. The polygamy is then at an end. The meaning of the law seems to be, that the master may divorce his slave-wife, but, if he does, he shall not retain her as a slave; he shall not keep her under the authority of his new wife, nor shall he sell her for money, for a reason assigned in the second text from Deuteronomy. The permission was probably a concession to men's hardness of heart, as in the case of the other law of divorce.

§ 13. The second of the seven texts is this: "If a man entice a woman which is not betrothed, and lie with her, he shall surely endow her to be his wife. If her father utterly refuse to give her unto him, he shall pay money according to the dower of virgins."[1] It is not easy to see what this law has to do with polygamy. It is only a provision, that a man who had seduced a young woman should marry her. Surely such a provision does not involve the lawfulness of polygamy. Such laws have actually existed in countries where it was unlawful. It might happen that the seducer was a married man, and could not comply with the law, but that involves no absurdity in the law itself. If polygamy were allowed, it might happen that the man could not comply with the law because the woman was related to him within the forbidden degrees.

§ 14. In the third of the seven texts the lawgiver is giving instructions about the kings, who would be set up at some future time. Among other rules is this: "Neither shall he multiply wives to himself."[2] This forbids that exorbitant polygamy, which was common among eastern kings, and was afterwards practiced by David, Solomon, and Rehoboam. It is addressed to kings, and is supposed to be directed against a particular vice, to which they, and they only, were tempted. But the prohibition to the king to multiply wives, cannot imply that every private man might have two or three. The text might more fairly be

[1] Exodus xxii. 16, 17. [2] Deuteronomy xvii. 17.

interpreted as restraining kings to one wife, than as allowing polygamy to other men.

§ 15. The fourth of the seven texts is this: "When thou goest forth against thine enemies, and the Lord thy God hath delivered them into thine hands, and thou hast taken them captive; and seest among them a beautiful woman, and hast a desire unto her that thou wouldst have her for a wife, then thou shalt bring her into thine house, and she shall shave her head and pare her nails. And she shall put off the raiment of her captivity from off her, and shall remain in thine house and bewail her father and mother a full month, and after that thou shalt go in unto her and be her husband, and she shall be thy wife. And it shall be, if thou have no delight in her, then thou shalt let her go whither she will; but thou shalt not sell her at all for money; thou shalt not make merchandise of her, because thou hast humbled her."[1] Here there is no allusion to polygamy. A man is allowed to marry his captive after certain delays, probably intended to act as checks upon his lust, and regulations are made for her protection. There is nothing from which it can be fairly inferred that the privilege of marrying a captive extended to married men. If polygamy be, and it certainly is, forbidden by the law in Genesis, the prohibition would control the permission, unless it were clear that the permission was intended to dispense with the prohibition. It is a rule that a law which forbids overrules one which permits, if the permission is only general, and the prohibitory law is not mentioned. It is another, that laws must be so construed that they shall not clash with each other. Both rules require that this privilege shall be confined to single men. If it had been expressly extended to married men, it would have been an argument in favor of polygamy; in its present shape it is not.

§ 16. The fifth of the seven texts immediately follows the one just cited; it is: "If a man have two wives, one

1 Deuteronomy xxi. 10–14.

beloved, and another hated, and they have borne him children, both the beloved and the hated, and if the first-born son be her's that was hated; then it shall be when he maketh his sons to inherit that which he hath, that he may not make the son of the beloved first-born before the son of the hated, which is indeed the first-born, but he shall acknowlege the son of the hated for the first-born, by giving him a double portion of all that he hath; for he is the beginning of his strength; the right of the first-born is his." [1] It has been said that this text does not necessarily imply that the man had two wives at the same time. It does not; but it is the more obvious and fair interpretation that he had. The passage implies polygamy, but it does not follow that it allows it. It assumes that there will be polygamists, and regulates their conduct. It forbids a man who has committed an injustice to his wife from committing another to his first-born son.

§ 17. The sixth of the seven texts is this: "If a man find a virgin which is not betrothed, in a field, and lay hold on her and lie with her, and they be found, then the man that lay with her shall give unto the damsel's father fifty shekels of silver, and she shall be his wife; because he hath humbled her he may not put her away all his days." [2] Here again there is no mention of polygamy. The true meaning is that she shall be his wife, if she may be so lawfully. The case of the ravished damsel is like that of the seduced one. The seducer or the ravisher must marry her if he can do so lawfully. But he could not lawfully marry her if she were his sister or his half-sister, or his aunt, or his niece, or on the supposition that polygamy was allowed, his his wife's sister.[3] In all these cases the law could not be acted upon without breaking another law. If polygamy were unlawful, it could not be acted upon if the man had a wife. If the law had provided that the damsel should be

[1] Deuteronomy xxi. 15-17. [2] *Ibid.* xxii. 28, 29.

[3] Leviticus xviii.

the man's wife, notwithstanding he already had one, there would have been an end of the question. Polygamy would have been lawful, at least in that case. But there is nothing of the kind. It would be as reasonable to infer that the laws in the eighteenth chapter of Leviticus had been abrogated by this law as that in the second chapter of Genesis. The same principles govern both cases. This law, like all others, could only take effect when it did not involve the breaking of any other law. Polygamy is contrary to the primary law of marriage. The two laws can be reconciled by applying that in Deuteronomy to single men. It will then furnish no evidence of the lawfulness of polygamy.

§ 18. One of the seven texts, which have been cited as giving countenance to polygamy, has not been considered in the place in which its position would seem to call for its consideration. It was reserved to be examined last, because of its importance and difficulty. It is: "Neither shalt thou take a wife to her sister, to vex her, to uncover her nakedness beside the other in her lifetime."[1] The most obvious meaning of this verse is that it forbids a man to marry the sister of his wife during her life. Two inferences have been drawn from it: one, that polygamy was allowed to the Israelites; the other, that a man may marry two sisters successively. Attempts have been made to escape from both these inferences by technical constructions, but they have not been very successful. With the second inference this is not the place to deal; it belongs to a subsequent chapter.

§ 19. It is agreed that the translation in the authorized version is the literal one, but the translators have introduced into the margin another rendering. It is: "Thou shalt not take a wife to another, to vex her, to uncover her nakedness beside the other in her lifetime." This merely forbids polygamy. The marginal translation has the advantage of being consistent with the primitive law of mar-

[1] Leviticus xviii. 18.

riage, which the other assumes to have been repealed or suspended, although the repealing or suspending law is not to be found. Still this will not be a sufficient ground for rejecting the literal translation, unless it can be shown that there is good reason for preferring another.

The argument upon which the marginal translation rests is this. It is an idiom of the Hebrew language to express the adding of one thing to another of the same sort, by the phrase of adding it to its brother or sister. It is said that this idiom occurs about forty times in the Old Testament. It is also said, and it is very probable, that in most of those cases it is impossible to understand the phrase literally, but no one has denied that in some of them it is possible to understand it literally. In reply, it has been said that the idiom is only used when the words are in the plural, but this looks very like an argument got up for the occasion.

The passage has been literally translated by Jews into Syriac and Greek, but it is easy to see that the literal sense would be attractive to other translators as well as to their own. The fact that the Jews practiced polygamy is urged in favor of the literal translation; but it no more proves that to be the true meaning of the passage, than it proves that polygamy is not contrary to the original institution of marriage, which was binding upon the Jews. Polygamy is inconsistent with the primary institution of marriage; the marriage of two sisters is inconsistent with the whole tenor of the same chapter; yet the literal translation allows both. This is a strong reason for preferring the idiomatic translation, which forbids one and says nothing about the other.

The words "to vex her," are an important part of the text, and must be taken into account in any sound interpretation. It seems certain that they imply that the forbidden action is forbidden during the life of the first wife and for her sake. In order to give these words a reasonable meaning it is necessary to adopt the idiomatic interpretation of the words "her sister." The literal translation leaves the man at liberty to marry any woman but his wife's sister, which would vex the first wife at least as much as if he married her sister. The text is then a direct prohibition of polygamy, in addition to the primary institution of marriage between one man and one woman.

§ 20. In answer to the argument that a woman would not be more vexed by the marriage of her husband to her sister than to a stranger, it has been supposed that the text in Leviticus owes its origin to the marriage of Jacob with two sisters. It is certain that Jacob was not happy in his domestic relations; but there is no reason for believing that the relation of sisters between his wives had any direct connection with that fact. The only way in which the two things can be said to be indirectly connected is, that the common parentage of the women led to the fraud, which was the cause of the polygamy. The fraud was perhaps felt as a grievance by Rachel. which she perhaps resented. Leah retaliated by taunts on the barrenness of Rachel, of whom she was jealous as the favorite wife. There is little or no reason to believe that Jacob's family was more disturbed than that of any other polygamist.

§ 21. Two interpretations of the text have been recently proposed. One of them, although in a somewhat different form, is really the same which has been already disposed of. In a debate in the Convocation of Canterbury,[1] Dr. Jelf said, with reference to this text, "If they took the words in their literal sense he would ask whether it must not be obvious that it related to a state of things not now existing, and was therefore not now applicable? It implied the prevalence of polygamy under the sort of half sanction given to it by the law of Moses, and prohibited the practice under particular circumstances." That is, it forbade marriage with a second sister in the lifetime of the first. In the same debate, Mr. Mayow said, "He thought they ran into a mistake if they took the marginal reading as an

[1] March 15, 1861.

absolute prohibition of polygamy. This, however, did not seem necessary to that reading, for it was very possible that the words 'to vex her' were more emphatic than was often supposed; so that the prohibition, taking the marginal reading, would then remain, that a man should take a wife to another in her lifetime to vex her, and this became almost a command that in the practice of polygamy a man should have reference to the wishes of a first wife, when he took the second. This would give a very good sense to the marginal reading, and would not clash with the law of Moses in which polygamy was winked at." The last proposition remains to be proved; and there are three other objections to this interpretation. It is quite new, it is very fanciful; and, what is of more importance than either, it clashes with the primitive law of marriage.

§ 22. In all discussions about polygamy in connection with the Mosaic law it is usual to assume that it was a very common practice among the Israelites who lived under that law. This seems to be a mistake. There were certainly some cases, chiefly among kings and great men. In the Book of Judges it is said that Gideon had threescore and ten sons, for he had many wives and concubines. Abimelech, one of his sons, was by a concubine, who was a maid-servant, or slave.[1] Jephthah seems to have sprung from the casual amour of a man who had but one wife.[2] Jephthah himself had but one child, and probably only one wife. Jair, Ibzan, and Abdon had each so many children that it is probable they were polygamists. But it is remarkable that Ibzan had thirty sons, for whom he took in thirty daughters from abroad. He took no more than one wife for each son.[3]

§ 23. These are all the cases of polygamy mentioned in the Book of Judges. In the Books of Samuel there is no instance of polygamy among private persons, except those

[1] Judges viii. 30, 31 ; ix. 18. [2] *Ibid.* xi. 1, 2.
[3] *Ibid.* x. 3, and xii. 8, *et seq.*

of Elkanah the father of Samuel, and David, who while still a private person had three wives. In fact there is no other instance, after the giving of the law, in any of the historical books. Elkanah "had two wives: the name of the one was Hannah, and the name of the other Peninnah, and Peninnah had children and Hannah had no children." [1] From the arrangement of the names it is probable that Hannah was the wife first taken, and that she proving barren, Elkanah took another for the sake of issue.

§ 24. The kings used polygamy freely, but it ought to be remembered that whether polygamy in other men were lawful or not, such polygamy as they practiced was specially unlawful for them. It cannot, therefore, be used as an argument for the lawfulness of polygamy. The prohibition follows: "When thou shalt come into the land which the Lord thy God giveth thee, and shall possess it, and shalt dwell therein, and shalt say, I will set a king over me, like as all the nations that are about me; thou shalt in any wise set him a king over thee whom the Lord thy God shall choose; one from among thy brethren shalt thou set king over thee; thou mayest not set a stranger over thee, which is not thy brother. But he shall not multiply horses to himself, nor cause the people to return to Egypt, to the end that he should multiply horses: forasmuch as the Lord hath said unto you, ye shall henceforth return no more that way. Neither shall he multiply wives to himself, that his heart turn not away; neither shall he greatly multiply to himself gold and silver.'" [2]

§ 25. There are some things in this passage which seem to refer to the election of Saul; but the precepts certainly were binding on all kings. It is not certain that Saul was a polygamist, although there is a Rabbinical tradition that he had six wives. In the Holy Scriptures there is no trace of them. It is said that the name of Saul's wife was Ahinoam, the daughter of Ahimaaz.[3] The form of expression

[1] 1 Samuel i. 1, 2. [2] Deuteronomy xvii. 14, *et seq.*
[3] 1 Samuel xiv. 50.

seems to imply that she was his only wife. No other equal wife of his is anywhere mentioned. He had three sons who were slain with him, and a fourth, Ishbosheth, who attempted to succeed him. He had also two daughters, Merab and Michal. This is not an unusual number of children for one woman. Saul had also a concubine, Rizpah, the daughter of Aiah; no other is mentioned, and he may have taken her after the death of Ahinoam. He had by her two more sons. A family of only eight children is not very consistent with the Rabbinical tradition of six wives. When David was called upon to put to death seven of Saul's posterity, to expiate the crime which Saul had committed against the Gibeonites, he could find none of his descendants in the male line, but the two sons of Rizpah, and Mephibosheth the son of his friend Jonathan. He therefore hanged, with the sons of Rizpah, five grandsons of Saul, by his daughter Merab, "whom she brought up for Barzillai, the Meholathite." [1]

It has been supposed that Saul must have had several wives, because Nathan reproached David that the Lord had given him his master's wives into his bosom.[2] Perhaps this is not to be understood literally. It seems to be a periphrasis for giving him the kingdom. It was a prerogative of an Eastern king to marry the wives of his predecessor, which no other person might do. Herodotus mentions instances of this among the Persians. The false Smerdis married the wives of Cambyses, and they were married a third time to Darius Hystaspes. That similar ideas prevailed among the Israelites, appears from two pas-

[1] 2 Samuel xxi. 7–9. The name of the unfortunate mother is Michal in our translation; but it was Merab who was married to Adriel the Meholathite, probably the same person with Barzillai.* Michal was the wife of David himself, and had lived for some time in adultery with Phaltiel the son of Laish, who was called her husband, until her return was demanded by David while he reigned in Hebron. She had no children.†

[2] 2 Samuel xii. 8.

* 1 Samuel xviii. 19. † 2 Samuel iii. 13–16.

sages in the Holy Scriptures. One is the anger of Ish-bosheth, because Abner had gone in unto Rizpah.[1] The other, which is more decisive, is the reply of Solomon to his mother when she asked Abishag for Adonijah, "Why dost thou ask Abishag the Shunamite for Adonijah? Ask for him the kingdom also." [2] Solomon considered the request so presumptuous that he put Adonijah to death for it.[3] David does not appear to have actually taken any woman who had been the wife of Saul; there is no mention of bringing the wives of Saul into David's house, nor is it said of any of his wives that she had been the wife of Saul. He could not have married Ahinoam, for he was married to Michal her daughter.[4] It seems certain that he did not take Rizpah. Upon the whole this passage does not prove that Saul was a polygamist.

§ 26. Many of his successors were certainly such. Those who carried the practice to the greatest extent were David, Solomon, and Rehoboam. After the death of Rehoboam there seems to have been comparatively little royal polygamy in Judah, although Joash is said to have had two wives.[5] The wives of some of the other kings are also spoken of in the plural number. Among the kings of Israel, Ahab is shown, by the number of his children, to have been a polygamist, in the sense of keeping concubines, though Jezebel seems to have been his only equal wife. There is little if any evidence of polygamy among the other kings of the ten tribes. It was the wife, not one of the wives of Jeroboam, who was sent to Abijah the Prophet.[6]

§ 27. It may then be concluded that although polygamy existed among the Israelites it was rather exceptional, especially after the irregular period of the Judges. It became an indulgence taken by kings, though directly against the

[1] 2 Samuel iii. 7.
[2] 1 Kings ii. 22.
[3] 1 Kings ii. 23–25.
[4] Leviticus xviii. 7.
[5] 2 Chronicles xxiv. 3.
[6] 1 Kings xiv.

law, and was sometimes adopted by the husbands of barren women.

§ 28. Whether polygamy were or were not common among the Jews, and whether it were or were not lawful for them, it is now, as has been already said, universally agreed among Christians that it is unlawful for them. The Scriptures furnish an abundant foundation for that opinion. Reference has been already made to the primary institution of marriage, and the commentaries upon it by the translators of the Septuagint and the inspired Prophet Malachi. It has been also mentioned, that our Blessed Saviour declared the primitive law to be Divine, and adopted the commentary of the Septuagint. It is thus sufficiently proved to be unlawful for a Christian man to have two wives at one time; but it may be well to say something more of the New Testament teaching upon the subject.

There are several passages bearing upon the question in the writings of St. Paul. One of them would by itself prove the unlawfulness of polygamy. It is: "Let every man have his own wife and every woman her own husband."[1] "The wife hath not power over her own body, but the husband: and likewise also the husband hath not power over his own body, but the wife."[2] In the second verse the Apostle expressly directs that each man shall have his own wife and each woman her own husband. The sexes are put upon an equality. It has never been supposed that it was lawful for a woman to have two husbands at once. Moreover, it is declared in the fourth verse, that she has the same power over, or interest in her husband, that he has in her. That interest is inconsistent with her having two husbands, and of course with his having two wives.

There are, notwithstanding, those who have cited other texts in St. Paul's writings, to show that polygamy is law-

[1] 1 Corinthians vii. 2. [2] *Ibid.* 4.

ful for lay Christians. The texts are these: "A bishop must be blameless, the husband of one wife;"[1] "Let the deacons be the husbands of one wife."[2] Instructing Titus as to the qualifications of an elder, he writes: "If any be blameless, the husband of one wife."[3] These texts nearly repeat each other. The result of the whole is that a clergyman may have only one wife. From this it has been hastily inferred that a lay Christian may have more. This can hardly be the true meaning. There is no mention in any writer, sacred or profane, of polygamy among the Jews after the Captivity. There is no reason to believe that it was either lawful or common among the Greeks. To the Romans it was utterly unknown throughout their whole history. The Christian converts at Ephesus belonged to one of those three nations. It would have been difficult to find among them, or indeed in the civilized world, candidates for orders who were polygamists. That interpretation is clearly wrong which regards those texts as imposing monogamy upon the clergy only. Another interpretation is that they forbid the ordaining of a man who, having divorced his wife for adultery, has married another in her lifetime. This, however, seems scarcely satisfactory.

The Eastern Church, from a very early period, if not from the first, has interpreted these texts as directing that a clergyman should have only one wife during his whole lifetime, although a lay widower might marry again. Perhaps this interpretation, though not without difficulties, is the true one. It has not, however, been received by the Anglican or any other Western Communion, and is practically disregarded by modern clergymen. It does not seem to be necessary to attempt a solution of the difficulty in the present treatise. It is sufficient to say that the non-existence of polygamy in the nations among whom the

[1] 1 Timothy iii. 2. [2] *Ibid.* 12. [3] Titus i. 6.

Gospel was first promulged, shows that the texts cannot be so interpreted as to give countenance to that sin.

§ 29. It may be well to conclude the chapter with bringing together the teaching of our Blessed Lord upon its subject. On one occasion He said: "Have ye not heard that He which made them at the beginning made them male and female, and said: For this cause shall a man leave father and mother and shall cleave to his wife; and they twain shall be one flesh."[1]

Another Evangelist reports Him as saying: "But from the beginning of the creation God created them male and female. For this cause shall a man leave father and mother and cleave to his wife, and they twain shall be one flesh; so they are no more twain but one flesh."[2]

This is sufficient proof that marriage cannot exist between more than two persons, but it is not all that can be adduced. There are four places in the Gospels, in which our blessed Lord speaks of marriage, and every one of them is conclusive against polygamy. Two of them have been just cited, but their whole force has not been brought out. In connection with the text just quoted from St. Matthew, our Lord said: "Whosoever shall put away his wife, except it be for fornication, and shall marry another, committeth adultery."[3]

So in connection with the passage quoted from St. Mark will be found the following words of our Lord: "Whosoever shall put away his wife and marry another committeth adultery against her; and if a woman shall put away her husband and be married to another, she committeth adultery."[4]

In the Sermon on the Mount, our Lord says: "Whosoever shall put away his wife saving for the cause of fornication, causeth her to commit adultery; and whosoever shall marry her that is put away committeth adultery."[5]

[1] Matthew xix. 4–6. [2] Mark x. 6–8. [3] Matthew xix. 9.
[4] Mark x. 11, 12. [5] Matthew v. 32.

In St. Luke's Gospel there is only one verse on the subject of marriage. Like the other passages, it is in the words of our Saviour: "Whosoever putteth away his wife and marrieth another committeth adultery: and whosoever marrieth her that is put away from her husband committeth adultery."[1]

In all four passages it is assumed that having two wives or two husbands at the same time is adultery; and it is declared that the putting away makes no difference in the sin. He who puts away his wife and marries, and she who is put away and married, and he who marries her that is put away, are all declared to be guilty of adultery. This can only be because the putting away does not dissolve the marriage. But if the old marriage, notwithstanding the attempt to dissolve it, rendered a second unlawful and adulterous, it must have had the same effect if there had been no attempt at divorce. The divorce could make no change in the original nature of the marriage. If it be adultery to marry a second wife in the lifetime of a first who has been put away, it must be adultery to marry a second woman without putting away the first.

This argument scarcely requires to be strengthened, but it does strengthen it to observe that it was never held lawful for a woman to have two husbands at once; and that in the passage in St. Mark's Gospel, the husband and wife are put upon the same footing. The strength of the argument against polygamy is this. It is four times declared by our Blessed Lord, that to marry a second wife in the lifetime of the first is adultery. The inference that polygamy is unlawful is irresistible.

[1] Luke xvi. 18.

CHAPTER VII.

OF THE PRACTICAL ELEMENTS OF MARRIAGE. — II. INDISSOLUBLENESS. 1. THE RULE.

§ 1. Another of the practical elements of marriage is indissolubleness. It entered into the primary institution of marriage, and it remained for a long time one of the customs of many nations. Divorce seems to have been unknown to the Greeks in the time of Homer. Among many other nations, however, the idea of indissolubleness was early lost. The law given by Moses does not very strictly enforce it, and it does not seem to have been much regarded among the Jews. It is now scarcely acknowledged by any non-Christian nation. It is losing ground among those Christian nations which claim to have made hte most progress in civilization, in the United States as well as in others. There is the more need of pressing upon the public the great fact that God has decreed that marriage shall be indissoluble.

Indissoluble means something more than permanent. Permanent means that the thing spoken of will endure under ordinary circumstances, but not that it may not be brought to an end. Indissoluble generally means that the thing spoken of cannot be dissolved or brought to an end. The marriage tie is divinely instituted, and can only be dissolved by Divine authority, and so is in a sufficient sense indissoluble. It cannot be dissolved by any human authority. It is not inconsistent with this that there should be a particular case, in which the Divine Law authorizes the dissolution of a marriage.

§ 2. The principle of the indissolubleness of marriage has become very unpopular. It is easy to account for this. There are two modes in which evils may be dealt with. One is to prevent their occurrence by suffering people to feel their consequences; the other is to mitigate their consequences at the risk of increasing the number of cases. The one looks to the general diminution of evil; the other to the comfort of unfortunate persons. The first seems to be the Divine, the second the human mode. God provides that suffering shall follow evil doing. Man seeks only to diminish human suffering.

The laws by which the world is governed annex suffering to evil-doing as its natural consequence, not merely as judicial punishment. The suffering grows naturally out of the conduct of the sufferer; sometimes out of conduct which men admit to be wicked; sometimes out of conduct which they regard as imprudent; sometimes out of conduct which they consider only mistaken. Where it arises from imprudence or mistakes, and even when it arises from misconduct, it often bears such a proportion to its cause as is very startling to the minds of men. Disease and death are sometimes incurred by actions or omissions which would scarcely be called ill-advised. Such are the laws of God, which men call the laws of nature; but which are really ordained of God. It is not enough to say carelessly, as men sometimes will, that they are ordained for wise purposes; it must be felt that they are ordained for good and wise purposes which man is utterly unable to comprehend.

God sees that those laws produce good, while they seem to man only to work evil. God at once sees and comprehends the whole universe and everything in it, and the connections and relations among them throughout all duration. Man is confined to a partial and one-sided view of a very few things, and to a very slender knowledge of their relations to each other, while he has absolutely no knowledge of their relations to the whole. It is therefore impossible for him to learn the reasons of the inflexibility of the laws of nature and the uniformity with which effects follow their causes, although they may crush sentient beings in their way. But it may be reverently conjectured that one motive of the Framer of these laws is to make men careful how they act.

§ 3. The Divine law, which decrees that a marriage once formed shall not be dissolved, has an analogy to the physical laws which have been just mentioned. It fixes upon those who enter into the marriage state the consequences of their irrevocable choice. It thus warns them that they must be careful how and with whom they form connections, which are at once close and indissoluble; but the lesson is not always learned. Some persons marry from improper motives, and some marry carelessly, without knowing anything of those to whom they commit their happiness in this world, and perhaps in the next. They thus unite themselves to persons who are unfit to be husbands or wives. The laws of nature follow their settled course. Misery ensues. Nothing, not even the dissolution of the marriage, can prevent or undo the evil. Yet it is supposed that in particular cases some mitigation may be found in a separation.

§ 4. Man is generally willing to relieve distress, especially in particular cases which touch his feelings; for he sees things only in their relation to the particular case. He can neither see nor understand the relations of anything to the whole. He would never enforce any inflexible law, because he could not see the beneficial effects of the rule, and would be moved by the sufferings of particular persons. He would never have ordained that marriage should be indissoluble. He sees the evils of ill-assorted marriages in particular cases, and in each case he desires to relieve the sufferers. He cannot see the effect of the inflexible rule upon the whole amount of happiness in the world; to measure that is beyond the compass of the human intellect. Men and women suffer from the consequences of their own guilty imprudence. They earnestly desire to be relieved, and other men desire to relieve them. Human law-makers sympathize with them, and laws are passed providing for the dissolution of marriages.

§ 5. The framers of such laws forget or deny the Divine institution of marriage, and reason on grounds of human knowledge and experience. They come to the conclusion, that ill-assorted marriages ought to be dissolved, because they see that there are many unhappy marriages. They do not know how many unhappy matches are prevented by the caution which the rule of indissolubleness enforces, or rather, how many would be prevented if the rule were not interfered with. If they did, they could not strike the balance; because no human mind could receive at one time all the particulars and compare them. All human reasoning must be inconclusive on such subjects, for all the facts cannot be collected; and if they could, they would be too many and too various to be dealt with by the human mind. There remains nothing but to rest in faith upon the Divine wisdom, as revealed in God's holy Word. Modern law-makers prefer their own, and so immoral laws will be made. This work is addressed to those who profess to receive God's revelation with faith, and to govern themselves by its precepts. It remains to show to such persons that the revealed Will of God declares marriage indissoluble.

In doing this, there will be occasion to do little more than to transcribe the very words of Holy Scripture. The passages will be very much the same as those which have been used to establish the exclusiveness of marriage. They will be taken in the order in which they occur in the Bible. The first will be the account of the primary institution of marriage which has so often been quoted in this work: "And the Lord God caused a deep sleep to fall upon Adam, and he slept; and He took one of his ribs, and closed up the flesh instead thereof; and the rib which the Lord God had taken from man made He a woman, and brought her unto the man. And Adam said: This is now bone of my bone and flesh of my flesh; she shall be called Woman, because she was taken out of Man; therefore shall a man leave his father and his mother, and shall cleave unto his wife, and they shall be one flesh." [1] It has been already observed that on this occasion Adam spoke by inspiration, and that our Blessed Saviour recognizes his words as those of God. The highest sanction is thus given to the doctrine of unity in marriage, which is so strongly expressed in the words, "they two shall be one flesh." Such an unity cannot, in the nature of things, be dissoluble.

§ 6. It is probable that this text was so understood from the first, and the idea prevailed for a long time that marriage was indissoluble. Throughout the whole Book of Genesis there is no allusion to divorce. Both Abraham and Isaac passed their wives for their sisters, lest they should be put to death by those who might desire them. The idea that the Gentile kings might compel them to divorce their wives does not seem to have occurred to them. Divorce was known and practiced among the Israelites soon after the Exodus, and was perhaps learned by

[1] Genesis ii. 21–24.

them in Egypt. Very little is known of other nations at that time.

§ 7. The words spoken by Adam received an inspired commentary from the Prophet Malachi. He says: "Yet ye say; Wherefore? Because the Lord hath been witness between thee and the wife of thy youth, against whom thou hast dealt treacherously; yet is she thy companion and the wife of thy covenant. And did not He make one? Yet had He the residue of the Spirit. And wherefore one? That He might seek a godly seed. Therefore take heed to your spirit, and let none deal treacherously against the wife of his youth. For the Lord, the God of Israel, saith, that He hateth putting away: for one covereth violence with his garment, saith the Lord of Hosts: therefore take heed to your spirit, that ye deal not treacherously." [1]

The prophet introduces God himself as saying that "the Lord God of Israel hateth putting away." This is to be connected with the creation of only one woman, and the oneness of the flesh, which Adam declared as between himself and his wife, and prophesied, or commanded, between all future men and their wives. Moreover, putting away is pronounced to be dealing treacherously. Perhaps the passage may receive emphasis from looking back to the verses which immediately precede it. The passage which has been transcribed is a kind of dialogue, in which the prophet supposes questions to be asked, to which he gives answers. It begins: "Yet ye say, 'Wherefore?'" To what does the wherefore refer? To the preceding verses; they are these: "Judah hath dealt treacherously, and an abomination is committed in Israel and Jerusalem; for Judah hath profaned the holiness of the Lord, which He loved, and hath married the daughter of a strange god. The Lord will cut off the man that doeth this, the master and the scholar, out of the tabernacles of Jacob, nd him that offereth an offering unto the Lord of Hosts.

[1] Malachi ii. 14-16.

And this have ye done again, covering the altar of the Lord with tears, with weeping, and with crying out, insomuch that He regardeth not the offering any more, or receiveth it with good-will at your hand." [1]

What is the treachery with which Judah is charged? Profaning the holiness of the Lord, which He loved, and marrying the daughter of a strange god. This has been supposed to have been a mode of speaking of idolatry. But idolatry did not prevail among the Jews after the Captivity. If they had been in the habit of committing idolatry they would not have asked the prophet wherefore he charged them with that sin. The offense was not merely marrying the daughter of a strange god; it involved cruelty. It covered the altar of the Lord "with tears, with weeping, and with crying out." This was the altar of the Lord, and not that of the strange god. The cruelty was not then the offering of human sacrifices, which, moreover, were not usual at that period. The offense also involved treachery, "Judah hath dealt treacherously."

After these statements, the prophet introduces the Jews as asking, "Wherefore?" This may mean: Wherefore do you bring these charges against us? or, wherefore will the Lord not regard our offering or receive it at our hands? The answer is, Because "the Lord hath been witness between thee and the wife of thy youth, with whom thou hast dealt treacherously." This treachery is explained to have been putting away a person, who is described as the wife of thy youth, "who was thy companion and the wife of thy covenant." Whatever may be the precise point of the question, it is clear that the Lord will not regard the offering of him that putteth away his wife. With this testimony to the indissoluble character of marriage the Old Testament leaves the subject.

§ 8. The Old Testament leaves it at its very close. The New Testament takes it up at its very beginning, in a man-

[1] Malachi ii. 11-13.

ner which is decisive of the question. Our Blessed Lord, in his Sermon on the Mount, says: "It hath been said, Whosoever shall put away his wife, let him give her a writing of divorcement; but I say unto you, that whosoever shall put away his wife, saving for the cause of fornication, causeth her to commit adultery, and whosoever shall marry her that is divorced committeth adultery." [1]

The man who puts away his wife is said by our Blessed Lord to cause her to commit adultery. But in what sense are the words to be taken? The man does not compel, or even solicit the woman to commit adultery. He can only be said to cause her to commit the sin because he exposes her to great temptation. But how is it possible that she can commit adultery? The man has done what he could to dissolve the marriage. If it be dissolved, she is no longer a married woman, and can only commit adultery with a married man, to which she is in no greater temptation than other women. But our Lord had specially in view a second marriage, for He says: "Whosoever shall marry her that is divorced committeth adultery." A second marriage, then, is for her adultery. The first has not been dissolved. The attempt of the husband to dissolve it failed, because it was indissoluble. If it were dissoluble, she would be a single woman, and she might marry whom she pleased. It may perhaps be said, that the word adultery is used for fornication, and that the divorced woman is placed in a situation in which she is liable to fall into fornication. But if she could marry, she would be no more liable to commit fornication than another woman; yet for her, marriage is declared to be adultery, or fornication, if that word is preferred. Why is this? Because she is under a bond of marriage, which has created that unity which cannot be dissolved.

§ 9. In another part of the same Gospel there is recorded a conversation between our Lord and certain Pharisees. "The Pharisees," says the Evangelist, "also came unto

[1] Matthew v. 31, 32.

Him, tempting Him, and saying unto Him: Is it lawful for a man to put away his wife for every cause? And He answered and said unto them: Have ye not read that He which made them at the beginning, made them male and female, and said: For this cause shall a man leave father and mother and shall cleave to his wife, and they twain shall be one flesh. . . . . What therefore God hath joined together, let not man put asunder. They say unto Him: Why did Moses then command to give a writing of divorcement, and to put her away? He saith unto them: Moses, because of the hardness of your hearts, suffered you to put away your wives; but from the beginning it was not so. And I say unto you whosoever shall put away his wife, except it be for fornication, and shall marry another, committeth adultery, and whoso marrieth her which is put away doth commit adultery." [1]

Our Blessed Lord here answers the insidious question of the Pharisees by recalling to their minds the primary institution of marriage, insisting on the unity involved in that institution, and thus showing that marriage is in its nature indissoluble. He draws the inference, that God hath united the married couple, and winds up with the solemn precept: "What God hath joined let not man put asunder." The whole taken together is perhaps as strong an assertion of the doctrine, that marriage cannot be dissolved, as could be framed.

The Pharisees so understood it and objected the authority of Moses. Our Lord replied, that Moses permitted divorce on account of the hardness of their hearts, but that it was not consistent with the primary institution. He then repeats, with some alteration, what He had said in the Sermon on the Mount: "And I say unto you: Whosoever shall put away his wife, except it be for the cause of fornication, and shall marry another, committeth adultery; and whoso marrieth her which is put away, committeth adultery." The

[1] Matthew xix. 3–9.

husband who puts away his wife cannot marry again without committing adultery, and none can marry her which is put away without committing adultery; because the first marriage has not been dissolved. He who put the woman away, and she who was put away, are still man and wife; for the marriage could not be dissolved.

The divorced persons cannot marry without committing adultery, and none can intermarry with either of them without committing adultery. There are many persons in American society who have been divorced according to the State laws. They are divorced for all civil purposes, but they are still married in the sight of God. It is for men and women to consider before they put themselves in such a situation; and it is for other men and women to remember that they cannot marry without committing adultery, and that none can marry them without committing adultery.

§ 10. Another Evangelist gives an account of a conversation, which is often supposed to be the same, although there are strong reasons for believing that it is a different one. St. Mark says: "And the Pharisees came to Him and asked Him: Is it lawful for a man to put away his wife? tempting Him. And He answered and said unto them: What did Moses command you? And they said: Moses suffered to write a bill of divorcement, and to put her away. And Jesus answered and said unto them: For the hardness of your heart he wrote you this precept, but from the beginning of the creation God made them male and female. For this cause shall a man leave his father and mother, and cleave to his wife, and they twain shall be one flesh; so then they are no more twain, but one flesh. What therefore God hath joined together let not man put asunder. And in the house His disciples asked him again of the same matter. And He saith unto them: Whosoever shall put away his wife, and marry another, committeth adultery against her; and if a woman shall put away her husband, and be married to another, she committeth adultery." [1]

[1] Mark x. 2–12.

§ 11. This passage is sometimes supposed to be another report of the conversation reported by St. Matthew. It is possible that it may be so, although there are great differences between the two reports; in fact they are absolutely unlike; so much so, that it is very improbable that they relate to the same conversation. The doctrine, with one remarkable exception, is the same, and it is not important whether it was promulgated once or twice. The forms of the two conversations are, however, very different. In one, what relates to the Law of Moses precedes, and in the other follows that which relates to the primary institution of marriage. But in both, our Saviour refers to the primary institution as conclusive of the question, and adds the precept, that man should not put asunder what God hath joined. Here St. Mark closes his account of the conversation with the Pharisees. St. Matthew adds the statement, that it is adultery for divorced persons to marry.

St. Mark introduces this doctrine into a private conversation with the disciples, which occurred after the more public discussion with the Pharisees. But the words are not the same as in St. Matthew, and the important exception to the rule is omitted. St. Matthew says: "Whosoever shall put away his wife, except it be for fornication, and shall marry another, committeth adultery; and whoso marrieth her which is put away doth commit adultery." St. Mark says: "Whosoever shall put away his wife, and marry another, committeth adultery against her. And if a woman shall put away her husband, and be married to another, she committeth adultery."

§ 12. There are three differences between those two statements, besides those relating to the persons to whom, and the place in which the words were spoken. One is the omission of the exception. This is the doctrinal difference, of which mention has been made. It is a matter requiring a good deal of consideration, which it will secure in another chapter. The second is, that the husband who puts away his wife and marries another is said, in St. Mark, to commit adultery against her. This is a stronger and more pointed affirmation of the continuance of the marriage, notwithstanding the divorce, than that in St. Matthew. The third is, that St. Mark says nothing of the case of a woman who has been put away, which is mentioned by St. Matthew. Instead of it, there is introduced the case of a woman who has put away her husband, and has been married again. Such a woman is declared guilty of adultery; which is a new illustration of the doctrine, that the marriage tie cannot be loosened.

The most remarkable differences between the Evangelists relate to the conversation with the disciples. They both give an account of such a conversation having taken place after that with the Pharisees, but they give it in very different forms. It has been just quoted from St. Mark. St. Matthew reports it as follows: "His disciples say unto Him: If the case of a man be so with his wife, it is not good to marry. But He said unto them: All men cannot receive this saying, save they to whom it is given. For there are some eunuchs which were so born from their mother's womb; and there are some eunuchs which were made eunuchs of men; and there be eunuchs which have made themselves eunuchs for the kingdom of heaven's sake. He that is able to receive it let him receive it." [1]

In St. Matthew the disciples begin by objecting to the doctrine of indissoluble marriage. In St. Mark they merely ask Him again of the same matter. In St. Matthew our Lord admits the difficulty with which His doctrine besets the entrance into marriage; but adds, that to a large part of mankind it is a necessity. There are those, He intimates, who either from natural constitution, or the effects of violence, or by the aid of Divine grace, are freed from that necessity. Such men can receive the saying, that it is not good to marry. Other men, who cannot receive that

[1] Matthew xix. 10–12.

saying, and to whom it seems good to marry, must take the Divine law, as He has laid it down. If they must, or will marry, they must marry indissolubly. According to St. Mark, our Lord merely delivered to the disciples the doctrine which, according to St. Matthew, He had delivered to the Pharisees, a little expanded. The marked differences in the accounts of the two Evangelists seem to prove that there were two different conversations. It would follow that there were two different conversations with the Pharisees. Both Evangelists, however, teach with one exception the same doctrine in nearly the same words.

§ 13. There is only one other verse in the four Gospels which touches upon this matter. It is part of a public discourse delivered by our Lord, and is in these words: "Whosoever putteth away his wife and marrieth another committeth adultery, and whosoever marrieth her that is put away from her husband committeth adultery." [1] This text does not require that anything more should be said of it, than that it is a repetition of the ninth verse of the nineteenth chapter of the Gospel according to St. Matthew, only omitting the exception therein contained.

§ 14. There are two or three passages in the writings of St. Paul which teach the indissoluble nature of marriage. One of them is this: "The woman which hath an husband is bound by the law to her husband so long as he liveth; but if her husband be dead, she is loosed from the law of her husband. So then if while her husband liveth, she be married to another man, she shall be called an adulteress; but if her husband be dead, she is free from the law, so that she is no adulteress though she be married to another man." [2]

§ 15. The greater part of the seventh chapter of the first Epistle to the Corinthians is a kind of treatise on marriage. Portions of this chapter may be passed over in this place, although they must be examined in another. But there are two which must be mentioned here. One of them is:

[1] Luke xvi. 18. [2] Romans vii. 2, 3.

"Unto the married I command, yet not I, but the Lord; let not the wife depart from her husband, but and if she depart, let her remain unmarried, or be reconciled to her husband, and let not the husband put away his wife."[1] The other is: "The wife is bound by the law as long as her husband liveth; but if her husband be dead, she is at liberty to be married to whom she will, only in the Lord."[2]

§ 16. There remains the remarkable passage in the Epistle to the Ephesians, in which the unity of the married pair is likened to that which exists between our Blessed Lord and his Church; it is a fair inference, that as one of those unities is indissoluble so is the other: "Husbands, love your wives, even as Christ also loved the Church, and gave Himself for it, that He might sanctify and cleanse it with the washing of water by the Word, that He might present it to Himself a glorious Church, not having spot or wrinkle, or any such thing; but that it should be holy and without blemish. So ought men to love their wives as their own bodies. He that loveth his wife loveth himself. For no man ever yet hated his own flesh, but nourisheth and cherisheth it, even as the Lord the Church; for we are members of His body, of His flesh, and of His bones. For this cause shall a man leave his father and mother and shall be joined unto his wife, and they two shall be one flesh. This is a great mystery, but I speak concerning Christ and the Church."[3]

The Apostle, in speaking of Christ and the Church, adopts the language of Adam when speaking of the relation between himself and his wife. "This," said Adam, "is now bone of my bone and flesh of my flesh." The Apostle says: "We," that is the members of the Church, "are members of His body, His flesh, and of His bones." Both then proceed to the precept which involves a doctrine, that a man shall leave his father and his mother and shall cleave unto his wife, and they two shall be one flesh.

§ 17. These are the principal, if not all the texts in the

[1] 1 Corinthians vii. 10, 11. [2] *Ibid.* 39. [3] Ephesians v. 25-32.

Bible, which teach that a marriage once entered into cannot be dissolved. It seems to be established by them as fully as any other doctrine of our holy religion can be established by any texts whatever. They all agree in forbidding man to put asunder what God has joined, and apply the precept to the case of a man and his wife. Our Blessed Lord utters the direct precept more than once. The context contains a prohibition of uniting either of the parties to another. But notwithstanding the common opinion, that is not the whole meaning of the text. What is directly forbidden is the separation; the unlawfulness of marrying again is the consequence of the unlawfulness of separation. The common notion that it is allowable for married persons to separate whenever they think fit, provided they do not marry again, is contradicted by the very words of our Saviour, "What God hath joined let not man put asunder." This is not generally observed, and it seems to be almost a universal opinion that the thing forbidden is the marrying another person after separation, and that the separation itself is lawful. Yet the separation alone is a direct breach of the precept.

§ 18. It involves moreover all the evils but one, which are involved in the permission to marry again. A man or woman who separates from his or her husband or wife and does not marry again, does not commit adultery; that is, does not add a second sin to the first. This is the only difference between separation and that which is called a divorce from the bond of marriage. The true bond of marriage is severed when the married couple begin to live separately. The separated couple do not cleave to each other. Neither has the comfort of the other's society. The wife does not help or advise the husband. The husband does not govern or protect the wife. The reason assigned by St. Paul, why men should have wives and women husbands, is disregarded.[1] The children lose all the benefits

[1] 1 Corinthians vii. 2.

to which they are entitled from one of their parents, and many of those to which they are entitled from the other. To restrain, therefore, as the public opinion of this country does, the text which forbids man from putting asunder what God hath joined, to such a putting asunder as will allow the separated persons to marry again, is to take an unwarrantable liberty with Holy Writ.

§ 19. Marriage involves an obligation not to marry again during the life of the person with whom it has been contracted; but it also involves a great deal more. When a married couple live separately, the marriage is, for all practical purposes, dissolved. This is not less true because they are restrained from marrying. The effect of the restriction is merely negative. All the positive duties of marriage are abandoned. Both the married persons are obliged to live in celibacy; they are married only in name. Such a condition involves great evils, which are, in this country, too little regarded. The great mass of the people do not know or do not regard the Divine prohibition to separate man and wife. Those who do, generally consider it as only a prohibition of marriage to the separated persons, a merely non-natural interpretation, which both formally disregards the words of Holy Scripture and renders them practically of none effect.

§ 20. It is frequently said that if people cannot agree they had better separate; but that is not the principle of Christian marriage. The Christian doctrine is that marriage cannot be dissolved, and that the parties must cleave to each other. Experience shows that people are less like to disagree when they must live and act together. When they have no other resource they will think of curbing their passions and of mutual concessions. The possibility of separation is an encouragement to obstinacy. It is the nature of man to exaggerate the present inconvenience, and to look with less dislike upon that which is not actually felt. It is therefore important that when married persons find it difficult to agree, it should be present to their minds that separation is sinful, and therefore impossible. The power of flying from the ills we have to others that we know not of, is a dangerous power. Some persons may object to this reasoning, that it is hardly within the compass of the human mind to measure the good and evil which arise from a rule of morals, and still less to measure those which may arise from changing one rule for another. This is true, but the rule which forbids the separation of man and wife is prescribed by Infinite Wisdom.

§ 21. The true intent of forbidding man to separate what God hath joined, is to prevent the separation of married persons, not merely to prevent them from marrying other persons after a separation. This may be proved by several texts. In the Sermon on the Mount, our blessed Lord said, "Whosoever shall put away his wife, saving for the cause of fornication, causeth her to commit adultery."[1] How does he cause her to commit adultery? By exposing her to temptation. Temptation to what, to marry? No, to commit adultery. True marriage is, in her case, a form of adultery; but it is not the only form. She who is separated from her husband is exposed to temptation to adultery in those other forms, and more, not less, if she cannot marry. To this temptation she is exposed by her husband who has put her away. She is living practically in an unmarried state, and thus she is exposed to temptations to the sins of the flesh, which in her are adultery. From those temptations she cannot escape like other women by marrying. It is the judgment of our Saviour, that to these temptations she is peculiarly liable. She cannot marry, but she can commit adultery. Her temptations to do so are so strong, that our Lord declares that he who exposes her to them "causeth her to commit adultery."

§ 22. It will be better, on several accounts, to give an exposition of this passage in the words of St. Paul, who

[1] Matthew v. 32.

writes thus: "Nevertheless, to avoid fornication let every man have his own wife and let every woman have her own husband. Let the husband render unto the wife due benevolence, and likewise also the wife unto the husband. The wife hath not power of her own body, but the husband; and likewise the husband hath not power of his own body, but the wife. Defraud ye not one the other, except it be by consent for a time, that ye may give yourselves to fasting and prayer, and come together again, that Satan tempt ye not for your incontinency."[1] Here is a direct prohibition of separation, without any reference to marrying again. The reason assigned for it seems to be the same with that which is given by our Lord in the Sermon on the Mount.

§ 23. In the same chapter is this passage: "Unto the married I command, yet not I but the Lord: let not the wife depart from her husband; but and if she depart, let her remain unmarried, or let her be reconciled to her husband, and let not the husband put away his wife."[2] The Apostle says: "I command, yet not I but the Lord:" by which he seems to mean that the words he is about to write are an inspired comment on some words of the Lord. The words commented on seem to be some of those recorded in the tenth chapter of St. Mark's Gospel: "What God hath joined together let not man put asunder." And again, "Whosoever shall put away his wife and marry another, committeth adultery against her; and if a woman shall put away her husband and be married to another, she committeth adultery." The text last quoted seems to contain rather the revelation of a doctrine than a precept. The prohibition to put asunder what God had joined had been already delivered, and our blessed Lord now reveals the truth, that putting asunder a man and his wife, does not release them from the guilt of adultery, should they marry again. St. Paul puts this doctrine into the form of a precept. He first delivers two precepts, which taken together

[1] 1 Corinthians vii. 2–5. [2] *Ibid.* vii. 10, 11.

repeat our Lord's precept: "Let not the woman depart from her husband." "Let not the man put away his wife." He then puts our Lord's doctrine into a third precept: "But and if she depart let her remain unmarried." This is in substance the same with, "If a woman shall put away her husband and be married to another she committeth adultery." St. Paul's arrangement throws light upon the words of our Lord, by showing them in a different point of view, and treating them all as precepts. It thus appears that there are two separate and distinct precepts involved in the words of our Lord. A woman must not depart from her husband; but if she be so ill-advised as to do so, she is met by another precept, which forbids her to marry. Marrying is forbidden in a distinct and separate precept. She is forbidden to leave her husband, and if she has done so, she is commanded to be reconciled to him. If she choose to disobey both of those precepts, she is still to remain unmarried.

§ 24. The verses which immediately follow those transcribed into the last section from St. Paul are these: "But to the rest speak I, not the Lord: If any brother hath a wife, that believeth not, and she be pleased to dwell with him, let him not put her away. And the woman which hath a husband that believeth not, and if he be pleased to dwell with her, let her not leave him. For the unbelieving husband is sanctified by the wife, and the unbelieving wife is sanctified by the husband; else were your children unclean, but now are they holy. But if the unbelieving depart, let him depart. A brother or a sister is not under bondage in such cases; but God hath called us to peace."[1] Here the Apostle says: "To the rest speak I, not the Lord." It is not to be supposed that by this he meant to admit that he was not writing by inspiration. He had before said, "I command, yet not I but the Lord." The two expressions are to be taken together. In the first instance

[1] 1 Corinthians vii. 12–15.

he was repeating a precept, which had issued from the lips of our Lord; but what he is now about to say is nothing more than an application of our Lord's doctrine to a particular case, — that of a Christian unequally yoked with an unbeliever. Even in this case, the Apostle decides that the law which forbids separation applies. The Christian woman is not to leave her heathen husband; the Christian man is not to put away his heathen wife. They have been joined by the God, whom then they knew not, and the bond is not dissolved because one of them has learned to know Him. They were joined, although they were heathens. They are not to be put asunder because one of them has become a Christian. All that the Apostle allows is that, if the heathen insist upon a separation, the Christian may acquiesce without sin; he or she is not under bondage. Such and so strict is the Christian Law which forbids the separation of man and wife. So far is it from countenancing the popular notion, that married persons may agree to separate, if they do not marry again.

§ 25. Such separations were not known in ancient times. The marriage tie seems never to have been left as a mere negative restraint. Whenever a woman was separated from her husband, she was regarded as at liberty to marry.

In the words of the Book of Deuteronomy: "She may go and be another man's wife." It is quite clear from an examination of the Mosaic Law, that the Divine lawgiver preferred an entire dissolution of the marriage tie permitting the parties to marry, to such a half dissolution as left a mere negative restriction, while all its positive obligations were taken away or disregarded.

The precept given by Moses, of which our Lord several times spoke, is this: "When a man hath taken a wife, and married her, and it come to pass that she find no favor in his eyes, because he hath found some uncleanness in her; then let him write her a bill of divorcement, and give it in her hand, and send her out of his house; and when she is departed out of his house, she may go and be another man's wife. And if the latter husband hate her, and write her a bill of divorcement, and giveth it into her hand and sendeth her out of his house; or if the latter husband die, which took her to be his wife, her former husband, which sent her away, may not take her again to be his wife, after that she hath been defiled, for that is an abomination before the Lord; and thou shalt not cause the land to sin, which the Lord thy God giveth thee for an inheritance."[1]

Any separation except one which involves the power of marrying is here forbidden. If a man have a wife who finds no favor in his eyes, and from whom he desires to separate, he must pursue a particular course, which is very precisely detailed twice in the compass of four verses. He may not send her out of his house without a bill of divorcement, and when he does send her out with such a bill, she may go and be another man's wife. In practice, the bill of divorcement was always written in a prescribed form which contains an express permission to the divorced woman to marry. The bill of divorcement was called in Hebrew, *Get.* The essential part of it, says the Mishna, is the following words: "Thou art herewith permitted to be married to any other man." The Rabbi Jehudah says the following is the essential part: "Thou hast here from me a writing of separation and a document of dismissal, that thou mayest go and be married to any man thou mayest like."[2] Whatever was the form of the writing, the law was express that the divorced woman might marry. When the husband had given it to his wife, he might send her out of his house. "And when she is departed out of his house, she may go and be another man's wife." If the latter husband divorce her, she may be married to any man except her former husband.

§ 26. This law is said by our Saviour, to have been

[1] Deuteronomy xxiv. 1–4.

[2] Robinson's *Evangelists and Mishna*, p. 33.

given by Moses to the children of Israel for the hardness of their hearts. Some writers have supposed that our Lord's meaning was that the hardness of their hearts was such that they would kill or ill-treat wives who had found no favor in their sight. If the cruelty of the husband during the marriage was the evil to be dreaded, a more obvious mode of protection would have been to give to the wife power to divorce her husband. It seems more likely that the grievance against which the law was directed, was that of sending a woman out of the house into the world, subject to all the temptations and hardships of single life, without the power of seeking protection from a husband. The Divine Lawgiver foresaw that the hardness of their hearts would be such that they would turn their wives out-of-doors. He preferred that women in that condition should have the power of marrying, although it was not so from the beginning. This was a departure from the Divine law of marriage which He only could authorize, and which He did authorize because men, in the hardness of their hearts, would not submit to the primitive law. The care which was taken to secure to the divorced woman the privilege of marrying, shows this.

§ 27. Our blessed Saviour does not authorize the cruelty which the law of Moses forbade. He recalls marriage to its primitive institution, when no separation of any sort was allowed. He renews the command that a man shall cleave to his wife, repeats the doctrine that they are one flesh, and introduces the precept that because of that doctrine men should not put them asunder. He thus forbids altogether any kind of separation. He further declares that if any one, disregarding his prohibition, shall put away his wife and marry another, he will be guilty of adultery.

In the Sermon on the Mount, he does not refer to the primitive institution, or deliver the precept which he elsewhere pronounces to be an inference from it. He there says: "It hath been said, whosoever shall put away his wife, let him give her a writing of divorcement; but I say unto you that whosoever shall put away his wife, saving for the cause of fornication, causeth her to commit adultery; and whosoever shall marry her that is divorced committeth adultery."[1]

Moses forbade all putting away without a bill of divorcement; that is, all putting away unless with the power of marrying. The bill of divorcement was a permission to take another husband. Our Lord forbids all putting away with or without a bill of divorcement, that is, with or without permission to take another husband. He abrogates the indulgence allowed by Moses, of putting away a wife, provided she were permitted to marry again, and declares that whoever puts away his wife, even in the way prescribed by Moses, causes her to commit adultery; and that whoever marries her commits adultery. He causes her to commit adultery, because he places her in a situation in which she is strongly tempted to commit adultery. This is all of the Sermon on the Mount which bears upon this part of the subject. The clause "saving for the cause of fornication," will be considered in the next chapter.

Subject to that saving, our Lord abrogates the law which allows a bill of divorcement; but He does not abrogate the law which forbade men from putting away their wives without one. That was an original part of the doctrine of marriage, and is reënacted in the words: "Whosoever putteth away his wife, causeth her to commit adultery." The temptations to commit adultery to which she will be exposed are the reasons why she is not to be put away. These temptations are greater, not less, if she be not allowed to marry.

[1] Matthew v. 31, 32.

CHAPTER VIII.

OF THE PRACTICAL ELEMENTS OF MARRIAGE. — II. INDISSOLUBLENESS. 2. THE EXCEPTION.

§ 1. Our Lord's Exception out of the Rule that Marriage is indissoluble. — § 2. Exceptions attempted to be introduced by Civil Laws. — § 3. Cruelty. — § 4. Desertion. — § 5. It is necessary to understand the Exception in the Gospels of St. Mark and St. Luke. — § 6. The Exception is not to be rejected because it is recorded by only one Evangelist. — § 7. It is not Local or Temporary. — § 8. The four Passages must be construed like Laws *in Pari Materia*. — § 9. The Rule that the more rigorous Law is to be obeyed does not apply. — § 10. Plainness of our Lord's Words in St. Matthew. — § 11. There is only one Way of giving effect to them. — § 12. The Word rendered Fornication is not erroneously translated. — § 13. Five Objections of the Rev. Hector Davies Morgan. — § 14. The Word translated Fornication means, in those Places, Adultery. — § 15. A Rhetorical Objection against the received Translation answered — § 16. It is not a Good Reason against the received Translation, that an Adulteress was to be put to Death. — § 17. Answer to the Objection, that Adultery was not a Cause of Divorce under the Mosaic Law. — § 18. The Word translated Fornication does not mean the Sin of Living in a Void Marriage. — § 19. It does not mean Antenuptial Fornication. — § 20. It does not mean Marriage with an Unbeliever. — § 21. It does not mean Incest. — § 22. The Exception cannot relate to Void Marriages. — § 23. It can be reconciled with the Tenor of our Lord's Discourse. — § 24. It can be reconciled with the Doctrine of St. Paul. — § 25. Mr. Keble's Opinion. — § 26. Analysis of 1 Corinthians vii. — § 27. Romans vii. 1-4. — § 28. The Exception is not inconsistent with the Drift of St. Paul's Arguments. — § 29. Pamphlet by an English Barrister. — § 30. The Mosaic Law for putting an Adulteress to Death. — § 31. Causing to commit Adultery. — § 32. Alleged Mistranslation of the Word rendered by "Saving." — § 33. Illustration from Acts xxviii. 19. — § 34. Illustration from 2 Corinthians xi. 28. — § 35. Alleged Mistranslation of the Word rendered by "Cause." — § 36. New Translations. — § 37. Paraphrases. — § 38. Analysis of Part of Matthew v. — § 39. Analysis of part of Matthew xix. — § 40. Alleged Corruption in the *Textus Receptus* of the Greek

Testament. — § 41. Conversation in St. Mark x. — § 42. The Exception is not a Declaration that our Lord was not speaking of Fornication. — § 43. Conclusion of the Chapter.

§ 1. Our blessed Lord four times promulgated with His own lips the rule, that the bond of marriage cannot be dissolved. Upon two of the four occasions he introduced an exception to the rule. The passages have already been several times quoted in this work, but it is proper again to transcribe them here, so far as to introduce the exception. The first is: "Whosoever shall put away his wife, saving for the cause of fornication, causeth her to commit adultery." [1] Another is: "Whosoever shall put away his wife except it be for fornication, and shall marry another, committeth adultery." [2] It seems clear that the rule of indissolubleness is laid down, and equally so that there is one exception, and but one to that rule. That exception is fornication. The word fornication is now understood, whatever may have been the case formerly, to mean sexual intercourse between unmarried persons. But it is agreed that the Greek word, which in these two places is translated by that English word, includes any kind of sexual sin. The plain literal and grammatical meaning then is, that a man may put away his wife if she commit sexual sin, but for no other cause. Various questions have been raised about the meaning of the word translated fornication, of putting away, and about other matters connected with the exception, all of which will be hereafter considered. It is however clear, that putting away a wife except for fornication, whatever that may mean, is forbidden, and that there is no other exception to the rule of indissolubleness. There is but one exception, the very form of the exception, or saving clause, excludes the idea that there can be more.

§ 2. It has been attempted to introduce other causes for putting away, by means of civil laws; and there are respectable writers who have attempted to shelter one of

[1] Matthew v. 32. [2] *Ibid.* xix. 9.

them under a perverted interpretation of Holy Writ. The two cases which most frequently occur, and in favor of which the most specious arguments are urged, are cruelty and desertion. These are not sufficient reasons for dissolving the bond of marriage; although they may be sufficient reasons why a person should be excused from performing the duties of a husband or a wife, because they may render it impossible to perform them. A real impossibility is a sufficient reason for not doing anything.

§ 3. There may be cases of cruelty which may render it impossible for married persons to live together. But the cases of technical cruelty which are sometimes heard of in courts of justice are not such cases. The cruelty must be real, and so great as to render it unsafe for the weaker party to live with the other. When such a case occurs, a woman has a sufficient excuse for not living with her husband, and may refuse to do so, and apply for protection to the courts. This is granted in the form which in England is called a sentence of judicial separation, and in this country a divorce *a mensa et thoro*.

§ 4. No person can live with one who refuses to live with them; so that obstinate desertion renders a performance of the marriage duties impossible, and the sin of the separation rests with the deserter. This idea receives the sanction of St. Paul, when he says: "If any brother have a wife which believeth not, and she be minded to dwell with him, let him not put her away. And the woman which hath a husband that believeth not, and if he be pleased to dwell with her, let her not leave him. For the unbelieving husband is sanctified by the wife, and the unbelieving wife is sanctified by the husband; else were your children unclean, but now are they holy. But if the unbelieving depart, let him depart. A brother or a sister is not under bondage in such cases; but God hath called us to peace." [1]

Some writers, as has been hinted, have interpreted this

[1] 1 Corinthians vii. 12–15.

passage as authorizing a dissolution of marriage on account of desertion. The view is not without plausibility if it be confined to such cases of desertion as those mentioned by the Apostle; but such cases can now scarcely occur. The Apostle implies that the marriages were heathen marriages between heathens, which when formed were not supposed by any one to be indissoluble. He also implies that the desertion is by a heathen, and that it occurs because the other party has become a Christian. The Christian is forbidden to separate from the heathen if the heathen be willing to continue the relation, because his or her faith sanctifies the other party, and the marriage. "But if the unbelieving depart let him depart; a brother or a sister is not under bondage in such cases." It may be asked: bondage to what? It may be said that the Apostle could not mean merely that the Christian was not bound to do an impossibility, and it was impossible for two persons to live together, if one were determined not to live with the other. Another interpretation is possible. It may be said that the Apostle meant that under such circumstances the Christian might marry. When the fact is taken into view, that at that time separations which left the bond of marriage unbroken were unknown, it does not seem impossible that St. Paul intended that the deserted Christian might marry. Not that he believed the bond of marriage dissoluble, but that he did not believe that in such cases it had ever been formed.

Whether this be so or not, the text has no application to modern cases of desertion, in which there has been a Christian marriage between those who were at least nominally Christians. In such marriages the unity of marriage has been formed. It cannot be broken by desertion, or by anything which does not fall within our Lord's exception. Desertion of a wife by her husband may render it probable that he has committed adultery; but it does not prove it. Moreover, it is at least doubtful whether the adultery of the husband is within the exception.

§ 5. To return to the one exception. It is denied that there is any exception, because St. Mark and St. Luke do not mention it in the accounts which they give of two other promulgations of the general rule. There is no contradiction about facts among the Evangelists; but there is a discrepancy in doctrine which must be reconciled. On the occasions mentioned by St. Mark and St. Luke, our Lord omitted to speak of the exception. He thus promulgated two rules, which can only be reconciled by understanding, as grammarians say, the exception in the places in which it is omitted. If this be not done, all force and operation are taken away from the exception. This is contrary to the rule of interpretation, that in any writing every word must have its meaning *ut res magis valeat quam pereat.* It is as certain as Scripture can make it that our Saviour spoke the words which make the exception, and some meaning must be found for them. They have been written for the edification of the Church, and preserved that men may read them, and be governed by them. This is as true of them as of any other portion of Scripture. It is impossible to disregard them. The only alternative is to consider them as understood in the narratives of St. Mark and St. Luke.

§ 6. In order to escape from this alternative some persons have insinuated, rather than maintained, that because St. Mark and St. Luke are two, and St. Matthew is only one, the majority of the witnesses is to be followed. Were the Evangelists mere uninspired writers, this would be very bad reasoning. If one credible person report a fact which he has seen, or words which he has heard, all men will believe him, although other persons who were present may not have seen the occurrence or heard the words. If the rules of evidence which apply to uninspired witnesses are to be applied to the Evangelists, it is also proper to remark that St. Matthew was present, and St. Mark and St. Luke were not. These preferences of the testimony of original witnesses over that of secondary witnesses, and of affirmative testimony over negative, are founded upon sound principles. But when witnesses are, like the Evangelists, speaking of different events, neither they nor the doctrine of preferring the testimony of two witnesses to that of one are applicable. But the Evangelists are not mere uninspired witnesses. The Holy Spirit guided them to all truth, and did not suffer any of them to write any falsehood. It is perfectly certain that our blessed Lord did on two occasions make the exception. It is part of the revelation intended for our guidance.

§ 7. Great efforts have been made to show that, admitting St. Matthew's statement to be true, it is not important. Very ingenious reasons have been found why our Lord should have introduced the exception, and why St. Matthew should have recorded it, although it is no part of the Christian Law. It is said that it was a mere local and temporary permission to the Jews. St. Matthew, who wrote for the Jews of Palestine, therefore preserved it. St. Mark, who wrote for the Hellenizing Jews, and St. Luke, who wrote for the Gentiles, did not mention it, because the permission did not extend to their readers.

It is also said that if the exception is allowed any force, those who read only the Gospels of St. Mark and St. Luke would be led into a grievous error, and be subjected to a more rigorous law, than those who had access to that of St. Matthew. It may be answered that those who read only St. Matthew, would, if the exception were not a part of the Christian Law, be led into a grievous error, and would be exposed to a dangerous laxity of practice. This would be a worse evil than the strictness imposed upon those who read St. Mark and St. Luke, and did not read St. Matthew. All the Gospels were written for the guidance of the Church in all ages. She has them all, and is bound to use them all. There is not a word in the Bible to show that St. Matthew's Gospel, or any part of it, is local or temporary, or addressed exclusively to the Jews of Palestine. No man has a right to set aside any part of it, or of any of the others. For "all Scripture is written by the inspiration of God, and is profitable for doctrine, for reproof, for correction, for instruction in righteousness, that the man of God may be thoroughly furnished unto all good works." [1]

§ 8. The whole Christian Law of divorce is contained in five passages; four of them are to be found in three of the Gospels, two in that of St. Matthew, one each in those of St. Mark and St. Luke. The other is the seventh chapter of St. Paul's First Epistle to the Corinthians. These passages must be regarded as laws *in pari materia*, that is, laws upon the same subject, proceeding from the same authority. The rule is, that such laws are to be all taken together and read as one law, of which no part is to be rejected. The statements of St. Matthew, St. Mark, and St. Luke, are all plain. In two places the exception is introduced, and in two it is omitted. It must be either understood where it is omitted, or erased where it is introduced. There is no middle course. It must be read as a part of the law, or not. If it be read, every word is made available; if it be not, the exception perishes, and some of the words of our blessed Lord are made of none effect.

§ 9. It has been said, that this course is not allowable, because when there are two laws, men ought to obey that one which is more strict, and less indulgent to human frailty. When two laws accidentally cross each other in a particular case, so that both cannot be obeyed, it is the duty of a conscientious man to obey that which is the less indulgent of the two to human frailty, lest he should make a mistake through following his own inclinations. But as a rule of interpretation, a means of finding out the meaning of one single written law, such a principle was never heard of. It would be still more absurd to use it as a reason for strik-

[1] 2 Timothy iii. 16, 17.

ing out of a Divine law an exception which Divine wisdom has inserted.

§ 10. Our Saviour uttered the words, "Whosoever shall put away his wife, except it be for fornication, and shall marry another, committeth adultery."[1] The meaning of these words seems to be very clear. If this were the only text on the subject, every one would agree that a man might put away his wife in the excepted case. For there is no other prohibition of putting away except that which must be inferred from the declaration, that marrying after putting away, is adultery. It can only be adultery because the putting away was unlawful, and so did not dissolve the unity of the married pair. But it is declared that in the excepted case the second marriage is not adultery. This can only be because in the excepted case the putting away does dissolve the unity.

But our Lord further said, "And whoso marrieth her which is put away doth commit adultery." Why? Because he has married the wife of another man. If the woman were not the wife of another man it could not be adultery to marry her. The second clause is then a reiteration of the rule, that a man cannot put away his wife and dissolve the bond of marriage. But does it contradict the first clause, which contains the exception? Must they not be made to agree? There is but one way to do this. The exception must be virtually incorporated, or, in the language of grammarians, understood, in the second clause. This reasoning is equally strong in favor of understanding it in the Gospels of St. Mark and St. Luke.

The passage in the fifth chapter shows the same thing, although perhaps less clearly: "Whosoever shall put away his wife, saving for the cause of fornication, causeth her to commit adultery." How? By exposing her to temptation. How is it possible that, being put away, she could still commit adultery. Because the bond of marriage being undissolved she is still a wife. But if she be put away for the

[1] Matthew xix. 9.

cause of fornication, she is not caused to commit adultery. Such is the plain meaning of our Lord's words. Why is it so? Because, like any other unmarried woman, she may marry. The bond of marriage has been dissolved by her being put away for that cause.

§ 11. If there were no Gospel but that of St. Matthew, there would be a plain law forbidding divorce except in one case, while in that case it would be allowable. But in the Gospels of St. Mark and St. Luke the prohibition of divorce is repeated in almost the same words, but without the exception. How are the two laws to be reconciled? If the words of St. Mark and St. Luke be without the qualification in St. Matthew, his peculiar teaching is, as it were, erased from the Holy Scriptures. It would be as if that which has been written had never been written, and the words which he records our Lord to have spoken had never been spoken. Some of our Lord's words would be made of none effect. Can men be justified in adopting such an interpretation? There is no alternative but to understand the exception in the two Gospels in which it is omitted.[1]

§ 12. But there are writers who contend that the exception does not mean that a man may put away his wife for adultery. They admit that the Greek word which has been translated fornication includes all sexual sins; yet they insist that in these places it does not mean adultery. Some of them think that it means that kind of fornication which is committed by persons who live together in a supposed

[1] It may be well to introduce in this place and way the following very neat argument, which is taken from a speech delivered in the British House of Lords, in 1820, by Archbishop Manners Sutton, of Canterbury. The Archbishop said: "I admit that the passages in Matthew are not in Mark nor in Luke; but in Matthew the exception is given, and Mark and Luke have the general institution without the exception. Now, I conceive that the passages in which the exception is omitted ought to be measured by the passage in which it is expressed; for it is impossible to believe that that was not intended, which was expressed, though that which was not actually expressed might yet be intended." *

* Tebbs *On Adultery and Divorce*, London, 1822, pp. 111, 112.

marriage, which is void, so that the exception only authorizes the nominal husband to declare that he will no longer respect a void marriage. One of these writers is the Rev. Hector Davies Morgan, an English clergyman who published a work on "Marriage, Adultery, and Divorce," in the year 1826. He admits that the Greek word which has been translated fornication is applicable to any sexual sin, but objects to its being applied to adultery. He maintains that in this place it means the fornication which is committed between a couple whose marriage is void. Other views have been taken by other writers, and in fact by Mr. Morgan himself.

§ 13. Mr. Morgan says: "In assuming the right of divorce upon proof of adultery, it is conceived that five capital objections have been overlooked. These objections cannot be removed, unless it is shown, — (1) that the word translated fornication does mean adultery; (2) that the clause of exception ought indeed and of necessity to be understood in the texts in which it is not inserted; (3) that the right and privilege of divorce can be fully collected from the clause of exception; (4) that the doctrine can be reconciled to the tenor of our Lord's discourse; and (5) that it can be made to harmonize with the doctrine of St. Paul, in arguing with the Corinthians upon marriage and divorce." [1]

These objections seem to include all those which have been made to the exception, though they are not very clearly put. It may be proper to interpret them. They are, — (1) that the word translated fornication does not mean adultery; (2) that the clause of exception ought not to be understood, where it is not expressed; (3) that the power of divorce cannot be collected from the exception; (4) that the doctrine cannot be reconciled with the tenor of our Lord's discourse; (5) that it cannot be reconciled with the teaching of St. Paul in the First Epistle to the Corinthians. The second objection in fact includes the fourth and fifth. It has been already disposed of in this

[1] Morgan *On Marriage, Adultery, and Divorce*, vol. ii. p. 87.

chapter, section five to section eleven both inclusive, but some remarks will, nevertheless, be made on the fourth and fifth objections. The third objection is really to the effect of the exception, and belongs to the next chapter.

§ 14. The first objection is, that the word translated fornication does not mean adultery. It is conceded that it is a large word, and may mean any fleshly sin, and adultery as well as any other. So interpreted it yields in these passages what is called a good sense, in fact a more natural sense than can be found in any other way. These considerations make it incumbent on Mr. Morgan to assign reasons why the word does not mean adultery, and to point out what it really does mean. He gives three reasons why it does not mean adultery; and says that its true meaning is that kind of fornication which is committed by persons who live together in a void marriage.

§ 15. One of his reasons for believing that the word does not mean adultery is that our Lord would not have used two words for the same thing in the same sentence. He would not have called it both fornication and adultery. This is a mere rhetorical reason, and is not entitled to much weight. It cannot outweigh the rhetorical or grammatical difficulty, which is inherent in the meaning which Mr. Morgan suggests. That difficulty is this: to put away for a thing, does not mean to put away to prevent a thing, but because it has been done.

§ 16. Another of the reasons which he assigns for not believing that the word means adultery is that by the Mosaic Law, an adulteress was to be put to death, and therefore could not be put away. But a man might not wish his adulterous wife to be put to death, and yet might not choose to live with her. He might then use the power which was supposed to be given him in the Book of Deuteronomy, and put her away without assigning any cause.[1]

This is the view taken by Bishop Jeremy Taylor. He

[1] See Matthew i. 17.

says: "As for the case of lapidation, it is true that the woman if she were legally convicted was to die; but the husband was not bound to accuse her; he might pardon her if he pleased, and conceal the fact. He might pardon her for his share, as Christ did the woman taken in adultery, or put her away privily, as Joseph, upon a mistake, intended to do to the blessed Virgin Mother."[1]

There is another answer to this argument. Our blessed Lord was not obliged to take any notice of the law which punished adultery with death. It was a judicial, or civil law which was not to be introduced into the Christian system. Our Lord was providing a rule to direct the consciences of men who were to live where there was no such law. His words were to bind the consciences of men in America, and in the nineteenth century, as well as in Judæa, and in the first. He forbids all divorces, except in the case of fornication. Men now say that the word translated fornication cannot mean adultery, because by the Law of Moses an adulteress was to be punished with death. Here and now she is not so punished, and the reason fails. Our blessed Lord knew that it would be so when He made the exception. It is astonishing how completely his Omniscience is forgotten, and how much he is treated as a mere human law-maker, who deals with the subject by the light of the age in which he lives.

§ 17. A third reason has been assigned why the word translated fornication cannot, in this place, mean adultery. It is, that adultery was not by the Mosaic Law a cause of divorce. It is said that our blessed Lord, when He was abolishing the Mosaic causes of divorce, could not properly have excepted that which was not one of them. Where is the evidence that He was abolishing the Mosaic causes of divorce? He was establishing the Christian law of marriage. In the Sermon on the Mount he announces a distinct law, which he contrasts with that of Moses, in

[1] *Ductor Dubitantium*, book i. chapter v., rule 8, § 8.

the particular of divorce as the Jews understood it. According to the prevailing opinion among them, the power of divorce was arbitrary, and rested in the will of the husband. There were no causes of divorce. Only one is mentioned in the law, that the woman found no favor in her husband's eyes, on account of some uncleanness. There was a question as to the meaning of the word uncleanness. One set of Rabbis held that it meant anything which the husband disliked, and the great body of the Jews held with them. Another held, that it meant adultery; and our Saviour seems practically to have agreed with these. He declared that the permission for men to divorce their wives because they found no favor in their eyes, was inconsistent with the primitive institution of marriage which He restored. That allowed of no divorce; but He as God could and did introduce an exception.

§ 18. Those who deny that the word translated fornication means adultery, are bound to assign some other meaning to it. Most of them, — and Mr. Morgan among the rest, — resort to the notion that it means that kind of fornication which is committed by those who live together in a void marriage. To this notion there are two objections. One that which has been set forth in the fourteenth section of this chapter. The other is that the exception cannot relate to void marriages. This will be more fully pressed hereafter. At present it will be sufficient to say that the rule relates to valid marriages, and therefore this exception cannot relate to void marriages.

§ 19. The notion about void marriages takes two forms. Perhaps the most common is to take the word fornication in its usual sense of ántenuptial sin, which is supposed to nullify the marriage. In order to account for this, it is asserted that fornication works a marriage between the fornicators. The authority given for this notion is this: "Know ye not that your bodies are the members of Christ? shall I then take the members of Christ and make them the members of an harlot? God forbid. What! know ye not that he which is joined to an harlot is one body? for two, saith He, shall be one flesh."[1]

This is an awful text and full of difficulty; but it can scarcely be necessary to consider it as making every act of fornication a marriage. The consequences of such an interpretation would be terrible. There would be many void marriages which are now supposed to be valid. Many innocent women would be living in unconscious adultery, and on making the discovery would be bound to leave their husbands. The Apostle is not treating of marriage in this place, but of fornication both spiritual and carnal, which he mixes together, using each as an illustration of the other. It seems more reasonable to suppose that he was merely putting in a strong light the sin of a Christian who was spiritually a member of Christ becoming even transiently one with a harlot. It is not likely that he would have announced in so indirect a manner the important doctrine that fornication is marriage. This doctrine would form the unity of marriage, without the consent of the parties to live together according to God's Word, without God's blessing, and consequently without sanctity. This can hardly be conceived. Such a marriage would be without the formative elements, and without their mysterious effects. It would be no Christian marriage.

The context does not favor the notion that fornication is marriage. Immediately after the words just transcribed, the Apostle says: "But he that is joined unto the Lord is one Spirit. Flee fornication. Every sin that a man doeth, is without the body; but he that committeth fornication, sinneth against his own body. What! know ye not that your body is the temple of the Holy Ghost, which is in you, which ye have of God, and ye are not your own? For ye are bought with a price; therefore glorify God in your body, and in your spirit, which are God's."[2]

[1] 1 Corinthians vi. 15, 16. [2] *Ibid.* 17-20.

§ 20. In this text Mr. Morgan finds another kind of void marriages to which he thinks the exception may apply. He suggests that the word harlot means alien in the sense of unbeliever, and that the word fornication means "spiritual fornication," that is, such unbelief as makes a person an alien from the Church of God. Marriage with such a person, he holds to be unlawful and void. A Christian, he thinks, may put away a woman who is such an alien, because she is not his wife, notwithstanding a form of marriage may have passed between them. According to this theory, St. Paul prohibits such marriages and thus makes them void. Unfortunately for the theory, the text does not make them void, if it forbids them; for it recognizes the unity which grows out of them. The recognition is the only foundation of the opinion that the passage has anything to do with marriage. In the next chapter, the Apostle recognizes the sanctity of marriages contracted between heathens, after one of the parties has become a Christian. This seems to be inconsistent with the notion that marriage with a heathen is merely void.

This interpretation embarrasses Mr. Morgan's argument not a little. It precludes him from interpreting the word fornication to mean antenuptial sin, because instead of the text making fornication marriage, it will forbid marriage for want of faith in one of the parties. If he take the ground that the text means a marriage with an unbeliever, he is met by his own translation of the text. If the word harlot there means an unbeliever, and the joining to which the text refers be marriage, that marriage is sinful but not void. "He that is joined to an harlot is one body; for two, saith He, shall be one flesh."

§ 21. Mr. Morgan's real theory seems to be that the word in the exception means incest. It follows, as he supposes, that a woman who had passed through the form of marriage with a man to whom she could not lawfully be married on account of consanguinity or affinity, may be put away to avoid continuing in the sin of incest. He does not assert that the only meaning of that word is incest, but admits that its classical meaning includes all sexual sins. It means incest, but it also means adultery. St. Paul uses it where it cannot possibly mean incest. He says: "To avoid fornication let every man have his own wife, and let every woman have her own husband."[1] The Greek word here translated fornication is the same which is so translated in the two passages in St. Matthew's Gospel. It is very clear from the words which have been transcribed, that it does not mean incest. The context makes it still clearer.

The word is applicable to any sexual sin, to incest as well as to others, but also to adultery. There is nothing in the construction of the sentence or in the context which would induce a belief that the meaning in this place is incest, but there is to induce a belief that it is adultery. If the word could only mean incest, the passage would be intelligible, though strangely worded. If it may mean adultery, that is the natural sense. If the putting away were to avoid living in incest, it would have been most natural to have said so directly. The exception might have been, except to avoid incest, in the nineteenth chapter; and in the fifth, saving to avoid incest. To put a woman away for adultery means to put her away because she has committed adultery; but to put her away for incest scarcely means to put her away lest she should continue in incest. If that were the idea to be conveyed, the natural form would have been saving or except to avoid incest.

§ 22. Before leaving this part of the subject it may be well to remark that no explanation of the exception which proceeds upon the idea that [it] relates to void marriages is admissible, for two reasons. One is that such an exception is no exception at all. Our Saviour was speaking of valid

[1] 1 Corinthians vii. 2.

marriages in which the parties had been joined together by God; void marriages in which they had not been so joined were not within the purview of his remarks. The rule applied to valid marriages; the exception cannot apply to void marriages, which, independent of the exception, are not within the rule. The other reason is, that as in void marriages there was no occasion for a divorce, there could be no occasion to speak of them.

It would be very singular that our blessed Lord should introduce the subject of unlawful marriages into a discussion about dissolving lawful marriages. The Pharisees ask: "Is it lawful for a man to put away his wife for every cause?" Our Lord refers to the primitive institution of marriage, declares that divorce for every cause is inconsistent with it, and promulgates His rule that man must not put asunder what God hath joined. Mr. Morgan makes him say, that a man who shall put away his wife and marry another, commits adultery, unless the original marriage were void. This is a new matter, entirely foreign to the question of the Pharisees, who seem to have desired a decision of the controversy whether divorce were lawful for any cause but adultery. They ask, is it lawful for a man to put away his wife for every cause, assuming that for some cause or causes it was lawful. They wanted an opinion from our Lord about the right of arbitrary divorce. To this inquiry He gave a precise answer: that it was not lawful to put away a wife except for fornication, that is, adultery. Anything about void marriages would have been new matter, unconnected with the question, unconnected with the permission of Moses, and unconnected with our Lord's own declaration, that man might not separate those whom God had joined. The whole context relates to lawful marriages only.

There is not such a context in the fifth chapter to show the incongruity of the notion about void marriages with the matter of the discourse. But there is no context which countenances the notion that the exception relates to void marriages. Our Lord introduces his doctrine into the midst of a discourse, in which He treats of almost everything belonging to Christian morals. The doctrine is that marriage is indissoluble. This He shows by declaring that, notwithstanding any putting away, the woman could commit adultery and could not marry without involving her new husband in adultery, that is, she was still a wife. To this rule He makes an exception, and announces it at the same time with the rule. It is, that the woman ceases to be a wife when she is put away for the cause of fornication. If this mean that a husband may dissolve a valid marriage if his wife have committed adultery, the whole passage is intelligible and consistent. There is an intelligible rule, and an intelligible exception, which make together a clear and consistent sense. This is not the case upon Mr. Morgan's interpretation, that if a man put away his wife saving when she is not his wife, he causeth her to commit adultery. Such an interpretation can hardly be maintained. None of the recent writers against the exception to the rule of the indissolubleness of marriage have taken this ground. It may be considered to be given up.

§ 23. The fourth objection is that the doctrine cannot be reconciled with the tenor of our Saviour's discourse, that is, that the exception is to be rejected because it conflicts with the general rule. This would be fatal to all exceptions. Every exception is inconsistent with the universality of the rule. But this does not affect this exception more than others. It does not reduce it to a seeming exception. It cannot be shown that it is inconsistent with the Divine nature to make an exception out of a Divine rule. If it had been asserted that the exception had been made by a General Council, or any other human authority, the case would not admit of doubt. The exception would be seen to be null, so soon as it was shown to be inconsistent with a Divine rule. But in this case the rule and the exception rest upon the same authority. Marriages might have been dissolved for any cause, or at the will of the parties, had it not pleased God to declare that a man and his wife are indissolubly one flesh. The rule rests on Divine authority, and the exception on the same authority.

Mr. Morgan says that the exception, in the sense of an allowance of divorce for adultery, is not authorized by the context, that is, it is an exception. An exception is never authorized by the context, except that the context makes it intelligible as an exception. In that sense this exception is authorized by the context. His own interpretation is far more within the scope of his objection. For an exception must be of matter, which without it would fall within the rule. But though an exception thus limits the operation of the rule, it is not inconsistent with it. If the rule were, that no tame animal should be shot, an exception of sheep would limit the rule; but it would not be inconsistent with the context. But if a law forbade the shooting of any tame animals except wolves, the exception would be inconsistent with the context, because wolves are not tame animals. It would also be nugatory, because it would make no change in the effect of the law. Suppose a law-maker were to enact that a man should not put away his wife, unless when she was not his wife, would not all men see that the exception was both inconsistent with the context and nugatory? Does it make any difference, if the exception should be, unless when the marriage is void? Suppose the exception were so ambiguously expressed that it might include void marriages with others, would it not be clear that it would be nugatory as to the void marriages, and operative on the others. In this case, Mr. Morgan attempted to show that there is such an ambiguity, and has not been very successful; yet he decides in favor of that interpretation which makes our blessed Lord's exception nugatory.

§ 24. Mr. Morgan's fifth objection is that the doctrine of divorce for adultery cannot be reconciled with the teaching of St. Paul. It is a very short and satisfactory answer, that the doctrine of St. Paul must be reconciled with that of the Saviour. Our Lord's teaching contains more than St. Paul's, and the reconciliation must be effected not by rejecting the surplus, but by using it to modify, or qualify the teaching of the Apostle. For no portion of Scripture is to be accounted inoperative, or without meaning, because it is not repeated in another place.

The teaching of St. Paul, to which Mr. Morgan refers, is to be found in the seventh chapter of the First Epistle to the Corinthians. The Apostle had no occasion to refer to the excepted case in that chapter. He was replying to certain questions which had been asked by the Corinthians. The chapter begins, "Now concerning the things whereof ye wrote unto me." The question about divorce for adultery was not one of those things, for he says nothing about it. He does not treat of any case within the exception, and does not mention it in any way. The general rule covered all the cases about which his advice was asked. About that rule there is really no difference of opinion among Christians. All the controversies relate to the meaning of the exception.

Mr. Morgan thinks that there can be no exception to the rule because St. Paul does not mention one, and that therefore the exception made by our blessed Lord must be treated as if it had never been made. He does this because to introduce an exception would contradict St. Paul, who mentions none when he was applying the general rule to cases outside of the exception.

§ 25. Mr. Keble, who takes the same general view with Mr. Morgan, also relies much upon the doctrine of St. Paul. He thinks it probable that St. Paul, writing to Corinth, a city remarkable for the prevalence of the sins of the flesh, would have said something about the exception had he regarded it as operative. This is at best but a conjecture, and one in which all will not agree. It is much more probable that he would have confined himself, as he professed to do, to the questions, a decision of which had been asked. These were, according to Mr. Keble himself, mixed marriages, second marriages, and some others. The question of divorce for adultery was not among them; had it been, the Apostle would have treated of it, which he has not.[1]

§ 26. The earlier portion of the chapter under consideration is occupied with the lawfulness and expediency of marriage, and the rights which married persons have over each other. These subjects are so treated as to show the unlawfulness of divorces *a mensa et thoro*, and of voluntary separations. This part of the chapter relates directly rather to marriage than divorce. It shows however that the mutual rights of married persons are such as to render permanent separations unlawful. Of divorce there is no direct mention; there was therefore no necessity for referring to the exception by which it is permitted in certain cases. This portion of the chapter occupies six verses. The next three speak of the inexpediency of marriage, which is afterwards explained to be connected with "the present distress."

In the tenth and eleventh verses, the Apostle lays down the doctrine, that it is the duty of married persons to live together, as a foundation for the teaching in the following verses to the sixteenth inclusive. These treat of mixed marriages, in which one of the parties was a Christian and the other a heathen. There again there was no occasion to speak of the exception.

One of Mr. Morgan's theories is, that it is to mixed marriages — which he thinks were void — that the exception applies. The scope of St. Paul's argument was to show that

[1] See Keble's *Argument against Repealing the Laws which treat Marriage as Indissoluble.* Oxford, 1857, p. 23 *et seq.*

they were not excepted from the rule of indissolubleness. The Christian converts who were married to heathens, were expressly forbidden to separate from their husbands or wives. Christians might innocently live in such marriages, and were bound to live in them if the heathen did not choose to dissolve them. Yet St. Paul says very plainly that they ought not to be contracted.

In the seventeenth verse, the Apostle leaves, for a time, the subject of marriage, and takes up that of accepting the dispensations of Providence. This seems to grow out of the mention of the duty of continuing in a mixed marriage; although it is spoken of in connection with other cases that have nothing to do with marriage. The subject is continued to the twenty-fourth verse inclusive.

The twenty-fourth verse, which in a certain sense closes the subject of submitting to the dispensations of Providence, is this: "Brethren, let every man wherein he is called therein abide with God." In the twenty-fifth verse, the Apostle speaks of virgins, whom he advises to continue such. He then glides into the subject of the inexpediency of marriage. He first speaks of the case of virgins, concluding the subject by saying, in the thirty-eighth verse, that he that giveth his daughter in marriage doeth well, but he that giveth her not doeth better. He then passes to the case of widows, in the thirty-ninth and fortieth verses. These Mr. Keble regards, perhaps rightly, as the answer to one of the questions which the Corinthians had asked about second marriages. They are certainly a continuation of the discourse on the inexpediency of marriage. The Apostle had discussed that subject in the case of virgins, and now treats of it in that of widows.

It may be observed that in the case of virgins St. Paul had been careful to exclude all idea of the unlawfulness of marriage. He thought virginity better for "the present distress," and more consistent with a highly devotional life; but he still taught thus: "If any man think that he behaveth himself uncomely toward his virgin, if she pass the flower of her age, and need so require, let him do what he will, he sinneth not: let them marry. Nevertheless he that standeth steadfast in his heart, having no necessity, but hath power over his own will, and hath so decreed in his heart that he will keep his virgin, doeth well. So then he that giveth her in marriage doeth well; but he that giveth her not in marriage doeth better." [1]

In the two last verses of the chapter the same principles are applied to widows. The verses follow: "The wife is bound by the law as long as her husband liveth; but if her husband be dead, she is at liberty to be married to whom she will; only in the Lord. But she is happier if she so abide, after my judgment: and I think also that I have the Spirit of God." [2]

The leading idea in the Apostle's mind seems to have been that in the fortieth verse: "She is happier if she so abide." One of the questions which the Corinthians asked was, perhaps, whether a widow might marry. The Apostle only answers it in this incidental way, in the course of his remarks on the temporary inexpediency of marriage. He considers her as on the same footing with a virgin; it is lawful but inexpedient for her to marry. Marriage binds only during the joint lives of the married persons. The law which bound her to her husband ceased to operate at his death.

But it is said: "The wife is bound by the law so long as her husband liveth;" and therefore there can be no divorce. Such is the general rule; but the question is about the exception which the Lord hath made. No man, whatever might be his opinions about divorce, would hesitate to lay down the general rule, that a woman could not marry during her husband's lifetime, and might after his death. The question about divorce was not before the Apostle, and this passage proves nothing for or against the exception.

[1] 1 Corinthians vii. 36–38. [2] *Ibid.* 39, 40.

§ 27. There is a parallel passage in the Epistle to the Romans. St. Paul is there using the condition of a widow and her right of marrying again, as an illustration of the condition of the converted Jews, who were under the dominion of the law until the death of Christ, but by their death to the law, at the time of His death, had been released from that dominion. He illustrates this by the case of a woman, who is released from the bond of marriage by the death of her husband; being freed from his dominion, she might be married to another. So the Jews being themselves dead to the law might be married to another, even to Christ. The passage is this: "Know ye not, brethren, for I speak to them that know the law, how that the law hath dominion over a man as long as he liveth? For the woman which hath an husband is bound by the law to her husband as long as he liveth; but if her husband be dead, she is loosed from the law of her husband. So then if, while her husband liveth, she be married to another man, she shall be called an adulteress; but if her husband be dead she is freed from the law; so that she is no adulteress, though she be married to another man. Wherefore, my brethren, ye also are become dead to the law by the Body of Christ; that ye should be married to another, even to Him that is raised from the dead, that we should bring forth fruit unto God." [1]

This passage does not at first sight seem very clear. The general meaning seems to be this: The Church, under the old dispensation, is regarded as the spouse of the law, as, under the new, she is of Christ. The law died with the human nature of Christ. This truth is taught under another figure in another place: "Blotting out the handwriting of ordinances, which was contrary to us, and took it out of the way, nailing it to His cross." [2] The law died, and so the Church, and each Jew as a part of it, was free from the law, and the Church became the Bride of

[1] Romans vii. 1–4.

[2] Colossians ii. 14.

Christ. This paraphrase, it must be admitted, is a little embarrassed by the expression, "ye also are become dead to the law by the Body of Christ." But that expression equally disturbs the illustration of the Apostle, which requires the sense of the paraphrase to keep up the analogy between the illustration and the thing illustrated.

To show that the passage is not inconsistent with the exception, it is sufficient to recollect that the Apostle wanted an illustration, for the transition of the Jews from their original condition in which they were under the law to that of Christians, members of the Body of Christ. The Church, which is the Body of Christ, is also his spouse, and as such bound to bring forth fruits unto God. He found what he wanted in the case of a widow, who, by the death of her husband, was left at liberty to marry another man. This principle was acknowledged by all nations. It was enough for his purpose, and it was unnecessary to advert to any exceptions to the rule, that "a woman is bound by the law to her husband as long as he liveth." It was the principle, that the woman was released from the bond of marriage by her husband's death, which was the point of the illustration. It was foreign to the purpose in hand, to inquire whether a woman might during her husband's life be released from the marriage tie by an exceptional permission extending only to a single class of cases.

§ 28. Upon the whole, there is no reason to believe that the exception is inconsistent with the drift of St. Paul's argument. It may not, therefore, be disregarded upon that account. It is no trifling matter to set aside an exception, which has been made on two occasions, by our blessed Saviour. If such an exception appeared to clash with the teaching of St. Paul, it would be necessary to seek some means of reconciling the two doctrines. But there is not even an apparent clashing. St. Paul is speaking of matters which did not bring the exception before his mind, and he had no occasion to say anything about it. This silence is no reason for blotting the exception out of the Scriptures, and thus mutilating our Lord's own teaching.

If a lawyer were asked whether a contract for the payment of an annuity during the life of a man were binding, he would answer yes, or no. He would not say it is binding if it be not released. If the question were whether it were binding after the death of the annuitant, it would be still more irrelevant to speak of a release. If the question related to the validity or the effect of a release, the lawyer would turn his attention to the law on that subject; but he would never think of bringing it into an inquiry into the effect of the contract itself. Marriage is binding for life, and cannot be dissolved unless under peculiar circumstances, and must therefore, for all ordinary purposes, be treated as continuing through life. St. Paul did so, even when writing to Jews who knew the law, and who consequently knew that by the Mosaic Law it might be dissolved. It was not necessary for him, in treating of the duration of marriage for life, to refer either to the Mosaic divorces or to our Lord's exception of the rule of indissolubleness.

Mr. Morgan's five objections have now been examined; and it appears that, so far as they are concerned, the exception made by our Saviour to the rule that marriage is indissoluble, is operative. The five objections cover the whole ground, but there are other writers who urge them with different arguments, of which it be may proper to take some notice.

§ 29. An English Barrister has published a pamphlet entitled, "Considerations on Divorce *a vinculo matrimonii*, in connection with Holy Scripture."[1] He contends that the parenthesis, which looks like an exception, is not really one, but has a quite different meaning. This theory is not new, but as old as Bellarmine. The Barrister who now revives it, is understood to be of high professional standing. His work is entitled to notice, because he is the latest advocate of these views; and his general ability, his

[1] London, 1857.

learning, and his professional habits enable him to bring out the whole strength of his cause. Although perhaps not the equal of Bellarmine, he has the advantage of seeing the latest phase of the controversy.

His argument is of the class which is called ingenious, but is not very convincing. He sets out with a conviction — probably founded on a decision of the Latin Church, to which he is a convert — that the dissolution of a marriage for any cause is unlawful. This idea underlies his whole argument, as the notion of the papal supremacy underlies most Roman Catholic arguments upon any subject. It is assumed as indisputable. This granted, the argument is unanswerable, and they so regard it. Yet it produces no effect on the mind of a Protestant, who does not accept the idea of the papal supremacy. That idea is the concealed foundation of the whole superstructure. Of this sort of begging the question the Barrister is clearly guilty.

§ 30. It so blinds him that he falls into gross fallacies. He supposes that the exception in the thirty-second verse of the fifth chapter of St. Matthew cannot apply to the second clause of the verse, because a woman guilty of adultery was, by the Mosaic Law, to be put to death. The same remark might be extended to the first clause, for if the woman were put to death, how could she be caused to commit adultery. Yet the exception must be applicable to the first clause, for it is contained in it. If it be applicable to one it must be applicable to both, for the second is only an application of the first. If it be not applicable to the clause, why was it inserted in it, and what is its use? To give it some meaning, the Barrister intimates that a woman guilty of adultery was to be put away before she was put to death. No ancient writer, sacred or profane, is produced to give countenance to this strange fancy.

§ 31. Another fancy, still stranger and founded upon a transparent fallacy, is that the exception meant, that a woman who was guilty of adultery might put be away without danger of causing her to commit adultery, because she had already committed it, as though it were a sin incapable of repetition. Yet she is not to be put away. The exception means nothing more than to intimate the impossibility of causing her to commit adultery.

§ 32. The Barrister's strong ground is, that the exception in the Sermon on the Mount is not really one, but is made to appear such by a mistranslation of two words — those which have been translated "saving" and "cause." [1]

In treating of the first, he refers to dictionaries and other authorities, to show that the word translated "saving" will bear other meanings; but he makes no attempt to show that it will not bear the meaning of saving. He produces from dictionaries several English equivalents for the Greek word. Among them are "out of," "without," "besides," "except," "exclusive of." It is obvious that almost any one, if not any one, of these might be substituted for the word "saving," without affecting the meaning.

§ 33. He calls in the aid of two illustrations. The first is St. Paul's reference to his bonds, in the twenty-sixth chapter of the Acts of the Apostles. In the authorized version it reads thus: "I would to God, that not only thou but all who hear me this day, were both almost and altogether such as I am, except these bonds." [2] It is clear that the sense of this passage requires some word equivalent to saving or except. Yet St. Luke used the same word which is translated "saving" in St. Matthew. That is, therefore, probably its legitimate meaning. Every one of the renderings, which the Barrister has selected from his

1 Page 16, *et seq.* In the Vulgate the exception is thus translated: *Excepta fornicationis causa.* Literally, "the cause of fornication excepted." The Rhemish translation is, "excepting for the cause of fornication."

2 Page 29. The Vulgate has: *Opto apud Deum, et in modico et in magno, non tantum te, sed etiam omnes qui audiunt, hodie fieri tales qualis et ego sum, exceptis vinculis his.* The Rhemish translation is: "I would to God that both in little and in much, not only thou but all who hear me this day, should become such as I am, except these chains."

dictionaries, would mean exactly the same thing with that chosen by the translators, although some of them would have expressed the meaning awkwardly. This text, then, furnishes no argument against translating the word by "saving."

But the Barrister says, that it ought to have been translated, "apart from these bonds," or "exclusively of these bonds," or "without reference to these bonds." What meaning is there in the last five words? The translation is very harsh, and does not give the idea which was in the mind of St. Paul. It is not easy to see what idea it does give: "I would to God that not only thou but all who hear me this day, were both almost and altogether such as I am, without reference to these bonds." What change do the last five words make in the meaning of the text, unless they are understood to mean saving or except? The other two proposed translations plainly do not change the meaning from that of the authorized version. "Apart from these bonds," "exclusively of these bonds," and "saving these bonds," all mean exactly the same thing.

If, the same words were inserted in the parenthesis under consideration, in place of the word "saving," the sense would not be changed. "Saving for the cause of fornication," "apart from the cause of fornication," "exclusively of the cause of fornication," are equivalent expressions, although the last two are somewhat awkward. The text will be very obscure if the parenthesis be made to read without reference to the cause of fornication. The Barrister thinks that that is the true translation, and that it means not saying anything about fornication. This might possibly mean the same thing as "saving for the cause of fornication." But the Barrister's idea is that our Saviour only intended to intimate that He was not speaking of fornication, and meant to exclude it from consideration. A question would then arise, Why should our Lord exclude all reference to fornication? Nothing had previously been said about it. It is much more natural to suppose that He meant to except putting away for the cause of fornication out of the general prohibition of putting away.

§ 34. The other illustration is from the writings of St. Paul. After enumerating his sufferings, he says: "Besides these things which are without, that which cometh upon me daily, the care of all the churches."[1] It seems that the word rendered "without" in this place, is the same which is rendered "saving" in St. Matthew. The Barrister thinks that it should not have been so translated, and that it might have been better rendered in one of several ways. It should have been either besides or independently of the things, "which are extraordinary or apart from any daily or constant care." He adds, that Dr. Burton, in his note to the passage, renders it, "Beside the things, which I have omitted." It is then proposed that the word which is rendered saving should be rendered by apart, or extraordinary, or independently, or which I have omitted. What is the context? St. Paul has been enumerating various external evils, which he has suffered, and then winds up by saying that, besides those things which are without, he had to sustain the care of all the churches. Beside external evils, he had to endure inward anxiety. This idea seems well expressed by the authorized version. That of Dr. Burton seems much looser, and less consistent with the context. The Barrister's would not much alter the meaning of the passage. If his first rendering, "apart," were introduced into the clause of exception in St. Matthew, it would not change the meaning; "extraordinary" could not well be made to give any sense.

§ 35. All his proposed changes in the rendering of this word will avail him nothing, unless he can also establish a mistranslation of that which is rendered "cause." Of this

[1] 2 Corinthians xi. 28. The Rhemish translation is scarcely intelligible English, but the word under consideration, "without," is precisely the same with that in the authorized translation. The Vulgate has, *extrinsecus*, "from without," "from abroad."

word he only says: "It is scarcely necessary for me to assert that it means a subject, a proposition, a question, a matter which is discussed or spoken of, as any reader of Greek must be aware of this, and any Lexicon will furnish authorities to prove it."[1] He does not deny that it may also mean a cause in the sense in which that word is used in the place under consideration, nor does he assert that the context is inconsistent with that sense.

It would take some twisting of the context to make either of the new renderings tenable. Fornication is not a matter which has been discussed or spoken of; the word only occurs in the saving clause. Adultery, the thing meant, had not been previously spoken of in connection with divorce. To speak of the proposition of fornication would be at least to use very strange language. Fornication had not been made the subject of any proposition. Nothing had been said about it.

The design of all the Barrister's criticism upon these two words is to make our Saviour say, "apart from the question of fornication," thus disclaiming that He was speaking of fornication. Why should any person suppose that He was speaking of that which had not been mentioned? Why should He have disclaimed that of which no one would have suspected Him? Besides, does not the express exclusion of the subject of fornication from his discourse, except that case from the rule which He was laying down as effectually as the word "saving?" Suppose that He had said, If any man put away his wife, — I am not now speaking of the cause of fornication, — he causeth her to commit adultery. What would that have meant?

§ 36. The Barrister introduces three new versions of the saving clause. He says: "It may be more correctly rendered, 'Apart from the question of fornication, without reference to the subject of fornication, or independently of a case of fornication.'"[2]

1 *Considerations on Divorce*, etc. p. 18, *et seq.*

2 *Ibid.* p. 17.

The last of these versions is identical in meaning with the old one, and admits that the word translated cause means case, which in the present connection is the same thing. But what is to be understood by "apart from the question of fornication, or without reference to the subject of fornication?" Do they not all mean very much the same thing? There had been no question about fornication; it had not been mentioned. Why, then, should it be referred to? In order, the Barrister would reply, to exclude it from consideration. Who would have taken it into consideration? If our Lord had omitted the parenthesis, the passage would have been plain. It is plain now, if the parenthesis be an exception. If it be not, it is very far from plain.

If our Lord had intended nothing more than to declare that he who put away his wife caused her to commit adultery, his object would have been fully attained without the parenthesis. If He proposed to make an exception, the parenthesis is fully accounted for; if He did not, it is a mere incumbrance. It is not easy to imagine anything less likely than that He should insert the saving clause, only lest He should be understood to be speaking of something which had no connection with His subject, and of which there had been no previous mention. This would seem to be a sufficient reason for preferring the authorized version. While there does not seem to be anything that can be said in favor of the new one, except that it suits the Barrister's argument, and falls in with his preconceived ideas.

§ 37. Perhaps it has not even these recommendations. In order to make the assertion, that it does support his notion, plausible, he finds it necessary to resort to this paraphrase: "Whoever shall put away his wife (saving for the cause of fornication, for which the law orders him to put her away in a particular manner, and for a particular purpose, which is, of course, independent of what I am saying), causeth her to commit adultery."[1] If this be a paraphrase it is an exceedingly loose one, introducing several ideas not to be found in the original. One of these is that the law ordered a man to put away his wife for adultery, in order that she might be put to death. This proposition is not true. The law orders that an adulterous woman shall be put to death, not that she shall be put away for that purpose. This whole so-called paraphrase is without the slightest warrant from the context.

§ 38. The subject of adultery was introduced in the twenty seventh verse, by a recital of the seventh commandment. In the twenty-eighth our Lord explains the spiritual nature of that commandment. In both adultery is considered as a sin against God; it is not spoken of as an injury to man, or as a civil offense liable to civil punishment. In the twenty-ninth and thirtieth verses, our Lord, leaving the former subject, teaches the necessity of men's parting with their sins, even though they should be as dear to them as their right hands or right eyes. He then, in the thirty-first verse, introduces the subject of divorce, and says: "It hath been said: Whosoever shall put away his wife, let him give her a writing of divorcement." Then follows the verse under consideration: "But I say unto you, that whosoever shall put away his wife, saving for the cause of fornication, causeth her to commit adultery, and whosoever shall marry her that is divorced, committeth adultery." In the next verse He passes to a different subject.

The idea of adultery in connection with divorce is introduced for the first time in the thirty-second verse. If the word fornication does not mean adultery, then adultery is not introduced until after the saving clause, and is only mentioned as a consequence of unlawful divorce. If the word translated fornication means, as is the better opinion, adultery, the sin is treated of in a new view as an injury

[1] *Considerations on Divorce*, etc. p. 23.

to man. Neither adultery nor fornication in any sense has been spoken of as connected with divorce in any part of our Lord's discourse, previous to the introduction of the saving clause. Yet that clause is said to be nothing more than a protest against the notion that the prohibition of divorce, with which it was connected, was intended to affect the civil punishment of adultery. It is difficult to understand how any one could suppose this. There seems to be no such connection between putting away and putting to death, as would make the forbidding of one a prohibition of the other. There is no allusion to the punishment of adultery in the whole Sermon on the Mount, except it be found in the alleged disclaimer — a disclaimer of meddling with a subject which had nothing to do with the discourse, and had never been mentioned, made in words, which will bear another and a much more natural signification.

§ 39. The Barrister finds the passage in the nineteenth chapter of St. Matthew harder to deal with than that in the fifth. He begins by showing that in the first part of his conversation with the Pharisees, our Lord laid down the broad rule that marriage is indissoluble.[1] It is not improbable that there should be an exception to a broad rule, and therefore it is not unlikely that a teacher should qualify a rule by admitting an exception. Yet this unlikelihood is used as an argument for virtually striking out the exception. The unlikelihood, if it exists, must yield to the fact. Our Lord uttered the words of the saving clause; if they import an exception, He made an exception. It must therefore be shown that they do not clearly mean an exception before the unlikelihood will be of much value.

The Pharisees ask, "Is it lawful for a man to put away his wife for every cause?" They assume that it was lawful to put her away for some cause. Our Lord answers

[1] *Considerations on Divorce*, etc. p. 24, *et seq.*

by referring to the original institution of marriage, and laying down the Divine law, that man may not separate what God hath joined. They retort the provision of the Mosaic Law. Our Lord tells them that Moses gave them that permission because of the hardness of their hearts, and adds: "I say unto you, Whosoever shall put away his wife, except it be for fornication, and shall marry another, committeth adultery: and whoso marrieth her which is put away, doth commit adultery."[1] The Pharisees ask whether a man might put away his wife for every cause, that is at his pleasure. Our Saviour gives a very emphatic answer in the negative. They quote Moses. Compare our Lord's answer with their original question. It will then mean: You ask whether a man may put away his wife for every cause. Certainly not; there is but one cause for which he may put her away. Everything is thus clear and consistent.

In the authorized translation, the saving clause in this place is: "Except it be for fornication." The translators have put the words "it be" in italics, thus showing that the literal translation is, "except for fornication." There is here no such word as that, which in the fifth chapter is rendered "cause," and which the Barrister translates "question" or "subject." There is, therefore, no room for his paraphrase. All the little strength of his argument as to the other passages, was in that word. In the discourse of which it made a part, adultery had been mentioned, although not in a way which would have called for a reference to it. But here there has been literally no mention of adultery or fornication, and no allusion to either of them, until they are mentioned in the saving clause itself. Here then it seems clear that the clause contains an exception.[2]

[1] Matthew xix. 3, 9.

[2] In this place the Rhemish version of the exception is word for word the same with the authorized version. The Vulgate is *nisi ob fornicationem*,

§ 40. The Barrister also attacks the *Textus Receptus* of the Greek Testament, and produces some commentators, who have changed the Greek word which is translated "except" for one which can only mean "though not."[1] It is a sufficient answer to this suggestion, that the words "though not" do not make sense of the passage. The word "though" has nothing to which it can refer Other commentators, he says, have held that the passage is altogether corrupt, and ought to be a mere repetition of that in the fifth chapter.

§ 41. In order to show that our Lord meant only to exclude the idea that He was speaking of fornication in a discourse in which it had not been mentioned, and on an occasion on which neither the word, nor any equivalent for it had been used by any one, the conversation on the same subject, recorded by St. Mark, is brought in. It is assumed that St. Mark is giving an account of the same conversation with the Pharisees which is recorded by St. Matthew. But St. Mark does not mention as a part of that conversation either the clause of exception, or the statement of doctrine in which it is included. In a private conversation with his disciples which St. Mark records, our Lord delivered the doctrine without the exception. This the Barrister supposes to have been done in order to convey the idea that the parenthesis was not an exception. This is purely a conjecture, and a very strange one. Supposing it true, it would still leave the fact that our blessed Lord used words which might bear the sense of an exception, and left them unexplained to those to whom He had addressed them. He afterwards repeated the sentence in which they had occurred, omitting them, but without explaining himself, even then. If the conversation with the

literally, "unless on account of fornication" or for fornication. There is appended to the exception, in a copy of the Rhemish translation, approved by the Roman Catholic Archbishop of Baltimore, this note: "In the case of fornication, that is, of adultery, the wife may be put away; but even then the husband cannot marry another as long as the wife is living."

1 *Considerations on Divorce*, etc. p. 31.

Pharisees be the same that is recorded by St. Matthew, which is more than doubtful, the explanation is, perhaps, that the disciples had just heard the exception made in public. They had difficulties about our Lord's doctrine, that marriage is indissoluble, for "they asked him again about the same matter," that is, about the unlawfulness of divorce, which they, like other Jews, were unwilling to receive. It does not appear that they then, or at any other time, had any difficulty about the exception.

§ 42. The Barrister again and again presses his notion that the parenthesis is nothing but a declaration that our Lord was not speaking of fornication. Suppose it to be so. Suppose that the true translation is: "Whosoever shall put away his wife and marry another, I am not now speaking of fornication, committeth adultery." What would it mean? Would it not mean that the declaration which I am now making does not apply to putting away for fornication? In this case there is no word which can be changed into "question" or "subject," and so give countenance to the notion that the clause is an exclusion of the subject of fornication. All that can be done is to propose a new meaning for the word translated "except." The writer asserts that the common translation, "except it be for fornication," is by no means free from objection, the passage may just as well, if not better, be translated, "if not for fornication," or, "though not for fornication."[1] This is in part true, "except for fornication," and "if not for fornication," mean exactly the same thing. If one is a good translation, the other must be so too. Whosoever putteth away his wife, if not for fornication, and marrieth another, committeth adultery, would be a full equivalent for the authorized translation. It would certainly not be a declaration, that our Lord was not speaking of fornication. Both the old and the new translation mean the same thing, that if the woman were put away for fornication, the case would not fall within the declaration, that

[1] *Considerations on Divorce*, etc. p. 31.

if her husband married again, he committed adultery. The other proposed translation is: "Though not for fornication." This is not admissible, because it has no meaning. There is nothing to which the word "though" can refer. Suppose there had been a previous prohibition of putting away a wife for fornication, and it had been added: Whosoever shall put away his wife, though not for fornication, and marry another, committeth adultery. What would that have meant? It would have meant, that putting away for any other cause was as much forbidden as for fornication. But there is no previous prohibition of putting away for fornication. That being the case, what does the new translation mean? It would not be an exception. What would it be? The Barrister thinks that both this translation, and that by "if not," "will only have the force of putting the case of adultery by way of exemplification or illustration, not by way of exception."[1] This seems a very strange idea, not founded upon the natural force of the words. What need was there to exemplify a general prohibition, and what need had it of illustration? If it had needed exemplification, neither of these forms would supply it. Whosoever putteth away his wife, though for fornication, and marrieth another, committeth adultery. This is intelligible, and an exemplification. But the word "not" takes away that character. It is neither, when that word is introduced, exception, exemplification, nor illustration. It is a mere incumbrance upon the passage. It has already been shown, that "if not," is nothing but an exception, and cannot be regarded as either exemplification or illustration.

§ 43. The whole matter may be thus summed up. Our blessed Lord used, on two occasions, words of which the literal and grammatical sense is, that the adultery of the wife is an exception to the general rule, that marriage is indissoluble, and that He has left no commentary upon them.

1 *Considerations on Divorce*, etc. p. 31.

CHAPTER IX.

OF THE PRACTICAL ELEMENTS OF MARRIAGE. — II. INDISSOLUBLENESS. 3. THE EFFECT OF THE EXCEPTION.

§ 1. Two Opinions on the Effect of the Exception. — § 2. The Exception is from the Declaration that Marrying again is Adultery. — § 3. Doctrine of the Church of Rome. — § 4. The Church of England, *Reformatio Legum*. — § 5. Two Opinions among the English Clergy. — § 6. Adultery does not dissolve a Marriage. — § 7. The Exception not a Partial One. — § 8. Ecclesiastical Law of Rome and England. — § 9. English Parliamentary Divorces. — § 10. Persons who had been so divorced had no Difficulty in finding Clergymen to marry them. — § 11. The American Church. — § 12. Two Opinions among the Jews. — § 13. The Mosaic Law. — § 14. The Exception must apply to the Rule. — § 15. Causing to commit Adultery. — § 16. Matthew xix. 9. — § 17. Divorces *a Mensa et Thoro* forbidden in the New Testament. — § 18. 1 Corinthians vii. 10, 11. — § 19. Mixed Marriages. — § 20. Does the Right to Marry extend to the Guilty Person? — § 21. Moral Arguments against it. — § 22. English Parliamentary Practice. — § 23. The Practice of the English Clergy. — § 24. The Bishop of Oxford and Lord Palmerston. — § 25. Scriptural Authorities against Separation without the Power of Marrying. — § 26. Our Lord's Words. — § 27. No Human Law should vacate such a Marriage. — § 28. Can a Woman divorce her Husband? — § 29. Such a Power would not promote the Happiness of Women. — § 30. The Sin is not equal in the Two Sexes. — § 31. The Equality of the Sin would not affect the Question. — § 32. Mark x. 11, 12.

§ 1. It has been said that the effect of our Lord's exception to the rule, that a man cannot put away his wife, is that he may put her away for adultery, but that the bond of marriage still continues unbroken. He may put her out of his house without authorizing her to marry again. This would be directly contrary to the Mosaic Law. The divorce is supposed to be of that kind which modern lawyers, who have invented it, call a divorce *a mensa et thoro*. Other writers maintain that the effect is to allow the bond of matrimony to be dissolved in cases of adultery. If the structure of the sentences in which the exception occurs be examined, it will appear that the latter is the true doctrine.

§ 2. It has been asserted that if the parenthesis, in two places in St. Matthew, be an exception at all, it is only from the prohibition to put away, and not from the declaration that whoever puts away his wife and marries another, commits adultery. Upon this interpretation the clause permits that which is now called a divorce *a mensa et thoro*, but not a divorce *a vinculo matrimonii*. It has been shown already that divorces *a mensa et thoro* are contrary to both the Mosaic and the Christian laws. There is no reason to believe that our Lord intended to authorize a partial dissolution of the bond of marriage, leaving it in force as a restriction, while all its uses were taken away. The man and woman would thus be married persons as to the rest of the world, but not as between themselves. But apart from this reasoning, the notion is inconsistent with the literal and grammatical interpretation of the passage. In one place the words are: "Whosoever shall put away his wife, saving for the cause of fornication, causeth her to commit adultery; and whosoever shall marry her that is divorced, committeth adultery." In the other place, they are: "Whosoever shall put away his wife, except it be for fornication, and shall marry another, committeth adultery; and whoso marrieth her which is put away committeth adultery."[1]

The exception in both cases must apply to the declaration that the women put away, and those who marry them, are guilty of adultery. There is nothing else to which it can apply. There is no prohibition of putting away but that. The whole sentence in one case is nothing more than a declaration, that putting away one wife and marrying another is adultery. In the other it is a declaration, that putting away a woman exposes her to temptations to commit

[2] Matthew v. 32, and xix. 9.

adultery. In both it is added, that he who marries a divorced woman commits adultery. In the midst of each of the two sentences, there is introduced an exception, which can be to nothing but the whole sentence.

It has thus been shown, that the exception must, from the form of words used, apply as well to the prohibition of marrying again, as to the prohibition of putting away a wife. But it may be said, that the prohibition to which it is an exception, is that against putting asunder those whom God hath joined. In the fifth chapter, this cannot be, for that precept does not appear there. It does appear in the nineteenth chapter, in the sixth verse, upon which the ninth may be regarded as a commentary. The exception occurs in, and is part of, the explanation. But a parenthesis included in a commentary can hardly be an exception from the rule in the text and not from the commentary.

§ 3. The Latin Church has practically taken up the opinion, that the exception is to the prohibition to put away a wife, and not to the declarations which amount to prohibitions of marrying again. Probably no stranger or more forced interpretation of our Lord's words could have been devised. Yet, if it be not the doctrine of the Latin Church, it has for ages governed the practice of her courts.

§ 4. The Church of England has retained in her courts the practice which she inherited from the Latin Church. The English Reformers in their private judgments rejected the Latin notion, and held that adultery was a sufficient cause for dissolving a marriage. They embodied this idea in the code called *Reformatio Legum.* They, however, held loose notions about the indissoluble character of marriage, which they also embodied in that code. It was happily never ratified by the authorities of either Church or State. The Church of England has never formally decided the question.

§ 5. A body of English clergymen, respectable for learning and numbers, has always — except perhaps immediately after the Reformation — adhered to the Latin rule. There has always been another set of clergymen, who have regarded the exception as a permission to dissolve the bond of marriage, when the wife had been guilty of adultery.

§ 6. It has been said, that adultery dissolves a marriage. Much has been written for and against that proposition. If it be meant that adultery of itself dissolves the tie of marriage, the proposition has nothing to do with the question of divorce. If adultery of itself annuls the marriage, there is no room for divorce. If it be established, as it easily may, that it does not of itself dissolve a marriage, it is still possible to maintain that it is a cause for which the injured person may dissolve it. This is the position of those who assert that our blessed Lord made an exception to the general prohibition of divorce. Their doctrine is, that our blessed Lord, while He republished the primitive law of marriage, according to which it cannot be dissolved, permitted the husband to dissolve it in case the wife had committed adultery.

§ 7. This doctrine can only be set aside in one of two ways. By showing either that the words of our Lord do not formally make an exception, or that the exception is not a real one. Neither of these positions is tenable. The notion now under discussion is not more untenable than they are; but it is stranger, although it is the prevalent doctrine among these who now deny the right of divorce for adultery. It admits a real exception, but mutilates it. It is that the exception only authorizes a divorce *a mensa et thoro*, that is, a separation, which leaves the bond of marriage unbroken, so far as it is an obstacle to another marriage, but no farther.

§ 8. It has been already remarked, that this was the doctrine of the ecclesiastical courts in the churches of Rome and England, and of a large body of English clergymen, while the doctrine, that adultery is a cause for which the marriage bond may be dissolved, has been always held by another body of English clergymen.

§ 9. The existence of the last-mentioned body of clergymen is proved in this way. A practice grew up, in the British Parliament, of dissolving marriages for adultery, by a legislative act. This practice continued until very recently, when it was put an end to by an Act of Parliament, which instituted a court to do the same thing judicially.

§ 10. These legislative divorces furnished means of ascertaining the opinions of the English clergy upon this question. If the Latin doctrine were true, they were only licenses to commit adultery; and any clergyman, who married a person who had been thus divorced, was an accomplice in adultery. Yet there was no difficulty in finding clergymen to officiate at such marriages. It has been attempted to weaken the force of this fact, by asserting that the clergymen who officiated on such occasions did not know the situations of the persons before them. This is very improbable. The cases of divorce were not numerous, and the expense of the proceedings confined them to the higher classes of society. Each case was notorious. The proceedings had to pass through several stages, at each of which they were mentioned in the newspapers, and the whole affair was eagerly discussed in society. English clergymen were not hermits, but moved in the very class of society to which the divorced persons belonged. The marriages were not numerous, for the divorces were but few, but the marriages bore a large proportion to the divorces. If the divorced husband had no children, he was almost certain to marry, in order that he might have heirs. If he were not passed the prime of life, he would probably marry, although he had children. Public opinion almost compelled the paramour of the divorced woman to marry her. A considerable number of such marriages took place.

When one happened it was always generally known that one of the parties to it had been divorced, perhaps for adultery with the other. It was very unlikely that a clergyman so well known to them as to be asked to marry them, should be ignorant of so remarkable a fact in the history of one or both of them. If he were not known to them, the application was enough to put him upon an inquiry, coming from persons prominent in society, who, strangers to him, must have had clerical acquaintances. It is exceedingly improbable, that any clergyman ever officiated at such a marriage in ignorance of the facts. There is no known case in which a clergyman hesitated to solemnize such a marriage. The inference is, that a large number of the clergy of the Church of England held that persons divorced for adultery might marry. In the year 1820, the then Archbishop of Canterbury, Manners Sutton, and several other Bishops, maintained the same opinion in the House of Lords.[1]

§ 11. The American General Convention, in 1808, passed a resolution which involved the same principle. It is in these words: —

"*Resolved*, That it is the sense of this Church, that it is inconsistent with the law of God; and the ministers of this Church therefore shall not unite in matrimony any person who is divorced, unless it be on account of the other party having been guilty of adultery." [2]

This resolution implies that the exception made by our blessed Lord related to adultery; and it authorized the dissolution of a marriage for that cause, or at least the setting

[1] Tebbs *On Adultery and Divorce*, p. 110. London, 1822. It was on this occasion that Archbishop Manners Sutton delivered the speech, an extract of which is given in a note on the eleventh section of the eighth chapter. On the same occasion, Bishop Howley, of London, afterwards Archbishop of Canterbury, said, that he entertained "no doubt whatever of the power of dissolving the matrimonial bond." Bishop Van Mildert, of Llandaff, afterwards of Durham, said: "According to the law of the land, he knew no other cause of divorce than adultery, and no other punishment of adultery than divorce. As to the Christian Law, it certainly provides that dissolution of marriage may take place in any case of adultery, for there is no qualifying clause in our Saviour's injunction." *Tebbs*, p. 112, *note*.

[2] *Journals of General Convention*, Hawks & Perry's edition, vol. i. p. 348.

at liberty of the innocent person. There are very few of the clergy of the American Church who dissent from its doctrine. The last clause involves some other principles, which do not bear upon this part of the subject.

§ 12. To return to the words of our Lord. He twice made an exception from the general rule, that marriage is indissoluble. In the nineteenth chapter of St. Matthew, the Pharisees ask, "Is it lawful for a man to put away his wife for every cause?" They assume that for some causes he might put her away, and only inquire whether he might do so for any cause. By putting away, they meant such putting away as dissolved the marriage, for the Law of Moses allowed of no other. There were two opinions among the learned Jews about putting away. Some of the Rabbis held that the text in Deuteronomy allowed the husband to put away his wife whenever she had found no favor in his eyes; that is, whenever he wished to do so. Others interpreted the passage so as to give effect to every word, and insisted that a wife could only be put away when she found no favor in her husband's eyes, because he had found some uncleanness in her. Uncleanness they interpreted to mean adultery. The Pharisees desired to compel our Lord to adopt one of these two opinions. Both of them related to such putting away as dissolved the bond of marriage. The Pharisees were not thinking of that modern mode of putting away, which leaves the bond of marriage, and excuses the married persons from performing the duties to which that bond obliges them. Of such a mode of putting away they had never heard. Our Saviour did adopt the construction of the stricter Rabbis. This accounts for his introduction of the exception, explains and adds to its force. The Pharisees must have understood Him to speak of the dissolution of marriage. His discourse would then be perfectly intelligible to them, and the grammatical construction of the sentence would fall in exactly with the ideas which were present in their minds. The Roman doctrine would have involved new ideas, and required explanations which our blessed Lord did not think proper to make. The inference is, that He intended to be understood as permitting a putting away "for fornication," which would dissolve the bond of marriage.

§ 13. Moses seems to have been anxious to exclude the notion of such a divorce. For he says: "When a man hath taken a wife and married her, and it come to pass that she find no favor in his eyes, because he hath found some uncleanness in her, then let him write her a writing of divorcement, and give it in her hand, and send her out of his house. And when she is departed out of his house she may go and be another man's wife." [1] This was the only kind of putting away of which the Jews had any experience. There was no such thing allowed among them as a separation between a man and his wife, who continued to be man and wife. The man must not send the woman out of his house until he had given her a writing of divorcement. When he had done so, she was at liberty to become another man's wife. In practice the permission to marry was expressed in every writing of divorcement. One in which it was not contained was not regarded as valid. To this it may be added that no ancient nation seems to have recognized a divorce which did not allow the divorced persons to marry. Such an idea was unknown to Jew and Gentile alike.

§ 14. Our blessed Lord made the exception under consideration twice. On both occasions it is included in the bodies of sentences, which contain no direct prohibition of putting away a wife, but only a warning of the consequences of so doing. The warning, however, involves the strongest prohibition. Yet it is said that the exception does not apply to the declaration of consequences, but only to the prohibition. How can it apply to one and not to the other, when both are included in the same words, into the midst of which it is introduced? — "Whosoever shall put away his wife, saving for the cause of fornication, causeth

[1] Deuteronomy xxiv. 1, 2.

her to commit adultery, and whosoever shall marry her that is divorced, committeth adultery." [1]

How can the exception apply to anything but the rule? What is the rule? That he who puts away his wife causes her to commit adultery, and that he who marries her that is divorced commits adultery. There is no other rule to which the exception can be applied. The same argument may be put in a slightly different form. The rule that a man shall not put away his wife, is involved in a declaration that putting away does not dissolve the bond of marriage, which is implied in a certain doctrine about adultery. But there is an exception introduced into the declaration. Can that exception be applied to the implied rule, and not to the expressed declaration in which the rule is implied?

Suppose that the text had been: No man shall put away his wife, saving for the cause of fornication, and if any put away his wife, he causeth her to commit adultery. It might then have been contended that the exception applied to the rule and not to the declaration of consequences. Such a proposition would scarcely have been tenable. But as the passage stands, there is nothing to which the exception can be applied but the declaration of consequences. There is no prohibition out of which the exception can be taken but that which is implied in the declaration of consequences. If the exception be taken out of that, it must also be taken out of the declaration in which it is implied.

§ 15. How does he who puts away his wife cause her to commit adultery? By exposing her to temptation. The temptation is not less when the woman has been put away for adultery, perhaps it may be greater. The excepted case does not, at first, appear to have much connection with the reason given why men should not put away their wives. The reason seems to be a good one for forbidding all separations of married persons.

What has the exception to do with the reason for for-

[1] Matthew v. 32.

bidding separations? He who puts away his wife exposes her to the temptation of committing adultery, by depriving her of that, which St. Paul regards as a safeguard against fornication, and fornication is for her adultery. There is only one way in which she, who is put away can "have her own husband," that is, by marrying. But this, too, is for her adultery; for it is written: "Whoso marrieth her that is put away, committeth adultery." By a parity of reason, a woman put away by her husband and married to another commits adultery; all the cases rest upon one principle, — that the putting away has not dissolved the marriage, the woman is still the wife of the first husband.

But if her husband put her away for fornication, he does not cause her to commit adultery. There is here no need of reasoning; our Lord says so expressly: "Whosoever shall put away his wife, saving for the cause of fornication, causeth her to commit adultery, and he that marrieth her that is divorced committeth adultery." The use of this language compels the belief, that if the woman be put away "for the cause of fornication," neither does her husband cause her to commit adultery, nor does he that marries her commit adultery. Why is this? It can only be, because in that case the marriage is dissolved. It is lawful for her to marry, and so having her own husband, she may have the Apostolic refuge against temptation. There can be no other answer. Marriage is then lawful for her as for other women. If it be so, the bond of marriage with her first husband must have been dissolved, when he put her away for the cause of fornication. The woman has ceased to be one flesh with her husband; the unity between them has been destroyed.

§ 16. In the nineteenth chapter the case is still plainer. The text there is: "Whosoever shall put away his wife, except it be for fornication, and shall marry another, committeth adultery." Here again there is no other prohibition of putting away a wife than that which is implied in the declaration that he who does so, and marries again commits adultery. There is nothing to which the exception can apply, if it do not apply to that declaration, for there is no other rule. Out of that rule the case of putting away for fornication is excepted. It is impossible to believe that if, in the excepted case, the man should marry again he would commit adultery. That must be because the marriage is dissolved. While he has still a wife who is one flesh with him, he cannot marry without committing adultery against her. The general drift of the passage, and of all the passages in the New Testament which relate to the subject, is that a marriage which takes place while either of the parties to it is joined in marriage to another person, is adultery.

If in the excepted case the putting away did not dissolve the marriage, our Lord would surely have explained his language. He would have said something like this: "Even in the excepted case, in which it is allowed to put away a wife, it is not to be understood that she may be put away, in the only sense in which you understand the phrase; even in that case the separated couple are still man and wife, and cannot marry." He gave no such explanation, although He was addressing men who had never heard of a separation which did not dissolve the marriage. They must have understood him to mean that in the excepted case, the divorced persons might marry. He took no steps to undeceive them. The irresistible inference is that they were not deceived.

§ 17. The New Testament fully agrees with the Law of Moses in the matter of separations without breaking the bond of marriage. It contains nothing which treats as lawful the permanent separation of man and wife while they continue one flesh. On the contrary, it can be shown that it is utterly unlawful.

§ 18. A single passage has been found in the writings of St. Paul which some persons have supposed to give countenance to such separations. The Apostle has just been treating of the duties of the married state, in a manner which cannot be reconciled to such separations. He then takes up the then present inexpediency of marriage. Having devoted some verses to that subject, he resumes the duties of married life, and says: "Let not the wife depart from her husband; but and if she depart, let her remain unmarried or be reconciled to her husband, and let not the husband put away his wife."[1]

There are three distinct prohibitions. The wife is forbidden to leave her husband; if she do leave him, she is forbidden to marry; the husband is forbidden to put away his wife. The woman is also exhorted to be reconciled to her husband. It is to be observed that the two prohibitions addressed to the woman are distinct. She is not to leave her husband, but if she be so ill-advised as to do so, she is not to marry. If she leave her husband, she disobeys one precept. If she marry, she disobeys another precept and is guilty of another sin. This is the plain meaning of the words. They give no countenance to the idea that it is ever lawful for a man and his wife to live separately.

Yet they are used as an argument to prove that in the excepted case, the putting away does not work a dissolution of the marriage; but is only a separation which, while it releases both the parties from the duties of marriage, leaves them restrained from new marriages. But the woman is not forbidden to leave her husband and marry. She is first forbidden to leave her husband, and then forbidden, if she have left him, to marry. The first clause forbids all separation; the third, which is addressed to the husband, prohibits all putting away without reference to marrying again. The two prohibitions seem to cover all cases of separation. St. Paul was treating of the subject generally, and cannot be supposed to have had any reference to the excepted case.

[1] 1 Corinthians vii. 10, 11.

Yet the advocates of the Roman doctrine insist that the twice repeated exception is inoperative because St. Paul did not repeat it in this place, or which is still stranger, that the omission gives countenance to their non-natural interpretation of our Lord's words. They need something which will countenance the interpretation, that these words only permit a putting away not a subsequent marriage. They seize on this text, and apply the first clause to leaving a husband who has been guilty of adultery, as if it were: Let not the wife depart from her husband except he be guilty of adultery; but and if she depart, let her not marry. The exception made by our blessed Lord, which is repudiated where He inserted it, is here interpolated without a shadow of authority. They do not propose to read the last clause with the exception understood so that it should mean: Let not the husband put away his wife except for fornication.

§ 19. In the next verse the Apostle enters upon the case of persons who had been converted after marriage, and whose husbands or wives remained heathens, and continues the subject through several verses; they are pervaded by the same ideas. He forbids a Christian husband from putting away his wife, and a Christian wife from leaving her husband under such circumstances. In speaking of the case of a heathen husband or wife who will not live with the convert, he says: "A brother or a sister is not under bondage in such cases."[1] A Christian must not separate from his wife or her husband, although she or he may be an unbeliever. If the unbeliever will separate, the believer has no choice, and is, therefore, not to blame; but the Christian must do what can be done to keep the peace.

§ 20. Another question connected with the effect of the saving clause, is whether the guilty person who has been put away is at liberty to marry. If it be true that put-

[1] 1 Corinthians vii. 15.

ting away for fornication dissolves the marriage, it will follow as a logical deduction, that the person so put away may marry. This logical deduction can only be overruled by revelation, and revelation is silent. One strong argument to show that such putting away dissolves a marriage, was found in the hardship which a woman would suffer if she were deprived of one husband and not allowed to take another. According to our Lord's words, to place her in that situation is to cause her to commit adultery. For this reason any putting away in any case but one is unlawful. Our Lord excepted that case, but the same objection lies to putting away in that case as in others, unless the putting away dissolve the marriage, and allow her that is put away to marry. It seems that by these two independent lines of arguments, the right of the person put away to marry, is sustained.

§ 21. The right has been much disputed on grounds connected with public morals. This has been particularly the case in England. In America, the General Convention of the Protestant Episcopal Church assumed in 1808, the unlawfulness of such marriages.[1] But public opinion in this country takes a different view of the subject, in which very many religious people concur.

§ 22. While the English law refused to allow any dissolution of marriage, a practice arose of dissolving particular marriages by the supreme power of Parliament. It was not done except in cases of adultery by the wife, and then as a general rule only after the fact had been established by judicial proceedings. Bills for divorces were considered to partake of a judicial character. The facts were recited in the preamble, and required to be proved either by the decisions of the courts, or where, from peculiar circumstances, that could not be done, before a committee of the House of Lords. The bill always originated in that House, which is a court of justice as well as a legis-

[1] *Journals*, Hawks & Perry's edition, vol. i. p. 348.

lative assembly, was attended by the judges, and had always some members who had been eminent lawyers. The practice was perhaps also connected with the presence of the Bishops in that House, which had thus access to theological knowledge. The House of Lords had the whole control of the framing the bills and of all the preliminary steps in the proceeding. It made a set of standing orders by which the whole matter was to be regulated. One of these was, that every bill for dissolving a marriage should contain a clause disabling the person who had been guilty of adultery from marrying, notwithstanding the dissolution. This order grew out of a notion that women would be less easily seduced if they could not be married to their seducers. The result was curious. The officers of the House continued to obey the standing order, and inserted the clause in every bill for a divorce. The House of Lords passed the bills, if at all, with the clause; the House of Commons invariably struck it out; the House of Lords invariably yielded. This continued until the passage of the law which authorized judicial divorces *a vinculo matrimonii.*

§ 23. It became a usage which was held to bind the honor of the seducer, that he should marry the divorced woman. Such marriages were constantly celebrated by clergymen of the Church of England, and no instance of a refusal is known. The inference is that the body of the English clergy held that such marriages were consistent with the Christian Law. It has been attempted to weaken this inference by dwelling on the fewness of such marriages, and the probability that the clergymen who solemnized them were ignorant of the divorces by which they had been preceded. The value of this argument has been examined in the tenth section of this chapter.

§ 24. When the Act of Parliament, authorizing judicial divorces *a vinculo matrimonii*, was pending in the House of Lords, the Bishop of Oxford moved and carried a clause forbidding a person, who had been divorced on account of his or her own guilt, from marrying. The clause was stricken out by the House of Commons, and the Lords yielded. Lord Palmerston denounced the clause in the House of Commons as immoral. On a question of morals, especially of Christian morals, between these persons, there must be a strong prejudice in favor of the Bishop. In this case, it is scarcely doubtful that such a prejudice would mislead him who was led by it.

The Bishop's view was that a woman would be less easily seduced if her seducer could not marry her. He looked at the case prospectively. Lord Palmerston looked at it retrospectively. He held the rule to be immoral because it left the woman exposed to temptation. Each was clearly right from his own point of view. The question is, Which is the true point of view? Perhaps that question cannot be decided by the human intellect. The general analogy of the Divine Law, which rather seeks to deter from sin than to allow an escape from its consequences, must be conceded to be with the Bishop of Oxford.

§ 25. On the particular question, Divine authority seems to be rather on the side of Lord Palmerston. Moses did not allow of any putting away in which the woman put away could not be married. Our blessed Lord assigns the temptations to which a divorced woman is exposed, as a reason against divorces. St. Paul assigns the same reason against separations of married persons, although only designed as temporary. The question seems thus to be decided by the highest authority, that a woman put away for fornication may marry.

§ 26. If a marriage cannot be dissolved for adultery, the guilty person cannot marry; but neither can the innocent person. If a marriage may be dissolved for adultery, both parties must be at liberty to marry. It cannot be dissolved as to one of the parties and not as to the other.

They twain were one flesh, and while they continue such, neither of them can marry. Had our Lord seen fit to direct that the guilty person should not marry, notwithstanding the dissolution of the marriage, it would be unlawful for such person to do so; but He has not given such a direction. It may be inferred that He did not intend that there should be any such restriction. His own words imply this: "Whosoever shall put away his wife, saving for the cause of fornication, causeth her to commit adultery."[1]

How does he cause her to commit adultery? By exposing her to temptation. Is the temptation less because she has committed adultery? No; but she may be presumed less able to resist it. The reason why she is not caused to commit adultery when she is put away for the cause of fornication, must be that she is at liberty to avoid temptation by marrying. If the saving clause mean that a man may so put away his wife for adultery, as to dissolve the marriage, it is a direct inference from our Lord's words, that the guilty woman may marry.

§ 27. If there be no Divine law against such marriages, no human law can vacate them. A man and woman who are joined in a marriage not divinely forbidden, are joined together by God, and man may not separate them. Any attempt, by any human authority, to vacate a marriage which is religiously binding, is a usurpation of Divine authority. If the civil authority were to declare such marriages void, the civil courts would be bound to respect the civil law, and the marriages would produce no civil effects; but they would be binding on the consciences of Christians. No one could intermarry with either of the parties to such a marriage, without being guilty of adultery. Still those who, by the civil laws, were placed under such a disability, would be bound to obey the law of the land, and the state would have a right to restrain them by

[1] Matthew v. 32.

civil punishments, if it were thought that it would contribute to the purity of public morals.

§ 28. The next question is, Whether the privilege allowed to the husband in the saving clause, extends to the wife. Can a wife under any circumstances put away her husband? This question has also been much discussed of late, in England. The form which it has there taken is a discussion, whether a marriage can be dissolved for the adultery of the husband. English divines have generally taken the negative side of the question; in this country their view is sometimes spoken of as absurd. It may be erroneous, but it is not absurd. It may not be easy to show that it is erroneous.

§ 29. Those who maintain that it is, take ground which seems rather sentimental. They say that our Lord must have intended to put the sexes upon an equality. It does not appear that He has expressed that intention. Nevertheless, it is certain that He did intend to put them upon an equality in everything in which equality would promote their true happiness. Whether a power in women to divorce their husbands for adultery, would promote their happiness, is another question. It will not be easily settled by the human intellect, and is, therefore, a very insecure basis for an argument.

In no age or nation have men been as chaste as women; nor has chastity ever been a point of honor among men as it is among women. A man who desired to get rid of his wife would seldom scruple to commit adultery to effect his object. A woman would rarely commit adultery merely to get rid of her husband. It is true that a man who committed adultery in order that his marriage might be dissolved, could not succeed without the aid of his wife. But suppose that she were willing to get rid of him, although not willing to commit adultery for the purpose. In such cases, to allow a divorce for the adultery of the husband, would be to allow a divorce by mutual consent.

There may also be cases in which a brutal husband who desired to be clear of his wife, would find means to compel her to give her aid. To allow divorce under such circumstances would be to allow divorce at the will of any husband who might be brute enough to add cruelty to adultery. The modern English law allows a divorce *a vinculo matrimonii* for the adultery of the husband, when joined with cruelty to the wife. This law of divorce will scarcely improve the condition of women.

§ 30. Another argument for giving the power of divorce for adultery to women, is that the sin is equal in the two sexes. This is not true; and if it were true, would not be relevant. Adultery is equally a sin in both sexes; but it is not an equal sin. Murder is equally a sin with parricide, and lying with perjury; but they are not equally great sins. So adultery in a woman is complicated with circumstances which do not exist in the case of a man, which enhances its guilt, just as parricide and perjury are complicated with circumstances which enhance their guilt above that of mere murder or mere lying.

§ 31. But if it be admitted that the guilt of adultery is the same in both sexes, it has nothing to do with the question as to the right of a woman to divorce her husband. Our Lord did not direct that a man should put away his wife as a punishment for the sin of adultery. He permitted him to put her away as a means of redressing the wrong done to himself, perhaps as a means of protecting himself against future wrongs. The wrong done to the husband by the adultery of the wife, is greater than that which is done to the wife by the adultery of the husband. Aggravate the wrong done to the wife as much as you will, it will still contain no element which is not also found in the wrong done to the husband. But the wrong done to the husband contains an element which is wanting in the other, — the danger of spurious children. It is quite probable that this danger may be the reason of the permission to a man to put away an adulterous wife.

Neither of the general arguments which have been adduced to show that our Lord must have intended to give to the woman the same power of divorce for adultery which He allowed to the man, is at all conclusive, though it must be admitted that there is no conclusive argument on the other side. Indeed, in the nature of things, there cannot be a conclusive argument on either side. Recourse must be had to our Lord's words.

§ 32. There is but one place in the Holy Scriptures in which any mention is made of a woman's putting away her husband. There are one or two places in which mention is made of a woman's leaving her husband, but it is only to forbid such a step. The only place in which a woman separating from her husband is mentioned without a direct prohibition, is in St. Mark's Gospel, and our Lord is the speaker. His words are: "Whosoever shall put away his wife and marry another, committeth adultery against her. And if a woman shall put away her husband and be married to another, she committeth adultery."[1]

It should be remembered that the Mosaic Law gave no power to a wife to divorce her husband, as it did to a man to divorce his wife. In our Saviour's day, some women had undertaken to put away their husbands, and our Lord's words seem to be an affirmative publication of a rule which was implied in the omission of Moses. This seems to imply that it was an absolute prohibition. Men were to have less power of divorce than they had under the common interpretation of the Law of Moses, and the saving clause was needed to show what power was to be left to them. Women had no power under the Mosaic Law, and none was to be given to them. So the prohibition was made without exception.

Those who deny that a woman may put away her husband for adultery, rely on the omission of the saving

[1] Mark x. 11, 12.

clause in this passage. If it had been inserted in the eleventh verse, the omission in the twelfth would have been conclusive; but it has not been inserted, and the omission has been regarded as an abrogation of the saving clause in St. Matthew. The lawfulness of divorce in any case can only be supported by supposing the saving clause to be understood in the eleventh verse. It will then be virtually incorporated in that verse. But for the present purpose, virtual incorporation is very different from actual insertion. If the words were actually inserted in one verse, the omission in the other would seem to have been designed, and to signify that the cases were not parallel to each other. A virtual incorporation does not preclude the idea that it was intended to be incorporated in both verses. In this view the facts stated in the last paragraph are important.

Those who advocate divorce for the adultery of the husband, insist that if the words be virtually incorporated in one verse, they must be virtually incorporated in the other. Their chief arguments are the equality of the sin, which is neither true nor relevant, and the intention of our blessed Saviour to put the sexes upon an equality, which is the very thing to be proved. The absolute equality of the sexes is a modern idea, and like all other absolute equality, receives no countenance from the Holy Scriptures. There does not seem to be any very strong argument either for or against incorporating the saving clause in the twelfth verse. But it may be remarked in addition to what has been said, that the saving clause in the letter relates only to the adultery of the wife, and is an exception from a rule which does not apply to the adultery of the husband. Upon the whole it may be said that the text is plain against a woman's putting away her husband and being married to another. The exception is not plain. It is therefore safest for all Christians to act as though divorces for the adultery of the husband were not lawful.

CHAPTER X.

OF THE PRACTICAL ELEMENTS OF MARRIAGE. — II. INDISSOLUBLENESS. 4. JUDICIAL PROCEEDINGS, AND THEIR RELATIONS TO THE CONSCIENCE.

§ 1. THERE remains a subject connected with the indissoluble character of marriage which must be treated of in a short chapter of its own, because it does not fall within the scope of any of the preceding chapters. It is the relation of judicial divorces to the conscience. Without something on this question this work would be incomplete, although it does not grow directly out of our Saviour's rule or exception.

§ 2. There is a very remarkable difference between the modes of divorce in ancient times, and since Christianity has been the acknowledged religion of civilized communities. Anciently divorces were arbitrary, depending upon the will of one of the parties, — generally the husband, — or at most upon an agreement between the parties to the marriage. In modern times they are judicially pronounced by a tribunal which acts by public authority, and has examined the subject. So soon as it was understood that divorces could only be allowed for certain causes, it became necessary that the community should be satisfied of the existence of those causes. The Church first, and afterwards the State, provided tribunals to inquire into all questions connected with divorce. In ancient times there was nothing of the kind. The idea of an application to a court of justice to examine into the truth of the facts upon which a claim for a divorce is founded is entirely modern.

At Rome, among the early patricians, marriages were celebrated by a peculiar religious ceremony called confarreation. Such marriages could only be dissolved by another religious ceremony called diffarreation. But the priest who presided upon such occasions did not inquire into the causes of the divorce. It was sufficient that the man and his wife were both willing to go through the ceremony. The plebeians were married by other forms, and the husband might divorce his wife when he pleased, without any cause, and with very little ceremony. It was sufficient to demand the keys, and put her out of the house in the presence of witnesses. In time the patricians adopted the practice of the plebeians, both as to marriage and divorce. But there was no such thing as a court to try matrimonial causes.

The Mosaic Law made no provision for such a tribunal. It only prescribed the formalities by which the husband was to signify his will that the marriage should cease to exist, and gave effect to that will when the formalities had been duly observed. It became customary to produce the writing of divorcement in a court of justice; and although it was not required by the law, it came to be considered a necessary formality. But the writing was only produced for the purpose of authentication, like the acknowledgment of a fine in England, or of a deed in the United States. A similar practice prevails among the Athenians, and probably among other ancient people. But that a divorce should be the subject of litigation was an idea never received by any heathen nation.

§ 3. Matrimonial causes are of several kinds. One which was, until lately, called, in England, a divorce *a vinculo matrimonii* — and is still so called in this country —

is not a divorce at all. It is really a declaration that there has been no marriage, — the ceremony having produced no effect on account of some impediment. Where the impediment is a subsisting marriage by which one of the parties to the new one is bound, it has not been considered necessary to have a judicial decision of the invalidity of the second marriage, which is regarded as merely void. The same rule is applied in the English courts to all marriages forbidden by act of Parliament. But in other cases of void marriages, which they distinguish as voidable, it is necessary that the impediment should be ascertained by a judicial sentence.

These ideas probably arose among the early Christians. Their consciences were tender, and they lived under a strict ecclesiastical discipline. When marriages occurred, which were forbidden by the Christian Law, the authorities of the Church would enforce separation by excommunicating the persons who had broken the law. They were not absolved until they ceased to cohabit. Should the Church see fit to restore lay-discipline, a similar course would be open to her, although it would meet with difficulties unknown to the ancient Church. At that time the civil law regarded divorce as arbitrary; and if the offenders thought fit to submit it to the decree of the church tribunal, it could produce no collision with the civil courts. The same thing is true now as to marriages forbidden in England by act of Parliament, and probably as to those forbidden by State laws in this country. As to the mere voidable marriages, so-called, it is possible that the ecclesiastical and civil tribunals might come to different conclusions in particular cases. In this country, too, the State laws do not recognize all the Christian impediments. In practice, the State has everywhere assumed and exercised the whole jurisdiction in matrimonial causes, which is in itself right. But the discrepancies between Divine and human laws may give rise to many cases of conscience.

In the primitive Church, if persons discovered or supposed that they were living in an invalid marriage, they would apply to the Bishop for his advice. Some such course would be necessary; for they would sin if they continued to live together in a void marriage, or if they separated when their marriage was lawful. The Bishops thus acquired a jurisdiction which they delegated to church courts, and which the courts exercised either at the instance of the ecclesiastical authorities, or at that of the persons interested. But after the jurisdiction had passed over to the courts it could only be exercised with forensic forms.

The State has now taken possession of the jurisdiction, and professes to exercise it through her courts. But no public authorities are appointed to invoke its exercise. It is scarcely an exception that some very gross cases of incest are punished as crimes. Persons who are living in void marriages are not likely to bring their cases before the courts, or to separate without troubling them, unless in the case of a quarrel. Hence it is very unusual to find American courts employed about such matters. Besides, the State, in many countries, does not regard, as impediments to marriage, many things which the Divine law has made impediments.

§ 4. That which is properly a divorce *a vinculo matrimonii* — a dissolution of a marriage which was once binding — is a very different thing. According to the Christian law, it can be allowed only for adultery. In the Western Church it was, for many ages, not allowed at all. In most countries the State has now revived it, applies it in cases of adultery and in some other cases, and administers the jurisdiction in her own courts.

The discipline of the primitive Church did not allow a married couple to separate at their own discretion. If a husband charged his wife with adultery, he was bound to prove it to the Bishop. In later times the Bishops exercised this, like all other jurisdiction, by deputy; but it was still the Bishop's jurisdiction. When the Bishop or the judge was convinced of the fact, he pronounced sentence of divorce. In the Western Church this was, as has been said, for many ages, only a divorce *a mensa et thoro.*

§ 5. This kind of divorce, which is a permission to one of the parties to a marriage to live separately from the other, is not very ancient. It was at first allowed only in the case of cruelty, by which was meant such cruelty as endangered life or limb. The Christian Law requires that men and their wives must live together. But it was thought that this rule could not always be enforced, and that some exceptions must be allowed. It seemed hard that a woman should be obliged to endanger her life by living with a brutal husband. The same rule prevailed, as in other matrimonial causes. The person desiring to separate must act under the advice of the Bishop. The proceeding was, at first, really before the Bishop; then before an ecclesiastical judge who was appointed by the Bishop, and who was at one time a clergyman, and afterwards a lawyer. The jurisdiction has now passed to the civil courts. Now, however, husbands and wives separate when they please, and come together again when they please. But divorces *a mensa et thoro* are frequently sought as a means of separating the pecuniary interests of men and their wives, for the protection of the latter. The civil courts look upon them very much in that light. In the United States, in England, and in most Protestant countries, the civil courts are in quiet possession of the jurisdiction, in matrimonial causes, and administer it according to the laws of the land.

§ 6. Questions still remain to be decided by private conscience. It is still necessary for a Christian to decide how far he may act upon the decisions of these courts. The general rule is that they may be acted upon just so far as is possible, without disobeying the Divine law. This is the rule as to questions of doctrine or law. As to questions of fact, the safest rule is to adopt the decisions of the courts as final. They have better means of ascertaining the truth than any private person can have. As to questions of law, the decisions of the courts are authoritative expositions of the law of the land. That law is to be obeyed whenever it can be obeyed, without disobeying the law of God.

This rule can be applied without much practical difficulty to all cases in which it is supposed that a marriage is void on account of some impediment. As yet the American States have not attempted to create any impediments to marriage. When any of them do so, it will be the duty of Christians to obey the law so far as not to marry where such artificial impediments exist. No Christian ought to form an union which is forbidden by the law of the land. But as such marriages would be valid in the sight of God, no Christian should intermarry with any person, who, having entered into such a marriage, has been released from it by the authority of the State.

With respect to marriages which the law of the land allows, but which the law of God forbids, no one ought to enter into them or to continue in them. The parties to them have not been joined by God, and man ought to put them asunder.

In some cases the civil courts undertake to dissolve marriages which were originally valid, for causes for which the law of God does not allow them to be dissolved. No Christian can consider a marriage which was once valid as dissolved by any power whatever, except only in the case in which our Lord has permitted such dissolution. No Christian can intermarry with any one who has been released from a valid marriage for a reason which was Scripturally insufficient, — for any cause "saving the cause of fornication," — without being guilty of adultery.

By following these few rules, a private Christian may

avoid being mixed up with the unchristian laws which have been adopted in America. He can thus keep a conscience void of offense in this matter before God and man.

§ 7. But the clergy may sometimes meet with embarrassing cases. They will come in one of two forms. A clergyman may be called on to solemnize a marriage which the law of the land allows, and the law of God forbids. There is no reason for believing that such a marriage can receive the Divine blessing, or possess the sanctity and unity of marriage. A clergyman should refuse to solemnize such a marriage, at whatever cost or risk to himself. Happily, an American clergyman can incur no danger from the State; for there is no law of the land which requires him to solemnize any marriage whatever. The only danger is that of giving offense to the public and to his parishioners. This is sometimes an important consideration; but we ought to obey God rather than men.[1]

At other times the question may present itself in the shape of a case of lay discipline, when a person who is living in a sinful marriage desires to be admitted to the Holy Communion. In the primitive Church, such a person would have been rejected until he or she separated from his or her partner in guilt. Whether a modern clergyman is called upon to revive this discipline by his own authority and upon his own responsibility, is a grave and difficult question which every clergyman must decide for himself, with the aid and counsel of his Bishop. It may be observed that the power of rejecting or suspending a communicant is very much limited by the first rubric of the Communion Service. It seems to require that the evil life for which a communicant may be suspended or rejected should be such as to give offense to the congregation.

[1] Acts v. 29.

CHAPTER XI.

OF THE PRACTICAL ELEMENTS OF MARRIAGE. — III. THE AUTHORITY OF THE HUSBAND AND THE SUBORDINATION OF THE WIFE.

§ 1. Unpopularity of Authority. — § 2. Unpopularity of Marital Authority. — § 3. Necessity of Authority. — § 4. Indissolubleness of Marriage. — § 5. Mutual Concession. — § 6. External Interference impracticable. — § 7. There must be some Rule as to who is to have Authority. — § 8. Submission must grow out of Principle. — § 9. The Romantic School. — § 10. The Amazonian School. — § 11. The Sentimental School. — § 12. There is a Divinely appointed Rule. — § 13. Primary Institution of Marriage. — § 14. Effect of the Fall. — § 15. Solomon. — § 16. St. Paul. — § 17. St. Peter. — § 18. The Bible the Rule of Life. — § 19. Conscience and Judgment. — § 20. Limits of Human Authority. — § 21. Limits of Marital Authority. — § 22. Mode in which the Husband should exercise his Authority. — § 23. Duty of the Wife.

§ 1. The authority of the husband and the subordination of the wife, which are two names for the same thing, constitute the remaining element of Christian marriage. It seems to be the most unpopular of the seven. All authority in this age is looked upon with dislike and apprehension. It is never forgotten that all authority is liable to abuse, and will be occasionally abused. It must always be that more persons are under authority than are entitled to exercise it. There will thus always be a majority against authority, who will forget that all liberty is also liable to abuse and will frequently be abused.

§ 2. The last remark does not specially apply to the authority of the husband; which, however, suffers from the unpopularity of authority in general, while it labors under special disadvantages of its own. The romantic and Amazonian theories of the relation between the sexes work against it. So does the idea that women are better than men. It rests upon revelation, and revelation has come to be thought a rule of doctrine, not a rule of life. The doctrine of marital authority has thus to contend with a large amount of prejudice, which is the greater because the authority of husbands has often been much abused.

§ 3. If men were left to the light of nature, it would not be easy to prove the authority of the husband, although it would be easy to prove the necessity that one of each married couple should have authority which would involve the subordination of the other. There might, however, be some difficulty in deciding which of the two should have the authority. Among non-Christian nations the knot has generally been cut by force. Among Christian people this rude solution of the difficulty does not satisfy public opinion. Yet the necessity that one of the married couple should have authority is very much increased by the Christian doctrine of the indissolubleness of marriage. The Prophet Amos asks, "Can two walk together except they be agreed?"[1] The common sense of mankind answers in the negative.

Men all admit that if two persons cannot agree, they must cease to act together. Two partners in business who can agree in nothing else, must agree to separate. If a master and his servant cannot agree, the relation between them must be dissolved. It is the same in nearly all the relations of life. There are but two exceptions. The relation of parent and child cannot be dissolved, and the difficulty is provided for by the Divinely given authority of the parent. The relation of husband and wife cannot be dissolved, and the difficulty is provided for by the Divinely given authority of the husband. In all other relations, the remedy for a serious disagreement is a separation. Just as if two friends set out for a walk, to use the Prophet's illustration, if they cannot agree as to the direction which they shall take, they must separate.

[1] Amos iii. 3.

§ 4. From this analogy is derived one of the strongest arguments in favor of the dissolution of marriage. It is frequently used in defense of absolute divorce, and still more frequently in justification of those separations in which the marriage formally continues, but which practically dissolve it, for they reduce it to a mere restraint from marrying again. Such a relation contains no blessing, and in fact nothing affirmative. It is only a negation of the power to marry.

People often say: If persons cannot agree it is better that they should separate. Religious people mean by this that the married persons who cannot agree, should live separately from each other, while they nominally retain a tie which has no reality. Another class more logically draw the inference that the marriage tie may be absolutely dissolved. But a Christian marriage is indissoluble in the highest sense, only subject to one Divinely appointed exception. It cannot be dissolved so that things shall be as if it had never been, and the parties to it be at liberty to marry new partners. Neither can it be practically dissolved so that there shall remain a merely nominal tie which has no reality, except as it is an impediment to marriage. Our blessed Lord said: "A man shall leave his father and mother and cleave to his wife; and they twain shall be one flesh; so then they are no more twain but one flesh. What therefore God hath joined together, let not man put asunder."[1]

The obligation of a wife to cleave to her husband must be the same as that of a husband to cleave to his wife. They twain are one flesh. Both are so joined by God that man is forbidden to put them asunder. Our blessed Saviour did not say, What God hath joined, let not man join to others; but He said, "What God hath joined, let not man put asunder."

§ 5. Married persons cannot then separate. It follows

[1] Mark x. 7–9.

that they must agree. How is the agreement to be brought about? Much may be done by mutual concession. Much is every day done by it in other relations. A master who has a good servant grants him many privileges, and allows him his own way in many things. A servant who has a good master does not oppose his will, although he may think it unreasonable in a particular case, because he is unwilling to lose the advantages of his place. When partners in business find their connection useful they mutually concede much.

Married persons have advantages over all these persons. They are supposed to be, and very frequently are, united by a warm affection for each other. They enjoy the benefits of the mysterious sanctity and unity of the married state. Under such circumstances very much may be done by mutual concession, so much that there may be little or no occasion for the use of authority. Where each of two persons is desirous of gratifying the other, mutual concession will have scarcely any limits. This is the secret which enables married persons to live together, without a wish to separate, and with little necessity for the use of authority.

But the principle of mutual concession may cease to work. The servant is discharged; the master is left; the partnership is dissolved; the time has come when two are no longer agreed, and can no longer walk together. Where the alternative of separation is impossible, mutual concession may be expected to hold out longer than when that door of escape is open. It will do so if it be fully understood that separation is impossible. Parents and children seldom come to the point of separation; although they often come to that at which authority must interpose. In the case of married persons, mutual concession must for reasons already mentioned, be a very enduring principle. But even between them it is possible that the spirit of mutual concession may be exhausted. There must be some remedy in such cases. God has forbidden the obvious course of separation. What shall supply its place?

§ 6. Shall it be arbitration or external authority invoked in any other way? It would be impossible to find any person who would possess so much of the confidence of the disputants as to be trusted with such an office. They would never be willing to impart to a third person the knowledge of the delicate questions which are involved in their disputes. If they could, the selection of the arbiter would be the last thing about which they could agree. Every one sees that the notion of deciding disputes between man and wife by external authority is absurd.

§ 7. There remains, then, no mode by which those who cannot be separated, can settle their controversies. They must have no controversies. They may be prevented by mutual concession. But cases may occur in which neither side is willing to give way. One of the parties must be bound to yield. Such yielding implies the authority of the other. Which is to have that authority? This question can only be answered by some definite rule, which shall give to one of the parties the right of deciding, and impose upon the other the duty of obeying. Very good reasons may be assigned why it is the duty of the wife to obey, although it can scarcely be expected that women should feel their force. In most ages and countries their submission has been compelled by brute force, or by the authority of human laws and social usages, or by the *ultima ratio* of arbitrary divorce. The man who had the power to drive a woman from her home and her children could extort an external submission to almost anything.

§ 8. But what is necessary for the happiness of married life is a submission which shall grow out of principle, not out of fear. Submission, to be valuable, must rest upon the idea of duty, and that upon the Divine Law. Women are to yield, but it should be to the Divine authority, delegated to the husband. If they do not, they will only yield to the fear of overwhelming evils. As it is they do not generally accept the idea of submission at all.

§ 9. Those of them who have adopted the romantic theory, — who are in this country the majority of the upper classes, — maintain that the man should always yield to the goddess. Some fortify this notion, by supposing that women ought to rule, because they are better and more conscientious than men. The fact may be admitted, but with some qualification, for it is certain that the consciences of women are easily swayed by their interests and feelings, so that a woman is very often practically very unjust, while she supposes herself to be very conscientious. Lawyers, who have had many female clients, know this well. But admitting the fact of their conscientiousness as fully as may be asked, the premises do not warrant the conclusion. Looking at the question practically, it will be seen that as a general rule, the dominion of the wife does not work well.

§ 10. The women of the Amazonian school do not formally claim dominion, though practically they do. Their theory is that there is to be no acknowledged superiority on either side, but that in each case the strongest intellect is to govern. In the opinion of each Amazon, her own intellect will be the strongest. The application of the rule thus gives dominion to the woman in every case, at least in the judgment of the particular woman who is interested. It is unfortunate that in each particular case the man will dissent from the judgment of his wife. He may concede the major proposition, that the strongest intellect should rule ; but it is nearly certain that he will deny the minor, that his wife's intellect is stronger than his own. This rule cannot work. Every man and his wife would have a new question to settle instead of settling the old one, and that perhaps the most difficult of all questions to be decided, and one the decision of which is more likely to irritate than to calm. Both would decide it, and "by decision more embroil the fray." They would be less likely to work together than before. Such a rule is practically inconsistent with the Christian doctrine, that marriage is indissoluble; one or the other must be given up. Unless the question of authority is settled, there can be no termination of the strife but separation. In fact the principle of separation is accepted by the Amazonian women.

§ 11. The ladies who receive the Christian theory generally receive it with some modification. They acknowledge the Christian principle, that marriage cannot be dissolved, but only in a qualified sense. They believe that it cannot be so dissolved as to make another marriage lawful. But they also believe that it can be so far dissolved as to make it lawful for the married couple to live apart from each other. They believe that this may be done by consent in every case, and, where a lady has been harshly treated, without [consent], — the lady herself being always the judge of what is harsh treatment. They forget the precept, that the married pair should cleave to each other, and read the prohibition to separate what God has joined, as if it only forbade persons who had been separated from being joined to others.

They do not accept the moral impossibility of separation, and therefore they do not apprehend the moral necessity that there shall be a rule binding one party always to yield. Such a rule settles every question and closes every altercation, effects which nothing else can produce. Some of these ladies adopt, to some extent, the romantic theory, and combine with it some facts of Christian history. Out of the two they form a theory, the holders of which may be called the sentimental school. It rests on the theory that women are better than men, and therefore ought to govern. On one of these theories, or on the Amazonian, or on some theory made up out of some or all of them, a lady is easily persuaded that at least in her own case, the wife ought to govern. Her husband, however, may be neither romantic nor sentimental, nor easily persuaded that his wife's judgment is better than his own, even if the fact should be so. Then comes the conflict, and sometimes the separation.

§ 12. A rule which will reach every case, is necessary. Human ingenuity could not invent a rule, which would be agreeable to both parties. Human authority could not, without recourse to physical force, enforce one which was disagreeable to either. Under rules of human invention woman has generally been a slave. No means of relieving her have been found, except making marriage dissoluble at her pleasure, which is as much contrary to the Divine law as the power of arbitrary divorce in the hands of man. Wherever the Divine rule has been neglected, men have ruled by the right of the strongest, or women have escaped by that craft which is the natural defense of the weak. Force is almost sure to be both abused and evaded. Hence in all non-Christian countries, women are in a state of slavery, while in those which are nominally Christian, they are often allowed a liberty, which is not good. There is a divinely appointed rule, which does not rest upon force, and has other limits than the will of the strongest. It is, that authority belongs to the husband, and submission is the duty of the wife.

§ 13. This is perhaps involved in the very primitive institution of marriage. It is recorded that woman was created to be the help of man, as well as his companion: "And the Lord God said, It is not good that the man should be alone: I will make him an help meet for him."[1]

The idea of a companion includes that of equality; that of a help includes subordination. Even in Paradise, both equality and subordination existed. The subordination could not have been slavish; the equality could not have been absolute. Perhaps the equality was nearer absolute, and the subordination less marked than after the Fall.

[1] Genesis ii. 18.

§ 14. Immediately after the Fall, the ideas of authority and subordination were largely developed, and that agreeably to the Divine will. When the Lord was passing sentence upon the offenders, He said unto the woman: "I will greatly multiply thy sorrow and thy conception; in sorrow thou shalt bring forth children: and thy desire shall be to thy husband, and he shall rule over thee."[1] This sentence has four members, of which the two first do not relate to the present subject. The third contains a prophecy, of the meaning of which, and of its very remarkable fulfillment, it is not expedient to speak. The fourth contains a law which is very plain: "He" that is, thy husband, "shall rule over thee." It is then the duty of the wife to obey, — a duty which is abundantly enforced by many texts in the New Testament.

§ 15. Before considering them, it may be remarked that Solomon, in speaking of the contentions of married life, invariably lays the blame upon the woman, thus assuming that submission is her duty. "A foolish son is the calamity of his father: and the contentions of a wife are a continual dropping."[2] Here he couples a contentious wife with a foolish, that is a rebellious son, implying that they are in the same position. A little further on, he remarks that: "It is better to dwell in a corner of the house-top, than with a brawling woman in a wide house."[3] And again: "It is better to dwell in the wilderness than with a contentious and an angry woman."[4] He nowhere speaks of the contentions or the brawling of a husband.

§ 16. In the New Testament, the doctrine of subordination and authority is yet more distinctly brought out. St. Paul writes to the Corinthians: "I would have you know, that the Head of every man is Christ; and the head of the woman is the man; and the Head of Christ is God."[5]

To St. Titus the same Apostle says: "Speak thou the

[1] Genesis iii. 16. [2] Proverbs xix. 13. [3] *Ibid.* xxi. 9.
[4] *Ibid.* 19. [5] 1 Corinthians xi. 3.

things which become sound doctrine: that the aged men be sober, grave, temperate, sound in faith, in charity, in patience; the aged women likewise, that they be in behavior as becometh holiness; not false accusers, not given to much wine, teachers of good things; that they may teach the young women to be sober, to love their husbands, to love their children, to be discreet, keepers at home, good, obedient to their own husbands, that the Word of God be not blasphemed." [1]

To St. Timothy he writes: "Let the woman learn in silence with all subjection. But I suffer not a woman to teach, nor to usurp authority over the man, but to be in silence. For Adam was first formed, then Eve. And Adam was not deceived, but the woman being deceived was in the transgression." [2]

To the Colossians he writes thus: "Wives submit yourselves unto your own husbands, as it is fit in the Lord." [3]

He treats the subject more fully in the Epistle to the Ephesians than in any other part of his writings. The latter part of the fifth chapter is a brief treatise on the duties of the married state. It begins and ends with the subordination of the wife, as if that were the foundation of the whole superstructure. He says: "Wives, submit yourselves unto your own husbands, as unto the Lord. For the husband is the head of the wife, even as Christ is the Head of the Church: and He is the Saviour of the body. Therefore, as the Church is subject unto Christ, so let the wives be to their own husbands in everything. Husbands love your wives, even as Christ also loved the Church, and gave Himself for it; that He might sanctify and cleanse it with the washing of water by the Word, that He might present it to Himself a glorious Church, not having spot or wrinkle, or any such thing; but that it should be holy and without blemish. So ought men to love their own wives, as their own bodies. He that loveth his wife

[1] Titus ii. 1–5. [2] 1 Timothy ii. 11–14. [3] Colossians iii. 18.

loveth himself. For no man ever yet hated his own flesh; but nourisheth and cherisheth it, even as the Lord the Church: for we are members of His body, of His flesh, and of His bones. For this cause shall a man leave his father and mother, and shall be joined unto his wife, and they two shall be one flesh. This is a great mystery: but I speak concerning Christ and the Church. Nevertheless, let every one of you in particular so love his wife even as himself: and the wife see that she reverence her husband." [1]

It would not be easy to frame a stronger statement of the doctrine of marital authority and wifely obedience, than that which is found in this passage. It is strengthened by the manner in which it runs into, and is, as it were, confounded with the statement of the authority of the Saviour over the Church. Whether the direct precepts, the illustrations, or the motives proposed be considered, they are strong, — so strong that nothing stronger can be conceived.

§ 17. St. Peter falls not behind St. Paul in the stress which he lays upon this doctrine. He writes thus: "Likewise, ye wives, be in subjection to your own husbands; that, if any obey not the Word, they also may without the Word be won by the conversation of the wives, while they behold your chaste conversation coupled with fear. Whose adorning, let it not be that outward adorning of plaiting the hair, or of wearing of gold, or of putting on of apparel; but let it be the hidden man of the heart, in that which is not corruptible, even the ornament of a meek and quiet spirit, which is in the sight of God of great price. For after this manner in the old time the holy women also, who trusted in God, adorned themselves, being in subjection unto their own husbands: even as Sarah obeyed Abraham, calling him lord: whose daughters ye are, as long as ye do well, and are not afraid with any amazement." [2]

[1] Ephesians v. 22, *et seq.*

[2] 1 Peter iii. 1-6.

This place is much more frequently quoted against what is called gay dressing, than as commanding the subordination of wives. The last is its true scope. Accordingly, the Church of England introduces it into that admirable summary of the duties of married life, which is the concluding exhortation in her marriage service. The outward adorning is only mentioned incidentally, and is not forbidden, but only disparaged in comparison with a meek and quiet spirit. The general drift of the passage is to instruct women in their wifely duties. The meek and quiet spirit is to be manifested, after the manner of the holy women of old, by being in subjection to their own husbands.

§ 18. This collection of texts establishes the doctrine of the authority of the husband and the subordination of the wife, not to use St. Peter's less courtly expression of subjection. They seem to be little regarded by public opinion. This proceeds in part, from the manner in which the Holy Bible is now regarded. It is no longer considered as the revealed rule of life. It is used as a supply of devotion, or as a store-house of doctrine, sometimes as a mere arsenal of polemic weapons. It is all these, but it is also a rule of morals. The popular theology ignores this, and thus separates morality from religion to an extent which its votaries do not perceive. The Bible is neglected as a moral guide, and public opinion has to seek another. So far as relates to the present subject, it is sought in speculations about the equality of the sexes and the best mode of producing happiness. This men fancy they find in associations without a head, in which each of the persons concerned does as he or she pleases; when they do not please to do the same thing, the association must be dissolved. Still the authority of the husband and the subordination of the wife continue to be fundamental principles of Christian morals, and are binding on the consciences of all Christian women.

§ 19. The authority of the husband is a part of Christian doctrine; but Christianity acknowledges no absolute human authority. All human authority is at an end when it comes in conflict with the Divine authority, from which it is derived. The province of the private conscience must be always respected. Yet the distinction between private conscience and private judgment must not be forgotten. The concern of the conscience is only with questions of right and wrong; while the judgment deals also with questions of expediency. Conscience belongs to the moral nature, and on all subjects inquires only what is right or wrong; judgment belongs to the intellectual nature, and may deal with any subject without reference to the distinction between right and wrong.

If any one deny this distinction, and assert that judgment deals with questions of right and wrong, or that conscience is only a function of the judgment, it may be conceded for the sake of argument. But the substance of the distinction will return upon him. There will still be judgment exercising its function of conscience, and dealing with the distinction between right and wrong, and judgment not exercising that function, neglecting that distinction, and exercising its other functions. The two phases of judgment will, practically, be two faculties. It is more convenient to distinguish them as judgment and conscience. There is a wide distinction between the judgment which deals with expediency, and the conscience which deals with right and wrong. This is so, whether they be two faculties or two functions of the same faculty. The distinction pervades the whole field of ethics. The reason for respecting the private conscience, is that it appeals to a law which it is bound to obey. When it ceases to do so, no matter by what name it may be called, it must submit to authority. In the family it must submit to the divinely appointed head of the family.

§ 20. Everywhere the question arises as to the limits of

human authority. Everywhere the answer is that human authority can have no dominion over the conscience. But the private conscience of one under human authority can have nothing to do with that authority, except to inquire whether its commands conflict with a law of higher authority, especially with the Divine law, from which all human authority is derived. When human authority forbids what God commands, or commands what He forbids, it is usurped and must be disobeyed. But it must be obeyed until it actually clashes with the Divine law in some particular case. It may forbid anything which God doth not command, or command anything which He does not forbid, and will be entitled to obedience. Within those limits it may be governed by its own views of expediency, otherwise it would not be authority. This is true of all human authority, and of that of the husband as well as of other human authority.

§ 21. Whether any human authority has transcended its limits is a question for the private conscience of those whom it calls upon to obey. It always resolves itself into another question, Is it possible to obey the human authority without breaking the Divine law? In the case of the marital authority, this question involves another. Can the husband be obeyed without breaking the law of the land or the law of the Church? Like every other Christian and citizen the husband is bound, as well as the wife, to obey both those laws, which are to them authoritative expositions of the Divine law. These questions are for the private conscience. If they are answered in the negative, we must obey God rather than man. If they are answered in the affirmative, the function of private conscience is at an end. The authority must be obeyed.

Conscience has nothing to do with questions of expediency, for about them the law says nothing; but it does say, "Let every soul be subject to the higher powers." "Submit yourselves to every ordinance of man for the

Lord's sake." Questions as to whether a particular course is agreeable, rank even lower than questions of expediency. They cannot appeal even to private judgment, but belong to the province of taste. Conscience has nothing to do with them, and it is only conscience which may oppose itself to authority.

§ 22. This view of the subject seems to be all that is necessary to guide the conscience of a married woman; but it is proper to speak of the duties of husbands as well as of their rights. Abundant instruction upon this subject is given in the texts of Scripture, on which the authority of the husband is founded. The long passage, which has been transcribed from the fifth chapter of the Epistle to the Ephesians (see § 16), dwells as much upon the love which is to temper the authority of the husband as upon the submission of the wife. They are urged upon parallel motives, and with the same illustrations.

The primary institution of marriage speaks more directly of the duty of the man than of that of the woman: "A man shall leave his father and his mother, and shall cleave unto his wife, and they shall be one flesh."[1] Solomon and Malachi repeat the lesson. The first says: "Let thy fountain be blessed: and rejoice with the wife of thy youth; let her be as the loving hind and pleasant roe; let her breasts satisfy thee at all times; and be thou ravished always with her love."[2] Malachi reminds the husband, that his wife is his "companion and the wife of his covenant."[3]

In the New Testament, precepts of affection for the wife addressed to the husband, continually occur in close connection with those which enforce the submission of the wife. This is the case in the passage which has been transcribed from the fifth chapter of the Epistle to the Ephesians. (See § 16.) It has already been observed, that that passage may almost be regarded as a summary of the Christian doctrine about married persons.

[1] Genesis ii. 24. [2] Proverbs v. 18, 19. [3] Malachi ii. 14.

To the Colossians, St. Paul writes: "Wives, submit yourselves unto your own husbands, as it is fit in the Lord. Husbands love your wives, and be not bitter against them." [1]

Again, in discussing the expediency of marriage, he declares that, "He that is married careth for the things that are of the world, how he may please his wife." [2]

St. Peter, after dwelling on the subjection and obedience of the wife, addresses husbands thus: "Likewise, ye husbands, dwell with them according to knowledge, giving honor unto the wife as unto the weaker vessel, and as being heirs together of the grace of life, that your prayers be not hindered." [3]

These texts sufficiently instruct the husband how he is to administer his authority. He is to remember that although as his wife she is bound to obey him, she is his companion, and therefore in a certain sense his equal, and is to be treated with respect. She is entitled to honor as the weaker vessel, and is the proper object of tender affection—of that love, which "suffereth long and is kind, is not easily provoked, thinketh no evil, beareth all things, believeth all things, hopeth all things, endureth all things." [4]

§ 23. These are the principles upon which the husband is to administer his authority, so that it may not be more burdensome than is necessary. But it still exists, and may be exercised in restraining extravagance and other follies. If the husband be imbued with the spirit of the texts which have been cited, and governed by the feelings which they inculcate, it will not be used harshly or without necessity. The wife will be allowed all liberty, which will not interfere with the welfare of the family. She will probably say and think that she desires no more. Yet there may be differences of opinion between her and her husband as to what will interfere with the welfare of the family. She

[1] Colossians iii. 18, 19.
[2] 1 Corinthians vii. 33.
[3] 1 Peter iii. 7.
[4] 1 Corinthians xiii. 4, 5, 7.

has a right to present and explain her own views; but those of the husband have authority, and must be submitted to if she cannot change them. If she do not submit, she does not walk after the manner of the holy women of old, who were in subjection to their own husbands.

CHAPTER XII.

A FEW GENERAL REMARKS UPON MARRIAGE.

§ 1. Introduction. — § 2. The Elements of Marriage. — § 3. Consent. — § 4. Popular Notion of Marriage. — § 5. The Practice of Separation.

§ 1. HAVING gone through the Christian doctrine of marriage, except with respect to impediments to marriage, it may be well to devote a very short chapter to a few general remarks, chiefly intended to recall to the mind things which have already been said.

§ 2. The elements of Christian marriage are seven, — consent, the Divine blessing, sanctity, unity, exclusiveness, indissolubleness, and the authority of the husband and subordination of the wife. The first two form the union by creating the two next, which are the mysterious essence of marriage. The three remaining are the logical and practical results of that essence.

§ 3. Consent is the first element; it is a necessary prerequisite for the Divine blessing, which creates the sanctity and the unity of the marriage. The true consent is to live with a particular person as a husband or wife, in the holy state of matrimony, according to God's holy ordinance. This implies an acceptance of all the seven elements of a Christian marriage. There is reason to fear that such a consent is rarely given. The greater number of those who come to be married, think little, or not at all, of God's blessing upon their union. The sanctity and unity of marriage are not believed in by great numbers. Many men have no idea of consenting to the exclusiveness of marriage, and have no scruple in indulging themselves in that which is practical polygamy. Few women give a hearty consent to the authority of the husband. They accept it, if at all, with a secret reservation, — that in their own case it shall never be exercised. The indissolubleness of marriage is a doctrine, which many of both sexes reject or at least accept in a very qualified sense. It is to this want of a sincere consent that many unhappy marriages are owing.

What is necessary, is a sincere consent to live together in God's holy ordinance of marriage. That people may give such a consent, it is necessary that they should understand the nature of Christian marriage, and how it is distinguished from that civil marriage, which is only a civil contract to live together according to the law of the land. The last may be marriage in the eye of the law; in the sight of God it is only concubinage.

§ 4. The true idea of marriage is not popular. The popular notion of marriage is that of a mere consent to cohabit, until something shall occur which shall make it unpleasant to do so any longer. Few persons, especially among women, look forward to an actual separation, because they do not expect anything unpleasant to occur. But great numbers have no notion of living together in case it shall become disagreeable to do so. This popular notion of marriage is at the bottom of many and great social evils. It leads to much misery, which it is in vain attempted to remedy by what are called voluntary separations. These are indeed putting asunder what God hath joined.

§ 5. The Apostles thought that the principle that marriage is indissoluble rendered it not good to marry. Our blessed Lord seems to admit that it so far renders it not good, that it is only good for those who are prepared for it. If any man cannot receive the saying, that a man and his wife are one flesh, so joined together by God that man cannot put them asunder, no person ought to marry unless he or she can accept this principle.[1]

[1] See Matthew xix.

The departure from this principle often leads to great hardships, which bear sometimes upon the man and sometimes upon the woman. A poor man can generally part with his wife without any intolerable inconvenience. He carries with him his means of subsistence, and perhaps finds his expenses lessened by the change. The case of the woman is very different; she loses that which the Scotch expressively call her bread-winner. If she has children she may either be deprived of them or find it difficult to support them. In every way her condition is pitiable. In a higher social position, where the lady has friends who can provide for her and her children, or compel her husband to provide her a separate maintenance, the separation is most frequently sought by the wife; while among the lower classes it is a rare occurrence for a woman to leave her husband. In the higher classes a hardship is often imposed upon the man, who is obliged to provide a separate establishment for his wife and children, while he is deprived of their assistance and of the comfort of their society. His expenses are increased, while his comforts are diminished. In every way these separations produce evil, but after all the greatest evil connected with them is that they are violations of the Divine law.

CHAPTER XIII.

OF THE IMPEDIMENTS TO MARRIAGE

§ 1. The Nature of Impediments to Marriage. — § 2. Two Classes of Impediments to Marriage. — § 3. The Necessity of an outward Consent. — § 4. Force. — § 5. Fraud. — § 6. Incapacity to Contract. — § 7. Unsoundness of Mind. — § 8. Practice of Civil Courts. — § 9. The Connection of Conscience with Judicial Decisions. — § 10. The Difficulty of finding a Rule. — § 11. The Rule for Christians. — § 12. Nonage. — § 13. Necessity for fixing an Age at which Capacity shall be presumed. — § 14. The Laws of England. — § 15. The Age of Consent. — § 16. Defect in the American Laws. — § 17. The Consent of Parents cannot supply the place of the Consent of the Persons to be Married. — § 18. Duty of Young Persons. — § 19. Impediments created by the Revealed Law. — § 20. An existing Marriage. — § 21. Incest. — § 22. Of Mixed Marriages. — § 23. Impediments attempted to be created by Human Laws. — § 24. Canonical Impediments; Consanguinity. — § 25. Affinity. — § 26. Spiritual Affinity. — § 27. Effects of these Prohibitions. — § 28. Of Dispensations. — § 29. State Prohibitions. — § 30. Marriage Act of George II. — § 31. Of Voidability of Marriage. — § 32. The True Rule. — § 33. The Royal Marriage Act. — § 34. Of the Marriage of First Cousins. — § 35. Duty of Christians. — § 36. Conclusion of the Chapter.

§ 1. All the elements of marriage gather about the unity to which some of them lead, while others spring from it. The unity, that is, the union of the twain into one flesh, is the central idea of marriage, and the basis of the precept against separation. Our blessed Lord, after stating the doctrine of the unity of the married pair, declares the unlawfulness of separation, which He expressly derives from that doctrine.[1] The consent of the parties and the blessing of God are the formative elements of marriage, the two factors, so to speak, by which it is made. Out of them arise the sanctity and the unity, which

[1] See Matthew xix. 5, 6; Mark x. 6–9.

are the parents of the other elements. God's blessing is the immediate cause of the sanctity and the unity. That blessing is not given when there has been no hearty consent, or when the consent, although given, is contrary to the Divine law. When there has been no Divine blessing, God hath not joined the twain so that they have become one flesh. The unity of marriage depends upon that junction which can be the work of no power but God. When it has not taken place there is no marriage, and man is not forbidden from putting asunder those whom God hath not joined. Persons who live together in such pretended marriages, live in sin. They not only may, but must separate.

This principle does not extend to marriages which have been entered into without the inward consent of one or both of the parties, to the elements of Christian marriage. If an external and formal consent has been given, man, who can only look upon the outward appearance, must inquire no further. All human laws, whether ecclesiastical or civil, must treat the marriage as binding. Nay, as between the parties themselves it is binding. The person who has withheld the consent has sinned, and has drawn the other party into a situation in which he or she would not have been but for the simulated consent. The sinner cannot, according to any law, Divine or human, take advantage of his or her own sin, but must submit to all the inconveniences of which it may be the cause. The deceiver should repent and amend, and give the consent which was improperly withheld. The blessing of God may then descend and supply what was wanting in the formal marriage. In the mean time the marriage is sinful, so far as the guilty person is concerned. But man has no warrant for treating it as other than a valid marriage.

§ 2. In this way, and perhaps in other ways, those may be sinful marriages which are displeasing to God, but which man cannot treat as void. But where no consent has been given, or where the marriage is in direct violation of a Divine law, and the absence of the consent or the unlawfulness can be shown by outward provable facts, man may separate those whom God hath not joined. It is plain that God hath not joined the parties, and that they are not married. There are then some things which make an outward marriage unlawful and void. They are called impediments to marriage, and are of two classes. The first are facts which prove that there has been no consent. The others are facts which prove that the marriage is of a class not allowed "by God's Word."

§ 3. Consent is the first element of Christian marriage; without it there can be no Divine blessing, and consequently no marriage. The case of an outward consent without an inward has been just considered. At present, the subject is the absence of an outward consent. Where there is an outward consent, men are bound to presume an inward one; but where there is no outward consent, there is no marriage. This truth is so clear to unassisted reason, that it has not been revealed. It is a logical inference from it, that where consent, although formally given, can be shown to have been only formal, the marriage is void. The cases to which this rule is applicable are those in which the consent has been obtained by force or fraud, or one of the parties has been incapable of giving an intelligent assent. Persons of unsound mind and children are under such an incapacity.

§ 4. Marriages have been sometimes brought about by force. In such cases there is no inward consent. The outward consent can be shown to have been extorted, and not to have been the index of an inward consent. Such marriages can be shown to be void, because it can be proven by evidence, of which man can judge, that there has been no consent.

§ 5. In other cases, persons have been induced to marry without knowing the facts about which they ought to have inquired. Here there is no internal consent, and in fact no external consent to the thing which has been done. When such a person has acted heedlessly, there has been sin, but not such sin as will annul the marriage. It is like any other marriage in which the outward consent has been given without the internal. The imprudent person has no remedy, and must give the internal consent whenever the facts are disclosed. But if a person has been deceived by the fraud and contrivance of the other party to the pretended marriage, it is a different case. It can then be proved that the formal external consent was obtained while the internal was withheld. The marriage can then be shown to be void. But the fraud must relate to the person, or at least to something which enters into the essence of the marriage. A fraud which relates to property, or to anything which is merely circumstantial to the marriage, will not affect its validity.

Under this head may be mentioned — although perhaps not with strict accuracy — the nullity of marriages in which one of the persons married labors under certain physical disabilities which unfit persons for some of the duties of marriage. On this subject it is perhaps best to say nothing more.

§ 6. It follows from the necessity of consent, that a provable incapacity to consent is an impediment to marriage. It is an impediment interposed by God himself, who requires consent by his unwritten law, and has, in the course of his providence, withheld from a particular person the power of consenting. All the writers on the subject of marriage, including those of the strictest principles, are agreed that an evident incapacity to consent is such an impediment as renders the outward consent ineffectual and the marriage void. Lawyers speak of three classes of persons who have not capacity to consent to a contract: idiots, lunatics, and infants. The progress of science is fast effacing the distinction between idiots and lunatics.

They may be included in one class, and called persons of unsound mind. The impediments to marriage arising out of incapacity are then two, — unsoundness of mind and nonage.

§ 7. Unsoundness of mind is the effect of a disease, or perhaps of several diseases, which interrupt in various ways the intercourse between the intellectual soul and the brain. Those who are thus affected are in a greater or less degree incapable of understanding the various relations of life, and consequently of governing themselves and taking care of their own interests. The law of the land interposes for their protection, and declares that they are not bound by any contracts which they may attempt to make; the rule applies to marriage as well as to other contracts. Its application is a very nice operation. Most persons have so much capacity as to understand, although perhaps imperfectly, something of the relations of life and the effect of contracts. But there are persons who are incapable of doing either. These are persons of unsound mind. The other class are persons of dull or slow or weak minds, and in some cases even of unsound mind. These are all figurative expressions. They all designate a certain, or rather uncertain amount of deficiency in the mind. The deficiency is very different in different persons. Whether the difference is in kind or degree is a very difficult question. If it be in kind, what is it? If it be in degree, where and how are lines to be drawn?

The nature and extent of these deficiencies cannot be ascertained, and rules deduced which can be applied to particular cases. Where the deficiency is very great, all men agree that the person is of unsound mind, while there are other cases in which all men agree that the person is of sound mind. But there is an interval in which it is difficult to decide whether the mind is sound or not. One man would pronounce a person of unsound mind, whom another would regard as only slow or weak.

§ 8. Civil courts are seldom inclined to annul contracts upon the mere ground of unsoundness of mind. Where there is an inequality in the bargain, which gives reason to suspect that undue advantage has been taken of the person alleged to be of unsound mind, they lean against the contract. They acknowledge no difference between marriage and a mere civil contract, and apply the same principles and rules to both. Few marriages would, therefore, be pronounced void upon the ground of unsoundness of mind. The courts would be unwilling to annul a marriage unless fraud were proved, and they could judicially see some inequality in the circumstances of the marriage. Moreover they would be unconsciously influenced by the sanctity of marriage, and consciously by the fact that the woman could never be restored to the condition in which she was before she was married. The question, however, seldom arises in the form of an application to have a marriage declared void. It generally comes up after the death of one or both of the parties to the marriage, in the form of a question as to the legitimacy of the children. In such cases, the courts lean in favor of the rights of the children and of the validity of the marriage.

The rule that marriage is void where there is an incapacity to consent, is never applied willingly by the civil courts, because they consider it as a civil contract. If a person has that amount of intellect which would qualify him to buy or sell a barrel of flour, the courts will hold him to be capable of contracting marriage. For all these reasons it is that there are not many marriages declared void for want of capacity to consent.

§ 9. The question, whether a Christian may lawfully intermarry with the sound-minded party to such a pseudo-marriage, is not likely to occur in practice. When it does arise, a presumption will arise out of the reluctance of the courts to set aside marriages, that one which they have set aside was really invalid. At the same time, it is probable that the transaction involved a defect in the morals of the sound-minded party to it. A conscientious Christian would not willingly intermarry with a person who had gone through the marriage ceremony with a person whom a court of justice had pronounced to have been at the time of unsound mind. No Christian, or person of right moral feeling, would think of entering into a marriage with a person who had been engaged in so doubtful a transaction.

On the other hand, the same tendency of the courts renders it certain that one who has been released from a pretended marriage on the grounds of his or her incapacity to consent is incapable of marrying. The decision should be received by the conscience of every one, as proving that it is unlawful to marry such person.

§ 10. Unsoundness of mind is a shadowy thing, and has no precise ascertainable limits, which can be reduced to definite rules. This is, in part, because the mind may be applied to subjects of unequal difficulty, some more and others less complicated. A mind may be competent to deal with one subject and not with another. Buying and selling is a very simple affair, to which an intelligent consent may be given by a very moderate capacity. A Christian marriage involves many considerations, to understand which requires much more intellect than will suffice to buy or sell. It would therefore seem reasonable that greater strength and clearness of mind should be required in marriage than in other less complicated contracts. There are many persons capable of buying and selling, who can only look upon marriage on its animal side. It is in the nature of law to deal in unbending rules and strict definitions. These are unattainable with respect to unsoundness of mind. The courts naturally lean to the idea that it is an absolute thing, and take no notice of degrees of unsoundness. They have abstained from laying down rules as to the degree of unsoundness, which will vacate a contract, and put all contracts on the same footing. They lean to the validity of all marriages, which have been solemnized with legal forms. For the purposes for which they exist, and from the point of view which they are obliged to take, they are right.

§ 11. In the court of conscience, the subject should be looked at in another way. A conscientious person, that is, one who exercises himself to have "a conscience void of offense towards God, and towards man," must "abstain from all appearance of evil." Such persons are bound to abstain from everything which is evil, no matter how slight the degree of evil may be, and to decide all questions about their own conduct by the strictest rule. Wherever there is any doubt of the soundness of any person's mind, it would seem to be inconsistent with the high tone of Christian morals to intermarry with such person. This rule, which is in part a rule of expediency, though of Christian expediency, can only be applied before marriage, as a reason for not marrying one who may be incapable of forming a Christian marriage. After marriage no such idea must be entertained for the purpose of escaping from obligations already assumed.

§ 12. The other class of persons who are unable to contract marriage, because incapable of understanding its nature and consenting to its obligations, are children, or, as they are called by the common law, infants. As to these the courts have adopted the same policy as in the case of persons of unsound mind. Their marriages are held valid, when their capacity to contract is only doubtful. Looking at the matter by the light of reason, it is clear that where there is an incapacity to give an intelligent consent, there can be no marriage. Here, as in the case of persons of unsound mind, the difficulty is to find a proper test of capacity.

§ 13. A child of a few months old, who has but just learned to speak, has certainly no such capacity. A young man or woman, whose mind has just attained maturity, certainly has. During the whole interval which has passed between these two periods, the intellect has been expanding. The capacity for understanding the nature of marriage, and of the consent by which it is constituted, has been continually developing. The germ, from which it has been developed, if it existed at the first period, could not be discerned. The development proceeds with greater rapidity in some cases than in others.

In different cases the development is complete at different ages; but for practical purposes it is necessary that there should be a definite rule. Definite rules are of the essence of law. One great function of human law-makers is to reduce the vague, because affirmative, precepts of the Divine laws to definite precepts by introducing negations to limit them. It is an analogous function to fix arbitrary periods at which capacity shall be presumed and before which incapacity shall be presumed. This is the only mode of escaping inquiries into the capacity of particular persons, which would be endless, and could never be satisfactory. Yet this course has its own insuperable difficulties. No period can be found which will apply to all cases; and that which is fixed upon will always appear, and in fact be, arbitrary. One young person is as competent to perform the duties of life at twenty as another is at twenty-one. A third at twenty-two may be less competent than either. The law, in order that there may be a definite rule, has fixed upon twenty-one, as the period upon which a young man enters upon his full rights and responsibilities. Yet it would be impossible to show that twenty-one is the average period of maturity. If the law had fixed upon twenty or twenty-two, it would have been equally impossible to show that either of those ages was or was not the proper period.

§ 14. The law of England fixes the time, at which young persons are allowed to act for themselves, at different ages for different transactions. It seems strange that children were allowed to consent to a marriage before they could bind themselves by any other obligation. This was probably connected with the mediæval notion, that parents had a right to dispose of their children in marriage, which was itself connected with the mediæval custom of early marriages. The mediæval laws assumed that a young lady ought to be married before she had completed her fourteenth year. In the time of the Tudors, and even later, there were cases of boys of fifteen and younger who married. In fact, there was no age at which children might not be and were not married, although a marriage before what was called the age of consent was considered only inchoate.

§ 15. In England the age of consent was and still is fourteen for boys and twelve for girls. It is strange that this law has never been changed in England, and still stranger that it has not been changed in this country. Early as the age of consent was fixed, marriages frequently took place at earlier ages. They were regarded as lawful but inchoate. The person who was under the age of consent might, on arriving at that age, disaffirm the marriage. The law was that, if it were not immediately and formally disaffirmed the marriage stood. If the husband died before the wife had reached the age of consent, she was, if she were nine years old, entitled to her dower.

The practice, however, was to affirm such marriages in the most solemn manner, by repeating the marriage ceremony. This has been done within less than two hundred years. Evelyn relates in his "Diary," that he was present at the marriage of the Duke of Grafton, a natural son of Charles II., with the only daughter of the Earl of Arlington, when the bride was about five years old and the bridegroom about nine. The Archbishop of Canterbury, Sancroft, officiated. Some years later Evelyn was present at their re-marriage, "the bride being now twelve years old."[1]

In these marriages of children, they were known to act under the direction of their parents, and to give no internal consent, although it is probable that there was no conscious dissent. Such marriages could not have been Christian marriages when they were celebrated, whatever they may have become afterwards. There is reason to believe that many of them turned out well. Evelyn's own marriage was a very happy one, although it took place before the bride was thirteen, the husband being about twice that age. The time for such things has passed. Little children are no longer married. At every marriage an outward consent is given and an inward one presumed. The outward consent is not now given under the pressure of paternal authority, though it may sometimes be yielded to maternal persuasion.

§ 16. In America, the age at which young persons are capable of marriage is not practically settled by law. It is not creditable to American law-makers that things are in such a state. The old notion of the age of consent, although forgotten, is still theoretically law. Boys and girls do not attempt to marry so early. If they did the marriages would be valid, although in some States the law attempts to prevent them by more or less stringent regulations. A marriage contracted by a young person who is incapable of giving an intelligent consent, is no marriage. What young persons are in that situation cannot be ascertained in each case. There is then a necessity for a rule which shall fix an age before which incapacity shall be presumed. The age actually fixed — the old age of consent — is absurdly early.

The Church and the State have each a right to establish such a rule for its own purposes; but if they adopted different rules, the consequences might be very awkward.

1 *Evelyn's Diary*, August, 1672, and November 6, 1679.

There would be civil marriages which the Church did not acknowledge, and ecclesiastical marriages which the State did not acknowledge. Moreover, a rule adopted by the Church would, practically, be binding on none but her members, and would be disregarded by many of them. She has therefore wisely abstained from acting upon the subject.

Were the State to make a rule, it would be the duty of the Church to accept it. The State, however, can scarcely be regarded as doing her duty while she gives no rule but one which is obsolete. Few things can be more absurd than that while a young man of twenty cannot contract a debt for five dollars, a boy of fourteen or a female child of twelve may enter into the marriage state without the least notion of its duties.

It would scarcely be right to postpone the age of consent until twenty-one. There are very few cases in which it is prudent for persons of either sex to marry before twenty-one. Yet most persons are as competent to understand the relation of marriage before they attain that age as they will ever be. But it is proper that some general rule should be laid down. Nothing short of this will prevent young persons from involving themselves in misery and perhaps in sin. In Europe the evil has been felt, and attempts have been made to remedy it, by making the consent of parents a condition of the validity of a marriage, if either of the parties to it were less than twenty-one. The British Parliament, moved by the strong objections to this law, have repealed it. In some other countries, still later periods have been fixed within which young persons could not marry without the consent of their parents.

§ 17. There is a religious objection to all this. The young person was or was not capable of giving an intelligent consent. If an intelligent consent has been given, there has been a Christian marriage, which cannot be dissolved by any human authority. The young couple have, so far as man can know, been joined by God, and man may not separate them for want of the consent of a parent. If the young person is not capable of giving an intelligent consent, the marriage cannot be made a Christian one by the consent of the parents. The consent of another person cannot be substituted for that of the person who is to be married. Such laws proceed upon the old error, that parents have a right to dispose of their children in marriage. It is scarcely necessary to repeat that parents have no such right; it is of the very essence of marriage that it should be free. Shakespeare spoke a deeper truth than he supposed, when he said, "Marriage is a matter of more worth than to be dealt in by attorneyship." It is also a matter of more worth than to be dealt with under compulsion. The rule of making the consent of parents necessary to the validity of the marriage of young persons has been laid aside in England. The experiment was not found to answer, and after the law had been in force for sixty-eight years it was repealed.

§ 18. It must not be supposed that, because young persons have the power of contracting marriage without the consent of their parents, it is right that they should do so. Piety and prudence both require that the parent should be consulted, though the power of acting is still in the child; but that power ought not to be exercised without the consent of the parents. A marriage contracted against the advice of a parent ought not to have been contracted, but being contracted it is valid, for there is no Divine law which makes the parent's consent one of the formative elements of marriage. The want of such consent is not such an impediment as can affect the religious validity of a marriage. Yet it is probable that few marriages, contracted by young persons without it, are really valid internally, for they are contracted in a state of mind not consistent with giving a really Christian consent to the union, and not very likely to call down the Divine blessing.

Marriages without parental consent involve young persons in sin. But the sin is a transient one, beginning and ending in the act of disobedience. It is not a continuing sin, like that of living in a marriage forbidden by the law of God, where the sin is continually repeated and renewed. It is, therefore, no reason for separating those whom God may have joined, although He has not approved all the circumstances of their union. This question will be further considered in another part of this chapter.

§ 19. In all the cases of void marriage which have been considered, the nullity has been connected with the want of consent. It is now proper to inquire into the other class of impediments, which arise out of the direct prohibitions of the revealed law. Of these there are two, — an existing marriage of either of the persons who desire to marry, and the sin which is called incest. It is of them that the Anglican Churches speak, in that solemn charge which they give to all candidates for matrimony: "I require and charge you both, as you will answer at the dreadful day of judgment, when the secrets of all hearts shall be disclosed, that if either of you know any impediment why you should not be lawfully joined together in matrimony, ye do now confess it; for be ye well assured, that if any persons are joined together otherwise than as God's law doth allow, their marriage is not lawful."

§ 20. The first of these two impediments is connected with the element of exclusiveness. Our blessed Lord said: "Whosoever shall put away his wife, and marry another, committeth adultery against her. And if a woman put away her husband, and be married to another, she committeth adultery." [1]

Our Lord assumes that it is impossible for a man to have two wives, or a woman two husbands, at one time, without committing adultery, and decides that the putting away a wife or husband does not alter the case. He uses

[1] Mark x. 11, 12.

the exclusiveness of marriage as a means of enforcing the doctrine that it cannot be dissolved. There is thus a revealed condemnation of both polygamy and polyandry. A living husband or wife is then an impediment, which arrests the Divine blessing on a marriage and deprives it of the elements of sanctity and unity. Such a marriage is adultery, although it may be connived at or licensed by the State.

§ 21. The other impediment growing out of revealed prohibitions is incest. It consists in sexual intercourse between persons whose relation to each other renders it especially sinful. Such relations are either of consanguinity or affinity. Consanguinity is the descent, within certain limits, from a common ancestor. Affinity grows out of marriage, and exists between each of a married pair, and those who are related to the other by consanguinity. The doctrine of incest rests chiefly upon the revealed law; but it may, to some extent, be discovered by the light of nature, for all nations have acknowledged that there is such a sin as incest. Marriage cannot make incest lawful, for an incestuous marriage is void, although connived at or licensed by the State. It always continues to be incest, just as an adulterous marriage always continues to be adultery. In both cases God refuses to bless that which He has forbidden, and the two persons are not joined by Him. This is an extensive subject, and will be reserved for further consideration in the next chapter.

§ 22. Some persons have supposed that there is another impediment to marriage growing out of a Divine prohibition. It may be proper to say something of it. It is the case of mixed marriages, as they are called, in which one of the parties is a Christian and the other is not. The general rule is that marriage is indissoluble, because those whom God hath joined man may not put asunder. The unlawful marriages which have been just mentioned, are not marriages, because of impediments growing out of the Divine prohibition. God has not joined those whom He has forbidden to be joined. Where the consent is a sin, the Divine blessing is withheld, and the marriage is void. This is the general rule; but there are exceptions. It is not every kind of unlawfulness which will render a marriage void. In this, as in other departments of the Divine law, there are cases within the law maxim: *Fieri non debet, factum valet.* It ought not to be done, but is valid when done.

The most prominent case of this sort is that of mixed marriages. It is not lawful for a Christian to marry one who is not in the Lord. The unlawfulness of such marriages rests mainly upon a single text. It is this, "The wife is bound by the law as long as her husband liveth; but if her husband be dead, she is at liberty to be married to whom she will; only in the Lord."[1] This text does not take the form of a prohibition, and there is nowhere any definition of what is meant by the words "in the Lord." There are many nominal Christians, of whom it can scarcely be said that they are in the Lord. Yet no one has asserted that such marriages are not religiously valid. It cannot be supposed that the full benefit of the Divine blessing is received, but they are so far blessed as to be binding. They are not continuing sins, and man cannot put asunder those whom God has joined. It is quite possible that the text may be only a counsel, and that may be the reason why a marriage is not void because one of the parties to it is not in the Lord. Whether it be law or counsel, there can be no doubt that it applies to all Christians, although in form it is only addressed to widows. If it be a counsel, counsel from such a quarter will be considered by conscientious Christians as equivalent to a law.

St. Paul elsewhere says, "Know ye not, that your bodies are the members of Christ? Shall I then take the members of Christ and make them the members of an harlot?

[1] 1 Corinthians vii. 39.

God forbid! What! know ye not that he which is joined to an harlot, is one body? For two, saith He, shall be one flesh."[1] Some divines have been of opinion, that the word which is here translated "harlot," ought to have been translated "alien," in the sense of one who is a stranger to the Church and commonwealth of Christ. This translation solves some difficulties, for which the authorized one leaves room. But there is not a sufficient weight of either argument or authority to make it safe to admit it. If it be admitted, it will follow that although intermarriage with Jews and Pagans was forbidden, yet such marriages, when they had taken place, were valid. The marriage of the Christian with the Pagan made them one flesh, by virtue of the primitive law of marriage. Yet, if the new translation be right, such marriages are forbidden.

There is a passage in Deuteronomy which has been applied to such marriages; but it is only a prohibition to intermarry with the Canaanites, and is closely connected with the command to extirpate them. It cannot be regarded as a portion of the permanent moral law. It is this: "When the Lord thy God shall bring thee into the land whither thou goest to possess it, and hath cast out many nations before thee . . . . And when the Lord thy God shall deliver them before thee; thou shalt smite them and utterly destroy them; thou shalt make no covenant with them, nor show mercy unto them. Neither shalt thou make marriages with them: thy daughter thou shalt not give unto his son, nor his daughter shalt thou take unto thy son."[2] The same remarks may be applied to the parallel passage in Joshua xxiii. 12.

§ 23. It is an important question, whether a mere human law of either the Church or the State can make void a marriage which has been solemnized with such outward forms, as involve an outward consent from which an inward may be presumed, and which does not contravene

[1] 1 Corinthians vi. 15, 16.

[2] Deuteronomy vii. 1–3.

any Divine law. If it could, a merely human law would prevent the operation of a Divine ordinance. This can scarcely be supposed. It follows that neither the Church nor the State can create an impediment to Christian marriage.

The State may forbid certain persons from intermarrying, and the law would bind the consciences of her subjects or citizens, as much as any other civil law, that is, they would be bound not to intermarry. This obligation might be enforced by penalties; but if a marriage took place, the State could not make it void, except so far as relates to the civil effects of marriage. The persons have sinned in contracting a marriage forbidden by the State. But the sin was transient, not continuing. It does not vacate the marriage; the parties to it cannot intermarry with other persons without both the parties to the new marriage committing adultery. They may not even separate, unless compelled to do so. A continuing sin renders a separation a duty, for God could not have blessed a marriage which involves continuing sin; but it has never been supposed that a transient sin, in the mere circumstances of a marriage, could prevent its being a valid marriage. Disobedience to a parental injunction and to a civil law are both sins; but neither will vacate a marriage because they relate only to circumstances. A marriage forbidden by a State law, is still binding on the conscience of a Christian.

§ 24. No human law, ecclesiastical or civil, can render a marriage so invalid as not to be binding on the conscience. Yet both the Church and the State have made laws, which attempt to annul marriages, thereby separating those whom God hath joined. The Church set the example, and created many merely canonical impediments to marriage. These generally related to persons connected by consanguinity or affinity. These terms have been explained in the twenty-first section of this chapter. The Levitical law forbade intermarriage in certain enumerated cases of consanguinity. From these enumerated cases, a rule has been deduced, that all persons more nearly related than first cousins are forbidden to intermarry. The Latin Church went farther. She forbade first cousins from intermarrying, and thus introduced a merely human impediment. The new principle was not allowed to stop here. It was at one time asserted that the words "near of kin," in Leviticus xviii. 6, included all persons who had a traceable descent from a common ancestor. Practically this would be a very vague rule, and would operate very unequally.

It was at last settled that no two persons could intermarry who were descended from a common ancestor through less than seven generations. The effect of this may be made plainer by observing that a man's son is removed from him by one generation, his grandson by two, his great-grandson by three, the son of his great-grandson by four, the grandson of his great-grandson by five, the great-grandson of his great-grandson by six, and the son of that very remote descendant by seven. Before the seventh generation is reached, the ordinary names of relationship in the descending line are exhausted, repeated, and exhausted again. Very few persons in this country, and not many in any country, can trace back more than four or five generations.

§ 25. The canonical impediments to marriage were extended yet more widely in the Latin Church. The Scriptural principle, that a man and his wife are one flesh, has been considered to make marriages between persons connected by affinity, unlawful to the same extent as those between persons related by consanguinity. This idea is very fully borne out by the special prohibitions in the eighteenth chapter of Leviticus. The Latin Church having extended the impediments of consanguinity to the seventh generation, which she calls the seventh degree, applied the Scriptural principle, that a man and his wife are one flesh, to them all. The blood-relations of a man were the kin of his wife, and hers were his. The number of cases in which marriage was forbidden, was thus greatly increased.

It was still further increased by a logical deduction. If a man and his wife are one flesh and her relations are his, it was inferred that the wives of her male relations must also be of kin to him. The same notion was applied to the husbands of the female relations of the husband. Thus arose the doctrine of a second degree of affinity, which had no foundation whatever in Scripture. It meant the connection which was supposed to exist between a man and woman, one of whom had affinity with a person who had affinity with the other. It was even attempted to introduce a third degree of affinity, between two persons, one of whom had affinity with a person who had affinity with the other in the second degree. This was seen to be absurd, affinity in the third degree was given up, and prohibitions on account of the second degree were reduced within narrower limits than in the cases of consanguinity and affinity proper.

§ 26. A third class of canonical impediments grew out of what was called spiritual affinity. By the law of Pagan Rome, a man might adopt a son. The adoption made the adopted person the son of him who adopted him, for all civil purposes and for all purposes connected with the heathen superstition. As the Romans regarded marriage as a civil contract, matters connected with it were no exceptions. It followed that the adopted son was the kinsman of all the kindred of the adopter. The Church borrowed these principles, and applied them to sponsors and those for whom they answered in baptism. Marriage between a god-parent and his or her godchild was considered unlawful. So was marriage between persons who had been sponsors for the same persons, and who were regarded as spiritual brothers and sisters. The connections thus growing out of baptism were called spiritual affinity, and it was held to make marriage unlawful among those thus connected, and also that of any of them with the near blood-relations of any of the others.

§ 27. The practical evil of these canonical prohibitions was enormous. In a small community, in which, as was usual in the middle ages, families remained stationary from generation to generation, all the persons who composed it would probably be descended from common ancestors within seven generations, and could not intermarry. Even if there were a few exceptions, they would be connected with their neighbors by affinity or spiritual affinity. It was impossible for the common people to find, within their reach, persons with whom they could intermarry. Persons of rank were subjected to the same inconvenience. The lesser nobility of each province, the higher nobility of each kingdom, and the royal and princely families of all Europe, were, each class within itself, connected within the prohibited degrees. This is apparent when one reflects that each person has in the seventh generation one hundred and twenty-eight ancestors. It may be further illustrated by recollecting that Queen Victoria is only in the eighth generation from James I.

Several great mischiefs arose from this state of things. Persons who wished to marry did not know whom they might canonically marry, while it was certain that they could not canonically marry within the circle in which they would naturally seek companions. Those who were married, very often did not know whether their marriages were valid. The Divine law, that marriage cannot be dissolved, was virtually made of none effect, as the Jews made the commandments of God of none effect by their traditions. Almost every marriage might be annulled. These consequences of the notion that impediments to marriage can be created by human laws, seem to show that the doctrine is a pernicious one, and that in policy, as well as upon principle, there should be no impediments to marriage which are not created by a Divine law.

§ 28. The Western Church endeavored to lessen these evils by means of dispensations. It was not a very effectual remedy; but it increased the revenue and the influence of the Popes. Much money and many other advantages could be obtained, when the passions or policy of a powerful prince, or even of a great noble, pointed to a marriage with a particular lady. When policy or domestic troubles, or a passion for another woman, inclined such a person to rid himself of his wife, even more money and greater advantages could be gotten. Much might also be had from those whose interests would be injuriously affected by such transactions. The system of dispensations began early, but was for a time confined to the merely canonical impediments. The prohibitions in the eighteenth chapter of Leviticus were called prohibitions by God's law, and were held not to be capable of dispensation.

Pope Alexander III., Roderic Borgia, is said to have been the first who broke through this rule. Julius II., who, although not such a moral monster as Borgia, was a very wicked man, granted the dispensation for the marriage of Henry VIII. to Catharine of Aragon, who had been the wife of his brother. This is said to have been only the second dispensation from an impediment created by the law of God. It was afterwards assailed upon the strong ground that the Pope could not dispense with the Divine law. But Clement VII. was induced by fear of the Emperor Charles V. to sustain the dispensation. The momentous consequences of this decision have compelled the Church of Rome to abide by the doctrine on which it rests. It may rest on either of two erroneous notions: one that the Pope can dispense with the law of God; the other that the sixteenth verse of the eighteenth chapter of Leviticus is not a part of the moral law of God. Unless one of these propositions is true, it is clear that a dispensation to marry the widow of a brother is void. The Council of Trent anathematized those who denied the efficacy of such papal dispensations; but did not entertain any question as to the ground on which they could be maintained.

§ 29. The State has also ventured upon creating impediments to marriage; although few or no laws of the kind have yet been passed in the United States. They have generally been connected with the maintenance and extension of parental authority. Some of the most remarkable cases of this usurped power have occurred in England, of which country only it will be convenient here to speak. Two remarkable laws of this sort were, during the last century, passed in England. They are known as the Marriage Act of George II., and the Royal Marriage Act.

§ 30. The first made void all marriages which might be contracted by persons who should be less than twenty-one years old at the time of the marriage, without the consent of their parents or guardians. The courts construed this to mean lawful parents or lawful guardians. An illegitimate child had no parents, and no person could consent to his or her marriage. If there were no parents, either in consequence of illegitimacy or death, the lawful guardian might consent to the marriage of his ward; if he did not, the marriage was void. It sometimes happened that the person who was supposed to be the guardian, and had consented to a marriage, had not been legally appointed. It also sometimes happened that the father or mother of an illegitimate child consented to a marriage, supposing that the law meant natural parents. In either case, the marriage was void. To obviate some of these difficulties, it was provided that marriages should be valid, although one of the parties was under age, if the bans, or notice of an intention to marry, were regularly published in the proper parish church. But the courts held that a fraud, or even a mistake as to names or residence of the parties, rendered a marriage by bans null.

The greatest hardship of all remains to be told. In all these cases of void marriages, the courts held that the children were illegitimate, and that their parents could not consent to their marriage. Thus the incapacity for marriage was transmitted from generation to generation. Persons who were believed by themselves and every one else to be lawfully married, were living in what the law regarded as fornication, and had no power to consent to the marriage of their children. The marriages of such of their children as were married before they attained the age of twenty-one, were void. This would lead to another set of void marriages. The result was that no one who had been married under twenty-one, or to a husband or wife who, at the time, was under twenty-one, could know whether he or she was married or not. For the marriage might be vitiated by the invalidity of that of some ancestor of one of the parties. An irregularity which was unknown and unsuspected at the time, might be discovered and used to vacate the marriage of some descendant a generation or two afterwards. Sometimes the defect, where it was discovered before the birth of a child, might be cured by a remarriage. But it was sometimes not discovered until it was too late, and persons were deprived of their inheritance by the legal, though unconscientious claims of their relations. Sometimes men took advantage of such defects, to get rid of their wives. But the great evil was the same as in the case of the canonical impediments, the breaking in upon the Divine law, that marriage is indissoluble. These evils led to a repeal of the act, after it had been in force nearly three fourths of a century.

§ 31. At the time of the repeal of this act, another expedient was proposed. It was that of making the marriage of minors what was called voidable. This consisted in giving a power to a parent to vacate the marriage of his or her minor child, by a suit in an ecclesiastical court, to be commenced within a limited time. If no such suit were commenced within the limited time, the marriage would become valid. This would have put an end to the treating as void, marriages in which there had been an actual consent given by persons who had not legal power to give it. All persons, except those who had been married under twenty-one without the actual consent of parents or guardians, would know whether they were married or not. But there would still have been a class who must live in doubt, and that of a very peculiar character. Their marriages would have been inchoate, and liable to be set aside by the parents of one of the parties. They would have borne a strong resemblance to the Roman marriages by *usucapio*, which might be dissolved at the pleasure of the lady's father. Such an arrangement would have been absurd, as well as inconsistent with the Divine law. Happily the notion of voidability was never incorporated into the law of England. In lieu of it, it was provided that the marriages of minors should be void under certain circumstances, which are not likely to occur. The law, however, still conflicts with the Divine rule of the indissolubleness of marriage.

§ 32. The marriage of children, who are incapable of understanding the nature of the relation, is a great evil. Such marriages are void in a religious view, for want of an intelligent consent. They should be treated as what they are, void marriages, which the consent of parents cannot make valid. Thus the imbecility of the child is protected against both himself and his parents. This is the rule in all other contracts. A boy or girl cannot sell his or her estate; the disability is absolute, and is not removed by consent of parents. By the existing law, a boy of fourteen or a girl of twelve may marry without the consent of any one. This is clearly wrong, but it would be no improvement, if the marriage were valid with the consent of parents and void without it. It would universally be thought absurd, if children were allowed to alienate their property with the consent of their parents. The true course is to make the age of consent later. If boys of fourteen and girls of twelve understand the nature of marriage, they have a right to marry. If they do not, the consent of parents cannot qualify them to enter into engagements which they cannot comprehend.

§ 33. What is called the Royal Marriage Act was passed in the reign of George III., and is still in force. It makes void all marriages entered into by any of the royal family, under the age of twenty-five, without the consent of the sovereign. After that age they may marry without the consent of the sovereign, if they have the virtual consent of Parliament; but this is in practice only nominal. Two violations of this law have been publicly avowed, and others have been suspected. The late Duke of Sussex, a son of George III., was twice married. Both his wives were of high position and respectable character. They lived with him openly, and were regarded by him, by themselves, and by the public as his wives, only they were not received at court, and were not publicly called by his title. After his death Queen Victoria created his widow a duchess by one of his titles; but the House of Lords decided that his dukedom did not descend to his son, because his mother's marriage was void. From these facts it may be inferred that public opinion in England had settled upon the true doctrine. The civil authority can vacate a marriage for civil purposes, but in a religious and moral view it still remains a marriage.

§ 34. The claims of the State to create impediments to marriage is a proper subject of attention, on account of a movement in this country to forbid the marriage of first cousins.[1] Plausible arguments against such unions are derived from the science of Physiology. There is little doubt that marriages between near relations tend to the deterioration of the species. The effect of such marriages, repeated in several successive generations, is very

[1] [Such marriages are now forbidden by the State of New Hampshire, and by some others. — Ed.]

observable. This is a very good reason why such marriages should be considered inexpedient and indeed sinful. It is a good reason why Christians should avoid them. It may also be a good reason that the State should forbid and punish them. But all this is very different from an impediment, which will prevent a marriage from taking effect. It is now acknowledged by every one that such marriages are valid. The only nominal dissentients are the Roman Catholics, and they consider them valid when contracted under a dispensation. If any legislature should undertake to declare them void, it would be a usurpation like those of the Church of Rome and the British Parliament. It would be creating an impediment which God had not ordained, and undertaking to separate those whom He had joined.

§ 35. This work is addressed to the consciences of Christians, and it is proper to say a word as to their duty with respect to such laws. It is to obey them. God has nowhere commanded that minors should marry, or that first cousins should intermarry. No Christian man is justified in contracting a marriage which is forbidden by the law of the land. The evils which such a marriage might produce to his wife and his children are sufficient reasons why he should not contract it, even if there were no other. The same reasons apply with even more force to Christian women. Yet the marriages, once contracted, are valid. No person is at liberty to treat them as void, either in his own case or that of another person. No Christian who has been involved in such a marriage can marry again. Nor can any Christian intermarry with a person who has been so involved.

§ 36. The whole doctrine of impediments, which render marriage impossible and marriage ceremonies of no effect, rests upon the idea that such impediments intercept the blessing of God. They divide themselves into two classes; one in which no blessing was given because there was no consent. This may be because the outward consent was extorted by force, or obtained by fraud, or was void through the imbecility of disease or childhood. In the other class, the blessing does not descend, because it is invoked upon a Divinely forbidden marriage. This class comprises only the cases of polygamy and incest. The Divine law of incest is contained in the eighteenth chapter of Leviticus. This law no human legislature, ecclesiastical or civil, is competent to change. It will be the subject of the next chapter.

CHAPTER XIV.

OF THE DOCTRINE OF INCEST.

§ 1. Of Incest in General. — § 2. Of the Eighteenth Chapter of Leviticus. — § 3. The Mosaic Precepts are either Ceremonial, Civil, or Moral. — § 4. The Moral Precepts are of Perpetual Obligation. — § 5. The Precepts in the Eighteenth Chapter of Leviticus are not merely Ceremonial. — § 6. They are not merely Civil. — § 7. They are Moral. — § 8. Consanguinity and Affinity. — § 9. The Degrees of Consanguinity and Affinity. — § 10. Impediments to Marriage growing out of Lineal Consanguinity. — § 11. Impediments growing out of Collateral Consanguinity. — § 12. Affinity is Kindred. — § 13. Impediments growing out of Lineal Affinity. — § 14. Impediments growing out of Collateral Affinity. — § 15. The Second Degree of Collateral Affinity. — § 16. Marriage with a Brother's Widow. The Sixteenth Verse of the Eighteenth Chapter of Leviticus does not merely forbid Adultery. — § 17. It is not a merely Civil Precept. — § 18. The Case of Ruth. — § 19. Deuteronomy xxv. 5, 6. — § 20. The Argument from that Law examined. — § 21. It is Civil and Exceptional. — § 22. The Prohibition to marry a Brother's Widow is a Moral Precept. — § 23. The Canon of Neo-Cæsarea. — § 24. Remarks upon it. — § 25. Marriage with a Sister of a Deceased Wife is forbidden. — § 26. Modern Notions. — § 27. The Eighteenth Verse does not touch the Question. — § 28. The Third Degree of Collateral Affinity.

§ 1. Incest is the sin of sexual intercourse between persons whose relation to each other is such as to make it especially sinful. Such relations are impediments to marriage. The law or doctrine of incest determines what relations are such. Most nations have accepted the general idea of incest, although they have not agreed upon the particular relations which make marriage incestuous. Marriages between persons one of whom is lineally descended from the other, as a granddaughter with a grandfather, have been rarely allowed, — never except perhaps among the Canaanites. But there is no other relation which has been universally held to make marriage unlawful. All collateral kindred have, in some nations, been allowed to intermarry.

The Holy Scriptures do not mention the creation of wives for the sons of Adam. They probably married their sisters, especially as Adam had daughters who could have no other husbands without a new creation.[1] Such unions must then have been permitted, perhaps specially for that necessity only. They were allowed by the laws of some ancient nations. But they were held in abhorrence by the more civilized races, although heathens, and are now so held by all Christians, and all nations which, although not Christians, are accounted civilized. The Christian law of incest is contained in the eighteenth chapter of Leviticus, which was also the law of the Israelites.

§ 2. It begins with a very solemn form of enactment, which occupies the first five verses. It is this: "And the Lord spake unto Moses, saying, Speak unto the children of Israel, and say unto them, I am the Lord your God. After the doings of the land of Egypt, wherein ye dwelt, shall ye not do; and after the doings of the land of Canaan, whither I bring you, shall ye not do; neither shall ye walk in their ordinances. Ye shall do my judgments and keep mine ordinances, to walk therein: I am the Lord your God. Ye shall therefore keep my statutes and my judgments: which if a man do, he shall live in them: I am the Lord."

Then follow seventeen verses which contain twenty-two prohibitions. Of these, nineteen relate to sexual intercourse, seventeen of them to incest, two to unnatural lusts, and one to idolatry. Among them there is but one which speaks directly of marriage. Sexual intercourse is forbidden between persons who bear certain relations to each other. It is inferred that persons so related cannot intermarry. For all sexual intercourse out of marriage is unlawful; unless, therefore, these prohibitions extended to marriage, they would be nugatory.

[1] Genesis v. 4.

After these seventeen verses the chapter concludes with a general prohibition of the actions forbidden in them, and certain reasons for the prohibitions. This conclusion, which begins at the twenty-fourth verse, is as follows: "Defile not ye yourselves in any of these things: for in all these the nations are defiled which I cast out before you. And the land is defiled; therefore I do visit the iniquity thereof upon it, and the land itself vomiteth out her inhabitants. Ye shall therefore keep my statutes and my judgments, and shall not commit any of these abominations, neither any of your own nation, nor any stranger that sojourneth among you: (for all these abominations have the men of the land done, which were before you, and the land is defiled;) that the land spew not you out also, when ye defile it, as it spewed out the nations that were before you. For whosoever shall commit any of these abominations, even the souls that commit them shall be cut off from among their people. Therefore shall ye keep mine ordinances, that ye commit not any one of these abominable customs which were committed before you, and that ye defile not yourselves therein: I am the Lord your God."

This solemn conclusion and the equally solemn commencement impart to the chapter a very decided unity, cutting it off from what goes before and from what follows. It may well be considered as an entire context, which governs a particular class of subjects. It very much resembles a modern law, having, as is common with modern laws, a preamble. It has also a conclusion, repeating and enforcing the preamble.

§ 3. The precepts of the Mosaic Law have been divided into ceremonial, civil, and moral. A ceremonial precept is one which relates to the outward forms of religion. It seldom takes the form of a prohibition, except in the case of those legal defilements which, according to the law of Moses, excluded the defiled person from public worship. Even in those cases, it generally takes the form of directions as to the ceremonies by which the defilement may be removed, and the time during which it must continue.

Civil precepts are those which relate to the duties of the *civis*, or citizen; as well those which he owes to his fellow-citizens as to the State itself. A great part of the Mosaic Law is the civil law of the nation of Israelites. Laws prescribing the punishment of offenses, or carrying into effect the policy which God had appointed for his chosen people, or regulating their polity or mode of government, are merely civil. Those which prohibit particular actions may be both civil and moral. They cannot safely be said to be one to the exclusion of the other, unless, like the law against usury, they plainly have reference to the policy of the nation.

Moral precepts are those which regulate human conduct, prescribing the duties of man as man.[1] Such precepts, being in no way connected with the ceremonies, the policy, or the polity of the Israelites, cannot come to an end with their religion and government.

§ 4. The seventh article of the Anglican Church declares that "Although the laws given from God by Moses, as touching ceremonies and rites, do not bind Christian men, nor the civil precepts thereof ought of necessity to be received in any commonwealth, yet, notwithstanding, no Christian man whatsoever is free from the obedience of the commandments, which are called moral." This declaration of the Anglican Church is the assertion of a Catholic principle which is acknowledged by all churches and all sects, and has been acknowledged in all ages of Christianity. It can bear the test of Vincentius Lirinensis: *Quod semper, quod ubique, quod ab omnibus.* That which has been believed always, everywhere, and by all churches, is Catholic truth. The next step is to inquire whether the precepts in the eighteenth chapter of Leviticus are ceremonial, civil, or moral.

1 [Cf. Bp. Butler's Analogy, part ii. chap. 1. — Ed.]

§ 5. They are not ceremonial. They are all direct prohibitions, and there is no intimation of any defilement or of any mode of removing defilement. There is but one allusion to worship in the whole chapter, and that not to the worship of the true God. The twenty-sixth verse is: "Ye shall therefore keep my statutes and my judgments, and shall not commit any of these abominations; neither any of your own nation, nor any stranger that sojourneth among you." The prohibitions were not addressed to the children of Israel only, but were expressly extended to others, who had nothing to do with the worship of the tabernacle or temple.

It has been asserted that the prohibition in the nineteenth verse is merely ceremonial, and therefore that the others must be taken to be of the same character. Even if this prohibition were merely ceremonial, it does not follow that the others are also ceremonial. Paley has furnished an argument against such a conclusion. It is true that he puts it in the shape of an argument, that the presence of moral precepts in a context must not be regarded as proving that the whole context is moral; but the argument, if it be worth anything, must be applicable for either purpose. His immediate object was to show that the presence of the fourth commandment in the Decalogue did not prove it to be moral. His reasoning is not very strong, but some of his examples are.

They are three; two of them being included in one text of Scripture.[1] In this text obedience to the prohibition. in the nineteeth verse of the chapter under consideration, is classed with obedience to precepts and prohibitions which are undoubtedly moral. Obedience to the prohibition of usury is mentioned in the same connection. Paley assumes that one of these prohibitions is ceremonial, and it is agreed that the other is civil. From these premises he infers that the fourth commandment may not be moral.

[1] Ezekiel xviii. 5–9.

The context of the five verses just referred to is continued for nine verses more, in which the prophet continues to treat of the same subject, but without further mention of the offense against the text in Leviticus, although he speaks again of usury. The case of usury and the other case too, if Paley be right in supposing that the prohibition is only ceremonial, are instances of precepts and prohibitions of different natures found in the Holy Scriptures in close connection with each other. It follows that the character of a precept cannot safely be inferred from that of its neighbors.

Paley's other instance is also very apposite. It is the Apostolic decree. "It seemed good to the Holy Ghost, and to us, to lay upon you no greater burden than these necessary things; that ye abstain from meats offered to idols, and from blood, and from things strangled, and from fornication."[1]

These instances are sufficient to prove that the presence of a ceremonial precept among others does not show that the others are also ceremonial. Whether it be so or not, it seems to be the better opinion, that the prohibitions in the eighteenth chapter of Leviticus are moral, and that the nineteenth verse is no exception. The same action which is forbidden in that verse, is mentioned in the thirty-second and thirty-third verses of the fifteenth chapter of the same book. It is there treated only as a ceremonial defilement, and a ceremonial purification is prescribed. It has been reasonably supposed that the passage in the fifteenth chapter relates to an accidental and unintentional occurrence, that in the eighteenth to a willful offense. The subject is again mentioned in the twentieth chapter, at the eighteenth verse, among other prohibitions of the eighteenth chapter, which are there repeated and enforced by penalties. The penalty denounced is to be "cut off from

[1] Acts xv. 28, 29. See Paley's *Moral Philosophy*, book v. chap. vii. p. 291, *et seq.*: Boston, 1810.

among the people." It is the same, which is denounced in the eighteenth chapter against disobedience to any of the precepts which it contains. The expression may mean put to death. It certainly means something more than a liability to undergo a ceremonial purification. That against which it is denounced, must therefore be more than a mere ceremonial pollution.

The same argument is applicable to all the other actions forbidden in the eighteenth chapter. For that reason, as well as for those stated in the beginning of this section, it seems that the precepts in the eighteenth chapter of Leviticus are not merely ceremonial.

§ 6. It has been said that some of the prohibitions in the chapter under consideration are of a civil nature. Some of them may truly be said to have their civil side, but it has never been denied that those very precepts are also moral. There is nothing to prevent a law from being both civil and moral. The sixth commandment is both; the seventh is a yet more apposite illustration, for a virtual repetition of it in the twentieth verse of this chapter, has been selected as especially a civil precept. Several of the precepts are repeated in the twentieth chapter, and death denounced against them. This passage may, perhaps, contain the civil precepts, which enforce by civil penalties the moral precepts of the eighteenth chapter.[1]

From the third verse it might be plausibly argued, that the law was intended as one of the means of separating the Israelites from their neighbors. For it is there said, "After the doings of the land of Egypt, wherein ye dwelt, shall ye not do; and after the doings of the land of Canaan, whither I bring you, shall ye not do; neither shall ye walk in their ordinances." This, taken without the context, forbids adopting the laws and manners of the Egyptians and Canaanites, and might show that the design of the laws — of the introduction to which the verse is a

[1] See Leviticus xx. 10–17.

part — was to separate the Israelites from those nations. That design once established, it might be contended that it was the sole reason of the prohibitions which follow. It might be answered, that there was nothing in any of the forbidden things, except one, which had any tendency to bring the Israelites into contact with the neighboring nations. The exception is the passing of children through the fire to Moloch. That is plainly a moral prohibition, whatever other purposes it may have been intended to serve. But the latter part of the chapter sets the question at rest; for the things forbidden are there declared to be evil in themselves and abominations.

§ 7. It is quite possible that some of the precepts in this chapter are ceremonial and some civil, but that they are all moral is shown in the chapter itself. The fifth verse — which, from the manner in which this chapter is cut off from what precedes and follows it, must be taken to have special reference to its contents — is as follows: "Ye shall therefore keep my statutes and my judgments; which if a man do he shall live in them." The incestuous actions forbidden in the seventeenth verse are declared to be wickedness. In the twenty-sixth, twenty-seventh, and twenty-ninth verses, all the forbidden actions are declared to be abominations, and in the thirtieth abominable customs. It is said in the twenty-fourth and twenty-fifth verses, that they defile the land, and were the causes for which the Canaanites were cut off. The prohibitions were not then merely intended to separate the Israelites from their neighbors, but must be taken to be moral and of perpetual obligation. Those of them which relate to incest are the Divine law upon that subject, and are binding upon Christians.

§ 8. The first of them is in the sixth verse, and is very general. It is: "None of you shall approach to any that is near of kin to him, to uncover their nakedness." This rule cannot be applied without knowing what persons are of kin to each other. Twelve verses follow, which contain particular prohibitions, and form a commentary upon the sixth verse.

These particular prohibitions relate to cases of consanguinity and affinity, and to both whether lineal or collateral. Consanguinity is the relation which subsists between two persons, who within certain limits are descended from a common ancestor. Lineal consanguinity is the relation which subsists between two persons, one of whom is descended from the other. Collateral consanguinity is the relation which subsists between two persons who are descended from common ancestors, but not one from the other. Affinity grows out of marriage, and exists between each of a married pair, and those who are related to the other by consanguinity. It is lineal or collateral, according to the nature of that consanguinity.

Thus lineal consanguinity exists, in the ascending line, between a woman and her father and grandfather, and in the descending line between them and her. Brothers and sisters are related by collateral consanguinity, for they have common ancestors in their father and mother. The same thing is true of first cousins, because they have common ancestors in their grandfather and grandmother. A child is connected with its stepmother, and she with it, by lineal affinity. A man is related by collateral affinity to his wife's sister, and by lineal to her mother or her daughter.

§ 9. Lawyers have arranged consanguinity and affinity under what they call degrees. This is done in two ways: one of which is according to the Civil or Roman Law, and the other according to the Ecclesiastical or Canon Law. A degree is a step, and two persons cannot be nearer to each other than one step apart. There is one step between father and son, and they are related to each other in the first degree. In the ascending and descending line, there are as many degrees, lacking one, as generations between any two persons. The father and the son are related in the first degree, the grandfather and the grandson in the second, the great grandfather and the great grandson in the third. In this the Civilians and the Canonists are agreed, though when they come to collateral consanguinity they have different modes of computing. Mr. Morgan illustrates the subject thus: "In the direct line of ascent and descent, they," the Civilians and the Canonists, " are agreed, counting so many degrees as there are generations, or as there are persons exclusive of the forefather. Thus Abraham, Isaac, Jacob, Dinah, — Dinah is in the third degree from Abraham, being the third person besides Abraham, or in the third generation from Abraham exclusively."[1]

In ascertaining the degrees of collateral consanguinity, the Canonists count the degrees from the common ancestor down to the more remote of the two descendants, whose degree of relationship is to be ascertained, and that gives the degree in which they are related. The rule seems to be that a man is related to all the descendants of his ancestor in the same degree in which he is related to his ancestor himself. Thus, two brothers are both in the first degree from their father, and therefore related to each other in the first degree. A granddaughter is two degrees from her father, and therefore related to her uncle in the second degree, and to her first cousin in the same. If the family be carried on, the grandchildren of one of the brothers are related in the third degree to the other brother and all his descendants.

The Civilians count the degrees from one of the two persons, the degree of whose relationship it is desired to ascertain, back to the common ancestor and then down to the other. Thus two brothers are each removed one step from the common ancestor, the father, which make two steps. They are therefore related to each other in the second degree, for there is one step from either of them

1 *Law of Marriage, Adultery, and Divorce*, vol. i. p. 258.

up to the father, and another from the father down to the other. It follows that according to the Civilians there is no such thing as collateral relation in the first degree. An uncle and his niece are in the third degree, for there is one step from the uncle up to his father, the common ancestor, a second down to the other brother, the father of the niece, and a third down to the niece herself. First cousins are in the fourth degree, there being two steps up to the common ancestor and two down to the other cousin.

The degrees of affinity are counted in precisely the same way as those of consanguinity, the husband or wife taking the place of the wife or husband. Thus, step-parents and children are related in the first degree; a man or woman, and the husband or wife of his or her brother or sister, in the second degree.

There is not much practical use made of the doctrine of degrees, except as it furnishes a convenient way of designating the relationship of persons who may not intermarry. When degrees of consanguinity or affinity are hereafter mentioned in this work, it is to be understood that they are computed according to the method of the Civilians.

There is no prohibition of marriage in the Levitical law between any two persons more distantly related than a nephew and his aunt. They are in the third degree, according to the computation of the Civilians. This has furnished a rule for the law of England. Statute and common law forbid marriages within the third degree, and allow them beyond it.

§ 10. In the case of lineal consanguinity, the Levitical prohibitions do not go beyond the second degree. Yet there seems to be no reason for doubting that all marriages between persons, one of whom is lineally descended from the other, are incestuous. They have been so considered by almost all nations. A man is forbidden to marry his mother in the seventh verse, his son's daughter and his daughter's daughter in the tenth. Marriage with a daughter is clearly although not directly forbidden in the seventeenth verse. It is an obvious rule of interpretation, that what is forbidden to one sex is forbidden to the other; thus when a man is forbidden to marry his granddaughter, it is a necessary inference that it is unlawful for a woman to marry her grandson. By the application of this rule, these prohibitions will include all cases of lineal consanguinity in the first and second degrees. The only blood-relations in the third degree, who are not forbidden to intermarry, are great grandparents and their great grandchildren. It seems to be agreed that the cases in which marriage is forbidden are put as instances, and that marriage is forbidden in all similar cases. Perhaps no other instances of marriage between lineal ascendants and descendants are forbidden in the Levitical law, because there is little temptation, or indeed opportunity to commit the sin beyond the second degree.

§ 11. There are no collateral relations in the first degree. In the second there are none but brothers and sisters. In the third there are none but uncles and aunts and nephews and nieces. The relations mentioned in the last sentence are collateral ancestors and descendants. A collateral ancestor is the brother or sister of a lineal ancestor, however remote. A collateral descendant is the descendant of a brother or sister, however remote. But all collateral ancestors and descendants beyond uncles and nieces, and all other collateral relations except brothers and sisters, are in the fourth or some more remote degree. Marriage between brothers and sisters is forbidden in the ninth verse, and the marriage of a nephew with his aunt, in the twelfth and thirteenth verses. There is no direct prohibition of the marriage of an uncle to his niece; but it is shown to be unlawful by the rule that what is forbidden to one sex is forbidden to the other. Moreover the reason assigned for the prohibitions in the twelfth and thirteenth verses apply also to this case. Those are all the cases of collateral consanguinity within the third degree.

There is little or no difference of opinion among Christians as to marriages between persons related to each other within the third degree of consanguinity. They are regarded in the words of Holy Writ as abominations. Even the laxity of American legislation has not permitted them. There is perhaps one exception : it is the marriage of an uncle with a niece. Such marriages are defended because there is no direct written prohibition of them, although they are forbidden by the strongest implication, and fall within the reason of the prohibition to marry an aunt. They are also defended by some fanciful arguments which are supposed to apply to this case and not to that of the nephew and aunt. The principal one is that the authority of a husband cannot be exercised consistently with the respect due to an aunt, while there is no similar anomaly in the case of a marriage between an uncle and a niece. Some German communities have taken these views; and the Church of Rome grants dispensations for such marriages, but not for marriages between nephews and aunts.

Nothing is said in the Levitical law of the marriage of collateral ancestors and descendants beyond the third degree. It may be said of more remote collateral ancestors and descendants, — as in the case of remote lineal ancestors and descendants, — that the cases are few in which such marriages are possible, and fewer still in which they are probable. Some writers have laid it down that as there is no express prohibition beyond the third degree, marriages between collateral ancestors and descendants, in the fourth and more remote degrees, are lawful. Although a man may not marry his aunt, he may marry his great aunt. There is no written law forbidding their intermarriage; but if the twelfth and thirteenth verses are examined, it will be found that the case is within the assigned reason of the rule. That reason is, that the aunt is the near kinswoman of the father or mother of the nephew. It is a case not likely to occur, but there may be a great aunt younger than her great nephew. There now is, or lately was, in the city of Baltimore, a young lady who has a great uncle younger than herself.

Upon the whole, it may be concluded that all marriages between blood relations within the third degree inclusive are unlawful and void ; and that it is doubtful whether marriages between collateral ancestors and their collateral descendants, even beyond the third degree, are valid.

§ 12. Affinity is the relation between a man and the blood relations of his wife, or a woman and the blood relations of her husband. It is inferred from the unity of marriage that persons who are related to one of a married couple are related to the other. Those who are one flesh must also have in some sense one blood. It follows that the prohibition in the sixth verse of the eighteenth chapter of Leviticus, — " None of you shall approach to any that is near of kin to him, to uncover their nakedness," — applies as well to those who are related to a man's wife or woman's husband, as to those who are directly related to the man or woman. The principle upon which all prohibitions of marriages between persons connected by affinity rests, is that a man and his wife are one flesh, and that whoever is of kin to the one is of kin to the other. This principle was first delivered by Adam, speaking by inspiration, in the second chapter of Genesis. It was fully adopted by our blessed Lord, when He said, " For this cause shall a man leave father and mother and shall cleave to his wife ; and they twain shall be one flesh." [1] And again, when He said, " For this cause shall a man leave his father and mother, and cleave to his wife, and they twain shall be one flesh ; so then they are no more twain, but one flesh." [2]

The unity of the husband and wife being thus established, the prohibition in the sixth verse comes in to forbid marriages with persons near of kin to a husband or wife. If it be said that the meaning of our Lord is not that

[1] Matthew xix. 5.

[2] Mark x. 7, 8.

because a man and his wife are one flesh they have the same relations, there is a sufficient answer. Among the cases enumerated as instances which fall within the rule are cases of affinity. The principle is directly recognized in the fourteenth verse: "Thou shalt not uncover the nakedness of thy father's brother, thou shalt not approach to his wife: she is thine aunt."

§ 13. It may be inferred from what has been said, that all the lineal ancestors and descendants of the wife are forbidden to the husband, and those of the husband are forbidden to the wife. The inference is generally accepted. There are eight cases of marriages between persons connected by lineal affinity, which are expressly forbidden in the chapter under consideration. A man is forbidden to marry his father's wife in the eighth verse, his daughter-in-law in the fifteenth, his wife's daughter, her son's daughter, and her daughter's daughter in the seventeenth. The same verse forbids marriage with the mother or grandmother of a wife. If to these prohibitions, the principle that what is forbidden to one sex is forbidden to the other be applied, it will be found that all possible marriages within the third degree of lineal affinity are forbidden.

§ 14. Another inference from the same premises is that marriages between persons connected by collateral affinity, within the third degree inclusive, are also unlawful and void; but this second inference does not meet with the same universal acceptance as the first. It is involved in the canon Law of the Roman Catholic Church. It is the law of the Church of England, and as yet of the British nation. It was recognized by the House of Bishops of the American Church in 1808, as a law derived by her from her English mother; but the law of the land in most of the American States regulates marriages without any reference to collateral affinity, and their laws are in perfect accordance with the prevailing, although erroneous, public opinion.

There are no collateral relations in the first degree; in the second, there are only brothers and sisters; in the third, only uncles and aunts and nephews and nieces. Consequently the only relations by collateral affinity in the second degree are husbands' and wives' brothers and sisters; and in the third, husbands' and wives' uncles and aunts and nieces and nephews. There is one Levitical prohibition applicable to the second degree and one to the third. The sixteenth verse forbids marriage with a brother's widow, the fourteenth with an uncle's widow.

If the rule that what is forbidden to one sex is forbidden to the other, be applied to the sixteenth verse, it will not be lawful for a woman to marry a sister's husband. The prohibition will then cover every possible marriage between persons related in the second degree of affinity.

§ 15. It has been already said that there are but two classes of persons connected by affinity in the second degree, and that both are forbidden to intermarry by the sixteenth verse; one by its letter and the other by necessary implication. Great efforts have been made to get rid of this text. As to one class of these marriages, those between a man and his deceased wife's sister, other arguments have been used to establish their validity. The remainder of this chapter will be occupied with the inquiry into these cases, which is not capable of being compressed into a single section.

§ 16. The case of marriage with a brother's widow will be first considered. It may be proper to begin by a transcript of the law by which such marriages are forbidden: "Thou shalt not uncover the nakedness of thy brother's wife; it is thy brother's nakedness."[1] The prohibition is clear and definite. It seems to put the case beyond doubt. Those who maintain the lawfulness of such marriages must get rid of it. This has been attempted in two ways.

The first is to assert that the text does not apply to

[1] Leviticus xviii. 16.

marriage with the widow of a deceased brother, but to adultery with the wife of a living brother. To this interpretation there are several objections. First, all adultery is directly forbidden in the twentieth verse, as well as in the seventh commandment. Next, there is upon that supposition no need for assigning the reason which is assigned. Again, the language is the same as is used throughout the chapter, when it is intended to forbid all intercourse whether within or without the pale of marriage. It is: "Thou shalt not uncover the nakedness of thy brother's wife; it is thy brother's nakedness." In the twentieth verse, which forbids adultery, very different language is used. That verse is: "Moreover thou shalt not lie carnally with thy neighbor's wife, to defile thyself with her." Moreover, if this interpretation be adopted in the sixteenth verse, it must also be adopted in the eighth, which is almost in the same words: "The nakedness of thy father's wife shalt thou not uncover; it is thy father's nakedness." This would take away the prohibition to marry a mother-in-law. Lastly, it is said in another place: "If a man shall take his brother's wife, it is an unclean thing; they shall be childless."[1] This text plainly relates to the marriage of a man with his brother's widow, and not to an adulterous intercourse with his wife, for he is forbidden from taking her, that is, from taking her to wife, not merely from having sexual intercourse with her. The penalty implies that the guilty pair expected to have children.

§ 17. The other mode of getting rid of the sixteenth verse is to treat it as a merely civil precept. To prove this, recourse is had to the law by which a man was obliged to marry the childless widow of his brother, and raise up seed unto his brother. Such a law or custom prevailed among the Hebrews before the giving of the law, as appears from the thirty-eighth chapter of Genesis. Had

[1] Leviticus xx. 21.

there been nothing more than this, the custom would have been abolished by the text under consideration, which taken together with the thirtieth verse of the same chapter, would have classed it with abominable customs. But the rule is republished in Deuteronomy. The passage is this: "If brethren dwell together, and one of them die and have no child, the wife of the dead shall not marry without unto a stranger; her husband's brother shall go in unto her, and take her to him to wife, and perform the duty of an husband's brother unto her. And it shall be, that the first-born which she beareth shall succeed in the name of his brother which is dead, that his name be not put out in Israel."[1]

§ 18. It appears in the Book of Ruth, that there was another similar custom, not exactly the same with that mentioned in Genesis, and not founded upon the law in Deuteronomy. It was probably an old Hebrew custom which is not mentioned in the written law. By this custom Boaz was bound to marry Ruth when the nearer kinsmen had refused, although he was neither the brother of her first husband, nor had dwelt with him.

In the second chapter Naomi tells Ruth that Boaz is a near kinsman, without alluding to the custom, which nevertheless she seems to have had in her mind. In the third chapter she develops her plan of calling upon Boaz to fulfill the obligation which she supposed rested upon him. He admits the principle, but denies the obligation, because there was a nearer kinsman. He then introduces a new idea, that if the nearest kinsman declined to perform his duty, or exercise his privilege, — for it seems to have been regarded in both lights, — it devolved on the kinsman who was next to him in blood. This position on this occasion, belonged to Boaz, and he was willing, if the proper person declined the duty, to take it upon himself. In the next chapter he offers the option to the next of kin,

[1] Deuteronomy xxv. 5, 6.

who declines to marry Ruth, whereupon Boaz marries her. Here another new feature appears. The kinsman was bound to purchase the land, and with it Ruth for a wife. He declines to do this, and thereupon Boaz does it.[1]

This is not according to the law in Deuteronomy, nor does it agree with the custom mentioned in the thirty-eighth chapter of Genesis. Tamar, in that chapter, seems to have had no claim upon any one but Shelah. Naomi, in the first chapter of Ruth, when she was thinking of the law, seems to have supposed that her daughters-in-law had no claim upon any one who was not the brother of their husbands. The transaction does not seem to have been under the law in Deuteronomy for another reason. The punishment there prescribed for a man who refused to perform the duty of a husband's brother, was not inflicted on the man who refused Ruth.

The custom in Ruth differed from the law in Deuteronomy in four particulars. It extended to all kinsmen, not merely to brothers who dwelt together. The kinsman might refuse without incurring any penalty. If he refused, the right or obligation devolved on the next kinsman in order. The kinsman was to purchase the property of the deceased, and with it the widow to be his wife. The custom in Ruth was independent of the law in Deuteronomy, and perhaps existed before it.

§ 19. If this custom existed before the time of Moses, the law in Leviticus rendered it unlawful for a brother to comply with it, but left it untouched in such cases as that of Boaz and Ruth. The law in Deuteronomy restored his obligation to its old footing, but only in cases where the brothers had dwelt together. Such cases were regulated by the law, other cases by the custom. In such cases only a man might marry his brother's widow. It has been denied that even in that case the woman was in a strict sense his wife, because she was taken for a special purpose

[1] Ruth iii. 10–13; iv. 5, 6, 10.

to raise up seed to his brother. It has even been supposed that after that purpose was answered the marriage was at an end. But that cannot have been so. Such a temporary association would be inconsistent with the Divine idea of marriage. It is directed that the first-born which she shall bear shall succeed in the name of her first husband, implying that there may be others who shall belong to the second. Moreover, the text in Deuteronomy expressly says that the surviving brother shall take her to wife. The question which the Sadducees asked of our blessed Lord, in the twelfth chapter of St. Mark's Gospel and the twentieth of St. Luke's, implies that the woman was equally the wife of each of the seven brethren. But the marriage was designed for a special purpose, and except for that purpose was clearly unlawful.

§ 20. The only argument from the law in Deuteronomy, which is of any value, is this: God cannot command what is in itself wrong, and therefore that which He commands under special circumstances cannot be wrong under any circumstances. This supposes a rule of right and wrong for man, which is independent of the will of God. If there be such a rule, it must be in the Divine nature of which man can know nothing but by revelation. For man, that is right which is consistent with the revealed will of God, that is wrong which is inconsistent with the same revealed will. God lays down general rules for our government, and no human authority can dispense with them, but God himself may dispense with them. He forbids killing human beings. Yet He commanded Abraham to sacrifice his son, and the Israelites to extirpate the Canaanites. No one has ever contended that these exceptional commands made human sacrifices or the indiscriminate slaughter of men, women, and children lawful. On the contrary, infidels have said that these particular commands could not come from God, because they clashed with his general law. But when He, by a general rule, forbids marriage with a brother's widow, and by a particular precept commands certain men, under certain circumstances, to marry the widows of their brothers, the argument is reversed. It is then said that the particular precept must stand, and the general rule be disregarded, or at least reduced to a temporary regulation.

§ 21. This is stranger, as the particular precept appears upon its face to be a local and temporary regulation, promulgated with reference to the civil state of the Israelites. It is beyond controversy a merely civil precept, which no human being supposes now to bind any one. If the prohibition in Leviticus be also civil, there are two civil laws, one of which is an exception to the other. An Israelite was not permitted to marry his brother's widow except in a particular case, in which he was obliged to marry her. There is no inconsistency, because the two laws fit into each other as rule and exception. Suppose the prohibition moral, do not the two laws still fit as rule and exception? But can a civil law make an exception out of a moral one? A human civil law cannot, but the civil precepts of the Mosaic Law rest on the same Divine authority as the moral. The exception may then be valid, but its existence will neither nullify the rule nor change its character. So long as the Israelites remained a nation, having a national polity, both were in force. When their polity fell, the exception, being only civil or political, fell with it, and is not now binding on any one. It does not follow that the rule, to which it was an exception, must fall with it.

§ 22. It is said that it is not morally wrong to marry a brother's widow, because it was once enjoined upon the Israelites, under certain circumstances, to do so, which injunction is not now binding upon Christians. Yet such marriages are plainly forbidden in the law of God. It is replied that the prohibition is not a part of the moral law. What then is it? It is not ceremonial, it has no connection with public worship or ceremonial defilement. It is not civil, it has no connection with the civil or political state of the Israelites. It certainly relates to the conduct of men. It must then be a moral precept. There are other proofs that it is so. The inspired Lawgiver includes the marrying a brother's widow, among the things which he twice calls abominations and once abominable customs, and which he says were among the sins for which the Canaanites were to be extirpated. Moreover, he says in another place: "If a man shall take his brother's wife it is an unclean thing; he hath uncovered his brother's nakedness; they shall be childless."[1]

§ 23. It may be then safely concluded that it is unlawful for a Christian to marry his brother's widow. That this was the sense of the early Christians appears from the second Canon of the Council of Neo-Cæsarea. This council was held in the year three hundred and fourteen, and is one of the earliest of which any records remain. It is also one of those, the canons of which were confirmed by the General Council of Chalcedon, in the year four hundred and fifty-one. The second Canon is this: "If a woman marry two brothers let her be cast out even unto death, if she will not be persuaded to dissolve the marriage; but for lenity's sake she shall be admitted to repentance at the time of death, if she says that in the event of her recovery she will dissolve the marriage. If, however, a woman or her husband die in such a marriage, penance is not to be easily allowed to the survivor."[2]

§ 24. Several remarks may be made on this Canon. The Levitical law forbids marriage with a brother's widow. The Canon provides for the punishment of a woman who marries two brothers. The punishment is excommunication, which is not to be removed even upon a death-bed, without what the Canon calls a dissolution of the marriage. This would have been proper, only because the marriage

[1] Leviticus xx. 21.

[2] Hammond's *Canons*, p. 159. New York edition.

was void and a continuing sin. It may be asked, How can a void marriage be dissolved? But technical accuracy is not to be looked for in the ancient canons. If it had been a valid marriage it could not have been dissolved; but being void, the connection between the parties, such as it was, could be dissolved by separation.

This proves that the fathers of Neo-Cæsarea believed that the Levitical prohibition of marrying a brother's widow was in force and binding upon Christians. It also proves that they did not understand the sixteenth verse of the eighteenth chapter of Leviticus, as merely forbidding an adulterous intercourse with the wife of a living brother. They thought that it forbade marriage with a brother's widow; for the Canon forbids marrying with two brothers, and also speaks of the sin which was to be repented and abandoned as, in some sense, a marriage.

The last clause of the Canon proves three things. First, the marriage was a continuing sin, for the parties were not to be admitted to repentance while it continued, but when it was dissolved by death the obstacle was removed. Again, the sin was a great one, for the survivor was not to be easily admitted to penance or repentance. Lastly, the man was equally guilty with the woman.

The Canon cannot be well understood without some knowledge of the practice of the Primitive Church as to excommunication and penance. When persons were excommunicated, the Church did not readmit them to the Holy Communion without something more than a mere verbal assurance of their repentance. They must prove the sincerity and earnestness of their desire for communion with the Church, by submitting to great humiliations in order to recover it. These were called penance, as being the evidence of repentance. If, however, a penitent died before his or her penance was completed, he or she might be restored to communion on a death-bed. But if the sin were a continuing one, the Church would never be convinced of the sincerity of the penitent until the sin was discontinued.

§ 25. The law in the sixteenth verse of the eighteenth chapter of Leviticus, and that in the twentieth verse of the twentieth chapter, being binding upon Christians and not being mere prohibitions of adultery, it follows that marriage with a brother's widow is incestuous. The two cases of marriage with a brother's widow and with the widower of a sister cannot be distinguished from each other. If one be unlawful so is the other; for that cannot be lawful for a woman which is unlawful for a man. A woman, then, cannot marry the widower of her sister, and it must be equally unlawful for him to marry her. The reason assigned for the prohibition is just as applicable to one case as the other. If it be unlawful for a man to marry his brother's wife, because the deceased brother and his wife were one flesh, it must be unlawful for a woman to marry the husband of her sister, because the deceased sister and her husband were one flesh. Thus it is shown that marriage with the sister of a deceased wife is unlawful.

§ 26. In most parts of this country, marriages with the sister of a deceased wife often occur. Public opinion does not recognize the Divine prohibition, although more or less respect is paid to it by religious persons. The late Judge Story asserted that such marriages are in this country regarded as especially praiseworthy. This may be so in Massachusetts; but in Maryland, and probably in most of the States, it is not true. They are not considered praiseworthy by any one; most persons let them pass without a thought, while some regard them as lawful, some as unlawful.[1]

[1] I am indebted for the following note to a very distinguished clergyman, whose name I do not feel at liberty to mention: "I am inclined to think the feeling against these marriages is *very strong*, but in each particular case, relatives and others who object are silenced by the silence of the Church, and by the complicity of the clergy. I have known clergymen, with the strongest repugnance against such marriages, to officiate in them,

It is in connection with such marriages, that the doctrine of collateral affinity has been most discussed, probably because the temptation to disregard the Divine law is stronger among persons filling that relation than in any other case of affinity. In most or all the States of the Union, the law of the land has been so altered as to allow such seeming marriages, and an attempt is making to bring about the same result in England. Those who desire the success of that attempt have felt the necessity of getting rid of the prohibition of marriage with a brother's widow, and, therefore, adopt one of the two untenable notions which have just been discussed. They assert either that the texts which contain that prohibition forbid only a particular kind of adultery, or that they are merely ceremonial or civil precepts. In maintaining the last opinion, they do not hesitate to use the passage in the twenty-fifth chapter of Deuteronomy, although that law is clearly exceptional, the case of the wife's sister clearly not within the reason for the exception, and the law itself is no longer in force. It is said that because a man was, among the Israelites, bound to marry his childless brother's wife, in order that his brother's name might not be lost, another man is, among Christians, to be allowed to marry his wife's sister, when the deceased wife was not childless, because she is the most proper person to take care of her sister's children. When they suppose that they have gotten rid of the prohibition to marry the widow of a deceased brother,

under various weak pretexts, and so give them a certain warrant in the eyes of the community. Public opinion depends much upon women, and women look for guidance to the clergy; when the clergy, therefore, give way, public opinion is debauched. In two cases that I have known in Baltimore, several ladies who *knew* nothing of the law, but had a strong instinctive feeling that the thing was wrong, yet *desired* to think otherwise, came to me in hopes that I could give them ground for a more lenient judgment, — in which, of course, it was not in my power to gratify them. In all such instances, I found it very easy to convert the vague feeling into a definite and grounded aversion. *Instruction* on the subject is very much needed."

they fancy that the whole strength of the case against them is in the eighteenth verse of the eighteenth chapter of Leviticus, which does not really touch the case. It will, however, be proper to examine it.

§ 27. That verse is thus rendered in the text of the Authorized Version: "Neither shalt thou take a wife to her sister, to vex her, to uncover her nakedness beside the other in her lifetime." In the margin there is a different translation of the words, so that the whole verse would read thus: "Neither shalt thou take one wife to another, to vex her, to uncover her nakedness beside the other in her lifetime." The last translation makes the verse to forbid polygamy, and so removes it altogether from the present subject. The passage has been examined in the eighteenth section of the sixth chapter, where it was shown that such was its true meaning. Whether it be so or not, those who maintain the unlawfulness of marrying a wife's sister need not quote this verse.

They rely upon the general prohibition in the sixth verse of marrying any one's near kindred, the sixteenth verse of the eighteenth, and the twenty-first of the twentieth chapter, the principle that a man and his wife are one flesh, the principle that what is forbidden to a man is forbidden to a woman, and the application of those two principles to those three verses. They also rely upon the idea, that all the prohibitions in the eighteenth chapter, which relate to incest, are examples intended to show how far the words "near of kin" in the sixth verse extend. If that be so, the prohibitions show that nearness of kin extends to the third degree of both consanguinity and affinity, while the sixteenth verse shows that the relation in question, which is only in the second degree, comes within the meaning of those words.

Those who contend for the lawfulness of such marriages generally stand upon the translation in the text, which they say, not without reason, is an authority on their side.

They say that it only forbids marriage with the sister of a living wife, and implies the lawfulness of polygamy and of marrying a second sister after the death of the first. If this were, as they assume, the only law upon the subject, the argument would be strong. But it has been shown, without reference to this verse, that such marriages are unlawful. If they be forbidden by other laws, this verse cannot take away the force of those other laws, and make the marriages lawful. If they were right in supposing that the sixteenth verse forbids adultery with a brother's wife, it would not, so long as the twentieth verse and the seventh commandment remain, make adultery with any other woman lawful. The fact, that marriage with a wife's sister is otherwise forbidden, is an argument that the eighteenth verse does not merely forbid polygamy with two sisters. But supposing that adultery and marriage with a wife's sister are otherwise forbidden, no one would say that forbidding adultery with a brother's wife, or polygamy with sisters, would make that which was otherwise forbidden lawful. If the eighteenth verse forbids polygamy with two sisters and not marrying the sister of a deceased wife, then he who marries two sisters, one after the death of the other, does not sin against the eighteenth verse, but he nevertheless sins against the sixteenth verse and the sixth, and against the twentieth verse of the twentieth chapter.

The eighteenth verse, about which so much has been written, may be left out of the controversy. If, as seems most likely, it only forbid polygamy, it has nothing to do with the question. The unlawfulness of marrying the sister of a deceased wife rests, whatever may be the meaning of the eighteenth verse, upon the sixth verse, the general drift of the chapter, the sixteenth verse, and the twenty-first of the twentieth chapter. It is also worthy of remark, that the marriage of a deceased wife's sister is within the reason of the prohibition in the sixteenth verse, and is not within the reason of the law in the fifth and sixth verses of the twenty-fifth chapter of Deuteronomy.

§ 28. If the rule, that what is forbidden to one sex is forbidden to the other, be applied to the fourteenth verse of the chapter under consideration, it will forbid all marriages between persons connected by affinity in the third degree, where the affinity is through the father of the younger. But in order to apply the prohibition to cases in which the affinity is through the mother of the younger person, it will be necessary to look to the reason for the prohibition which is assigned in the fourteenth verse. That reason applies to relations on both sides, and with the rule, that what is forbidden to one sex is forbidden to the other, will make the fourteenth verse forbid every possible marriage between persons related in the third degree of collateral affinity.

In the twentieth verse of the twentieth chapter of Leviticus, there is a direct prohibition, which, in the English translation, extends the prohibition of marrying the father's brother's wife to the mother's brother's wife. It is this: "If a man shall lie with his uncle's wife, he hath uncovered his uncle's nakedness; they shall bear their sin, they shall die childless." The word uncle in English means as well a mother's brother as a father's brother, but the Latin language has a separate name for each. This enables the Vulgate to be more explicit by using both words. It says: "Qui coierat cum uxore patrui vel avunculi sui, et revelaverit ignominiam cognationis suæ, portabunt ambo peccatum suum; absque liberis morientur."

This verse may be regarded as a commentary on the sixth and fourteenth verses of the eighteenth chapter. It strengthens the argument for that interpretation of the sixth, which regards the doctrine, that a man and his wife are one flesh, as involving the idea that they have the same kindred. It so expounds the fourteenth, that with the aid of the principle, that what is forbidden to one sex is forbidden to the other, it forbids every case of marriage between persons related in the third degree of collateral affinity.

CHAPTER XV.

SUPPLEMENTARY: — OF THE MOTIVES TO MARRIAGE AND THE CHOICE OF A PARTNER.

§ 1. Introductory. — § 2. Motives to Marriage. — § 3. Companionship. — § 4. Help and Protection. — § 5. Another Motive mentioned by St. Paul. — § 6. An Affection for a Particular Person. — § 7. The Continuation of the Species. — § 8. Marriage sometimes Sinful. — § 9. How far Wealth is necessary to a Prudent Marriage. — § 10. When Marriage is a Duty. — § 11. Choice of an Associate. — § 12. Nature of Christian Marriage. — § 13. Careless Marriages. — § 14. Nature's Damnatory Clauses. — § 15. Indissoluble Character of Marriage. — § 16. Duties of Husbands and Wives. — § 17. Love. — § 18. The Emotional Nature. — § 19. Spirit, Soul, and Body. — § 20. — Passions and Affections. — § 21. The Affection of Love. — § 22. The Passion of Love. — § 23. It is not irresistible. — § 24. Its Connection with Malevolence. — § 25. Mediæval Notions about Love and Marriage. — § 26. Early Marriages necessary for Ladies in the Middle Ages. — § 27. Notions in the Sixteenth and Seventeenth Centuries. — § 28. Romantic and Unromantic Marriages. — § 29. Sir Walter Scott's Opinion. — § 30. Importance of Character — § 31. Wealth not a Proper Motive to Marriage. — § 32. Nor the Passion of Love. — § 33. Marriages, Wicked, Tolerable, or Right. — § 34. Love, the Lower Affection. — § 35. Love, the Higher Affection. — § 36. Moral Worth. — § 37. Religious Principle. — § 38. Agreement in Religious Doctrine. — § 39. Difficulties.— § 40. The Prudent Course. — § 41. Christian Conjugal Love.

§ 1. It seems to be a prevalent notion among young persons, especially among young women, that marriage is to be a fixed and uniform state. There is no better reason for this than that is the usual catastrophe of a novel. It is really a new phase of ever-changing human life, which, like every other, brings new duties, new cares, new anxieties, new labors, and new pains. It also brings new enjoyments. Whether the pleasant or the unpleasant circumstances preponderate, is a question which cannot be decided. Every one would answer it according to the circumstances of the moment, and the mood of his mind. It is as impossible to settle the question, as it is to settle the same question with respect to human life. Marriage is a phase of life, and like every other and like life itself, is continually changing its aspect. All its aspects with all that relates to them cannot be taken in at any one moment, by any human mind, so as to compare the good and evil of the state.

In the economy of the world, marriage is the formation of a new family, which is to endure for a time and then be dissolved. It will make way for others, which have perhaps grown out of it. In the economy of grace, it is a new sphere of duty, in which the faith and obedience of the young couple are to be tried, and which is to produce good or evil in time and in eternity, according to the result of the trial. It is a serious thing to enter upon it, and perhaps few persons would do so, except under the influence of some strong emotion.

But marriage is a Divine institution, and God has provided inducements to overcome the natural hesitation. He has declared that it is not good for man to be alone. Marriage is therefore, in itself, better than celibacy. Yet there is abundant evidence that it sometimes produces great evils. It will always do so unless it be entered into upon proper motives and with proper caution. The present chapter will be devoted to considering the motives to marriage, and the principles upon which a partner should be chosen.

§ 2. Marriage is a Divine institution designed to promote the happiness of the human race, which it is expressly revealed would be incomplete without it. Still there may be particular cases in which it is inexpedient to marry. Such dispensations of Providence, like all His dispensations, must be submissively received; but the general rule that it is not good for man to be alone is still true.

The conviction of this truth is one legitimate motive to marriage. There are others, which generally correspond with the Divine reasons for the creation of woman and the institution of marriage.

§ 3. One of the reasons for the institution of marriage, and of course, a legitimate motive for marrying, is the supplying the natural desire of companionship: "It is not good for man to be alone." He or she who desires a companion has a sufficient motive for marrying. But he or she would not desire to marry a person who could not be a companion. Such a person has no business to marry. A man who is immersed in business, may well require the comforts of companionship, and may properly seek them in marriage. But if he be so absorbed in his business as not to be able or willing to be the companion of his wife, he ought not to marry. A woman, who is so devoted to [what] she calls the pleasures of society, that she will not be willing to be the companion of her husband, has no business to marry. If such persons do marry, it will be their duty to overcome the taste for business or pleasure, and fulfill the obligations of their new position. The wisest course is to overcome the taste and to marry. But if the taste cannot be overcome, or the person be unwilling to encounter the struggle, such a person ought not to marry.

§ 4. Another motive to marry, which is connected with one of the reasons for the institution of marriage, is the providing a help meet for the man. The correlative motive is providing a protector for the woman who shall defend and maintain her. These are legitimate inducements to marry, when the want of help, protection, or support is felt. But they are not inducements to marry a person, who is incapable of furnishing the help, protection, or support. On the contrary, such incapacity is a reason why one who labors under it should not marry.

§ 5. There is another motive mentioned by St. Paul, of which nothing need be said, beyond referring to the second verse of the seventh chapter of the First Epistle to the Corinthians.

§ 6. An affection for a particular person is also a legitimate motive for marriage. Romantic young ladies believe that it is the only one. In this they are mistaken, although no other motive can be sufficient unless a suitable person, a proper object of affection, can be found. All motives must be restrained if there be circumstances which render the act to which they prompt improper.

§ 7. The continuation of the species was one of the reasons for the creation of woman and the institution of marriage. It is perhaps never the motive for a particular marriage. The continuation of a particular family has often been the motive. Among the old Romans no doubt men married upon such motives. A Valerius Publicola, or a Cornelius Scipio, felt an interest in the continuation of the Valerian or Cornelian gens, and in that of the race of Publicola or Scipio. Kings and nobles now marry that they may have heirs, but not lest the human race should become extinct.

There have been states of society in which the best, or only means of protection consisted in a numerous family. In such a state of society it was said: "As arrows are in the hand of a mighty man; so are children of the youth. Happy is the man that hath his quiver full of them; they shall not be ashamed, but they shall speak with the enemies in the gate."[1] Under such circumstances men married to strengthen themselves, as in modern times they marry to provide heirs to their titles and estates. In neither case is there any care for the continuance of the species as such. In the present state of civilization, men look to the law and the State for protection. Children, except in particular cases, are not desired. On the contrary, they are regarded, at least until they are born, as causes of trouble and expense, which most men would rather be without. Men accept the

[1] Psalm cxxvii. 4, 5.

possibility of children as incident to a marriage desired upon other grounds, but they rarely marry in order that they may have children.

§ 8. It may perhaps be well to repeat, that none of these motives, or indeed any motives, should induce any person to marry one who did not possess the qualifications for a happy marriage. All motives must be restrained, as has just been said, if there are circumstances which render the action to which they prompt improper. Marriage is honorable in all men, but there may be circumstances surrounding particular persons which may render it inexpedient for them, and the inexpediency may be so great as to render marriage sinful.

§ 9. Poverty is such a circumstance. Children will come into the world, and will have claims upon their parents for maintenance and education. So far as education consists in home training, this is only an inducement to be careful in the choice of an associate. But the maintenance of a family, and the instruction which children in the ordinary course of things must receive from paid teachers, require the expenditure of money. People have no right to marry who have not a reasonable prospect of being able to meet that expenditure. A reasonable prospect is not an absolute certainty. There are no absolute certainties in human life. It is not necessary, to make a marriage a proper one, that either of the parties to it should possess accumulated wealth. Nor is it necessary that the intended husband should have a large business income. But it is necessary that there should be such an income as will provide for the present wants of the family, and a reasonable prospect that it will increase as the family increases. There should be on the part of the man, at the very least, industry and the capacity to labor. In all situations in life, except the very humblest, there should be some capital to render labor profitable. There must be no tastes or habits, in either the man or the woman, which lead to such a consumption of time as will interfere with business, or of money as will render needful a larger income than there is good reason for believing can be provided.

§ 10. Where the necessary qualifications for marriage exist, and a suitable associate can be found, it may be considered that it is generally a duty to marry, for marriage conduces to the virtue and happiness of the community, as well as of the married persons themselves. It is a duty which men and women are generally willing enough to perform, so far at least as entering into matrimony and assuming its obligations performs it. But there is danger that they may do it without proper precautions, and without properly considering the responsibility which they are assuming.

§ 11. It is scarcely necessary [to say] that in the choice of an associate, one must be selected who is at liberty to marry, and to marry the person who has the matter under consideration. No man or woman, who has been divorced, except for the cause of fornication, is at liberty to marry. Our blessed Lord has said that whoever marries such a person commits adultery: "Whoso marrieth her that is put away doth commit adultery." "Whosoever shall put away his wife and marry another, committeth adultery against her. And if a woman shall put away her husband and be married to another, she committeth adultery." [1]

No marriage valid in the sight of God can be contracted between persons who are connected by consanguinity or affinity, in the degrees which are forbidden to intermarry in the eighteenth chapter of Leviticus. Such pretended marriages are not marriages, and no human authority can make them marriages.

There are cases in which the choice of a particular person for a husband or wife is a direct breach of the law of God, and Christian marriage with him or her impossible. In other cases there is room for much deliberation, in which the necessity of conforming to the laws of Christian

[1] Matthew xix. 9; Mark x. 11, 12.

marriage must never be lost sight of. The question to be asked is, always, Can I live with this man (or this woman), as my husband (or wife), after God's ordinance in the holy state of matrimony? It is to be feared that this question is too often neglected.

§ 12. Many unions take place, in every country, of which it can scarcely be hoped that there is an intention of carrying out those ideas which enter into the true notion of a Christian marriage, and which cannot be enforced by human laws. It was this which led to the remark of Dr. Johnson: that the marriage service of the Church of England was only intended for the best sort of marriages, and that there ought to be another provided for ordinary marriages. The Church in this, as in other cases, has chosen to set before her children the highest form of virtue, to which, if they cannot attain, they must labor to approach. The office recognizes, in a very impressive manner, the nature of a Christian marriage. In the promises made to the Church, before the minister proceeds to the marriage, there is notice taken not only of the general idea of love, but of its fruits, of honor, comfort, and fidelity on both sides, and of obedience on that of the woman. Moreover, the unity of marriage is recognized on both sides, by the promise to forsake all others and keep only to the person at the altar, and its indissolubility by the continuance of the promise so long as they both shall live. In the troth-plight the same promises, with some variations of expression, are made by each of the parties to the other.

Those who have been thus joined are truly said to have been joined by God, and men are forewarned against putting them asunder. They have assented to the conditions of a Christian marriage, and are entitled to the Divine blessing, which has been promised to the holy state; they have become "one flesh" according to the law of God in both Testaments. God has enjoined these laws of marriage, and the Church has recognized them as the means of constituting the marriage state holy, and therefore happy. It would be so, were all marriages entered into in strict conformity with the laws and requirements of God and the Church, and did all persons, when once united as husbands and wives, live in obedience to those laws and requirements. But it is too notorious that the best sort of marriages, as Dr. Johnson called them, are very rare, and that ordinary marriages are very common. In consequence there has arisen a proverbial saying, that marriage is a lottery. The provision made by God himself, to secure the virtue and happiness of His creatures, is, after all, only a game of chance, in which happiness and virtue are the stakes, and are at least as likely to be lost as won. This can only be because the Divine idea is not followed out, and the union is formed in the same careless manner in which lottery-tickets are purchased. Under such circumstances, it is too true that marriage is a lottery, and one in which no prudent man or woman would be willing to take a ticket. The inference is, that there must be a reform in the mode of selecting husbands and wives, or the propagation of the human race must be left to the imprudent and the vicious; the better portion of the race remaining in that condition, concerning which the Divine wisdom pronounced that it was not good, even in Eden.

§ 13. It is feared that in practice marriages are not contracted upon Christian principles, or so as to entitle them to the Divine blessing. The service is gone through as a form required by law and public opinion; but no hearty assent is given to its promises, and no reverent attention to its lessons. It is undoubtedly true, that marriages entered into without due deliberation and a proper knowledge of the character of the party with whom they are about to be contracted, are not likely to be happy. They are almost certain to draw the blanks in the lottery. It is also true, that the requisite knowledge of the character of the other party is not of easy acquisition. But this only renders the obligation more stringent, to take great care to obtain the information.

The American Church declares in the address with which her office opens, that marriage is "honorable among all men, and therefore is not by any to be entered into unadvisedly or lightly; but reverently, discreetly, advisedly, soberly, and in the fear of God." The Mother Church of England, whose service was set forth in a less fastidious age than that which saw our revision, is yet more explicit. She says, that marriage "is commended of St. Paul to be honorable among all men; and therefore is not by any to be enterprised or taken in hand unadvisedly, lightly, or wantonly, to satisfy men's carnal lusts and appetites, like brute beasts which have no understanding, but reverently, discreetly, advisedly, soberly, and in the fear of God, duly considering the causes for which matrimony was ordained." Such is the Church's doctrine of holy matrimony.

§ 14. It has been said, not unhappily, that nature has her damnatory clauses as well as the Athanasian Creed.[1] By this remark it was meant, that whoever violates the physical laws of nature, whether willfully or through ignorance, will be met by certain penal consequences, from which he will scarcely be able to escape. Whoever habitually exceeds the laws of temperance in eating or drinking, will, when his excesses have been numerous enough and long enough continued, be met by dyspepsia or *delirium tremens*. The moral law, even when it does not so directly connect itself with the physical laws of nature, has its own damnatory clauses; which are as sure to be enforced against the violators of that law, as dyspepsia is to punish the glutton, or *delirium tremens* the drunkard.

But this is a benevolent age, and one in which men are wiser than their Creator. The damnatory clauses, whether in faith, morals, or physics, are unpopular. It is thought very hard that people should suffer on any account. It is

[1] [Compare Bp. Butler's *Analogy*, Pt. I. ch. 2, towards the end.]

forgotten that those damnatory clauses are made and promulgated by Divine wisdom and goodness, and that they are designed as guards and cautions to prevent men from violating his laws. The intention of the Almighty is, that men should be, by those penalties, induced to avoid doing the things against which they are denounced. But in this age, it is thought that they ought to stand "like forfeits in a barber's shop, as much in mock as mark." It must be an understood thing that the penalties shall not be enforced. Everything which is wrong is an imprudence, and everybody must be, so far as it is possible, relieved from the consequences of imprudence. There must always be a *locus penitentiæ*, even after the evil action has been fully committed. The evils of imprudence are to be met and obviated, not by caution, the only mode recognized by the Governor of the world, but by taking away the natural consequences of imprudence.

§ 15. Thus God has decreed that marriage shall be indissoluble. His Church has taken care to call the attention of every person who enters into the state to this law, and, moreover, cautions them that they should not enter into their new condition unadvisedly. But many persons reject her cautions, disregard her warnings, turn her solemn office into an occasion of jesting, and then find themselves unhappy. It is held to be a great pity that they should suffer for their folly. So modern philanthropy undertakes to reverse the law of God, by what are falsely called human laws, but which are in truth, nothing more than abuses of human power. Marriage is thus pronounced, but not made, a dissoluble contract, and human tribunals undertake to dissolve the ill-assorted union, which God has not blessed, because His blessing has not been truly sought. Nevertheless, the Divine law is, that "a man shall cleave to his wife, and they shall be one flesh." And again: "They twain shall be one flesh: so then they are no more twain, but one flesh. What, therefore, God hath joined together, let not man put asunder."[1]

But the laws of Heaven are not so easily evaded. The separation, so far as human laws are concerned, puts an end to the union; yet its consequences remain. The parties have been man and wife; and that fact influences the rest of their lives, in a way not conducive to their happiness. This alone would seem to import a necessity for more caution than is usually exercised in contracting marriages. We fear, however, that it is true, that by much the larger portion of the marriages which take place in this country, are entered into with very little care or deliberation. One continually sees, in the newspapers, accounts of marriages concluded, or narrowly escaped, by young women, with men who already have one or more wives. The women are undoubtedly objects of commiseration; they would be more so had they given evidence of more Christian and lady-like principles and feelings. But it generally appears, that the engagement, and perhaps the marriage, has been contracted, after an acquaintance of a very few weeks, with a man of whom neither the woman nor any of her friends or relations knew anything. No doubt many other matches take place under similar circumstances, in which no prior wife appears, or perhaps exists. But the marriages may nevertheless be very unhappy. In some cases the husband disappears, and perhaps goes to deceive some other incautious woman. In others, the marriage is an unhappy one, because the man is a very unfit person to be a husband. In all such cases, it may be added that the woman is a very unfit person to be a wife.

§ 16. What then are the qualities to be sought for in a husband or a wife? This question may best be answered by ascertaining what are the duties of a husband or a wife. Those of the husband may be all summed up in one word, — love. Those of the wife in two, — love and obedience.

[1] Mark x. 8, 9.

The difference is of Divine appointment, and pervades the whole both of the Old Testament and the New. If one may reverently conjecture the reason of the difference, it may be supposed to be that in the fallen state of our race, there is a necessity for an authority to decide questions, which might otherwise lead to interminable disputes. In Paradise there was, perhaps, no danger of disputes, and consequently no need of authority. This theory is supported by the fact, that it is not until after the Fall that there is any direct mention of the husband's authority. It was after the Fall that God said unto the woman: "Thy desire shall be unto thy husband, and he shall rule over thee." The first part of this remarkable sentence seems to be designed as the means of bringing about the other. It accounts for the extraordinary phenomenon, that women will bear the most cruel usage from unworthy husbands, and still retain an affection for them. Such affection, no doubt, sweetens an otherwise bitter lot. But it is better not to put one's self in a position where such a compensation will be required. Moreover, this sort of affection does not come until after marriage.

§ 17. What are the proper inducements by which young persons should be governed in the choice of a husband or a wife? Should this question be put to a young lady, the answer would of course be, love. Many young gentlemen would answer, — if there were no young lady within hearing, — money. The ladies are right, although they may not have very accurate ideas as to what love is, or the kind of love which is requisite as a good reason for entering into the married state. They are generally possessed with a peculiar notion of love, which is learned from the sentimental novel writers. This emotion, which they allow to be called a passion, is supposed to be irresistible, undying, incapable of being felt more than once, and to be the evidence of the possession of every other good quality. Men know very well that this is entirely erroneous, and that there is nothing answering to it in the human heart. Marriage soon reveals to the woman that there is nothing like it in the male heart; and it is well if it does not also reveal its absence from her own. The idea is in fact made up of exaggerated notions taken from various emotions, which are confounded under the name of love. The largest portion of them are derived from that attachment of the wife to the husband, which has been already mentioned as a beneficent provision of the Almighty, intended at once to secure and to compensate her subordination. But this does not and cannot exist before marriage. Moreover, it is a female attribute, and does not belong to the male.

§ 18. What is the love which is the prerequisite to marriage? For the soundness of the theory of the ladies is not to be doubted. To answer this question, it may be proper to refer to the diagram in the second chapter of this work (pp. 72, 73). It is there shown that the inciting instincts, of the merely animal nature, are the developments of three primary instincts,—self-love, benevolence, and malevolence. These primary instincts, when transplanted, as it were, into the human nature, and combined with the intellectual faculties of memory and imagination, become the germs out of which are developed all human emotions. The emotions, considered together, constitute what is sometimes called the emotional nature, and, both theologically and popularly, the heart. The emotions are divided into three classes, as they are developed from the three primary instincts. Those which are developed from the selfish or malevolent instincts, are known as passions, sufferings, on account of their violence. Those which are developed from the benevolent instincts, are called affections, and are, in the present depraved state of human nature, far inferior in strength to the passions. The affections are also known by the generic name of love. Most of them have no other specific name than a specific epithet added to the generic name, as parental love, filial love, conjugal love. There are exceptions to this rule, such as gratitude, friendship, pity. But it is common to the whole of both classes, that they are kindly feelings, seeking their gratification in the well-being of objects without ourselves. The principle which is common to all, is kindness. This word is more commonly applied to the outward manifestation of the feeling, which in itself is called love. The love which prevails between young persons who have chosen, or are choosing each other to fill the relation of husband or wife, has no specific epithet, or name. It is designated absolutely as love; and it differs from friendship by its combination with the passion of love.

There is another matter connected with the emotions which requires some notice. In the mere animal nature, the instincts which answer to them are occupied solely about the immediate and present interests of the animal. In the human nature, when the primary instincts are combined with the intellectual faculties, the emotions acquire breadth, depth, and permanence. It is by those qualities that passions and affections are distinguished from mere animal instincts. But they are still conversant about the interests, so to speak, of the individual.

§ 19. There are, however, in human nature elements which have a still higher character than the intellectual and the emotional possess. St. Paul speaks of the spirit as well as the soul and the body. In this loftier region are to be found the faculties of the higher reason and the conscience. The soul may be considered as consisting of the mind and heart, of the intellectual and emotional portions of our nature. The spirit is the seat of conscience, or the moral nature. This faculty draws to it the higher reason, which is distinguished from the lower reason, sometimes called the understanding, by its power of dealing with spiritual matters, which the lower faculty wants. But this higher reason is itself, after all, only the handmaid of conscience, the queen of all the faculties, and the highest part of our nature.

The emotional nature is as capable of being elevated into this moral region as the intellectual; at least the affections and the passions connected with the malevolent instinct are so; for the selfish or concupiscible passions do not seem capable of any such connection. It is not to be supposed that conscience has no authority over or connection with the selfish passions; they are clearly subject to her dominion. But they do not seem to be capable of being dignified in such a way, that they are to seek their proper objects under the direction of conscience. Her authority over them is merely restrictive. They are the pariahs of the emotions, incapable of being ennobled. The philosophical reason of this is, that they can by their nature have no other objects than self: while the affections and the irascible passions, although having an ultimate object in self, have other intermediate objects, in whose well or ill being the self is interested, and of whose sentient existence the affection or passion, from its very nature, takes cognizance.

The same idea may be further illustrated, by remarking that the affections and the irascible passions regard their objects as persons, even although they may be only things; while the concupiscible passions regard their objects merely as things, although they may be really persons. The affections and the irascible passions always involve the notion of good or bad desert. The concupiscible passions look at everything only as it may contribute to the gratification of the desires of him who is under their influence.

The irascible passions and the affections always regard their objects as persons, and as capable of good or bad desert. This quality enables them to associate with conscience. Without that association, they look only at the good or bad deserts of their objects, with reference to the interests of the individual. He who has treated me kindly is a proper object of my affections. He who has treated me unkindly is a proper object of my malevolence. But both are so, without any reference to the distinction between right and wrong. But when the passions and affections are elevated into the moral region, then they are excited and appeased with reference to the right and wrong doing of the persons who are their objects. In the first case, the good or bad desert of such persons is regarded with reference to the interests of an individual; in the other with reference to the great principles of right and wrong as administered by conscience.

§ 20. The emotional nature, or heart, is thus divided into three regions, by different lines from those which have been already spoken of. These lines may be metaphorically considered as horizontal, while the former division is vertical. The selfish or concupiscible passions are incapable of rising above the first and lowest line of demarcation. The second stratum is occupied by the irascible passions and the affections, which are in their own nature higher than the merely selfish feelings, and are capable of rising above even the second line of demarcation. The third stratum is composed of the affections and the malevolent feelings which have actually risen above the third line of demarcation. In this elevated region, it may be observed that the irascible emotions lose the violent character which entitles them to the name of passions, and assume the character of affections, emotions, that is, which affect us without carrying us away by their force. No man is ever excited to that vehemence of emotion which we call passion by moral motives only. But he is *affected* with feelings towards the wrong-doers akin to the passions which he would have felt, had the wrong been done to himself. The term irascible or malevolent passions has ceased to be applicable; but there are now unkind[1] as well as benevolent affections. The heart is thus divided into three strata.

[1] Perhaps this expression requires some explanation. The word affection is now most commonly used for a benevolent emotion. The coupling it with the word "unkind" will seem strange to most readers. But in the text the word "affection" is used in another sense. An affection may be

§ 21. The present business relates to all these three strata. The distinction is commonly enough taken between the passion of love and the affection of love, when we are speaking of those emotions which are introductory to the marriage state. It is to the affection that the honor belongs of bearing as its specific designation the generic name of the affections, without a specific epithet. It is a true affection, which, like other benevolent affections, has its natural place in the second stratum. In or-

considered as an emotion which is not a passion, because it is not extremely violent. It affects us, but not to the point of suffering. It is precisely because the benevolent affections are of this sort, not violent, that they are called affections. The name may therefore be properly applied to any emotions which do not transcend the same grade of moderation. But the emotions connected with the malevolent instinct, when excited merely by the sense of wrong in the abstract, not connected with a sense of personal injury, do not advance beyond the same grade of moderation, which is reached by the benevolent emotions. They can, therefore, hardly be called passions, and the term "affection" may properly be applied to them.

The older writers used the word "affection" in a sense sufficiently broad to justify this application of it. Johnson's second definition is, "passion of any kind;" and he cites as authorities the following passages from Spenser and Hooker: —

"Then 'gan the Palmer thus: Most wretched man,
That to *affections* does the bridle lend;
In their beginning they are weak and wan,
But soon through sufferance grow to fearful end."
Faery Queen.

"*Affections* (as joy, grief, fear, and anger, with such like), being (as it were), the sundry fashions and forms of appetite, can neither rise at the conceit of a thing indifferent, nor yet choose but rise at the sight of some things." — *Hooker.*

But the malevolent emotions, however moderated and elevated, are not benevolent; they involve no good-will to their object. They are connected with the malevolent instinct; yet the word malevolent seems too harsh a one to be applied to them. Some milder epithet is wanted which may distinguish them from the benevolent affections, and intimate that they are not benevolent. The last two words form one of Johnson's definitions of the word "unkind." It has therefore been adopted, and the emotions in question called "unkind affections." The substantive indicating the moderation, and the adjective the character of the emotions. By whatever name they may be called, they are a very important part of human nature. They are intimately connected with conscience and the higher reason, which deals with abstract ideas. Moreover, they lie at the roots of the sterner virtues, as the kindly affections do at those of the milder. Without them, a man might be amiable, but could never overcome evil.

dinary minds it regards, as all affections do, the person who is its object as a person having good or bad desert; but it considers the good or bad desert solely with reference to the individual who loves his or her person and interests. But like all the other lower affections, it is capable of being brought into connection with the higher reason and conscience, and so elevated into the moral region, in which good and bad desert is judged of by moral rules, with reference to the great principles of right and wrong, and not to the person and interests of the loving person. Thus there may be said to be a higher and a lower affection of love, which may coëxist in the same mind towards the same person, and which unite in forming the highest kind of conjugal love. The union of these two grades, rather than kinds of love, is therefore the best preparation for entering into the marriage state.

§ 22. But besides the affection of love in its two grades, there is also a passion of love. What sort of a passion is it? To which of the three classes of emotions does it belong? It is conceded to be a passion; therefore it cannot be an affection, and belong to the benevolent class of emotions. It is called love, and so if its name at all expresses its nature, it can hardly belong to the malevolent class of passions. It follows that it must be one of the concupiscible passions which grow out of the instinct of self-love. As such a passion, it must belong to the lowest of the three grades of emotions, and be incapable of regarding its object, although really a person, as other than a thing only to be considered as it may contribute to the gratification of the self-lover, incapable of good or bad desert, either with respect to the self-lover or with respect to moral worth. The person so regarded is, of course, not reduced to such a condition, even in the imagination of the self-lover; but that is his or her condition looked at exclusively with regard to the passion called love. This passion is, in truth, only the sexual appetite determined by the imagination to a certain object, and dwelt upon until it becomes habitual. The sarcastic account which a poet has given of it is a just one: —

> "Lust, through some certain strainers well refined,
> Is gentle love, and charms all womankind."

Such is the passion of love in its nakedness; but like most other passions it has a power of combining itself with other feelings. It readily combines with other concupiscible passions, such as vanity, the love of admiration, and the desire of success. The last emotion is not to be confounded with the desire of the fruits of success. Mysterious as it seems, it is also capable of being combined with affection. In very affectionate natures it produces affection, although this may be accounted for by a process which will presently be explained. Where the affection exists between persons of opposite sexes, the passion is very apt to be its consequence. This is so generally understood, that the idea of Platonic love, that is, of an affection subsisting between persons of different sexes, without passion, where the parties are not so connected by blood as to render the passion unlawful, is regarded as only a subject of ridicule.

It is out of the confusion of this passion with the mysterious attachment, which, as has been already mentioned, a woman conceives for her husband after marriage, that poets, whether writing in verse or prose, have framed the idea of that sentimental or romantic love which has misled so many young people to their ruin. From one of these elements its violence has been taken, from the other its undying nature, for the passion of love seldom long survives marriage. Its blindness is found in both.

§ 23. The notion that the passion of love is irresistible, has led to many unhappy marriages. It is as false as it is mischievous. Love is no more irresistible than hatred. It is, as has been very well said, a very manageable passion. What is the reason that it is held disgraceful for a lady to fall in love with a married man? Why is it that no one falls in love with his sister or her brother? It is because love is a manageable passion. Anger and fear take people by surprise, and hurry them from their propriety. There is a passion which is sometimes called love, that does the same. That kind of love receives little favor. It is universally agreed that it is to be kept out of the heart, or if it make its appearance there, that it should be instantly stifled. It rarely looks to marriage, for it is as transient as it is violent. The love which, like hatred, produces permanent effects, is of slow growth. It is the offspring of the imagination, and may be controlled by controlling the imagination. Until it has become thoroughly rooted, it can be kept from growing, and in time destroyed by resolutely turning the thoughts in another direction. Of this truth tens of thousands of persons have had experience. Yet women who would be shocked to hear any one say that he could not help hating a particular person, will fancy that they cannot help loving a man whom they ought not to love.

Nothing can be more absurd. It is not possible to love that which does not present itself in an agreeable light; but it is very possible to withdraw the thoughts from that upon which they ought not to dwell, unless the wrong direction has become habitual. Young persons, especially young women, should never suffer any person of the opposite sex to become habitually present to their thoughts, unless they are well assured of the fitness of such person for a husband or wife.

§ 24. It is one of the mysteries of our nature, that the passion of love is always accompanied by a feeling allied to the malevolent instinct. This feeling is kept in check by the desire to conciliate, which the passion of love itself induces, and still more by the affection, which in some degree generally coexists with the passion. It exists, nevertheless, and shows itself in various ways. It is connected with some forms of dalliance, and with the proverbial tendency of lovers to quarrel. Their quarrels are sometimes sportive, sometimes semi-sportive, and sometimes in earnest, although not permanent; but in one form or other they have a strange disposition to jangle. When their jangling is in earnest they are easily reconciled, a fact which is as proverbial as the other. Those alternate ruptures and reconciliations are the alternate triumphs of two antagonistic yet inseparable principles. But when the passion of love has been gratified or crushed, if there has been no affection, or if that also has disappeared, the malevolent feeling is apt to survive, and manifests itself in some way, sometimes in acts of gross cruelty. There are many facts which bear out these views; but from their nature they cannot be here detailed. A very remarkable one is, however, recorded in Holy Scripture, in the thirteenth chapter of the second book of Samuel. It is obvious that this malevolent accompaniment of the passion of love, and the transitory nature of that passion itself, combine to render the passion a very insecure basis on which to erect the fabric of domestic happiness.

§ 25. Until within a few generations, our ancestors did not regard love as the gate of marriage. In the Middle Ages, the state of society was such as to leave a young lady no choice but between marriage and a nunnery. It was only by the power of a husband, or by the authority of the Church, that she could be protected from lawless violence.

There were also great difficulties about her subsistence, for an income could not be provided for her. Interest, which was then called usury, was proscribed by the laws both civil and ecclesiastical, and by public opinion. It was practiced by the Jews and Lombards. In their hands, it was a hazardous business, returning great profits at uncertain intervals, but was liable to great losses. It could not be made the source of a regular and punctually paid income, such as a single woman requires. Joint stock companies were not invented, and could not have existed; for many of them depend more or less upon interest, and all upon a confidence in the integrity and punctuality of men, for which there were no grounds. Small parcels of land could not be bought, and would have yielded very uncertain returns. Ladies had no means of investing money; whatever a father could give to his daughter, he could only employ as a marriage portion, or in buying for her a place in a nunnery. If she married, her husband would protect and support her during his life, and at his death she would be entitled to dower in his lands.

§ 26. In most cases, marriage was a necessity for a lady, and it was generally important that it should take place early in life. She was not in a situation to live single or to choose her own husband. It was therefore held to be her duty to accept one chosen by her friends. This duty almost every young lady was ready to perform cheerfully. She was generally called upon while still a child. Two things combined to lead to frequent marriages of children. Fathers were anxious to see their daughters married, since that was their only security. If the young ladies were heiresses, their fathers had an additional motive for marrying them early, that they might not fall into the hands of a guardian in chivalry, that is, into those of the king, the intermediate feudal lord, or any person to whom the king or the lord might give or sell the guardianship. Guardians were anxious to receive the value of the marriage, lest they might lose it by the death of the ward, or by her attaining the age of sixteen, and also because she generally wanted money. Guardians, and, it is to be feared, fathers paid little or no attention to anything but their own interests. This was the great defect of the system, and no doubt had much to do with the deplorable unchastity which prevailed during the ages of chivalry. Nevertheless, there is reason to believe that mediæval marriages not unfrequently turned out well.

§ 27. The Reformation took away the alternative of a nunnery, before the modern means of providing for single women were developed. This made marriage still more necessary to women. It seems to have been so regarded in England for a long time. The usage of marrying children still continued. Fathers had still nearly the same motives for marrying their daughters early as in the Middle Ages. The legal right of a guardian in chivalry to dispose of the hand of his ward, remained until the Civil War; and almost to the close of the seventeenth century, parents continued to provide husbands for their daughters while still very young.

Even when the young people were grown up, the passion of love had little to do with bringing them together. The choice of a husband or wife was rarely made for any reason which was not connected with property or political influence. A young man in choosing a wife rarely thought of love. He was much guided by the advice of his parents and friends. The strongest recommendations of a young lady were wealth, position, birth, that is, descent from ancestors of high position, and a careful mother. If she possessed these four things, especially if she added to them beauty, she might be married to any man whom her friends might select. If any of them were wanting, her choice of a husband was more limited, although she might still hope for an advantageous marriage, unless she was poor. Public opinion, immediately after the Reformation, allowed a young lady no right of refusing the man whom her friends had chosen; but in the course of the seventeenth century such a right gradually grew up, though it was not thoroughly established until some time in the eighteenth. Ideas about marriage similar to those of the Middle Ages long prevailed in the Roman Catholic countries of Europe, and are perhaps not yet quite extinct. Royal and princely houses, whether Roman Catholic or Protestant, still arrange their marriages upon the same principles.

It is the fashion to speak very harshly of our ancestors for their mode of match-making. It is true that young persons were not much consulted in the matter, and it is generally supposed that their feelings were often rudely treated. Such cases no doubt occurred; but the arrangement was generally made before they had any feelings upon the subject, perhaps before they were old enough to have any. In the last case they acquiesced, grew up together, and entered upon the married state without passion, but perhaps not without a certain habitual affection. When the young persons were grown up our ancestors acted upon an unromantic theory. It was, that any man and woman, who are married, will in time become so assimilated to each other that a liking will grow up, perhaps a strong affection. According to the then notions, it was not very important, when a person was to be married, to whom he or she was joined.

§ 28. Such was the theory of our ancestors, which is not yet extinct either as a theory or as influencing practice, although it is vehemently disowned. Many marriages are still entered into upon these principles. The result of a marriage, whether formed on the romantic or the unromantic theory, really depends upon the character of the parties to it; for it depends upon the state of feeling into which they may finally settle. This in marriages of passion, is something very different from the passion which led to the union. It may be true affection, or it may be the same kind of liking which often supplies its place in other marriages. It may, for a reason which has been already given, be hatred. Marriages on the other principle may lead to a true affection, if the persons married are capable and worthy of such a feeling, or they may produce in less amiable and affectionate natures the contented liking which grows out of habit, and which is the usual substitute for happiness, happiness itself being a rare blessing. Perhaps comfort and happiness may be as attainable in such marriages as in marriages of passion. The chance of this was, however, better before the romantic theory had taken root in the imaginations of women.

§ 29. These ideas have been well expressed by Sir Walter Scott. He says: "Let not those who enter into a union for life without the embarrassments of an enthusiastic passion, augur worse of their future happiness, because their alliance is formed under calmer auspices. Mutual esteem, an intimate knowledge of each other's characters, seen as in their case undisguised by the mists of partial passion, a suitable proportion of parties in rank and fortune, in tastes and pursuits, are more frequently found in a marriage of reason, than in the unions of romantic attachment, where the imagination, which probably created the virtues and accomplishments with which it invested the beloved object, is frequently afterwards employed in magnifying the mortifying consequences of its own delusion, and exasperating all the stings of disappointment."[1]

§ 30. The true objection to the old system is that the parents were too much influenced by considerations of property or other external advantages, which are not proper inducements to enter into the holy state of matrimony. The true objection to the romantic system is that the young people are too much influenced by personal appearance, accomplishments, manners, and other personal advantages, which are not proper inducements to enter into the holy state of matrimony. In both it is forgotten that the first thing to be considered in choosing a husband or wife is character.

§ 31. A return to the old system is by no means to be recommended; but it may be as well not to be too sure that our own is so very superior to it. There are still a good many marriages which are merely or chiefly the result of pecuniary motives. Most men are willing to admit that the

[1] *Redgauntlet*, vol. ii. ch. 18.

idea enters into their calculations, until they have fixed on the person whom they design to marry; and then to be sure their only motive is pure love, sentimental, romantic love. Nor is it to be supposed that the ladies are all insensible to the charms of wealth. Not a few of them are believed annually to sacrifice themselves to the splendor in which their intended husbands are able to maintain them. The goodness of the match is, on both sides, generally estimated by the wealth of the spouse. There is reason to believe, that even where that which can be regarded as wealth is out of the question, there are many ladies who become wives with reference to the support to which a wife is entitled.

§ 32. But passing from the pecuniary part of the subject, is the love, which is now regarded as the proper incentive to marriage, a more proper or a safer inducement than the desire of wealth, or of a maintenance? This question can scarcely be answered in the affirmative. What is the history and nature of a modern love-match, from which pecuniary motives have been carefully excluded? It begins on the man's side with the passion of love. This becomes so strong that he determines to attempt its gratification by marriage. Taken alone, it is scarcely the proper inducement to marry; although, were it not for the existence of the passion, probably very few matches would take place. Whether proper or not, it is very often the sole inducement on the part of the male, and sometimes on that of the female. It would be absurd to deny that females are liable to this passion; although the proprieties of life compel them to conceal it, and it is, in an overwhelming majority of cases, weaker than in men. But it is only in exceptional cases that it is the primary inducement by which a lady is governed in the choice of a husband. Its place is supplied by an affection which is very apt to produce the passion.

This affection has not itself, however, a very elevated

origin. It grows out of that which is sometimes called the instinct of coquetry, and more generally, in society, the love of admiration. This is one of the concupiscible or selfish passions, the object of which is the good opinion or kind feelings of other persons, more especially those of the opposite sex. It exists in both sexes, but is stronger among females. When the nature is hard and selfish, it produces that odious character, a coquette; where the nature is more affectionate, it furnishes a motive for kind feelings. The very fact that a man has fallen in love with a woman, that is, has experienced the passion of love for her, is a tribute to this passion, and has a tendency to excite a feeling of kindness. The attentions and flatteries of the man under the influence of the passion of love, tend in the same direction, and the lady soon feels an affection for her admirer; which is not very noble in its origin, and is not, according to the ordinary laws of human nature, likely to remain altogether Platonic.

Whether it do or not, it gives rise to a kindliness of deportment on her part, which tends to strengthen the feeling of affection on the part of the man, where it exists, and to originate it where it does not. The manifestation of affection on the part of the man, in turn, strengthens the affection on the part of the woman. Thus the parties are indefinitely acted upon and act. It is by such means that an affection grows up between a man and a woman. But this affection is without any reference to the moral worth of either. It is grounded on the notion of good desert; but that good desert consists in deserving well of the other party, not in deserving well of the Almighty. It is kindness to the individual, not obedience to the laws of God. It is not the higher affection which is connected with conscience and with the higher reason. The lower affection is the highest motive, upon which marriages are usually founded.

§ 33. But too many are founded upon yet lower bases.

It may be on the mere passion of love on the man's side, and on a feeling of kindness, growing out of a gratified love of admiration, on the woman's. It may be on the passion of love on the man's part, and on the desire of support, or of wealth and splendor, on the woman's. It may be on the passion of love on both sides. That this passion is not a proper foundation for marriage, the Church of England very distinctly teaches in her office for the solemnization of matrimony. She there declares, that that holy state is not "by any to be enterprised, nor taken in hand unadvisedly, lightly, or wantonly; to satisfy men's carnal lusts and appetites like brute beasts that have no understanding." That pecuniary motives are not the proper ones all are agreed, and entering into marriage upon them would be clamorously censured, even by those who have done so or are on the point of so doing. The affection which is the consequence of gratified vanity is not much better. Its basis will soon fall from under it. The attentions out of which it grew will cease to be paid so soon as the desires which prompted them are gratified,— whether those desires were for wealth or for anything else. No marriage which has for its basis any of the four which have been mentioned in this paragraph, is likely to be happy. They may turn out well; because it is within the compass of possibility that an affection may grow up after marriage, if the man be of an affectionate disposition; that is a forlorn hope. Yet it is to be feared that by far the greater part of the marriages which take place in this age and country rest on one or other of these four bases. Such marriages ought not to be contracted.

Others may be divided into two classes, those which may be allowed, or are tolerable, and those which are right in a Christian view. These last are what Dr. Johnson meant by the best marriages; the tolerable class are what he meant by ordinary marriages. The several species which have been spoken of in the last paragraph, may be classed together as wicked marriages; although it is to be feared that they are, in one sense of the word, ordinary marriages.

§ 34. Those, however, to which that term has been above applied, and which may be called allowable marriages, being those which grow out of that lower kind of affection, which springs from reciprocal kindnesses, have their dangers. So long as the affection continues, they will, so far as temporal matters are concerned, be very happy. But the affection which springs from mutual kindnesses requires to be sustained by the same nutriment. So long as the passion of love continues this will probably be the case, and even after that is worn out, the affection itself will produce the kindnesses upon which it feeds. But there will arise cases in which the irascible passions will be more or less excited, and thus there may occur words and actions of an unpleasant nature, the recollection of which tends to counterbalance that of the kindnesses which have produced and sustain the affection. The cares of life, too, call off the attention from the affection itself, and interfere with the showing such kindnesses as involve the expenditure of time. Under the pressure of poverty, all these evils are increased and aggravated, and the affection is apt to be severely tried. It has long been a proverb, that, "when poverty comes in at the door love goes out of the window." "Love and a cottage" is a phrase which sounds very well; but it is an idea hard to realize, unless both parties are prepared, by habit or character, to put up with the cottage without reference to love.

§ 35. There is a higher kind of affection which is based on the moral qualities of the beloved object. This may, and probably often does arise after marriage. It is not incompatible with the lower affection, which looks only to the relative desert of the object, that is, to the kindly relations between the parties. In fact, it can hardly exist separated from it. For in a worthy character, the affections must be strong, and will manifest themselves in kindly actions. A good man must be more or less an amiable man, and so the food of the lower affection will be abundantly supplied. The existence of this higher affection is not incompatible with that of the passion of love. In fact, it has the same tendency to excite it, with the lower affection, although, perhaps, in a lesser degree. Even this kind of affection can only in exceptional cases exist between young persons of opposite sexes in the Platonic form; unless where there are impediments to marriage, which are well understood to be insuperable.

§ 36. The higher affection has, then, so many possible helps that it is not easy to be sure that it is the moving principle. Still the person who desires to contract a marriage should first be sure that he or she believes in the moral worth of him or her with whom the union is designed. It is true that, on this point, there may be self-deception. The virtues may be the effect of the attachment, not its cause. This may be true in two senses. They may be assumed for the purpose of deceiving the inquirer; and they may exist only in the imagination of that inquirer. It is, therefore, better in such cases to rely on the judgment of others than on our own. Parents, friends, and even the public have better means of judging in such cases than the person immediately interested. But where the inquiry is omitted altogether, and a lady, for instance, marries a man known to be immoral, in the hope of correcting his vices by her post-matrimonial influence, this rule is grossly violated, and the marriage is, to say the least, highly imprudent. Not only is the proper basis of marriage wanting, but it is an absolute certainty, that the attempt to exercise such influence will put an end to even the lower affection, the only one of which such a man is capable.

§ 37. The only sure basis of a good moral character is a sound religious belief, and that involves a public religious profession. Such a profession may be hypocrisy, or it may be self-deceit. The ladies have this advantage, that in the case of a young man, the state of public feeling is not such as to render a hypocritical profession of religion a likely occurrence. It must be conceded that a religious profession gives no absolute certainty of a religious character; but it is certain, that he who makes no religious profession gives no guarantee of a religious character, and in an immense majority of cases does not possess it. No Christian man or woman is then justified in entering into the marriage state with one who does not profess to be guided by religious principle.

§ 38. This involves another rule. There is really no religious principle that does not grow out of some definite faith. It is necessary to the perfection of a Christian marriage that both parties should profess Christianity in the same sense. It would be very difficult, if not impossible, to perform the highest duty of the marriage state, the religious education of the children, under other circumstances. Ladies sometimes depart from this rule in the hope of being able to bring their intended husbands over to their way of thinking, and they even extend this notion so far as to try a similar experiment upon men who make no religious profession at all. Such conduct is like to that of her who marries an immoral man in the hope of reforming him. He who makes no religious profession has not given any evidence of his religious character, upon which a prudent woman can rely. She will, if she tries the experiment, find that her influence is much more likely to be outwardly successful before marriage than after it. Moreover, she may find that if it succeed before marriage, the spell will be dissolved very soon after the new state is entered into. He who makes a religious profession which is not founded upon a definite faith, is not a suitable husband for one whose faith is definite. His foundation is too insecure to be trusted. He who makes such a profession, upon a definite faith, will scarcely change that faith under the influence of his wife.

This principle applies to all persons who have any definite faith, whether it be the true faith or not. It has nothing to do with soundness of doctrine, but depends exclusively upon the sincerity and earnestness with which it is held. Two persons holding irreconcilable doctrines, which are both false, are as liable to all the inconveniences indicated in the last paragraph, as if one of them held the truth. Two persons holding the same doctrine, although a false one, would not be liable to them. The substance of this rule is that husbands and wives should be of one mind.

§ 39. It will be readily seen that upon the principles which have been laid down, it is not very easy for Christian men or women to find husbands or wives. The difficulty on the part of the women is undoubtedly the greater of the two. For there are more women than men who make public profession of a conformity to religious principles. But it must be remembered on the other hand, that there is much more certainty that the religion of a young man is sincere and deep than that of a young woman ; because he has fewer inducements to make a profession upon light grounds, and more difficulties to overcome.

The conclusion of the whole matter is, that those who desire to enter into the marriage state upon Christian principles, and will not depart from those principles, will find it very difficult to marry at all. This is one of the difficulties which in our age and country besets the Christian course. It is, however, no reason for joining in the light and unseemly view, which is generally taken of the holy state of matrimony. Nothing is more certain, than that it should be thought of reverently and entered into cautiously. Everything which may lead to it should be carefully watched, and a guard set upon the thoughts, until the most careful measures have been taken to learn the true character of the suggested person. Such a course is by no means romantic or sentimental. But if it were adopted, and carried on even upon worldly principles, there would be fewer bigamies and fewer unhappy marriages. At present marriage is a lottery; because nothing is done to make it otherwise. The plan said to have been adopted by some Christian sects, of marrying by the actual lot, is not more hazàrdous than a system which brings couples together without any other knowledge of each other than can be gained by the frivolous battle of fashionable society, or in the more intimate intercourse of what is called courtship, when mercenary views, or a fancy, which may be a passing one, or the love of admiration or flattery, may produce a deception not always quite involuntary.

§ 40. No person ought to select an associate in marriage without sufficient reason for believing that the person selected has good principles, is pious and amiable, and agrees with the person who is about to choose as to the great doctrines of religion. The greatest care should be taken to ascertain the truth upon these points. For that end it is desirable and a duty to take the advice of parents and prudent friends, and to be governed by it. Such advisers are in less danger than the person immediately concerned of being blinded by passion or flattery. In order that there may be parents and friends who are capable of advising, it is very desirable that a long acquaintance between the parties to a proposed marriage and their respective families should precede the very first movement towards the union.

§ 41. Above all it is important that persons who are about to marry should bear in mind the sacred nature of the engagements which they are about to assume. This work will now conclude with a statement of this, in the words of Dr. Pusey. He says: —

"Since marriage is this high and wondrous image of the union of the soul with Christ, how holily ought it to be compassed, entered upon, lived in!

"What is the pattern, and measure, and model of the mutual love of the husband and the wife? What but the love of Christ himself, and of his redeemed Church for Him its Head? 'Husbands, love your wives even as Christ also loved the Church.' St. Paul stops short in no created being; he lifts us to Him who is God and Man, the All-Holy, the All-Loving. And how then did Christ love the Church? More than Himself, more than his own life; 'He gave Himself for her.' In what condition did Christ love the Church? For her beauty, her goodness, her holiness, her graces? Nay, ye know well what this our human nature was before Christ came; how defiled, how full of all evil and deformity. And to what end did He love her? That He might array her with all beauty, that He might do away with every spot and wrinkle, and make her like a bride ordained for her husband, holy and without blemish.

"This plainly cannot belong to us. Christ is the pattern to us, not as to power or gifts of grace, but in His love. 'Love your wives,' he saith, 'as Christ loved the Church.' The love of Christ was with power; we cannot imitate the power; but we can, through His grace, imitate the love. Christ loved in the Church an undying beauty which He would give her. He loved all souls, not for what they were, but for what He would make them. We love after the pattern of Christ when we love in one another that deathless beauty of the soul which Christ gives; when we love in despite of defects which Christ will by his grace remove; when we are patient and forbearing with what Christ has not yet removed, looking and longing for His transforming grace now, yet onward still to that mighty working whereby He shall subdue all things unto Himself. To love the beauty of the body, save as the soul shines through it, is not to love like Christ. Poor, fading, a shadow only of that which shall never fade, is any beauty of the body. Beautiful above the stars of heaven, more piercing than their lustre, and undying, is the beauty of the soul in grace. Look then to that in one another which shall live on and shine on in the heavenly courts, when all which is of this earth shall be dissolved, yea, when what is now of this earth, but from our Maker's hands, not from our marring of His work, shall be transformed into the glory of Christ.

"Live then, day by day, for that day; love day by day with that day before you; love as ye shall wish that ye had loved in that day; love that which shall abide in that searching day, when wood, hay, stubble shall be burned up. But love meanwhile with a tender, forbearing love, as Christ is tender and compassionate with us, bearing with our decay, and beholding us as what, by his grace, we shall one day be; cherishing one another, encouraging one another, helping one another along the narrow road which leadeth unto Him; denying, each, self for the other, as Christ loved our souls more than Himself, in that He poured out His own soul to death for us. This love shall grow with years, as the love of Christ and the grace of Christ, which is the beauty of the soul, grows and is enlarged in each. This love shall be refined and purified by sickness and the wasting of the body, as the soul shall, through God's chastening, purifying Hand, lay aside its dross and glow the more with the beauty of the grace of Christ. This love shall not decay, much less die, even after the body's death. For souls which are united in Christ shall not be separated from Christ; they shall live on still, one in the one love of Christ." [1]

[1] *The Sacredness of Marriage.* Parochial Sermons, vol. ii. pp. 391–393, English edition.

APPENDIX.

It has been thought advisable by friends of the author of this volume, whose judgment is entitled to respectful deference, that a few words should be added about the question of the re-marriage of divorced persons. The object of Dr. Evans, in the ninth chapter of this Treatise, was to ascertain the true meaning of the disputed texts in Holy Scripture on this subject. This object will, perhaps, be furthered by reprinting (for the first time in this country) the comparatively rare tract of Bishop Andrewes on this topic, and by giving some references to other books which may assist the general reader in pursuing the investigation of this question, which is too momentous to admit of any one's forming a hasty opinion upon it.

A word first in explanation of the interpretation of Dr. Evans. In a letter to the editor dated June 5, 1868, he says: "The difference between the Editor of 'The ——' and myself about divorce, is precisely the same as that between Bishop —— and myself. The view of the Bishop and the Editor rests upon human notions of expediency, not upon any fair interpretation of the Saviour's words. They have been interpreted by an overwhelming weight of authority to mean that neither party can marry, but I think it clear that both can marry. At any rate the marriage must either continue or be dissolved. It cannot be binding on one and not on the other."

In 1857 Dr. Evans wrote thus of the Resolution of the House of Bishops in 1808: —

"Very strong reasons may undoubtedly be urged in favor of the rule as it stands, and the present writer is not prepared to urge a change. But if it be true that the danger of incontinence is the reason why divorces are prohibited, it would seem that they who had already shown an inherent tendency to that vice ought not to be placed in a situation which the highest authority has declared to be one of peculiar danger. Logically, too, it is not easy to see how a marriage can exist as to one party and not as to the other. If the adulteress is still the wife of her injured husband, after he has put her away, he must be still her husband, and so unable to take a second wife. If she be not his wife, it is not easy to see why she should not marry, unless a direct Divine prohibition could be found, which is not pretended.

"Yet the danger of inducing the commission of adultery as a means of dissolving a hated marriage, and bringing about an union with a new and preferred partner, is very obvious. The proper remedy for that is, however, the infliction of penalties by the State upon the adulterers, not the treating a marriage not divinely prohibited as a nullity. If the Church had any lay discipline, it would be a very proper occasion for its exercise, if parties committed adultery, and the censure might not improperly be made more severe if the object of the adultery appeared to be to procure a divorce, with a view to a second marriage. But it does not seem clear that the Church has a right to pronounce such second marriage void." [1]

About the time of the passage of the present English Divorce Law, in 1857, Dr. Christopher Wordsworth (now Bishop of Lincoln), so well known on this side the water for his "Commentaries on Holy Scripture," published a sermon on "Marriage with a Divorced Person," with learned notes, in which he argues against the position of Mr. Keble and the English barrister, which is that marriage is absolutely indissoluble, but also differs as decidedly from the

[1] *American Church Monthly*, May, 1857, pp. 334, 335.

doctrine which Dr. Evans holds to be the logical consequence, that *both* parties, after a proper divorce, may marry. His words are: —

"On the whole it is respectfully submitted to the consideration of the reader, whether the great cause of Holy Matrimony can be safely grounded and successfully defended on the plea of *indissolubility*.

"Our appeal must be to the original text of Holy Scripture. And, to say the least, it is very doubtful whether Holy Scripture, understood in its plain grammatical sense, will bear any one out in urging the plea of [absolute] indissolubility.

"If it does not, let not Holy Scripture be invoked as if it did sanction it.

"If the cord is strained too tightly, it will break in our hands. If, in dealing with this grave and solemn question, we endeavor to apply Holy Scripture where it is not fairly applicable, we shall not be able to apply it where it ought to be applied. We shall strengthen the hands of our enemies. The ground of Holy Scripture will be cut away from under us, and then where shall we have any footing left?

"We cannot find it in a few sentences from some Latin fathers. And we shall find no benefit, but rather the contrary, from finding ourselves in the company of the Council of Trent. [This style of argument is (with due deference to the respected writer) surely questionable, and it is difficult to see what force it can have except to one who would rather be in the wrong than hold the truth, if so be, with the Council of Trent.]

"Rather let it be humbly suggested, that all who desire to maintain the sanctity of matrimony should unite in defending that common ground whereon they can all stand together as allies and brethren, and that they should combine in maintaining the two following propositions: —

"1. That it is necessary to restrain the present prevailing recklessness in contracting marriage; and it is inexpedient to give facilities to divorce; and that Christian husbands and Christian wives should endeavor to bear one another's burdens; and that even if the one be separated from the other, a new marriage should not hastily be contracted; but that time be allowed for repentance, and, if possible, for restoration.

"2. That marriage with a person divorced for adultery is adulterous."[1]

The reader will find a valuable collection of authorities and quotations in the notes to Bishop Wordsworth's Sermon.[2] He quotes, in support of his view that marriage may be dissolved for adultery so as to leave the innocent party free to marry, besides many of the Fathers, Bishop Hall, Dr. Hammond, "Of Divorces," vol. i. p. 595, chap. ii.; Herbert Thorndike, "On the Laws of the Church," book 3, chap. xiii., 29; Bishop Jeremy Taylor, "Ductor Dubitantium," chap. v. rule viii., and others.

Mr. Liddon, on the other hand, maintains, in the sermon quoted in the preface to this volume, the opinion of Mr. Keble and the English barrister which Dr. Evans discusses in the ninth chapter of this work. It coincides with the doctrine of the Council of Trent, that there can be no divorce except in cases where the marriage was void *ab initio*, which are not, properly speaking, divorces. He quotes largely from the tract of Bishop Andrewes, which is herewith reprinted, and from Döllinger's "First Age of the Church," translated by Mr. Oxenham, p. 424 (2d edition). He holds that in the texts in St. Matthew our blessed Lord "proclaims the indissolubility of the marriage tie. Alluding to the Jewish law [Deut. xxii. 20, 21], He rules that if an unacknowledged act of fornication on the part of the woman had preceded the contract, the apparent tie may be dissolved. I say the apparent tie, because in reality the con-

[1] *Sermon*, pp. 12, 13, note.

[2] There are two other sermons on this subject by the same author in his *Occasional Sermons in Westminster Abbey:* No. XL., *On Divorce*, and No. XLI., *The Restoration of Holy Matrimony*.

tract was vitiated from the first; one of the contracting parties was deceived as to its real terms. Yet, even here, to marry the woman is adulterous, for she knew the terms on which she had bound herself. But when a contract is perfect it is altogether beyond recall, at least before God. A separation from bed and board may subsequently become necessary, but no suspension of the enjoyments of married life can cancel the indissoluble bond itself; and therefore much more than in the Jewish sense referred to, 'Whoso marrieth her that is' in this sense 'divorced, committeth adultery.'"[1]

The tract of Bishop Andrewes, which follows, was first published at Oxford in 1854, in the last volume of his works, — pp. 106–110. It is selected for reprint here because of its comparative rarity, and the great celebrity of its author. The notes (with the exception of those in brackets) are by the Oxford editor.

"A DISCOURSE,

WRITTEN BY DR. ANDREWES, BISHOP OF ELY, AGAINST SECOND MARRIAGE, AFTER SENTENCE OF DIVORCE WITH A FORMER MATCH, THE PARTY THEN LIVING.

In Anno 1601.

"THE question is, whether upon adultery proved, or sentence recorded, a man be set at liberty, that he may proceed to contract with another.

"First. I take the act of adultery doth not dissolve the bond of marriage; for then it would follow, that the party offending would not, upon reconciliation, be received again by the innocent to former society of life, without a new solemnizing of marriage, insomuch as the former marriage is quite dissolved, which is never heard of, and contrary to the practice of all churches.

"Secondly. The sentence, as I take it, doth not relieve, for there is no lawful sentence of any court in case of di-

[1] *Christ and Human Law*, pp. 15–18.

vorce, but it ever containeth an express inhibition to either party to marry with another, with intimation in flat terms, that from the time that either of them shall go about any other marriage, *quod ex tunc prout ex nunc, et ex nunc prout ex tunc* (it is the style of the court), that present sentence shall be void to all purposes, and they in the same case as if it had never been given.

"These both failing, the word of God is sought to; where let me tell you first, that during the Primitive Church, ever till now of late, the judgment of the divines and the present practice of the law ecclesiastical were both one; and great reason why; for well-known it is, that the authority of the fathers was the ground of the ancient canons, by which the law in this case is ruled. So that but for the conceit of some latter divines, there need not be sought any opposition between law and divinity in this question, nor that pitiful distraction happen, which we daily see, Divines to give their hands for licence to that, for which law will convent men and censure them too.

"But in my opinion second marriages (where either party is living) are not warranted by the word of God. The ground of which opinion is, that one may not in any wise have two wives at once; for by the original institution there can be but two in one flesh. But a man having one wife already, which notwithstanding she hath profaned marriage with another, is not thereby become the wife of him with whom she now liveth, but remaineth his wife whose first she was, and whose only she can be while she liveth.

"The word of God is plain for this in St. Paul, Romans vii. 2: *The woman is bound to the man so long as she liveth, so that if while she liveth she become another man's, she shall be holden an adulteress;* from which words the vow of marriage seemeth to have been framed, which is solemnly made in the congregation by either party, *forsaking all other to keep only to her so long as both shall live.* And again, *to have and to hold, for better for worse, till death:* these plainly show the band is only broken by death, and that though she become another man's, yet is she not become his wife.

"Now upon this dependeth the next rule of the word of God (1 Cor. vii. 11), that a woman of herself departing, or put away by her husband, is commanded either to be reconciled, or to remain unmarried: which commandment of the Apostle's must be understood of the case of adultery; for were it any other cause but that wherein Christ hath given leave to depart or to put away, the Apostle would not have put it upon either, or upon one, but would simply and absolutely have commanded her to be reconciled, as indeed in all other cases she is bound to seek it, and is not less at liberty. You may imagine that favorers of those kind of marriages will say somewhat to these places, by way of evasion; for what is so plain, but by man's wit somewhat may be said to it? But that his meaning is the direct meaning of the ancient writers, and that these in this sense understand these places, and that both when they were met together in councils, and in their several writings, I refer you to the Council of Eliberis (which is as ancient as the first General Council of Nice), the 9th Canon;[1] and to the Council of Milevitum, where St. Augustine and Optatus were present, and subscribed the 17th Canon;[2] and to Origen's 7th Homily upon Matthew;[3] and to St. Hierome's

1 "Item fœmina fidelis, quæ adulterum maritum reliquerit fidelem, et alterum ducit, prohibeatur, ne ducat; si duxerit, non prius accipiat communionem, nisi quem reliquerit, prius de sæculo exierit; nisi forte necessitas infirmitatis dare compulerit." — Conc. Elib. Can. ix. — Conc., tom. i. col. 971. D.

2 "Placuit, ut secundum Evangelicam et Apostolicam disciplinam, neque dimissus ab uxore, neque dimissa a marito alteri conjungantur." — Conc. Milev. Can. xvii. — Conc., tom. ii. col. 1541. E.

3 Ἤδη δὲ παρὰ γεγραμμένα καί τινες τῶν ἡγουμένων τῆς ἐκκλησίας ἐπέτρεψάν τινα, ὥστε ζῶντος τοῦ ἀνδρὸς γαμεῖσθαι γυναῖκα, κ. τ. λ. — Orig. *Comm. in Matt.* xix. *Op.*, tom. iii. p. 647. Paris, 1740. It is called *Tractatus in St. Matt.* vii. in Editt. Vett. Latt. Erasmi, tom. ii. p. 67. Basil, 1571.

Epistle to Amandus;[1] St. Ambrose upon the 1 Cor. vii.;[2] to Innocentius the First (who lived a little before St. Augustine), in his Epistle to Ereusius, 9th section;[3] to St. Augustine's book, 'De Adulterinis Conjugiis ad Colentium' [*leg.* Pollentium], lib. ii. cap. 4,[4] whose meaning and interpretations I prefer, and wish all (I may prevail with) to lean to, rather than opposite ones of latter times.

"Likewise, it cannot be denied, but that the Fathers do allege and understand these two places, the one in Mark x. 11, the other in Luke xvi. 18, as they stand in plain and full terms, that a man having put away his wife cannot marry again. For as for the place in Matt. xix. 9, where it seemeth to be qualified with (*unless it be for adultery*), which place is all the show that can be made for these marriages, they follow the rules both of divinity and reason (which is) when there is any diversity in places, first to expound the lesser number by the greater, and not contrary; that is, one evangelist by two, and not two by one;

1 "Quamdiu vivit vir, licet adulter sit, licet sodomita, licet flagitiis omnibus coöpertus, et ab uxore propter hæc scelera derelictus, maritus ejus reputatur, cui alterum virum accipere non licet." — S. Hier. *Ep.* lv. (al. cxlvii.), ad Amandum, § 3. *Op.*, tom. i. col. 296. A.

2 "Non . . . . permittitur mulieri, ut nubat, si virum suum causa fornicationis dimiserit." — S. Ambr. (seu potius Hilar. Diacon.) in 1 Cor. vii. 10, 11. *Op.*, tom. ii. Append. Col. 133.

3 "Qui ergo vel (quæ viro vel, *in marg.*) uxore vivente, quamvis dissociatum videatur esse conjugium, ad aliam copulam festinarunt, neque possunt adulteri non videri." — Innoc. I. *Epist.* iii. *ad Exuperium* (sic), § 6. — Conc., tom. ii. col. 1256. C.

4 "Nullius viri posterioris mulier uxor esse incipit, nisi prioris esse desiverit. Esse autem desinet uxor prioris, si moriatur vir ejus, non si fornicetur." — S. Aug. *de Conj. Adult.* lib. ii. cap. 4. *Op.*, tom. vi. col. 686, B. C.

[When S. Augustine is appealed to on this question, it is fair to add what he himself says in his *Retractations* (lib. ii. c. lvii. tom. i. col. 653, ed. Migne, quoted by Bishop Wordsworth, l. c. p. 6): "Scripsi duos libros de Conjugiis Adulterinis, quantum potui secundum Scripturas cupiens solvere *difficillimam quæstionem.* Quod utrum enodatissime fecerim, nescio; imo vero *non me pervenisse ad hujus rei perfectionem sentio,* quamvis multos sinus ejus aperuerim, quod judicare poterit quisquis intelligenter legit." — H.]

secondly, to expound the former writer (which it is granted Matthew was) by the latter, as both Mark and Luke were, and not contrary, especially where both may stand, as here, they interpreting it thus: He that putteth away his wife (which but for adultery is not lawful) and marrieth another, committeth adultery himself.

"Now, if you ask why that exception might not have been left out in Matthew (seeing it maketh the matter ambiguous), they answer, that in Matthew it was necessary that our Saviour Christ should add it, for that these very words (*he that putteth away his wife, except it be for adultery*) contain the direct answer to the Pharisees' question, Whether a man for any cause might put away his wife? whereunto but for this clause no answer had been made. But in the other two Evangelists, where no such question is moved, nor like occasion offered, there it is left out, both in St. Mark, where the disciples asked him about it, and in St. Luke, where He simply delivereth the doctrine, no man moving any doubt about it to Him.

"Some of the reasons why the ancient writers cannot favor this exposition, which giveth liberty to second marriages, be these: —

"First, our Saviour Christ meant plainly in that place to restrain the commonness of divorces among the Jews; but divorces are not restrained, this exposition holding, inasmuch as He hath left it still in the pleasure of every lewd man or light woman, who committing the sin with another, may dissolve as many former marriages as they like: for being weary of the first, it is but to be lewd of her body, and presently the bond is broken, and liberty given to make a new choice of another, and being weary of that, of a third, and fourth. Jerome in Matt. xix.[1]

[1] "Ubiquumque est igitur fornicatio, et fornicationis suspicio, libere uxor dimittitur. Et quia poterat accidere, ut aliquis calumniam faceret innocenti, et, ob secundam copulam nuptiarum veteri crimen impingeret, sic priorem dimittere jubetur uxorem, ut secundam, prima vivente, non habeat." — S. Hier. *Comm. in S. Matt.* xix. 9 (lib. iii.). *Op.*, tom. vii. p. 146.

"Secondly, it is not our Saviour Christ's will to make the committing of sin gainful or beneficial to any offender. But this exposition holding, the guilty person must gain thereby; for so the committing of adultery do dissolve marriage, then maketh it the persons in the same case they were before they were married; and so may either, as well the guilty as the innocent, marry, which is the very benefit the adulterer propounds to himself. Ambrose.[1]

"Thirdly, this exposition holding, and adultery dissolving marriage, not only that absurdity would follow (which I in the beginning mentioned), that no Christian might receive his wife, having been faulty, except a new marriage were celebrated between them (a thing never heard of); but that which is more gross, that the innocent party, if he could have knowledge of his wife's body, having been false this way, should in so doing commit adultery himself, inasmuch as he hath had the use of her that now is none of his. None of his (I say), because their marriage was utterly dissolved by the act precedent of his wife. Augustine.[2]

"Now, to conclude: there be two divers things in that place of St. Matthew: the putting away of his wife, and the taking of another. And in the midst of these standeth the exception (if it be not for adultery).[3] To speak truth, it

1 The reference seems to be to S. Ambr. *Expos. S. Luc.* (cap. xvi.) lib. viii. § 4. *Op.*, tom. i. col. 1471. B., though the meaning appears to be mistaken.

2 S. Aug. *de Conj. Adult.* lib. i. cap. xii. (§ 13). (*Op.*, tom. vi. col. 668. B. C.), is probably the passage intended. Compare *de Nupt. et Concup.* lib. i. cap. x. (§ 11). *Op.*, tom. x. col. 615. B.

3 [Mr. Liddon and Dr. Döllinger press the use of πορνεία instead of μοιχεία in this text; the former, they contend, must mean unchastity before marriage and not adultery. (See *Christ and Human Law*, pp. 15, 34, etc.) Those who may be inclined to make too much of Dr. Evans's ignorance of Greek, in judging of his argument on this head, may be reminded that on this point he is supported by the high authority of Bishop Andrewes, who does not hesitate to translate the word by *adultery* (the authorized version of King James was not yet published). It appears from a note to Mr. Liddon's sermon that one of the first of modern English scholars, the late Prof. Conington, has also maintained in some strictures on Mr. Liddon's argu-

cometh a little too soon, for if it had been stayed till the end of the sentence, thus: He that putteth away his wife, and taketh another, committeth adultery himself, except it be for adultery, it had sounded for them. But now it cometh in thus: *He that putteth away his wife, except for adultery, and marrieth another*, etc.; that is, the exception standing behind the first, and going before the second. Sure it is not clear and plain; for as it may by some be understood to limit the former only (and so the old writers do generally restrain it, as before it hath been said). Therefore, here it is doubtful at least, since divines differ about it.

"LANCELOT ANDREWES.

"*Anno* 1601."

The following *Canon* was drawn up by Dr. Evans a few months before his death, and sent to the Church newspapers with the following note:—

ment, in the *Contemporary Review* for May, 1869, that πορνεία is a large word and may include μοιχεία. Other Greek scholars confirm the interpretation of Bishop Andrewes and Dr. Evans. Dean Alford says: "πορνείας must be taken to mean sin, not only before marriage, but after it also, in a wider sense, as including μοιχεία likewise." (Gr. Test. *in loc.*)

Bishop Wordsworth also has no doubt that the word means adultery; he says further: "It is generally supposed by divines of Rome that ἀπολύω does not here signify to *divorce*, in its strict sense of severing the *vinculum matrimonii* (which they suppose to be in all cases indissoluble), but means only to separate *a mensa et thoro*, and that matrimony is in all cases pronounced indissoluble by our Lord in Mark x. 11; Luke xvi. 18. But the conversation here with the Pharisees is concerning divorce *a vinculo*; and ἀπολύω is used in the natural sense of *dissolutio vinculi*, as expressed in the bill of divorce (Deut. xxiv. 1), ... and the exception contained in παρεκτὸς λόγου πορνείας is repeated by our Lord in Matt. xix. 9. And it cannot be supposed that anything taught by our Lord in the 'Sermon on the Mount' has been *repealed*." . . . . (Gr. Test. on St. Matt. v. 32).

Kuinoel is no great authority as a philologist, but his collection of examples is worth examination: "Πορνεία latissime patet, et omnis generis impudicitiam indicat; h. l. intelligi debet *adulterium*, quo vinculum matrimonii dissolvitur, v 1 Cor. vi. 16; Matt. xix. 6–9, nam est de uxore sermo. . . . . etiam Hesych. atque Auctor Etymol. M. τὸν μοιχὸν dicit πόρνον, et de uxore, quæ Hos. iii. 1, vocatur μοιχαλὶς, ib. iii. 3, adhibetur verbum πορνεύειν. Amos vii. 17, ἡ γυνή σου ἐν τῇ πόλει πορνεύσῃ." . . . . —Kuinoel, Comm. *in loc.*—H.]

"The mind of the Church is now much occupied about some important questions touching the sanctity of marriage, and there seems to be a wide-spread opinion, that the coming General Convention ought to deal with the subject. These questions have occupied much of my thoughts for about eleven years. I have, therefore, ventured to prepare a project of a Canon, which I shall (D. V.) offer in my place in the Convention. I will thank you to insert it in your paper, in order that the members of the Convention may have an opportunity of examining it beforehand.

"It will be observed that the section which treats of divorce, merely repeats, as it were, the words of our blessed Lord, without meddling with any question of interpretation.

HUGH DAVEY EVANS.

TITLE II. CANON 13.—OF MARRIAGE AND DIVORCE.

"§ 1. (1.) Whereas, Almighty God hath in the Holy Scriptures forbidden all intermarriages between persons near of kin to each other, and hath explained that nearness of kin exists between persons who are connected with each other in certain relations of consanguinity and affinity. And whereas, our mother Church of England hath, ever since the Reformation, held that the persons so forbidden to intermarry are those mentioned in a table, which was set forth by authority in the year 1563, and is still in force in the Church of England. And whereas, it was declared by the House of Bishops in the year 1808, that the said table was obligatory upon this Church, and would remain in force, unless there should thereafter appear reason to alter it, without departing from the Word of God or endangering the peace and good order of this Church. And whereas, the said table is in the words following:—

"'A man may not marry his grandmother, grandfather's wife, wife's grandmother, father's sister, mother's sister, father's brother's wife, mother's brother's wife, wife's father's sister, wife's mother's sister, mother, stepmother, wife's mother, daughter, wife's daughter, son's wife, sister, wife's sister, brother's wife, son's daughter, daughter's daughter, son's son's wife, daughter's son's wife, wife's son's daughter, wife's daughter's daughter, brother's daughter, sister's daughter, brother's son's wife, sister's son's wife, wife's brother's daughter, wife's sister's daughter.

"'A woman may not marry her grandfather, grandmother's husband, husband's grandfather, father's brother, mother's brother, father's sister's husband, mother's sister's husband, husband's father's brother, husband's mother's brother, father, stepfather, husband's father, son, husband's son, daughter's husband, brother, husband's brother, sister's husband, son's son, daughter's son, son's daughter's husband, daughter's daughter's husband, husband's son's son, husband's daughter's son, brother's son, sister's son, brother's daughter's husband, sister's daughter's husband, husband's brother's son, husband's sister's son.'

"Therefore, any communicant of this Church, who shall hereafter intermarry with any person connected with him or her in any of the relations mentioned in the above table, shall be suspended from the reception of the Holy Communion in this Church, until he or she shall separate from the person with whom he or she shall have intermarried contrary to the divine prohibition.

"(2.) No person, not already a communicant of this Church, who shall be living as husband or wife with any person connected with him or her in any of the relations mentioned in the above table, under pretense of any marriage ceremony hereafter performed, shall be received to the Holy Communion in this Church, until he or she shall separate from the person with whom he or she shall be so living contrary to the divine prohibition.

"§ II. (1.) Whereas our blessed Lord and Saviour Jesus Christ, hath declared that whosoever shall put away his wife, except for fornication, and shall marry another, committeth adultery, and whosoever marrieth her that is put away committeth adultery, and also that if a woman put away her husband and is married to another, she committeth adultery. Therefore, any communicant of this Church who shall, hereafter, intermarry with any person who has been divorced from any person still living, except for fornication, or who having been himself or herself divorced from any person still living, except for fornication, shall, hereafter, intermarry with any person whatever, shall be suspended from the reception of the Holy Communion in this Church, until he or she shall separate from the person with whom he or she shall have intermarried contrary to the divine prohibition.

"(2.) No person not already a communicant of this Church, who shall be living as husband or wife, under pretense of any marriage ceremony which may be hereafter performed, with any person who shall have been divorced, except for fornication, from any husband or wife still living, or who having been himself or herself divorced from any husband or wife still living, except for fornication, shall, under pretense of any marriage ceremony hereafter performed, be living as husband or wife with any person whatever, shall be received to the Holy Communion in this Church, until he or she shall separate from the person with whom he or she shall be so living contrary to the divine prohibition.

"§ III. (1.) No minister of this Church shall hereafter solemnize matrimony between persons, either of whom shall have been divorced from any person then living, except for fornication, or between persons who shall be connected with each other in any of the degrees of consanguinity or affinity mentioned in the table above set forth in the Canon.

"(2.) If any minister of this Church shall be called upon to solemnize matrimony in any case in which he may think that the contemplated marriage is forbidden by any of the provisions of this Canon or by the Divine Law, he may lay the case before the Bishop or Ecclesiastical Authority of the diocese, who shall forthwith issue a commission of two clergymen and one lay communicant, to examine into the case. The commissioners shall inquire into all the facts and circumstances, and shall as soon as may be convenient, report to the said Bishop or Ecclesiastical Authority all the facts and circumstances which have come to their knowledge, and also their opinion or opinions whether the contemplated marriage can or cannot be solemnized consistently with this Canon and the Divine Law, and the reasons for such opinion or opinions. The Bishop or Ecclesiastical Authority having considered the report, may forbid or permit the solemnization of the said contemplated marriage, as to such Bishop or Ecclesiastical Authority may seem right."

The death of Dr. Evans having occurred before the meeting of the General Convention, his Canon was not discussed. The Canon passed by the Convention, which is now the law of the Church, is as follows: —

"No minister of this Church shall solemnize matrimony in any case where there is a divorced wife or husband of either party still living; but this Canon shall not be held to apply to the innocent party in a divorce for the cause of adultery, or to parties once divorced seeking to be united again."

For some friendly criticisms upon this Canon, see President Woolsey's "Essay on Divorce," etc., pp. 249, *et seq.* New York: Scribner & Co. 1869.

INDEX.

[The Roman numbers refer to the chapters, the figures to sections of chapters ; where no Roman number is given, the preceding one is to be understood.]

TEXTS SPECIALLY REFERRED TO.

[The references in this Index are to pages.]

www.ingramcontent.com/pod-product-compliance
Lightning Source LLC
LaVergne TN
LVHW021128110826
845150LV00005B/961

* 9 7 8 1 4 2 5 5 5 0 2 7 1 *